Psychological Assessment

Psychological Assessment

by

N.C. Rawat

MD Publications Pvt.-Ltd.
B/231-E, Greater Kailash - I
New Delhi-110048

ISBN 81-7533- 099-6

Published by

MD Publications Pvt. Ltd.
B/231-E, Greater Kailash - I
New Delhi-110048.

Showroom
"MD House"
11, Darya Ganj
New Delhi-110002

Printed & Published by
MD Publications Pvt. Ltd.
B/231-E, Greater Kailash - I
New Delhi-110048.
email : contact@mdppl.com
www : www.mdppl.com

Contents

PREFACE

Psychological Assessment is often interchanged with the terms occupational testing or psychometric testing. These terms are used to describe tools which are essentially sophisticated devices designed to measure individual difference in a number of areas such as intelligence and ability. Psychological Assessment are used for a number of purposes in various circumstances including: career counselling, team building, development and recruitment. However, the most common use of tests is in the process of selecting individuals at the point of entry into an organisation. Testing has been in use for more than 50 years, but there has been a significant rise in test use in the last decade and, as the selection process becomes ever more sophisticated, testing has assumed a more and more prominent role for a number of organisations.

Most tests are designed and developed by occupational psychologists and are accompanied by detailed manuals providing the data to establish the reliability of the test and the normative information against which test results may be compared this is the information that allows employers to compare their test candidates against the scores of a normal population of similar people. Administering tests and analysing the results is a skilled task. Scoring of tests is often complex and how it is done will depend on what a test is trying to measure. With personality tests there are no right or wrong answers as they are designed to present a profile of an individual.

Psychological Assessment are tests which can be systematically scored and administered, which are used to measure individual differences. They are supported by a body of evidence and statistical data which demonstrates their validity and are used in an occupational setting.

Psychological Assessment conduct a comprehensive psychological evaluation. It provides a complete review of the most commonly used assessment instruments and the most efficient methods for selecting and administering tests, evaluating data, and integrating results into a coherent, problem-solving report.

This is a careful and thoroughly updated revision of the most highly acclaimed and successful undergraduate text in testing. Psychological testing and assessment examines the philosophical, historical, and methodological foundations of psychological testing, assessment, and measurement, while helping students appreciate their benefits and pitfalls in practice.

The chapters of the book are central to the diagnostic process and are used to inform parents, clients and clinicians, among others, about academic problems, personality functioning, neuro-psychological strengths and weaknesses, behavioral problems and the like.

This book is designed to help busy mental health professionals quickly acquire the knowledge and skills they need to write effective psychological assessment reports. Each concise chapter features numerous callout boxes highlighting key concepts, bulleted points, and extensive illustrative material, as well as test questions that help you gauge and reinforce your grasp of the information covered.

This practical guide focuses on efficiently and effectively communicating referral and background information, appearance and behavioral observations, test results and interpretation, summary and diagnostic impressions, and treatment recommendations.

N.C. Rawat

1

Psychological Assessment: Measurement of Profile Validity

Introduction

The original intent of Hathaway and McKinley in developing the traditional validity scales was to aid in determining the test-taking attitude of the subject. Some individuals are motivated to distort their responses to the test items, either to minimize the presentation of their psychological problems or to exaggerate their psychopathology. Others may present a distorted picture of themselves by answering the items without fully comprehending their meaning or perhaps by simply not reading the items and responding randomly or with a true or false response bias. It is, therefore, important to ascertain the participant's test-taking disposition before interpreting the clinical scales. Although the validity scales were designed for this purpose, they have also been shown to correlate with personality traits and behaviors. Hence, the validity scales can enrich the clinical interpretation of the profile by providing the clinician with other psychological descriptors as well as an index of self-description accuracy.

The accurate assessment of a participant's test-taking attitude on the MMPI-2 (or any other personality inventory) is a complex issue. Some individuals believe they are giving an honest picture of themselves through their responses but in fact are distorting their presentations by overly positive self-evaluations, exaggerated perceptions of control or mastery, or unrealistic optimism (S. E. Taylor & Brown, 1988). These self-illusions may serve them well in coping with life's stresses but will affect their responses to inventory items. Paulhus referred to those participants who believe in their positive self-reports as engaging in self-deception and those who consciously attempt to manipulate others' views of themselves as "impression managers." There appears to exist a continuum of accurate self-reporting that ranges from underreporting to over reporting psychological problems and concerns, although Lanyon, Dannebaum, Wolf, and Brown conceptualized underreporting and over reporting as independent dimensions. It is up to the clinician to assess the validity of the participant's self-report before making a detailed analysis of the clinical and supplementary scale scores. To this end, the following validity scales should be considered as indispensable in assessing the individual's self-report style and test-taking attitude.

Cannot Say Score (?)

The Cannot Say score is the number of items an individual did not answer or double marked, thereby leaving the response unscorable. A response could also be unscorable if it is uncertain to the test scorer whether a true or false response was given to the item. On the original MMPI, Cannot Say was plotted as a scale and assigned an arbitrary T -score value. However, technically it did not qualify as a scale because scales have a set number of items or a consistent item pool. On the MMPI-2 profile sheet, a space exists for recording the raw score value of omitted or double-marked of unscorable items, but the score is not transferred to the clinical profile as it was for the MMPI. The MMPI-2 manual considers a profile invalid with a Cannot Say score of 30 or higher, whereas raw scores between 11 and 29 are of questionable validity. Scores between 0 and 10 are probably valid, but the psychologist should examine the content of omitted items.

The reasons for the lack of a response to an item are numerous. Perhaps some of the items lack personal relevance, or an individual filling out an answer sheet could accidentally skip an item. Different motivational factors, such as test-taking resistance or suspiciousness, have been associated with high Cannot Say scores. Not answering an item may be related to decisional ambiguity, which is the inability of the participant to decide how to respond to an item. In addition, intellectual or reading deficits may make it difficult to comprehend an item, leading to its omission. However, most test takers respond to all of the items, although some individuals may object to various items. For example, those in personnel selection situations are more likely to react negatively to items if they feel there is no job relevance. If participants omit items, it is always desirable to encourage them to complete the omitted ones, and to assess why they chose to leave them out. Although in many cases the omission may have occurred accidentally, other omissions may have occurred because the item was ambiguous or offensive to the reader or, as implied earlier in the case of adolescence, semantically confusing. It is likely, however, that the improved item wording on the MMPI-2 will lead to fewer item omissions.

Archer summarized the findings of Ball and Carroll, who examined correlates of Cannot Say scores among 262 ninth-grade, public school students in Kentucky. Archer stated that, in general, the adolescents who omitted greater numbers of MMPI items also had lower IQ scores and grades that were below average. This seems to suggest that intelligence and reading limitations are associated with Cannot Say scores as much as negativistic attitudes toward the testing. An inverse relationship between reading grade level and raw scores on the Cannot Say measure was also found by Archer and Gordon. In a sample of 495 normal adolescents who were administered the MMPI-A and the Ohio Literacy Test, a measure of reading comprehension, they found that adolescents who have difficulty reading MMPI or MMPI-A items tend to omit items at a higher frequency than other adolescents. Archer also pointed out that, unfortunately, many adolescents also attempt to respond to items that they have difficulty reading or understanding, which often results in invalid test protocols. This emphasizes the necessity to evaluate carefully an individual's reading ability before he or she is administered the MMPI-2.

Usually 10 or fewer omitted items or less will not affect the validity of the profile. When between 5 and 30 items are omitted, Greene recommended a procedure called "augmenting" the profile. In this procedure, the items that were omitted are endorsed in the deviant direction, scored, and reinterpreted. The test should also be scored without the items marked in the deviant direction so that the two profiles can be compared. More than 30 item omissions renders the test record highly suspect, if not completely invalid. If items are omitted, then the scale on which they are scored will be lowered, thus compromising the validity of the profile. The omission of items can also change the MMPI's high-point pairs (highest clinical scales), which could significantly alter the interpretation of the profile. It should be noted that the validity and clinical scale items are all contained within the first 370 items of the test. Thus, if the item omissions occur after Item 370, the standard scales will not be affected. However, the supplementary and content scales, which are scored after Item 370, could be affected.

Clopton and Neuringer conducted a two-phase study to address the issue of item omission and its effects on profile configuration. In the first phase, they examined the occurrence of omitted MMPI items from Veterans Administration (VA) psychiatric patients being admitted to the hospital, outpatients at a regional mental health center (MHC), and police and firefighter applicants who had completed the MMPI. In each of these three groups, the majority of test participants completed all 566 items, with the percentage of participants omitting 5 or fewer items being 93.7% for the job applicants, 88.9% for MHC clients, and 85.6% for the VA patients. The corresponding number of mean items omitted was 2.45 for job applicants, 2.24 for MHC clients, and 4.68 for the VA patients.

The second phase of Clopton and Neuringer 's study involved inspecting the effects of randomly omitted items on profile elevation and configuration (high-point pairs). A subset of 180 randomly selected VA patient MMPI profiles, which were completely filled out, were then rescored with 5, 30, 55, 80, 105, and 130 items randomly omitted. The original MMPI profiles were compared with the different rescored profiles with different levels of omitted items. As more MMPI items were omitted, there was a corresponding reduction in the profile elevation and, perhaps more importantly, changes occurred in profile configurations. The mean reductions in T scores across the clinical scales for the six levels of omitted items fell an average of 0.45, 2.74, 5.61, 7.70, 9.09, and 11.54 points, respectively. Randomly eliminating 30 MMPI items from complete answer sheets in their study led to a change in the high-point pair in more than 25% of the profiles and an average reduction of nearly 3 T-score points in the clinical profile. Thus, profile configuration, rather than specific T -scale scores, is more importantly affected by a large number of item omissions.

Although most people rarely omit a significant number of items, the consequences of doing so are such that the clinician should inspect the answer sheet carefully for a completed test record. Failure to check an answer sheet having a large number of item omissions can mislead the test interpreter to underestimate the degree of psychopathology revealed in the profile. As suggested earlier, whenever possible it is good practice to ask examinees why items were omitted and to encourage them to complete those items. A recent example illustrates the importance of checking the answer sheet for item omissions. An MMPI had been completed by a security guard applicant during a pre employment screening. The clinical psychologist who interpreted the profile failed to examine the answer sheet and instead relied exclusively on the profile for making his recommendations. The profile was well within the normal limit range. However, the applicant had omitted approximately 77 items from the first 370 items on the MMPI. Because the psychologist failed to look at the answer sheet, he recommended that the security guard be hired for employment. The numerous item omissions came to the attention of this text's first author when the security guard later became involved in a shooting incident that led to litigation in which the guard was sued for brutal and aggressive force. Clearly, the MMPI should have been either considered invalid or given back to the job applicant to complete his responses to the items. This kind of oversight can be avoided if clinicians routinely look at the Cannot Say score on the profile sheet or, if it is not reported, examine the answer sheet directly.

Variable Response Inconsistency Scale

The VRIN scale is a 67-item scale designed to detect inconsistent or contradictory responding. It is a new scale designed for the MMPI-2 and resembles the function of the shorter Carelessness scale on the MNPI developed by Greene. One major difference between the VRIN scale and the Carelessness scale is the greater scale length of the former. The VRIN scale is also seen as a replacement for the TR index on the MMPI, which consisted of 16 repeated items and for which four or more inconsistent responses raised the question of profile invalidity due to inconsistent responding.

The content of the VRIN item pairs have similar or opposite meaning. Some pairs of items are scored as inconsistent if one item receives an opposite endorsement (true or false as the case may be) from the other item in the pair, whereas others are scored as inconsistent if both pairs are scored as either true or false. As Butcher has stated, "the score in the VRIN scale is the total number of item pairs answered inconsistently". High scores raise the possibility that the test taker did not respond carefully to the content of the inventory, thereby rendering the profile uninterpretable. The scoring direction for the VRIN items is based on the frequency of item endorsements by the contemporary normal sample; hence, many apparently contradictory response patterns are not scored. The following examples from the VRIN scale illustrate the scoring directions for inconsistency and the item content of the VRIN scale.

3. I wake up fresh and rested most mornings. (True) 39. My sleep is fitful and disturbed. (True)

If an individual answered true to both Items 3 and 39, he or she would receive a raw score point of 1 on the VRIN scale.

9. My daily life is full of things that keep me interested. (False)
56. I wish I could be as happy as others seem to be. (False)

Both Items 9 and 56 need to be endorsed false in order to receive I point on the VRIN scale.

349. I am never happier than when I am alone. 515. I am never happier than when I am by myself.

Both Items 349 and 515 need to be oppositely endorsed (True-False or False-True) in order to be scored on the VRIN scale. Greene pointed out that the VRIN scale actually consists of 49 pairs of unique items because two separate response patterns (i.e., True-False or False-True) are scored for 18 of these 67 item pairs, as with Items 349 and 515.

Because scoring is configural for the VRIN scale, the user must be especially careful if hand scoring the scale because mistakes could easily be made. Iverson and Barton recently investigated the hand-scoring accuracy of the VRIN and TRIN scales and compared these results to the reliabilities of the other clinical and validity scales. Despite high reliabilities across most of the scales, clerical errors were common (7% of the scales were scored inconsistently), although for the most part these errors only "represented one or two raw score points and did not affect the clinical interpretation of the scales". However, there were three times as many scoring disagreements for the VRIN scale than for any other scale, suggesting that the configural nature of the scale is much less of a scoring handicap if a computer-scored program is used. If this is not possible, clinicians should carefully check their hand scoring of this scale.

For the MMPI-2 to be clinically interpretable, it is necessary for the individual to respond to semantically similar items in similar ways. A high rate of inconsistent responses usually indicates difficulties in understanding the content of the inventory or a lack of cooperation (noncontent responding). The VRIN scale (along with the TRIN scale) was designed to complement the interpretation of the L, F, and K validity scales. The MWI-2 manual states that, for example:

> *a high F score combined with a high VRIN score is more Rely to indicate a profile that is uninterpretable owing to carelessness, confusion, etc. than if VRIN is not elevated. On the other hand, in the case of high F and low VRIN, carelessness, etc. can be ruled out and a high F score can be interpreted in terms of its actual content which could, then, reflect either true psychopathology or deliberate efforts to fake bad.*

More recent research findings also support this strategy of interpreting an elevated F scale by referring to the VRIN score.

Note that a participant could shift his or her test-taking attitude at any point during the test administration. For example, an individual could become fatigued and less motivated to read the content and then resort to random, all-true, or all-false responding. If the participant answered cooperatively during at least the first 370 items, all of the clinical and validity scales could be accurately interpreted. However, after Item 370, if a participant adopts a random-response bias, the content and supplementary scales could be unduly affected. Greene pointed out that the VRIN scale items are fairly evenly distributed throughout the MMPI-2. If the clinician wanted to take the care and time to score the validity scales in blocks of items rather than for the entire test, it could be determined where a participant began randomly or inconsistently responding. This approach would be particularly helpful for intermediate scores on the VRIN scale.

The MMPI-2 manual suggests that a raw score of 13 (T = 80) on the VRIN scale indicates inconsistent responding, which is consistent with more recent research focusing on validity scale cutoff scores. Greene, however, suggested a more graduated interpretation. He suggested a raw score cutoff of 16 for the VRIN scale and that scores between 8 and 15 could indicate either consistent or inconsistent responding, thereby necessitating the examination of other measures. More recently, Nichols and Greene stated the following:

> *Unfortunately for VRIN raw scores in the range of 11 to 16, a relatively large number of inconsistent cases may be inappropriately judged consistent, whereas many consistent cases, particularly in psychiatric samples, may be inappropriately judged inconsistent. In some cases, especially where there is a large imbalance between the proportion of items marked "true" and those marked "false," lower VRIN raw scores (e.g., 7-12) may lead to incorrect judgments of consistency. In these cases, TRIN (true response inconsistency) may prove to be a more appropriate indicator of response consistency because of its greater sensitivity to extremes and "true" versus "false" responding.*

Additional indices of consistency may usefully supplement VRIN and should always be used when VRIN falls within the indeterminant range of 11 to 16, inclusive, and we encourage their examination when VRIN exceeds a raw score of 6.

The main number of VRIN items earned by men and women in the MMPI-2 standardization group was approximately 5 (SD = 2.5). Test-retest correlation coefficients for these participants over about a 1-week interval was .54 for men and .51 for women.

Recent research data supports the validity of the VRIN scale. Berry recently investigated the tendencies of normal participants who completed the MMPI-2 to randomly respond, although they were given the test with standard instructions. The participants were asked to estimate the extent to which they randomly responded to questions, and their self-reports were compared with their VRIN, F, and FB scores. The major findings showed that partial random responding occurred with some frequency and that self-reports of random responding correlated significantly with MMPI-2 random-responding measures. This study supports the construct validity of the VRIN scale and its sensitivity to random responding.

In another investigation of the sensitivity of the validity scales to detect random responding and malingering, Wetter instructed college students to either randomly respond to the entire MMPI-2 or to fake various levels of psychiatric disturbance. Their results showed that the VRIN scale was elevated only in the random-responding group. The F and FB scales were elevated in both the random and malingering groups. It appears that the VRIN scale is essential to examine when the F or FB scale is elevated.

Although random responding elevates the VRIN scale, a high or intermediate VRIN score may not always indicate carelessness or uncooperativeness. Bond suggested that individuals with higher inconsistencies scores tend to endorse more maladjustment items. This view is consistent with data presented by Greene, who demonstrated that 43% of 68/86 code types could result from inconsistency. In fact, he pointed out that most code patterns that include Scale 8 frequently could result from inconsistency. This makes sense, given that seriously thought-disturbed individuals such as those obtaining the 86 or 68 profile (e.g., individuals with schizophrenia) are likely to have difficulty maintaining the consistent set that normal have during testing. Another possible explanation for in determinant range scores on the VRIN scale (raw scores of 7 to 13) involves not carelessness or lack of cooperation but rather indecisiveness. If an item is clearly applicable or inapplicable to an individual, it will be relatively easy to respond with certainty and consistency. However, an item with ambiguous application to the person involves a complex judgment process that can change on a repeated presentation of an item. Bond studied the MMPI responses of college students and found that indecision, rather than carelessness, may be a more important determinant of inconsistency on repeated items. Even though Bond was studying the repeated items on the Carelessness scale and the TR index, it may be valid to generalize his findings about semantic inconsistency to the item pairs on the VRIN scale. Bond offered three possible reasons for which items may elicit indecision: (a) the degree of ambiguity in an item perceived by the respondent, (b) the perceived degree of relevance an item has to the respondent, and (c) the degree of conflict aroused in a respondent by an item that is applicable but of an undesirable nature. Whereas carelessness may be one factor for elevated scores or inconsistency measures, other factors, such as indecision and maladjustment, could also be important contributing determinants.

Examination of the MMPI-2 manual shows that for the contemporary normal men and women there is a small but significant correlation between the VRIN scale and recent life changes and a social readjustment rating scale. There is also a small but significant correlation between dysphoria and hostility and the VRIN scale for a subsample of men and women, as rated by their life partners on an adjustment scale. The implications raised by Bond and gleaned from the MMPI-2 manual data are that indeterminant scores of normal and psychiatric patients on the VRIN scale may not reveal inconsistent or careless responding as much as indecisive responding, a result that would suggest quite different empirical correlates and meaning. This issue needs more study in order to make interpretive sense out of scores in the indeterminant range on the VRIN scale.

True Response Inconsistency Scale (TRIN)

The TRIN scale is a new scale consisting of 23 item pairs designed to assist in the interpretation of the traditional validity indicators. Like the VRIN scale, the TRIN scale reflects the tendency of a participant to respond to items in a contradictory or inconsistent fashion. Although VRIN items can have either similar or opposite content, TRIN items consist exclusively of pairs that are opposite in content. According to the MMPI-2 manual, inconsistency is scored as follows:

> *If a participant responds inconsistently by answering true to both items of certain pairs, one point is added to the TRIN score; if the participant responds inconsistently by answering false to certain item pairs, one point is subtracted. Consequently, a very high*

TRIN score indicates a tendency for the test participant to give true answers to the items indiscriminately ("acquiescence") and a very low TRIN score indicates a tendency to answer false indiscriminately ("non-acquiescence")(negative TRIN scores are avoided by adding a constant to the raw score). In other words, very low or very high TRIN scores are warning that the test participant may have been answering the inventory indiscriminately so that the profile may be invalid and uninterpretable.

The following examples of TRIN items, with the scored direction in parentheses, illustrate the scoring characteristics of the scale.

3. I wake up fresh and rested most mornings. (True) 39. My sleep is fitful and disturbed. (True)

This pair of items is one of the 14 item pairs to which the inconsistent response is "true." A test participant endorsing both of these items would receive 1 raw score point. The following pair of items illustrates an inconsistent response if both items are answered "false." A total of nine pairs of items are scored in the false direction.

9. My daily life is full of things that keep me interested. (False)
56. I wish I could be as happy as others seem to be. (False)

For this pair, or any pair of items scored false on the VRIN scale, 1 point is subtracted from the total raw score. A score of 9 points is always added to the final score to avoid the possibility of negative scores. For example, a client endorsing only falsely scored pairs of items on the TRIN scale and no scored items in the true direction would obtain a negative score if it were not for the constant being added.

The MMPI-2 manual shows that the contemporary sample of men and women averaged approximately 9 raw score points on the TRIN scale. Test-retest reliability data in the MMPI-2 manual for about a 1-week interval show normal men and women to have a correlation coefficient of .34 and .52, respectively. The manual also recommends that a TRIN score of 5 or less or 13 or greater would suggest inconsistent responding. A low raw score reflects a false-response bias, whereas higher scores reflect a true-response bias. The contemporary normal sample is used as a reference group for converting the raw scores on the TRIN scale to linear T scores.

Interpretation of the TRIN scale often can clarify the validity of a particular profile. For example, a high F score in conjunction with the markedly elevated TRIN score suggests indiscriminate responding, whereas an elevated T score with a low to moderate TRIN score reveals a possible magnification of symptoms or marked psychopathology. The TRIN scale, like the VRIN scale, should always be assessed when interpreting the validity of any MMPI-2 profile.

Infrequency Scale (F)

The F scale was designed to measure the tendency of an individual to respond to the test items in an unusual manner, such as in the case of not comprehending the items. On the MMPI-2, it consists of 60 items (64 items on the MMPI) to which at least 90% of the normals in the original standardization group responded in the same direction (either true or false). Whether an F scale item is answered true or false is irrelevant; the point is that the items are said to have high community agreement in most cases. According to Marks, Seeman, and Haller, "every time a participant responds in a rare direction, they are deviating from the community on some participant in which it is in exceedingly high agreement". For this reason, the scale has come to be called the Frequency or Infrequency scale. Because the probability is .90 or better that for any given item the normal participant will answer in the popular direction, it is not surprising that the mean number of deviant responses for the F scale is relatively low for the MMPI-2 normative sample (mean score for men = 4.5, mean score for women = 3.7). Normal individuals responding to the test with the usual care and understanding usually will not obtain raw score values above 6 or T -score values higher than 55 on the MMPI-2 (Butcher et al., 1989). However, individuals suffering from situational distress (e.g., loss of a loved one or relationship or job-related problems) or psychopathology often will elevate their F scale score as high as T -score values of 65 or greater.

The F scale items represent a broad range of content that obviously suggests deviant behavior, making it relatively easy for individuals either to deny symptoms or to over claim problems, depending on their motives. Examples of F scale items, with the item numbers and keyed responses, are as follows:

> *24. Evil spirits possess me at times. (True) 30. I have nightmares every few nights. (True) 36. When I am with people, I am bothered by hearing very queer things. (True) 78. I am liked by most people who know me. (False) 126. I believe in law enforcement. (False) 168. I have had periods in which I carried on activities without knowing later what I had been doing. (True)*

The F scale underwent some changes in the restandardization, with 12 modifications to the 60 items, including six grammatical changes, five modernizations of idioms and usage, and one change in sexist wording. The content of the F scale remains diverse and includes psychotic-type experiences and strange sensations, social maladjustment, poor physical health, hostility, and unconventional beliefs. Because 25 of the 60 items overlap other scales, and because about one third of the scale items are scored on the so-called psychotic tetrad scales (Scales 6, 7, 8, and 9), increasing elevations on the F scale are usually associated with increasing psychotic scale elevations. Greene pointed out that 15 F scale items overlap with Scale 8 (Schizophrenia) and 9 items overlap with Scale 6 (Paranoia).

The F scale when elevated is considered one of the most sensitive scales of the test for indicating severity of maladjustment and generally tends to correspond to the overall elevation of the clinical scales. For this reason, seriously or acutely disturbed individuals tend to obtain elevated scores on this scale. Also, people who exaggerate their concerns and psychological problems by over claiming symptoms elevate the F scale, whereas individuals wishing to appear free of psychological problems tend to produce low scores. Numerous studies have supported the validity of the F scale in detecting people who over claim symptoms or malinger, with the general result that the F scale is elevated above a T score of 90. Cutoffs vary for this scale according to the setting, but scores above 90 generally should raise the concern of the clinician to look for other indications in the MMPI-2 of exaggeration or random responding as well as in non test data, such as interviews, life history data, and observations from people familiar with the participant. In a recent review of the MMPI with a focus on the validity scales, Berry, Baer and Harris meta-analytically reviewed 28 studies that used the

NCVTI to detect malingering. The multiple comparisons contrasting malingering and honest groups on the raw and T -scaled F scores showed that this scale (particularly raw score values of F) is one of the most powerful measures on the test in detecting faking. The F scale was elevated slightly over 2 SD s above scores of participants answering honestly. Although their study identified other measures in the test for detecting malingering, the F scale was clearly the measure of choice for detecting "faking bad." It is recommended, however, that the reader not rely on any one scale in deciding about an individual's test-taking attitudes. Rather, a combination of measures coupled with non test data should be considered in the clinical decision-making/ inference process.

Elevated F scale scores may result from either a single factor, such as poor comprehension, random responding, severe psychosis or malingering, or a combination of these factors. Therefore, it is important to consider the F scale as serving three important functions. First, the scale should be considered as an indication of the openness or guarded approach of the test taker. Next, if the profile appears valid and the F scale score is in the patient range, it may roughly indicate the person's level of distress or maladjustment. Last, scores on the scale can serve to suggest behavioral correlates about the individual. Numerous recent studies and reviews have provided useful guidelines for interpreting elevations on this scale.

Test-retest correlation coefficients for 82 men and 111 women from the contemporary normative sample are reported in the MMIPI-2 manual. These participants were retested at an average interval of 8.58 days (Mdn = 7 days), with men and women showing test-retest values of .78 and .69, respectively. Although the MNWI-2 manual does not present similar data for psychiatric patients, Dahlstrom reported test-retest coefficients for psychiatric cases on the F scale that range from.80 to.81 with a 1-to 2-day interval between tests and from .63 to .76 with a 1-year interval between tests. In a large-scale meta-analysis of MMPI reliability studies using a wide variety of populations conducted between 1970 and 1981, Hunsley found an average internal consistency of .77 across 70 studies of the F scale. They also reported an average test-retest reliability of .70 for 15 studies, with time intervals from 1 day to 2 years.

F-Back Scale (FB)

The FB scale was developed on the MMPI-2 to operate in a manner similar to the F scale, but the items appear later in the inventory. The 60-item F scale is scored within the first 361 items, with 82% of the items scored between Items 1 and 299. The last F scale item is 361, which indicates that this sensitive scale prematurely stops its measurement function short of the entire instrument. Therefore, the restandardization committee for the MMPI-2 designed a 40-item F -Back scale (so named because of the location of the items in Form Ax) to pick up where the F scale left off. FB begins at Item 281. Although the basic validity and clinical scales are all scored within the first 370 items, many of the content and supplementary scale items occur after Item 370. Therefore, a scale similar to the F scale was needed for the latter part of the test to detect random or faking-bad/faking-good tendencies that could affect the content and supplementary scale scores.

Items on the FB scale were selected if they were endorsed by less than 10% of the contemporary normative sample in the deviant direction. The majority of FB scale items (95 %) are concentrated between Items 300 and 5 67, making the scale sensitive to a response set or shift in responding due to fatigue or a change in cooperation during the latter part of an MMPI-2 administration. In this regard, the FB scale serves a parallel function to the earlier occurring F scale, with a wideband sensitivity to different response sets, including symptom magnification or fabrication, random responding, and severe psychopathology. The following are examples of FB scale items, with the scoring direction indicated in parentheses:

> *281. I dislike having people around me. (True) 291. I have never been in love with anyone. (True) 303. Most of the time I wish I were dead. (True) 311. I often feel as if things are not real. (True) 407. I deserve severe punishment for my sins. (True) 463. Several times a week I feel as if something dreadful is about to happen. (True) 383. When things get really bad, I know I can count on my family for help. (False) 404. I have no trouble swallowing. (False)*

It should be noted that the FB scale, although similar in its construction to the F scale, is somewhat different in its content. The predominant content theme in the F scale appears to be psychoticism, whereas the main theme for the FB scale appears to be acute distress and depression. Therefore, clinicians should consider this content difference when making any interpretive inferences from the two scales.

Because the FB scale was constructed to appear later in the test, it shares little item overlap with the standard clinical scales. The FB scale shares two items each with Scales 6 (Paranoia) and 7 (Psychasthenia) and nine items with Scale 8 (Schizophrenia). However, because most of the items are scored between Items 300 and 567, there is significant overlap with the content scales and, to a lesser degree, with the supplementary scales. For example, the FB scale shares as many as 6 items with the content scales DEP (Depression) and FRS (Fears) and as few as one item with SOD (Social Discomfort), ANX (Anxiety), ANG (Anger), and HEA (Health Concerns).

As mentioned above, although some content differences exist between the FB and the F scales, examination of the partner ratings in the contemporary normative sample shows that the FB scale is similar to the F scale in that it shows significant positive correlations with dysphoria, hostility, impulsivity, and antisocial behavior and negative correlations with sociability and conformity. It should be noted that almost the entire FB scale is keyed in the "true" direction (37 of the 40 items), so a "true" response bias will tend to elevate the scale. A very high score should be checked against the TRIN score, VRIN score, and the answer sheet itself.

Internal consistency estimates for the FB scale is .71 for a subsample of 82 men in the normative sample and .75 for a subsample of 111 women. Test-retest reliability coefficients for the same participants are .86 for men and .71 for women, with a mean test-retest interval of 8.5 days. F scale test-retest correlation coefficients are much lower for men (.78) and about the same for women.

Although the construction method was similar for the F and FB scales, the same raw score values will yield more extreme T scores on the FB scale than on the F scale because the FB scale has a smaller standard deviation than the F scale. This is, in part, because the FB scale has fewer items (40 items vs. 60 on the F scale) and, more importantly, because the FB scale, unlike the F scale, has been derived on the basis of the contemporary MMPI-2 norms and as a result has a higher proportion of items with extreme endorsement frequencies.

Berry found that a raw score of 9 on the FB scale out predicted the ability of the VRIN scale to detect random profiles (the VRIN scale is described later in this chapter). Berry had 180 college students complete the MMPI-2 under standard instructions prior to having their test booklets removed and the remaining blanks on the answer sheet randomly completed. Groups of students had their booklets removed after 100, 200, 300, 400, or 500 items were completed. The more random responses that were given, the higher the FB scores (as well as those for the F and VRIN scales). Thus, the scale appears to be sensitive to random responding. Berry also found the FB scale to be sensitive to random responding in job applicants and community volunteers; a significant number of these normal participants taking the MMPI-2 admitted to answering some of the MMPI-2 items in a random manner. The range of average random responses was between 12 and 38. Positive correlations between the FB scale (and other validity scales) and the participant's self-estimations of random responding support the sensitivity of the FB scale to non content responding.

Further support for the sensitivity of the FB scale to detect not only random responding but also malingering comes from an investigation by Wetter, Baer, Berry, Smith, and Larsen. These researchers explored the effects of both random responding and malingering on the validity scales of the MMPI-2 using four groups of college students. One group completed the answer sheet in a random manner, two other groups were told to complete the MMPI-2 so as to appear moderately or severely disturbed, and the last group answered honestly. The FB scale was sensitive to all four conditions and performed as well as the F scale. The FB scale scores increased in elevation with the level of feigned disturbance. The fake-severe disturbance group produced the highest FB score (M =119, SD = 4.2), followed by random responders (M = 116.5, SD = 6.0). The values for the F scale followed the same pattern and were only slightly higher, except for the fake-severe group, which had an almost identical value (M =119.4, SD =3.7) to the FB scale.

The efficacy of the FB scale to detect the over reporting of symptoms is further illustrated in a study by Wetter, who instructed two groups of normal adults about the characteristics of posttraumatic stress disorder (PTSD) and paranoid schizophrenia and then asked them to simulate these disorders on the MMPI-2. To determine if the information about the disorders helped them to feign a realistic profile, Wetter compared their scores with actual groups of paranoid schizophrenic and PTSD patients. Having specific information about the psychological disorder did not enable the fakers to simulate actual patient profiles with the validity scales, including the FB scale. Specifically, the PTSD patients produced a mean FB T -scale score of 85 (SD =23.6), whereas the simulators produced a mean T - score value of 110 (SD =20.3). The paranoid schizophrenic patients produced a mean T -score value of 74.2 on the F(B) scale (SD =19.0), with the simulators earning a mean T -score value of 119.3 (SD =2.0). Clearly, the fakers tended to grossly over claim symptoms relative to the actual patients, a trend consistently seen in the faking-bad literature. Malingerers reliably score in the upper T -score ranges on both the F and FB scales.

Although the FB scale is a new scale, it has received significant research attention since its publication and appears to be a useful and valuable addition to the MMPI-2. In a recent meta-analysis of malingering scales and indexes on the MMPI-2, Rogers found that the FB scale yielded strong effect sizes for controls and psychiatric comparison groups. They did point out that large ranges of cutting scores exist for the FB, suggesting that clinicians need to exercise the same caution in interpreting this scale as they do for the other validity measures. Greene suggested interpreting the elevation on the FB scale in a similar manner to the F scale because the construction of the two scales is so similar. This appears to be a practical suggestion, but readers should be aware that they could encounter profiles in which the FB scale may be significantly more elevated than the F scale (e.g., a participant may produce an FB scale T score of 110 with an F scale T score of 65). Such a difference suggests the possibility of fatigue, uncooperativeness, or random responding in the latter portion of the MMPI-2 rendering the content and supplementary scales uninterpretable. However, because the person responded consistently in the earlier part of the test, the standard clinical scales can be meaningfully analyzed. It is rare to see the converse situation a high F scale score but a within-normal-limit-range FB scale score.

Such a protocol would suggest standard interpretation of the content or supplementary scales, but caution should be exercised in interpreting the clinical scales. In general, a multivariate approach to profile validity is suggested, with the examination of the FB scale being an important part of this process. It is important to recall that the difference in content between the F scale (which emphasizes psychoticism) and the FB scale (which emphasizes acute distress) may also account for discrepancies between elevations on these scales.

Cutoff scores for validity measures in the MMPI-2 vary from study to study as a function of local base rates and participant characteristics, such as educational level and intelligence. Therefore, the psychologist would be wise to examine each protocol on an individual basis while considering different factors, including, but not limited to, the participant's motivation or test-taking attitude (e.g., over reporting in an attempt to gain sympathy or monetary gain as in a personal injury litigation case), socioeconomic factors, reading ability (which could affect comprehension), and psychopathology (which can operate independently or in concert with any of the above-mentioned factors). Guidelines for determining an invalid profile are described in this chapter; however, in general, the same T -score values that apply for the F scale should be used for the FB scale in suggesting profile invalidity.

Measures of Response Style

The usefulness of the standard validity scales can be enhanced by examining additional measures of reporting or response styles, which can be distinguished as self-favorable or self-unfavorable in nature. Self-deception and impression management tendencies are factors important to consider in clinical, forensic, and personnel settings, where motivation can affect the test results.

The DS and F(p) scales are categorized as measuring the reporting of self-unfavorable traits, attributes, and dispositions that the participant believes to be false. Scales L, K, S, Mp, Sd, and Ss are measuring the displaying or mimicking of self-favorable traits, attributes, and dispositions. These scales are not meant to be inclusive of all available scales for use but rather represent what we recognize to be the mainstream measurements or those with the potential to develop into useful adjuncts to the standard validity scales.

Self-unfavorable Scales

The Infrequency-Psychopathology Scale: F(p): The F(p) scale was designed by Arbisi and Ben-Porath for the NIMPI-2 as an additional self-unfavorable or over reporting measure, particularly for use with patient populations in which a high rate of endorsement of psychological disturbance is expected. They suggested that the F(P) scale be used to understand elevations on the F scale, which may be elevated for several reasons, including random responding, poor reading comprehension of the items, genuine psychopathology, or an attempt to fake bad (i.e., attempt to portray one's self as more impaired than is actually the case). As previously described, the F scale contains items that were endorsed by less than 10% of the normal standardization group of the original MMPI; it was not constructed of items that were endorsed infrequently by psychiatric patients (a common misconception about the scale). Therefore, an elevated F scale score cannot automatically be assumed to be an indication of malingering of illness or of an invalid profile. The F(p) scale was constructed of items endorsed rarely (20% or less in the keyed direction) by two separate groups of patients with known psychiatric disturbance and by members of the MMPI-2 restandardization sample. As noted by Arbisi and Ben-Porath, there are overlapping items between the F(p) scale and certain clinical scales, especially Scale 8 (Sc), with which it shares five items in common. The item overlap between the F(p) scale and the other clinical scales is substantially less than that between the F and FB scales and the clinical scales. The F(p) scale contains 27 items, of which 15 overlap with the F scale. The following items represent examples of the content on this new scale, with the direction of scoring following the item in parentheses:

66. It would be better if all laws were thrown away. (True)

93. Sometimes when I am not feeling well I am irritable. (False)

162. Someone has been trying to poison me. (True)

252. Everything tastes the same. (True)

478. I hate my whole family. (True)

Arbisi and Ben-Porath suggested that when the F(p) scale is elevated along with the F scale, the clinician can more confidently attribute the high scores to a patient's attempt to over report psychopathology if other validity measures such as the VRIN and TRIN scales are not elevated significantly. More recent investigations have found that the F(p) scale is less influenced by diagnostic membership and the confounding effects of distress and psychopathology than is the F scale and is more effective than the F scale in distinguishing groups with genuine psychopathology from those asked to feign psychiatric impairment. However, Bagby, Rogers, Buis found that the F(p) scale was more effective in distinguishing patients with schizophrenia from participants feigning that disorder whereas the F and FB scales were better able to identify patients with depression from participants feigning depression. This finding is not surprising, given that the F(p) item content is more relevant to psychoticism than it is to major depression. Nicholson found that the F(p) scale failed to outperform the F scale in their malingering comparisons. Even so, Nicholson noted "that F(p) may be the preferred index of fake bad responding when the two indicators perform comparably because interpretation of elevated scores appears more straight-forward in the case of F(p) than F".

Rothke provided normative data for the F(p) scale with a large variety of clinical and forensic samples, including psychiatric inpatients with borderline personality disorder (BPD), paranoid schizophrenia, PTSD, and alcoholism, as well as pain management patients, TBI patients, and Social Security disability-benefit applicants. In addition, data were provided for non litigating TBI patients and normal simulating BPD, PTSD, and paranoid schizophrenia. The results showed that elevations on the F(p) scale are infrequent in most clinical samples; elevations are much more common when malingering or exaggeration of psychopathology is expected. Consistent with the findings of Arbisi and Ben-Porath, Rothke 's study supports the finding that the F(p) scale is relatively independent of psychiatric diagnoses and is less sensitive than scale the F or FB scale to specific psychopathology.

It is recommended that the F(p) scale be studied further, but its applied use should be governed by using a sequence of steps, as well as observing cautions about its potential limitations. Arbisi and Ben-Porath recommended that the following sequence be followed in interpreting an elevated F scale: (a) Rule out random responding and acquiescence by eliminating profiles with elevated VRIN (T ? 100) or TRIN (T ? 80) scores; (b) rule out malingering or exaggeration by considering whether F(p) is elevated; and (c) if the results of steps a and b are negative, then a high F scale can be considered consistent with psychopathology. An elevated FB score should be interpreted with the same sequence.

When an elevated F(p) scale is encountered, we recommend that an examination be made of which items are endorsed before a conclusion about exaggeration or malingering is made. For example, four of the items on the F(p) scale (Items 90, 192, 276, and 478) deal with participants' views of their mother and father and whether they love (loved) their parents and family. Rothke reported a case of a patient with no other signs of malingering or secondary gain issues who endorsed all four of these items, consistent with a very significant history of impaired family relationships. Despite the fact that these items were rarely endorsed by the clinical derivation sample or the normal standardization group, we suggest that the clinician be mindful of a history of significant family problems before interpreting an F(p) score inflated by the endorsement of two or more of these four items. Given that it takes very few item endorsements to inflate an F(p) score, these types of concerns should be addressed to avoid over interpreting the meaning of an elevated F(p) score.

It is important to recognize that because the F(p) items extend almost throughout the inventory (up to Item 555), an elevated F(p) score could be due to item endorsements fairly evenly distributed or concentrated early or late or even in the middle of the instrument. To address these types of concerns, the MWI-2 restandardization committee added the FB scale to cover infrequently endorsed items that occur later in the MNEPI-2 (as described earlier, the F scale stops its measurement function at Item 361). This was done with the awareness that individuals may change their approach (e.g., because of fatigue, uncooperativeness, or boredom) to answering the items during the test administration. The utility of the FB scale lies in the fact that many important scales (e.g., content and supplementary) occur later in the inventory and warrant interpretive caution should the FB scale be significantly elevated.

Similarly, Arbisi and Ben-Porath and Arbisi, McNulty, Ben-Porath and Boyd recognized that the F(p) scale could be applied in a similar way as the F and FB scales. That is, by dividing the F(p) item content into items occurring earlier versus later in the test, they could identify differences on these subcomponent scales, which could help explain an elevated FB or F score. These component subscales are named F(p)1 and F(p)2. The F(p)1 subscale begins with Item 51 and ends with Item 252; the F(p)2 subscale begins with Item 270 and ends with Item 501. The following examples should help illustrate how scoring for the F(p)1 and F(p)2 subscales could assist in the interpretive process. Consider a participant who obtains an acceptable VRIN and TRIN score, indicating consistent responding, but significantly elevates the FB scale with a normal-range F score. Examination of the F(p) score for possible exaggeration might reveal a slightly elevated scale score (e.g., raw score of 3 or 4) but not one which is considered exceedingly high in terms of a T - score value. By scoring the F(p)1 and F(p)2 subscales, the clinician could discover that all three or four items were endorsed on the F(p)2 subscale, thereby raising the distinct possibility that the respondent began exaggerating his or her complaints in the latter part of the inventory. This should alert the clinician to be careful to not over interpret the content and supplementary scales that occur later in the inventory. When the F and F(p) scales are elevated without the FB scale also being elevated, an inspection of the F(p) subscales can help the clinician feel confident to interpret the content and supplementary scales if the F(p)2 subscale is not significantly elevated.

Clearly, research is needed to better understand the operating characteristics of these new components subscales, but they appear to have promise in assisting test interpreters to identify response sets occurring early or late in the test administration process. It is important to remember that specific clinical settings reflect different base rates of psychopathology; it is therefore critical that clinicians understand the nature of their population with regard to frequency and type of psychopathology before interpreting the F(p) scale or any other scale score. Arbisi and Ben-Porath recommended that additional studies be conducted in settings in which clear incentives to feign symptoms exist. Rothke suggested that future investigations of samples of psychiatric or injured patients control for motivation to appear impaired (as might be the case in patients involved in litigation, seeking disability compensation, or attempting to avoid criminal prosecution) by carefully interviewing the patient or by record review as the F(p) scale appears sensitive to efforts to over report symptoms. In the Rothke study, participants who were either in the process of litigation and seeking compensation, or feigning psychiatric conditions produced elevated F(p) scores, supporting the construct validity of the scale. This is not to suggest, however, that all litigating participants exaggerate their complaints. When used with clinical judgment, the F(P) scale can be a useful addition to the assessment of MMPI-2 profile validity.

Dissimulation Scale (Ds)

Gough developed the 74-item Ds scale by identifying MMPI items that empirically differentiated a group of patients classified as psychoneurotic from a group of test normal (college students and professional psychologists) instructed to take the MMPI simulating the role of a neurotic patient. The items separating the simulators from the patients were further studied in a cross-validation procedure. The simulators tended to score much higher than the actual neurotic patients, suggesting that individuals prevailing stereotypes about neuroticism were not a good fit to the actual construct of neuroticism as measured by the MMPI. The Ds scale is intended to be used for assessing the intentional overstatement of psychological disturbance or faking sick. The function of the scale is similar to the F and FB scales, although the content of the Ds scale is much more subtle than the latter scales, where "what is the rare and atypical response" is consistently obvious. The Ds scale does not have the extreme or psychotic-related item content of the F and FB scales and overlaps neurotic exaggeration as much as psychotic malingering. It is therefore useful in assessing the intentional exaggeration of a variety of symptoms for financial gain or manipulative intent. Rogers also pointed out that the scale is multifaceted and extends beyond neurotic symptoms. Gough indicated that the Ds items covered the following: physical complaints and dysfunctions; feelings of victimization, injustice, and discouragement; irritability, fear, and anxiety; lack of independence and self-sufficiency; discontent with childhood and family background; sexual conflicts and preoccupations; and bizarre ideation and religiosity.

The MMPI-2 has retained 58 of the original 74 Ds items (78.4%) of which 19% were altered. The following items are examples of the Ds scale content, with the direction of scoring in parentheses. Note that the majority of the scale items are scored as "true" (48), with 10 items scored as "false."

17. I am sure I get a raw deal from life. (True)

22. No one seems to understand me. (True)

57. I hardly ever feel pain in the back of my neck. (False)

72. My soul sometimes leaves my body. (True)

75. I usually feel that life is worthwhile. (False)

In providing a general review of the Ds scale with a few specific research examples, we wish to convey the point that the basic findings are consistent across studies; that is, that the Ds scale appears to measure exaggerated claims of psychopathology. There are a number of recent and older studies and reviews supporting the construct validity of the scale.

Anthony instructed 40 nonpsychotic U.S. Air Force male clients, after taking the MMPI under usual administration conditions, to exaggerate the troubles that had brought them to treatment so that their read ministered MMPI would reflect a more severe condition than they were actually experiencing. They were also asked to exaggerate in a way that was not clearly obvious. The 74-item Ds scale was scored, and the results showed an optimum hit rate of 86% in identifying exaggerated MMPI profiles. This hit rate was higher than the F -- K (81%) and F raw-score (81%) hit rates. The findings support the utility of the Ds scale in discriminating exaggerated MMPIs from authentically produced deviant profiles. In support of Anthony's findings, Greene stated that the Ds scale appears useful in identifying fake-bad profiles.

Walters found support for the use of the Ds-r scale, an abbreviated version of the Ds scale, in an inmate population for identifying genuinely disturbed inmates. In the first part of a two-phase study, Walters et al. were interested in how the standard validity and clinical scales performed against the Ds-r scale (and other indexes). The participants were 72 male inmates with maximum security status at a U.S. penitentiary. A structured psychiatric interview was administered to the inmates, generally within one day of an administered MMPI. A 4-point rating scale was created to evaluate an inmate's proneness to exaggerate psychiatric symptomatology. The ratings were made by two psychologists familiar with both the inmates and their contact with others (e.g., work supervisors). The average length of time between the psychiatric interview and the rating assignment was 7.6 months. A rating of 1 on the scale reflected malingering, whereas a rating of 4 indicated no malingering or embellishment of symptornatology. The base-rate estimate for psychopathology in this setting was estimated to be 60%. An abbreviated MMPI was scored (first 400 items of Form R), so only 28, rather than 40, Ds-r items could be scored. Therefore, prorated T-scores were calculated for the Ds-r scale. The results showed that the MMPI validity and clinical scales (with the exception of Scale 1) could not accurately discriminate the malingerers from the nonmalingerers. Although the Ds-r scale failed to improve on the base-rate criterion in the study without the assistance of an indeterminant category, it could differentiate malingering from genuine psychopathology. Low scores on the Ds-r scale were predictive of authentic pathology, but high scores failed to correlate with malingering.

More recently, Berry, Baer and Harris meta-analytically reviewed 28 studies that used the original MMPI to detect malingering. The contrasting of several malingering and honest groups on several reporting measures showed the original Ds scale to be one of the most effective measures in detecting over reporting and one of the indexes of choice for identifying malingering. The mean effect size in T -scale value was approximately 2 SDs (d = 2.17) for the Ds scale. For the original Dissimulation scale (Ds), a raw cutting score of 35 was common across studies and had a hit rate of about 88%. The revised Dissimulation scale (Ds - r) had much lower effect sizes when contrasting faking and honest groups, suggesting caution in its use.

Whereas Berry, Baer and Harris focused on findings with the original MMPI, Rogers examined different faking indicators specifically for the MWI-2. Rogers et al. reported that although the meta-analysis by Berry, Baer, and Harris demonstrated the efficacy of the Ds scale in assessing malingering, unfortunately most of the MMPI-2 studies had relied on the shortened 34-item version of the Dissimulation scale, sometimes referred to as Ds - r 2. The Ds - r 2 yielded only a moderate effect size in the meta-analysis. The longer 58-item version of the scale is likely to be more discriminating in its detection of dissimulated profiles. Berry found the Ds 2 scale (58 items) to be effective in detecting the over reporting of closed-head injury symptoms by nonclinical participants instructed to fake such a syndrome and by compensation-seeking (vs. non-compensation-seeking) closed-head injury patients. Berry cautioned that an unelevated over reporting scale score, such as on the Ds - r 2, does not automatically rule out the possibility of feigning of neuropsychological problems was administered to the inmates, generally within one day of an administered MMPI. A 4-point rating scale was created to evaluate an inmate's proneness to exaggerate psychiatric symptomatology. The ratings were made by two psychologists familiar with both the inmates and their contact with others (e.g., work supervisors). The average length of time between the psychiatric interview and the rating assignment was 7.6 months. A rating of 1 on the scale reflected malingering, whereas a rating of 4 indicated no malingering or embellishment of symptomatology. The base-rate estimate for psychopathology in this setting was estimated to be 60%. An abbreviated MMPI was scored (first 400 items of Form R), so only 28, rather than 40, Ds -r items could be scored. Therefore, prorated T-scores were calculated for the Ds -r scale. The results showed that the MMPI validity and clinical scales (with the exception of Scale 1) could not accurately discriminate the malingerers from the non malingerers. Although the Ds - r scale failed to improve on the base-rate criterion in the study without the assistance of an indeterminant category, it could differentiate malingering from genuine psychopathology. Low scores on the Ds - r scale were predictive of authentic pathology, but high scores failed to correlate with malingering.

Berry, Baer and Harris meta-analytically reviewed 28 studies that used the original MWI to detect malingering. The contrasting of several malingering and honest groups on several reporting measures showed the original Ds scale to be one of the most effective measures in detecting over reporting and one of the indexes of choice for identifying malingering. The mean effect size in T -scale value was approximately 2 SDs (d = 2.17) for the Ds scale. For the original Dissimulation scale (Ds), a raw cutting score of 35 was common across studies and had a hit rate of about 88%. The revised Dissimulation scale (Ds - r) had much lower effect sizes when contrasting faking and honest groups, suggesting caution in its use.

Whereas Berry, Baer, and Harris focused on findings with the original NUVIPI, Rogers examined different faking indicators specifically for the MMPI-2. Rogers et al. reported that although the meta-analysis by Berry, Baer, and Harris demonstrated the efficacy of the Ds scale in assessing malingering, unfortunately most of the MAVI-2 studies had relied on the shortened 34-item version of the Dissimulation scale, sometimes referred to as Ds - r 2. The Ds - r 2 yielded only a moderate effect size in the meta-analysis. The longer 58-item version of the scale is likely to be more discriminating in its detection of dissimulated profiles. Berry found the Ds 2 scale (58 items) to be effective in detecting the over reporting of closed-head injury symptoms by nonclinical participants instructed to fake such a syndrome and by compensation-seeking (vs. noncompensation-seeking) closed-head injury patients. Berry cautioned that an unelevated over reporting scale score, such as on the Ds - r 2, does not automatically rule out the possibility of feigning of neuropsychological problems.

It is possible that a participant fabricating or exaggerating closed-head injury symptoms might not conceptualize the syndrome as including psychiatric, as opposed to physical and cognitive problems. Thus, they might feign deficits on neuropsychological. testing but not on the MMPI-2 and hence not elevate oyer reporting scales.

We suggest that the 58-item version of the Dissimulation scale (Ds) is a useful additional scale in evaluating the validity of an MMPI-2 profile. However, more research is needed, especially with adolescents and actual samples of malingerers versus analogue study participants. Research findings vary regarding cut scores as a function of the population studied, the methodology used, and the sample size employed. For these reasons, it is recommended that an assessment of protocol validity be based on the examination of multiple MMPI-2 measures as well as rely on other clinical data beyond the MMPI-2, such as record reviews, life history data, and interview findings.

Self-favorable Scales

Factor studies of various measures of self-favorable responding to the MNPI have repeatedly produced findings indicating that defensiveness cannot be subsumed under a single dimension. In Wiggins analysis and expansion of these reports, he distinguished between Alpha, a dimension consistent with A. L. Edwards' interpretation of faking good on personality inventories without special instructions to do so and Gamma, which Wiggins interpreted as "social desirability in role-playing". Nichols and Greene, for example, found a strong tendency for scales developed under fake-good instructional sets to be highly correlated with each other but only weakly associated with scales like K and A. Paulhus proposed a two-factor model of social desirability responding that distinguishes between self-deception, the tendency to bias inventory responses brought about by the person's belief that such responses are true and justified, and impression management ("other deception"), a self-conscious and deliberate attempt to tailor responses so as to create a favorable impression and mislead the clinician in the direction of an overly benign personality description from test results. The Gamma dimension has been labeled variously as "lying", "propagandistic bias" and "impression management"; these labels converge on the theme of a self-conscious, or intentional, motivation to promote a favorable impression of the self. The Alpha dimension is largely coextensive with the first factor of the MMPI/MMPI-2, with the high end of this dimension being marked by scales that reflect distress, discomfort, and maladjustment and the negative pole marked by scales such as K, Es, S, and Ss. In the Wiggins and Paulhus analyses, this factor was marked by the K scale and Edwards' Social Desirability scale (So - r). Two of the scales described later, Butcher and Han's Superlative Self-Presentation scale (S) and S. E. Nelson's Socioeconomic Status scale (Ss), also are related to this dimension. The other two scales, Cofer, Chance and Judson's Positive Malingering scale (Mp) and Wiggins' (1959) Social Desirability scale (Sd) marked, along with the L scale, the Gamma dimension in the Wiggins and Paulhus studies.

Lie Scale (L)

The L scale consists of 15 items, all of which are scored in the false direction. The scale was designed as a validity indicator to detect intentional efforts to underreport problems. Underreporting of problems can occur in many settings and is often referred to as "faking good" or as defensive or socially desirable responding. Circumstances and settings that "promote" this response set include personnel selection situations, child custody litigation and other forensic cases, prison inmates wishing a transfer to a more desirable setting, patients wanting a release from a forced hospitalization, and clients coerced into marital or family treatment who want to look psychologically healthy. The L scale items had their origin in previous research on honesty and deceit by Hartshorne and May. Because the items for the L scale were borrowed from previous work and rewritten, they compose the only scale in the original MMPI that was not empirically constructed. The L scale provides 15 opportunities throughout the test for the participant to endorse certain virtues. The items represent socially virtuous behaviors (e.g., denial of dishonesties or aggressive feelings) that may be desirable for many people but are rarely true for most people. For this reason, the "items constituted a fairly subtle trap for anyone who wanted to give an unusually good impression of himself". The following are examples of L scale items, with the direction of scoring following the item in parentheses:

41. I do not always tell the truth. (False)

51. I do not read every editorial in the newspaper every day. (False.)

102. I get angry sometimes. (False)

203. I gossip a little at times. (False)

260. Once in a while I laugh at a dirty joke. (False)

Individuals are expected to claim some feelings of virtue, and most do, in fact, answer some items in the "lie" direction. The mean number of items answered in this direction by the contemporary normative sample was 3.5 for both men and women. The original MMPI Lie scale T -score values were arbitrarily established and did not provide separate validity scale values for men and women. However, the MMPI-2 Lie scale (and other validity scales) T -score values were established according to the new normative data with separate T -scores by gender.

Most often, higher raw scores on the L scale reflect the tendency to put oneself in a favorable light. Consequently, the clinical scales are expected to be suppressed because the individual is tending to deny basic human frailties and "look good." In addition to its sensitivity to detect obvious efforts at looking good, the L scale is also related to psychopathology when elevated, especially paranoid symptoms in some cases and certain neurotic conditions. Interpretive guidelines for the L scale.

Because all the items on the Lie scale are scored in the false direction, an all-false response set will elevate the L scale as well as Scales 1, 2, and 3, for which the deviant response is usually false. An extremely low raw score on the L scale could likewise reflect an all-true response bias. When this is suspected, the TRIN scale should be investigated. In the MMPI-2 revision, the L scale lost no items, although the sexist wording on some items was changed and one item was changed to reflect more modern usage. The majority of the items on the L scale (n = 9) do not overlap the other MMPI-2 scales. The largest overlap occurs with Scales 2 and 9, each sharing two items in common with the L scale.

Moderator variables (e.g., SES, education, and occupation) can greatly affect scores on the L scale. The item content of the scale is fairly obvious, and sophisticated individuals rarely elevate the scale, perhaps because they realize it would be unconvincing to give such a distorted response to the items. College educated individuals and those with a higher SES infrequently obtain T scores above 50; thus, elevated L scale score for a college-educated individual should be carefully evaluated. Individuals of lower SES with less education tend to earn higher scores on the L scale because the items reflect a more obvious form of test-taking defensiveness.

Test-retest reliability coefficients on the L scale for the MMPI-2 over an approximate 1-week interval shows coefficients of .77 for men and.81 for women in a subset of the contemporary normal sample. Retest data are not available in the manual for psychiatric patients on this scale. However, the earlier data on the original MMPI can be applied to the present MMPI-2 scale because its composition has not changed significantly. On the MMPI L scale, test-retest correlation coefficients for psychiatric cases range between .74 and .78 with a 1-to 2-day interval between tests and between .35 and .61 with a 1-year interval between administrations. In a large-scale meta-analysis of MMPI reliability using a wide variety of populations conducted between 1970 and 1981, Hunsley, Hanson, and Parker reported an average internal consistency of .77 across 70 studies of the L scale. They also reported an average test-retest reliability of .63 for eight studies with time intervals from 1 to 2 years.

Additional reliability data on the MMPI-2 are presented by Matz, Altepeter, and Perlman, who examined the temporal stability and internal consistency of the MMPI-2 in a sample of 128 students. Moderate to high stability coefficients were obtained (range=.60 to .90, Mdn =.74), with alpha coefficients ranging from .39 to .91 (Mdn =.62).

In a recent meta-analysis of 25 studies in which participants who responded honestly were compared with participants who underreported psychopathology, Baer et al. (1992) found that the L scale, relative to other special scales or indexes designed to detect underreporting, is a valid measure. In general, their review indicates that participants known to be underreporting problems tend to score about 1 SD above average on the L scale.

Correction Scale (K)

The original purpose for developing the K scale was to improve the sensitivity of the clinical scales to detect psychopathology by adding a correction or suppressor factor to the scaled scores. Without this correction factor there were too many false negatives or low-ranging MMPI scores among psychiatric patients whose psychopathology should have elevated certain clinical scales. The efforts of Meehl, Hathaway, and McKinley in the development of the K scale were directed primarily toward the reduction of false negatives without significantly affecting the number of accurate diagnostic identifications, or test hits. Experience with the MUTI also demonstrated that although the L and F scales were adequate in detecting extreme test-taking attitudes or distortions, they were less sensitive to more subtle expressions of defensiveness or the underreporting of problems. Recognizing that test scores are considerably influenced by test-taking attitudes, Meehl, Hathaway, and McKinley identified two important general test-taking approaches: (a) the tendency to be self-critical and overly self-disclosing ("plus getting") usually referred to as faking bad, and (b) the tendency to be defensive or to over portray one's virtues, often referred to as faking good. Proper interpretation of the validity scales, particularly the K scale, should aid in assessing the presence of a fake-bad or fake-good test attitude. Another way to conceptualize the function of the validity scales is along a continuum: One end measures an individual's willingness or capacity to be open to admitting problems, including an over declaration. of symptoms, and the other end measures the strong tendency to minimize problems or to be closed to admitting any problems at all.

The K scale was developed by selecting 25 male and 25 female psychiatric inpatients who obtained normal scale elevations (no T score over 70). These patients had L scale T scores of at least 60, indicating test-taking defensive and psychiatric diagnoses (e.g., alcoholism, personality disorders, or behavioral disturbances) rather than psychotic or neurotic disorders. The responses of these patients (who apparently were answering these test items in a defensive manner) were compared with those of some of the Minnesota normative cases used in the original standardization group. Item analysis yielded 22 items (common to men and women) that discriminated the "true and false negative profiles and their item endorsements by at least 30%". High scores on these items indicated more defensiveness and a greater likelihood of a false negative (e.g., a patient who should have generated an abnormal profile but who actually obtained a normal one). Low scores on these items were important in detecting false positives (i.e., cases in which normal obtained abnormal test scores). Because the 22-item K scale was insensitive to some depressed and schizophrenic patients who tended to produce normal-looking profiles, an additional 8 items were included to assist in separating the original normative group from these two patient groups and resulted in a final scale of 30 items. In addition to meeting the criterion of differentiating the normals from the abnormal (e.g., schizophrenic and depressive patients), the items also had to meet another criterion. Specifically, these items also had to be insensitive to participants who were instructed to fake good or fake bad, thereby implying that their content was not obvious.

By adding differential proportions of raw K scores to five of the clinical scales, Meehl, Hathaway, and McKinley were able to improve the ability of these scales to differentiate between the normal and criterion groups. The standard profile sheet is based on T scores corrected for the K additions, and test users are advised to make certain that they add the K -correction factor to five clinical scales. However, the MMPI-2 manual provides conversion tables for plotting non- K -corrected profiles, and many computer programs provide both K and non- K -corrected profiles for the test user. The raw K scale addition for Scale 1 (Hs) is 0.5 and 0.4 for Scale 4 (Pd), Scale 7 (Pt) and Scale 8 (Sc) have 1 full raw score value of K added, and Scale 9 (Ma) receives 0.2 K. The K -correction values remain unchanged in the MMPI-2. It is important to note that the K -correction value for any given clinical scale is related to the proportion of subtle items contained in the scale.

Because the K corrections were developed with adult psychiatric patients, it may not always be appropriate to use the K corrections with dissimilar populations. Greene reviewed the literature on the use of the K scale in various settings and concluded that, in general, little research justifies the continued widespread use of the K correction of the clinical scales. Greene stated that clinicians probably need to avoid using K corrections in settings in which normal persons are being evaluated with the MMPI-2, but they should use the K corrections in settings in which psychopathology is suspected, keeping in mind the potential inaccuracies that K corrections may introduce. More recently, Butcher studied the MMPI-2 profiles of airline pilot applicants. He noted that the majority of these participants tended to score above the clinical cutoff of T = 65 on the K scale, suggesting an overly favorable response pattern in a group of well-adjusted individuals. Because high K scale scores are common in many other personnel selection populations, the addition of the K correction to the profile may be inappropriate in situations assessing normals, given that the scale was developed to detect defensiveness in psychiatric populations. However, it does appear that most clinicians -- and most researchers continue to use the K correction despite this limitation. It is recommended for adults (e.g., those 18 years and older) that the reader apply the K correction and plot T scores with and without the K correction with normal populations until future research clarifies the appropriate parameters of its use. As Archer noted, "the raw score K -correction is not used in profiling T -scores for adolescents with either the original test instrument or the MMPI-A". It appears that adolescent MMPI profiles are more accurate without the K correction.

Most recently, Archer, Fontaine, and McCrae examined the accuracy of the K correction procedure in a large sample of psychiatric inpatients. Their results indicated that the K correction procedure with the MMPI and the MMPI-2 did not result in higher correlations with external criteria in comparison with non- K -corrected scores. They suggested that the reason that the original K -correction weights were retained for use in the MMPI-2 was because the massive research literature generated for the original MMPI was based on K -corrected scores. This raises a considerable dilemma, as researchers and clinicians can either use the K - or non- K -corrected scores:

> *They can use K -correction procedures with standard weights, which link their result7s to a large research literature, or the non- K -corrected scores, which relates to a much smaller literature but produces stronger evidence of concurrent validity. This dilemma can be resolved if future researchers report results of analyses using non- K -corrected scores (perhaps in addition to K -corrected scores), so that a comprehensive non- K -corrected research literature can eventually be developed for the MMPI-2.*

As pointed out by Putzke, Williams, Daniel and Boll, there is a relative dearth of studies examining the effectiveness of the K - correction procedure. Investigations are needed to examine various adult patient populations, as well as different clinical settings that vary in regard to the prevalence of defensiveness.

Twenty-nine of the 30 items on the K scale are scored in the "false" direction making the scale sensitive to the effects of an all-false or all-true response set, as well as reflecting the scale's function to measure the denial of problems. The mean number of K scale endorsements for men and women in the contemporary normative sample was approximately 15. The K scale contains five unique (non overlapping) items, with the remaining 25 items distributed somewhat equally across the clinical scales. The K scale content is wide-ranging and covers issues of self-control, family and interpersonal relationships, and the denial of problems. The following items from the K scale illustrate the wide-ranging content; the scored responses are indicated in parentheses:

29. At times I feel like swearing. (False)

83. I have very few quarrels with members of my family. (True)

116. Often I can't understand why I have been so irritable and grouchy. (False)

127. Criticism or scolding hurts me terribly. (False)

167. I find it hard to make talk when I meet new people. (False)

The K scale did not lose any items in the MMPI-2 revision, although one item was slightly altered for modernization purposes. Test-retest correlation coefficients based on the MMPI-2 contemporary normative sample for the K scale are.84 for men and.81 for women over an average interval of about 1 week. Internal consistency estimates for the MMPI-2 K scale are.73 for men and.71 for women. The MMPI-2 K scale does not appear to have lost any reliability in the revision process as the K scale is essentially unchanged. As expected, reliability coefficients for psychiatric patients are lower than those of normals. Test-retest correlation coefficients for psychiatric cases on the MMPI K scale range between .46 and .56 for a 1- to 2-day interval between tests and between .42 and .72 for a 1-year interval between tests. In Hunsley large-scale meta-analysis of MMPI reliability studies using a wide variety of populations conducted between 1970 and 1981, an average internal consistency of .82 across 71 studies of the K scale was reported. They also reported an average test-retest reliability of. .77 for 15 studies with time intervals from 1 day to 2 years.

Various elevations on the K scale are associated with different interpretations or personality correlates. Very-high-scoring participants (T score greater than or equal to 65) are generally described as maintaining a defensive posture and unwilling to admit to psychological problems. However, well-functioning individuals also describe themselves in similar terms, which may simply reflect that their lives are in order. For this reason, it is critical that the K scale score be assessed in the context of as much other information as possible, including the referral context and the person's past and current life situation. In general, elevated K scale scores are positively correlated with SES. The MMPI-2 manual points out that individuals with more status stand to lose more by making disclosures that reveal incompetence, ineffectiveness, and insecurities. Therefore, these individuals may try to slant their responses in such a way as to protect their self esteem and the impressions that others will form about them. The use of the K scale weights serve to correct for this type of defensiveness. Very-low-scoring participants on the K scale are often seen as being overly self-critical in confessing many psychological difficulties. In general, elevated K scores are associated with lower ranging clinical scale scores, whereas the converse is true for under elevated K scores. When there are clinical elevations in a high K profile, they tend to be associated with a neurotic triad. Individuals faking bad tend to over claim symptomatology, and the resulting low K scores are often associated with peaks on the psychotic tetrad scales. Socioeconomic factors, age, race, culture, and intelligence all affect the interpretation of the clinical and validity scales and must be considered when interpreting a profile.

It is important to recognize that a high T score on a clinical K-corrected scale could be due to the addition of a large K correction or due to a high raw score on that scale. Therefore, it is critical to examine the raw score values on the elevated scales. For example, a T score of 65 on Scale 7 (Pt) could be achieved in several ways. One way could consist of a male participant endorsing (a) 20 Scale 7 items in the deviant direction and 13 K scale items or (b) 10 Scale 7 items and 23 K scale items. The latter endorsement pattern reflects significantly more defensiveness or ability to cope with symptoms than does the former pattern. Inferring worry or tension from the T score values of 65 in the latter case may be misleading because the individual with the lower raw score value on Scale 7 is less likely to be experiencing worry and tension.

Interpretation of the validity scales is discussed more completely in chapter 5, but it should be pointed out that general psychiatric patients with bonafide disorders tend to score higher on the K scale than do normals instructed to feign a psychiatric disorder. A number of studies have supported this finding, with the implication being that scores on the K scale below a T score of 35 should be checked against other validity measures to ascertain the possibility of a faked or "over reported" profile. A recent study also illustrates that when test participants are instructed to fake a closed-head injury and are given specific information on how to manipulate the validity scales (including the K scale), they are able to lower their validity scale scores. Although these results show that coaching can have an important impact on MMPI-2 results in analogue-malingering participants, the implication is that test instructions and test-taking attitudes can greatly affect the scores that clinicians interpret.

Superlative Self-Presentation Scale (S)

Since the restandardization of the MMPI (i.e., the MMPI-2), Butcher and Han developed a new scale to assess "the presentation of self in a superlative manner". This scale, S, was developed by contrasting the item responses of 274 male airline pilot applicants with the 1,138 men from the MMPI-2 restandardization sample. Fifty items were identified that both differed significantly (.001) in their endorsement frequency between the two groups and contributed to the internal consistency of the scale. In separate factor analyses of the S scale items for the men and women of the MMPI-2 restandardization sample, Butcher and Han developed and named five component subscales: Belief in Human Goodness (S1, 15 items), Serenity (S2, 13 items), Contentment with Life (S3, 8 items), Patience and Denial of Irritability and Anger (S4, 8 items), and Denial of Moral Flaws (S5, 5 items).

The component subscales afford a good idea of the content of the S scale, with their emphasis on benevolence, serenity, and freedom from impatience and irritability. Butcher and Han presented external correlates gleaned from the couple's data collected in the restandardization project. These portray the high scorer as emotionally stable and well controlled, calm and relaxed, and patient and easygoing, as well as agreeable, cooperative, and trusting in relations with others.

These descriptors suggest a close relationship between the S scale and the K scale. Indeed, the two scales share 10 items (5 on S1, 3 on S2, and 1 each on S3 and S4) and intercorrelate in the.80s. Butcher and Han found additional positive correlations between the S scale and the R, Es, Re, O - H, and L scales, and negative correlations with the A, Pt, CYN, Mt, ANG, ANX, and Sc scales. These correlates indicate that the S scale, like the K scale, incorporates high levels of first-factor and, to a lesser extent, second-factor variance. Both the S and K scales are negatively correlated with all of the MMPI-2 content scales, but the correlations are generally somewhat higher for the S scale than for the K scale. Moreover, judging from the 39 items of the S scale and the 30 items of the K scale for which social desirability ratings are available, the S scale appears to indicate slightly (9% or 10%) more social desirability than the K scale. These factors would suggest that the S scale is somewhat more likely than the K scale to suppress content scale scores and the endorsement of obvious items in general. In this sense, the S scale appears to possess good construct validity.

Although the empirical strategy used to develop the S scale is not, as such, especially objectionable, it does tend to conflate the means and motives by which the pilot applicants manifested their "superlative" adjustments. Thus, some may have emphasized a deliberate strategy of claiming extraordinary adjustment; others of denying relatively common weaknesses, character flaws, worries, and habits; and still others, those of truly superior adjustment, may have merely marked the items in a manner consistent with that adjustment, without seeking to overstate it. Moreover, for those participants who may have exaggerated their adjustment, some may have approached the task in a self-conscious fashion, whereas others may have achieved similar results through less conscious, self-deceptive means. In this sense, then, the construct validity of the S scale remains ambiguous.

Although the availability of subscales for the S scale affords some degree of insight into the content of the items favored by particular respondents, these subscales do not necessarily correspond well to the strategies of response undertaken by the pilot applicants to yield the different rates of endorsement that determined which items would compose the scale as a whole. Regardless of these potential problems and their implications for the interpretation of S scores, the S scale has performed well in several research trials involving the discrimination of a variety of samples instructed to fake good on the MMPI-2 from samples given standard instructions. Among these, two studies incorporated features that permitted the evaluation of the incremental contribution of several scales and indices that have been proposed for the detection of underreporting. In hierarchical regression analyses, Baer, Wetter, Nichols found that only 2 of the 11 underreporting scales and indexes they investigated demonstrated incremental validity beyond the L and K scales: the S scale and Wiggins' Sd scale. A similar analysis by Bagby, Rogers, Nicholson found that, depending on the samples compared, only S, Sd, So-r (Edwards' Social Desirability scale), and Nichols and Greene's Other Deception scale (Od) could demonstrate incremental validity over the L and K scales. Furthermore, in both studies, the S scale was among those scales showing the largest effect sizes. More recently, Bagby, Nicholson, Buis, Radovanovic and Fidler found that a composite based on the raw score sum of the S and Sd scales substantially outperformed the L and K scales in a study of underreporting and non underreporting child custody litigants.

As already noted, the S scale belongs to a class of scales that are known to be saturated with the first factor. As such, it is likely to suppress most of the clinical and content scales, bias the profile toward a negative slope, and push up K, Es, GM, and similar scales. Butcher and Han presented several empirical correlates for S scores gleaned from spousal ratings gathered during the MMPI-2 restandardization project. Partners of high S scorers tend to describe them as pleasant and relaxed, as slow to express annoyance, as disinclined to worry or fret about minor matters or to become irritable or grouchy over such things, as not moody, and as not suspicious or argumentative in their approach to others. In other words, the unusual freedom from emotional discomfort and interpersonal conflict claimed by high S scorers tended to be confirmed as realistic attributes in ratings by their spouses. It will require further investigation to establish reliable empirical correlates in other samples, both normal and abnormal, and to ascertain more precisely its position in relation to other, better established response-style measures. For the time being, however, the S scale does show promise in the detection of certain common types of underreporting of psychopathology.

Positive Malingering Scale (Mp)

Cofer had 81 male and female college students complete the MMPI under three instructional sets: under standard instructions (i.e., honestly) and then (a) under instructions to malinger (to avoid induction into the Army), (b) under instructions to create the best possible impression of themselves (to be accepted into a midshipman training program), and (c) under standard instructions a second time. The second administration intended to eliminate the regression-toward-the-mean effect of the trend of slightly greater normality on the average that is expected on a second standard administration. Thirty-four items (one a duplicate) were found to be stable under the two standard administrations and the fake-bad instructions but to be endorsed more frequently under the fake-good instructions. These constitute the 33 items of the original MP scale. In keeping with the tendency of these items to change only under fake-good instructions, the MP items can be understood as flaws that most people admit when responding candidly but deny when seeking to create a highly favorable impression.

In their meta-analysis of MMPI underreporting scales, Baer found an average effect size of 1.42 across 11 studies, making it among the best performers among the 10 scales and indexes examined and substantially better than the L scale (.94), the K scale (.90), and the F - K scale (.71). For example, Otto, Lang, Megargee and Rosenblatt found that the MP scale correctly classified 80% of a sample of alcoholic participants, half of whom were instructed to conceal psychopathology and half of whom followed standard instructions, the best of several measures that included L, K, F - K, and Sd.

The MMPI-2 version of MP is reduced by 7 items to 26. It overlaps the Sd scale by 13 items, the L scale by 6, the S scale by 6 (4 of these on S2), and the K scale by 4 items. Correlations between the MP scale and these scales in a large psychiatric sample were .75, .65, .56 (.66), and .50, respectively.

Content is quite variable, with masculine interests; freedom from worries, fears, and internal struggles or changes of heart; sexual inhibition or circumspection; and high confidence in oneself and in one's leadership potential emerging as discernable themes.

High scores are best considered in relation to scores on the L, K, Sd, Ss, and S scales. Scores at or above T = 60 should raise the question of a deliberate effort to exaggerate one's level of adjustment, especially when accompanied with similar elevations on the Sd scale. When both the MP and Sd scales exceed T = 65 or are higher than the K scale, and when Ss scores are average or low, a conscious attempt to fake good is strongly suggested. High L scores tend to push up the MP and Sd scales. When scores on the L scale are significantly higher than those for the MP and Sd scales, however, the respondent's approach may be more naive than deliberate, a reaction to the fear of moral judgment rather than an attempt to mislead the examiner into a belief or judgment that the respondent is free of maladjustment and psychopathology. S scores exert considerably greater upward pressure on the K and MP scales than on the L or Sd scales, such that the S scale is usually high, along with the K scale, when the MP scale is significantly elevated but the Sd and L scales are not.

Social Desirability Scale (Sd)

The responses of 72 male and 106 female Stanford University undergraduates instructed to answer each item in terms of whether people in general would consider a true or a false response more desirable were compared separately with 55 male and 85 female Stanford University controls following standard instructions. Participants given the desirability instructions were further given to understand that they were to make their judgments on the basis of "the general values of American culture." Wiggins found 40 items that separated the desirability group from the standard instruction group at.001 or less, for both men and women. In their meta-analysis, Baer found an average effect size for the Sd scale of 1.60 across six studies making it the best performing of the scales and indexes they reviewed.

The MMPI-2 version of the Sd scale is reduced by 7 items to 33. It overlaps the MP scale by 13 items, the L scale by 7, the S scale by 2 (both on S2), and the K scale by 1 item. Correlations with these scales of .75,.54,.35 (.49), and .28, respectively, were found in a large psychiatric sample.

Whereas the items of the MP scale are biased toward the denial of shortcomings and distress, the items of the Sd scale tend to emphasize the assertion of positive attributes. The content of the Sd scale affirms broad interests: conventional, if not conservative, socially responsible moral values; a high level of drive and energy; persistence and decisiveness; sociability, extraversion, and an absence of self-consciousness; and an absence of health concern. In keeping with the instructions to judge desirability in terms of the values of people in general, the content of the Sd scale converges on a portrait of an idealized model citizen, one who is extraverted and outgoing, free of worry and self-doubt, assertive, self-directed and in full control of his or her mental faculties; who is orderly, confident, capable, decisive, cool under pressure, and oriented to success; and who is composed but friendly, buoyant, energetic, up-to-the-task, and actively engaged in living; but one who is also over conventional, hypervirtuous, prudish, and unrealistic in terms of self-portrayal.

Unlike the S scale and other Alpha-type scales, which appear to conceal psychopathology directly by suppressing test expressions of neuroticism and psychoticism, the MP and Sd scales, as scales of the Gamma dimension, appear to achieve their results by somewhat different and more indirect means. Although these means are not thoroughly understood, both scales appear to mask psychopathology through the substitution of a highly favorable social image. High scorers on the MP and Sd scales deny flaws and assert virtues that most people do not feel the need to deny or assert when taking the MMPI-2. In the case of the MP scale, this image emphasizes virtue and stability in the context of relaxed, pacific, quiet self-assurance, and a placid if not imperturbable emotionality, whereas the image conveyed by the Sd scale emphasizes virtue and vitality in the context of a strong-willed, outgoing, constructive, engaged, and poised social presence.

As with the MP scale, scores at T = 60-65 on the Sd scale should raise the question of a deliberate attempt to portray oneself in terms of an idealized social image, and Sd scores that exceed the K scale strongly suggest such, especially when Ss scores are average or low.

Socioeconomic Status Scale (Ss)

Rescued from obscurity by Alex Caldwell, S. E. Nelson's Ss scale was inspired by the insight that various aspects of abnormal psychology and symptomatic behavior may be related to social stratification. As an example, Nelson mentioned that such behaviors as wife beating, heavy drinking, improvident spending habits, siding with and covering for his children vis-à-vis school authorities, and relocating the family's domicile to avoid creditors may be easily construed as psychopathic by mental health service providers, a group typically if not uniformly of high social status, even though such behaviors may be all but normative in some segments of the lower-lower class.

From an initial sample of 710 male patients who had been treated at the Ft. Snelling VA Hospital, S. E. Nelson simultaneously rated patients for years of education and occupational level, as determined by the Warner seven-step scale of occupational status categories. Forty-one participants with 13 or more years of education and occupations within the highest two status categories (e.g., engineer or manager) constituted the high-status group; 43 participants with 8 or fewer years of education and occupations within the lowest status category (e.g., laborer or dishwasher) constituted the low-status group. Eighty-seven items were found to separate the two groups at the .01 level or less, and these became the Ss scale; 73 of these items remain on the MMPI-2.

The scale was validated on new samples of patients for which highly significant correlations were found with education (.47), occupational level (.45), and intelligence (.41). The Ss scale was unrelated to age in both the scale development and later validation samples. In a cross-validation sample, the Ss scale misclassified only half as many participants as Gough's Status scale (St), although both scales correctly classified most of the participants. W. L. Jenkins found that the Ss scale was related to better prognosis in paranoid schizophrenia.

Nelson divided his scale into 12 groups of items according to content: physical complaints (13 items), sleep difficulties (3 items), psychological deficit (4 items), phobias and obsessive-compulsive traits (9 items), delusions and misperceptions (6 items), paranoid traits (5 items), affective states (5 items), self-insight (3 items), rigid moral code (2 items), interest in intellectual pursuits (2 items), other interests (6 items), and a miscellaneous category (15 items). The direction of scoring is such that high scorers tend to deny somatic complaints; dysphoric mood; fears and phobias; cynicism, suspiciousness, paranoia, and psychoticism; problems with cognitive functioning; nonintellectual interests and occupations that depend largely on physical (vs. mental) activity; introversion; and impulsiveness. They portray themselves as alert, concerned about their social presentation, fallible, inclined toward candor, mature, discreet, and morally flexible and tolerant.

A scale of the Alpha type, the Ss scale shares considerable variance with both the K and S scales, correlating with both at about .65, despite sharing only two items with each. Although such correlations would naturally raise the question of defensiveness, albeit of a rather subtle kind, there is little doubt that higher status members of society, in general, possess a degree of insulation from stresses and sources of instability that is unavailable to those at lower socioeconomic levels. Their better reputations and the greater financial resources and respect they command confer considerable flexibility and a wider range of alternatives for managing interpersonal conflict, situational difficulties, and economic reverses indeed hardships and misfortunes of most kinds. Moreover, and in the main, such people tend to possess the kinds of abilities, intelligence, knowledge, and skills that enabled them to attain higher SES in the first place, as compared with those who fail to attain such status. In the face of difficulty, then, the higher status person tends to have a wider network and greater access to social support; better and more reliable problem-solving skills; greater access to information and expertise; more money and more discretion as to how it is spent; and more time to assess, plan, and implement measures for its alleviation. In the light of such advantages, it is not surprising that such persons would have a higher threshold for experiencing feelings of inadequacy and insecurity, developing symptoms of maladjustment and psychopathology, and expressing distress over their problems, even when present, than would persons lacking these advantages.

Although the validity and performance characteristics of the Ss scale have been little explored since its initial development, Caldwell has argued that this scale can play a helpful role in the interpretation of K scores, along with the Gamma scales L, MP, and Sd. When high K scores are accompanied by high Ss scores, and L, MP, and Sd scores are unelevated or low, Caldwell suggested that the elevation on the K scale should not be construed as a deliberate attempt to mislead the examiner or to frustrate the purposes of the evaluation; rather, the elevation should be understood to reflect the portrayal of favorable adjustment over which the examinee has little conscious control. By an extension of this reasoning, a deceptive or defensive interpretation of elevated scores on the S scale should be attenuated when these are accompanied by high Ss scores. When the K score is high along with elevations on the Gamma scales and the Ss score is average or low, Caldwell recommended that the K score be interpreted as indicating an intentional fake-good approach to the evaluation.

Conversely, when the Kand Ss scores are both low, the MP, Sd, and Ds scores are average, and the F score is not higher than T = 80, "a low-status candor, lack of sophistication, and genuine self-negativity in the absence of any 'faking bad'" is suggested. When the K and Gamma scale scores are low, the F and/or Ds score is high, and the Ss score is within an average range, Caldwell argued that there existed "an excessive self-criticalness or deliberate faking bad with the low K not being due to low socioeconomic status".

In keeping with Caldwell's view that the Ss scale achieves its positivizing of test performance without any conscious effort to convey a more favorable impression on the MMPI-2, it is noteworthy that its correlations with the Gamma scales are close to 0, the highest being with the MP scale at. 17.

Validity Indices

In a valid profile, the F and FB scales should have similar scores, given that both scales consist of infrequently endorsed items. Nichols and Greene recommended that the absolute raw score difference between the F and FB scales provides a crude measure of consistency of item endorsement on both halves of the test. If the raw score for the FB scale exceeds the F scale by 6 or more and there are no content reasons to explain the difference, it becomes important to consider that the second half of the test may be invalid. As stated earlier, the F scale ends with Item 361 and the FB scale begins at item 281. The FB scale is useful for detecting random or faking-bad/faking-good tendencies that could affect, for example, the content scales concentrated in the last 150 items of the inventory.

On the basis of a random sort of scores for the VRIN, F, and FB scales, Greene reported that 75% of these random sorts had a raw score of 7 or higher on the F-FB index. With VRIN scores in the intermediate range (8-15), he reported that less than 26% of the random sorts had scores of 6 or lower on this index. Greene stated that the "clinician can be fairly confident that the client has endorsed the items consistently if this index is 6 or lower when VRIN is in the intermediate range of 8-15". It is recommended that the F- FB raw difference score be routinely examined in assessing the validity of an M MP I-2 profile.

Dissimulation Index (F - K)

The F - K index was derived by Harrison Gough as an additional validity indicator for the original MMPI to assist in determining whether an individual completed the test in an appropriate manner or attempted to simulate or exaggerate psychopathology. Gough found the F - K index to be a more accurate classifier of simulated or faked profiles than the F or K scale alone. The F - K index is derived by subtracting the raw K score from the raw F score. When the raw F score is greater than the K score, the index takes on a positive numerical value; when the reverse is true, the index takes on a negative numerical value. According to Baer, "individuals over reporting psychopathology should obtain elevated F and low K scores, resulting in positive scores on this index, while those underreporting psychopathology should obtain low F and high K scores, resulting in negative scores". In general, elevated F scores have been attributed, in part, to psychotic conditions, cries for help, general maladjustment, random responding, and partial or pure malingering. Participants with low F scores have been described as free of psychological problems or denying difficulties (faking good) when the K scale is significantly elevated. Elevated K has usually been interpreted as suggesting defensiveness, cautiousness, or emotional reserve, with low K scores reflecting a tell-all attitude and lack of emotional modulation or reserve.

In creating the index, Gough had a group of 11 clinical workers feign two psychiatric syndromes:

> *The first syndrome was defined as "an acute, severe, anxiety neurosis which would lead to separation from the service, but not to commitment to a mental hospital," and the second as "a non-deteriorated, acute, paranoid schizophrenic psychosis." Skilled judges were able to identify eight of the eleven psychoneurotic patterns which intermixed with 68 authentic psychoneurotic records, and were able to identify all of the psychotic simulations when they were intercalated with 24 authentic profiles. At the same time, a simple combination of the F raw score minus the K raw score was able to pick out ten of the eleven simulated records in each of the two situations. The F -K cutting scores proposed at that time were plus 4 and over for neurotic profiles, and plus 16 and over for psychotic profiles.*

Gough later suggested that F - scores of more than 9 indicated a fake-bad attitude (i.e., the participant attempted to present him- or herself with serious psychopathology). Scores of less than 0 on the F - K index indicated a fake-good profile, whereby the participant attempted to deny the presence of any type of psychological disturbance. Gough stated that the F - K index was less efficient in detecting fake-good profiles as compared with fake-bad profiles at any particular cutoff score. He pointed out that the problem in establishing an F - K cutting score is one of minimizing false positives and false negatives.

What is considered to be over versus underreporting is often subject to the interpretative skills of the clinician as cutoff guidelines using clinical and normal groups have varied considerably among researchers and reference groups. Most investigations on the F - K index have used analogue participants who were asked to simulate various disorders or normalcy and whose profiles were then compared with those of authentic normal and patient profiles. College students have constituted the majority of these participants, and Dahlstrom noted the differences in conducting faking studies with college students. For example, it is known that well-educated individuals tend to score higher on the K scale by almost 1 SD.

Therefore, their elevated K scores will tend to bias their F - K index scores in the fake- good direction. Greene indicated in his review of the F - K index that it has been difficult to identify any specific F - K score for the detection of students instructed to fake good under usual administration instructions for the MMPI. Presumably, students who are for the most part free of psychopathology find it difficult to look even better than they already are when instructed to fake good. Greene also acknowledged that another problem in detecting fake-good profiles in college students (or any one else) is that a person who is effectively handling his or her problems and who is well-adjusted would be expected to score low on the F scale and high on the K scale, indicating an absence of distress. Therefore, Greene stated that normal persons taking the MMPI often will be inappropriately classified as producing underreported profiles.

Greene's review contains some important conclusions. He stated that the usefulness of the F - K index in detecting fake-bad profiles may be more limited with actual clinical patients who exaggerate their problems than with students. He recommended interviewing those who obtain a high F score and hence a high F - K index, to determine if their self-report of distress is accurate or exaggerated. He also questioned the utility of the index in detecting fake-good profiles among psychiatric patients. He pointed out that psychiatric patients and inmates have difficulty producing normal-appearing profiles when instructed to do so. Recently, Bagby, Rogers, Nicholson found that a sample of schizophrenic outpatients in the residual phase were in fact able under fake-good instructions to reduce their clinical scale elevations as well as, if not better than, students, thereby suggesting that patients are as capable as students to manipulate their MMPI-2 clinical scale scores. The Marks study of projected discharged profiles seems to supports Greene's call for additional research to examine whether normal profiles produced by clinical participants instructed to fake good are generally positive prognostic signs.

Clear limitations have also been reported on the utility of the index for separating profiles of patients simulating or exaggerating illness from authentic patient profiles. Hedlund and Won Cho found that psychiatric patients achieved a mean F - K index score near 0 compared to the -10 noted with normal, which is clearly in contrast to what Gough had indicated earlier about the index not being affected by the presence of psychiatric disturbance per se. In light of this, interpretation of a profile as that of malingering or exaggerating psychopathology must be made with caution as it does appear that the presence of psychiatric disturbance has a bearing on the resulting F - K score.

It is generally reported that scores on the F - K index increase significantly as the degree of simulated disturbance increases. Berry, Baer and Harris conducted a meta-analysis on 28 studies that used the original MMPI to detect malingering in order to quantify how much higher malingerers or simulators score on the various over reporting scales and indexes, including the F - K index. They noted a wide variability in cut scores used across studies, with cut scores between 7 and 16 yielding the highest classification rates. On the basis of their review of various scales and indexes, the F - K index was recommended as a choice for identifying malingerers. Overall, the results showed that participants malingering or over reporting their symptoms scored almost 2 SDs higher on the F - K index than participants answering honestly. Rogers also found the F - K index to be a powerful indicator of malingering in their meta-analytic study of MMPI-2 fake-bad measures and recommended that it be used in conjunction with the F scale and the obvious-subtle subscale differences as a screening indicator.

Along the same lines as the above-reported investigation, Baer meta-analytically reviewed the empirical literature on the detection of underreporting psychopathology (faking good) on the original MMPI. Twenty-five studies in which participants were responding honestly were compared with participants underreporting psychopathology. Several indexes were examined, including the F - K index. By computing mean overall hit rate (percentage of total participants correctly classified) for each index of underreporting by collapsing across cutting scores, the investigators were able to gain a general impression of which measure best detected underreporting participants. The F - K index correctly classified 77% of the participants, and the highest mean overall hit rate of 84% was obtained for the Sd scale. As with the malingering participants reported earlier, there was considerable variability in hit rates; the percentage of honest participants correctly classified ranged from 62% to 100% with the best overall hit rate being 95% with an F - K index score of -11. In general, the results indicated that underreporting participants and honest participants differ on the F - K index by just less than 1 SD (d = 0.71). It appears that the F - K index is less accurate in correctly classifying under reporters versus over reporters of psychopathology, a finding consistent with other investigations. The considerable overlap in distributions between honest and undeffeporting participants is likely an important factor in these differences. The reader interested in more details about methodologies used in these type of studies is referred to the studies by Baer; Baer, Wetter, and Berry; Berry, Baer and Harris; and Baer, Wetter, Nichols, Greene, and Berry.

Note that the study and use of the F - K index is primarily focused on adults. Adolescent inpatient respondents score significantly higher on the F scale than adult psychiatric inpatients, and outpatient adolescents score similarly to adult inpatients on the F scale. Given the higher F scale value among teenagers, Archer suggested that the F - K index criterion should be used very cautiously with these respondents when the MMPI-A is administered.

The revision of the MMPI necessitates the establishment of new norms for the F -K index for several reasons. Four items were deleted from the original F scale (resulting in a scale of 60 items), and 12 modifications were made to the remaining items, including 6 grammatical changes, 5 modernizations of idioms and usage, and 1 change in sexist wording. The K scale was less affected, as it lost no items in the revision and only one item on the scale was modified. Participants in the contemporary group of normals were screened out if their item endorsements on the F scale were too elevated (raw score greater than 20). No such limitations were imposed on the collection of participants for the normative sample of the original MMPI. Inspection of the item endorsement frequencies of the contemporary and original normative groups shows distinct differences on many items, especially on the K scale, which may reflect societal and cultural changes since the time of the development of the original MMPI.

The purified standardization sample of the original MMPI contained 225 men and 315 women from which the T-score conversions for clinical profiling were derived. The male group had a mean age of 33.1 years, a mean level of education of 9.7 years, and a mean F - K score of -8.56. The female group had a mean age of 33.9

years, a mean level of education of 10.0 years, and a mean F - K score of -8.91. For the standardization sample of the MMPI-2 consisting of 1,138 men and 1,462 women, the mean age of the combined sample was 41.0 years, with mean level of education of 14.7 years. The mean F - K score was -10.77 for men and -11.37 for women. This is about 2 full points more in the negative direction for both groups compared with the purified standardization sample on the original MMTI and about 1 full point more in the negative direction for men. It is also about the same for women compared with the recent norms of Osborne for the original MMPI.

Data are now available from several investigations on the F - K index from the MMPI-2. Graham, Watts and Timbrook examined the utility of the MMPI-2 validity scales and the F - K index for identifying fake-bad and fake good profiles. A cutoff score of 12 or higher for women and 17 of higher for men correctly classified 90% of fake-bad profiles by college students but also misclassified approximately 16% of psychiatric patients as having produced a fake-bad profile. For detecting fake-good profiles, the index was not as useful, a finding consistent with previous research with the original MMPI. As previously stated, recent meta-analyses on the original MMPI corroborates the finding that the F - K index is much more useful for detecting fake-bad than fake-good profiles. Iverson, Franzen and Hammond examined the ability of the new FB scale and the F K index to discriminate prison inmates instructed to malinger mental illness from actual psychiatric patients. The inmates instructed to malinger psychopathology produced much higher scale scores, including higher F and lower K scores than inmates and psychiatric patients who were given standard instructions. The mean F -K index was 24.8 (SD = 13.0) for malingerers, -4.9 (SD = 8.1) for inmates given standard instructions, and -4.5 (SD = 8.9) for psychiatric patients. The F - K index and the F scale produced comparable overall rates of correct classification, and both were more effective than was the FB scale.

With the revision of the MMPI-2, Rothke reported MMPI-2 norms for the new standardization group on the F - K index and presented data for samples of psychiatric patients, head-injured patients who were litigating and not litigating, individuals seeking disability benefits, job applicants for police and priest positions, and substance abusers. These investigators chose to approach the establishment of normative guidelines for detecting over-or underreported profiles by selecting scores that separated the upper 2.5% and lower 2.5% from the overall score distribution (i.e., ±2 SDs from the mean, assuming a normal distribution of scores). This approach is viewed as preferable to the use of cutoff scores derived from analogue studies (i.e., those in which participants are asked to fake bad or fake good), in which the assumption is made that analogue participants actually reflect how malingerers would respond. Wetter noted that analogue participants often are not given specific information about the diagnosis they are attempting to feign, nor are they told that successful malingering involves selective and not mass endorsement of symptoms. This may result in analogue malingerers obtaining an overly positive F - K index value, leading to exaggerated cutoff scores. Rothke 's approach of setting guideline scores based on the extremes from the distribution of scores of a particular diagnostic or applicant group is similar to the concept of using local norms as a way of enhancing the generalizability of cutoff scores to a particular participant. This is an important point because the F - K index is not only used for clinical decision making but also for making decisions about whether a participant may be malingering in a litigation or forensic context or whether someone should be denied a job because they excessively denied psychological weaknesses or difficulties in an employment context. Thus, these interpretations have real-life implications for individuals.

Table 1.1 lists the MMPI-2 F - K scores at the approximate lower and upper 2.5 percentile of the distribution reported for various samples. This should allow a specific comparison of a participant's score to the general population from which the individual derived:

These scores should not be viewed as specific cutoffs for fake good or fake bad profiles. This is due, in part, to the fact that some of the samples are small in size and these "cutoff" scores could easily be affected by a single extreme score. These scores should serve as a reminder that F - K scores will differ across clinical samples necessitating future normative studies on these clinical populations.

The importance of comparing a single participant's score to an appropriate reference group is suggested by Table 1.1 :

> *For example, in a competency-to-stand trial evaluation in which the defendant presumably would have an interest in appearing*

impaired, it would be important to consider using F - K scores for psychiatric patients (if that individual had a history of psychiatric disturbance) as they may differ from those of the normative population. Thus, an interpretation of the validity of the profile should not be based solely on the guidelines for the normative population. The same would hold true of a patient with traumatic brain injury (TBI) involved in personal injury litigation; the sample scores for patients with TBI should be considered.

As can be seen in Table 1.1, very different conclusions would be drawn about whether a participant was feigning or exaggerating a disorder if cutoffs based on the normative sample were used, as opposed to making adjustments from the specific diagnostic group. Rothke suggested that the clinician use the guidelines from the normative group but make adjustments for the specific diagnostic group in order to address how a participant's score compares with that of the general population in a manner that is mindful of the impact of a particular condition on the F - K index score. This is similar to the practice of using general cutoff scores on neuropsychological tests for identification of impairment and then modifying interpretations based on adjustments for age and education, which are well known to affect neuropsychological test performance.

The Rothke data show that the scores on the F - K index are generally more in the negative direction (underreporting direction) on the MMPI-2 than on the original MMPI, where comparison scores were available, except for the psychiatric sample. This could be due in part to the fact that the mean raw K scale scores for the MMPI-2 normative group were approximately 15 (for both men and women) compared with approximate means of 13 for the original normative group. This is likely to have been an effect of the MMPI-2 normative group having a higher mean level of education than the original normative group. Rothke 's findings also indicate the need to maintain separate guidelines for male and female participants in fake-bad assessments, a finding consistent with other studies. For example, Graham, Watts, and Timbrook found that a cutoff score of 12 for women and 17 for men produced the highest correct classification rates.

In summary, the research to date with the F - K index for both the MMPI and the MMPI-2 suggests that the index is much more useful for identifying fake-bad than fake-good profiles. The cutoff scores derived from the original MMPI that exist in the clinical lore should be replaced with cutoffs from the MMPI-2 research.

Table 1.1. MMPI-2 F - K Scores at the Lower and Upper Extremes of Different Diagnostic and Participant Groups

Participant Group and Gender	N	Approximate Lower 2.5% (Fake Good)	Approximate Upper 2.5% (Fake Bad)
Normals			
Male	1,138	-22	4 a
Female	1,462	-22	3 a
Psychiatric			
Male	215	-18	27
Female	241	-20	22
Substance dependent			
Male	168	-19	10
Female	96	-22	10
Traumatic brain injury			
Male	50	-23	17
Female	29	-22	-1
SSD/SSI benefit applicants			
Male	217	-11	37
Female	74	-22	30
Police applicants			
Male	49	-25	-11 b
Female	12	-24	13 b
Priest applicants			
Male	38	-25	-8 b
Female	30	-24	-7 b

Note. SSD = Social Security disability; SSI = supplemental security income.

a These "cutoffs" might have been higher had the normative group not excluded participants with raw F scores of 320.

b Scores in this direction more likely reflect a willingness to acknowledge difficulties (in these participant groups) than an attempt to feign a disorder.

From "MMPI-2 Normative Data for the F - K Index: IMPlications for Clinical.

It is recommended that a determination of profile validity not be made on the basis of a single score or index value alone. Rather, an examination of various measures, as well as of overall clinical scale elevation (mean profile elevation), in conjunction with interview findings and the participant's history and current circumstances is recommended. Future research should focus on specific diagnostic groups in order to maximize generalizability to individual cases. This would also minimize the potential impact of differing base rates of elevated and low index scores within different groups on the sensitivity and specificity of guideline scores. Research exploring the outcome (e.g., treatment, job selection, and litigation status) and recovery correlates of the F - K index would make it a much more useful clinical tool. Specifically, Rothke suggested that investigations on the use of the F - K index as a validity indicator need to include independent measures (either other tests or criterion measures if available) of malingering, exaggeration of illness, defensiveness, denial of illness, and effects of litigation and/or of the job selection process on test performance.

2

Clinical Scale Development and Its Uses

Introduction

The clinical scales were the first scales to be constructed from the test items and have been the focus of most of the MMPI research done in the past 50-plus years. They form the basis of all of the coding systems and the core of all the clinical uses of the MMPI-2. Traditionally, Scales 1, 2, and 3 are referred to as the neurotic triad, and Scales 6, 7, 8, and 9 are referred to as the psychotic tetrad. The modifications made in the restandardized MMPI-2 left the clinical scales essentially intact, with only nine deleted items from Scales 1, 2, 5, and 0.

Once the clinician has ascertained through an analysis of the validity measures that a profile is valid, an interpretation of the clinical scales is possible. Interpretation of the clinical scales is primarily focused on scale elevations and configuration with attention to item content being an important adjunct in the process. Typically, clinicians examine each scale elevation to form an initial impression of the test taker prior to examining the score combinations and the profile code. After examining the clinical scales, the psychologist typically examines the different content scale scores.

Table 2.1. T-Score Classifications and Percentile Values

Uniform T Score	Classification Percentile	Equivalent
30	Very low	<1
35		4
40	Moderately low	15
45		34
50	Average	55
55		73
60	Moderately high	85
65		92
70	High	96
75		98
80	Very high	> 99
85		
90	Extremely high	

Harris-Lingoes and Subtle-Obvious subscales. These subscales were derived from many of the clinical scales in order to help clarify the meaning of individual scale elevations. Because these subscales are discussed within the context of the clinical scales, we present an overview of their derivation and meaning before the clinical scale descriptors. Moderator variables, such as age, education, and SES are discussed in relationship to MMPI-2.

The T -score value at which clinical significance is generally assumed is at 65 and above (as compared with 70 on the original MMPI). This does not mean that individuals with scores below 65 are always free of psychopathology or concerns. The guideline cutoff score of 65 should be considered a demarcation to assist the clinician in interpreting the MMPI-2 profile rather than as an absolute standard. Although considerably less research has been conducted on low-scale elevations, it is still important to examine the lowest scores in a profile to ascertain if there is significance attached to the score. Keiller and Graham studied partner ratings in a sub sample of the MMPI-2 standardization sample and compared low, medium, and high scores on the MMPI-2 clinical scales. They reported that for this non clinical sample, low scores on most MMPI-2 scales provided valuable information. In general, low-scoring non clinical participants showed positive characteristics and greater than average adjustment, which will usually be the opposite of those traits typically associated with high scores on a particular scale. Their findings did not suggest that low scores indicate negative characteristics or adjustment problems that were poorer than average.

More recently, Graham, Ben-Porath and McNulty recognized that Keiller and Graham's findings might not generalize to the clinical settings in which the MMPI-2 is most typically used. They therefore, studied the meaning of low scores on both the clinical and supplementary scales in an outpatient mental health population. Low scores were defined as being below a T score of 41. Graham reported the following results:

> *Our results indicate that the meaning of low scores on the MMPI-2 scales that we were able to study differs from one scale to another. For some scales, low scores seemed to provide no useful information. For other scales, low scorers appeared to have fewer symptoms and negative characteristics than within normal limit scorers. In some cases, these characteristics are specifically related to the construct that the scales were designed to measure; in others, they indicate better overall adjustment. Perhaps the most consistent finding was that for none of the scales that we studied did low scores indicate more negative characteristics or poorer overall adjustment than within normal limit scorers.*

Graham recommended that low MMPI-2 scales in an outpatient mental setting be interpreted cautiously; it should not be assumed that a low score necessarily indicates the converse of a high score on that scale.

It is clear that more research in multiple populations is needed concerning the correlates of low scores on the clinical and supplementary scales. We believe it is important to note unusually low scores on any of the clinical or supplementary scales in any population as it can raise important interpretive hypotheses. For example, if a psychiatric patient who recently suffered multiple losses obtained a very low score on the Depression scale, the clinician should consider whether the patient is pathologically attempting to deny depression and whether suicide precautions should be considered. Any statistically deviant score is worthy of consideration and should be attempted to be understood in the particular context of the individual's situation.

On the profile sheet where MMPI-2 scores are plotted, the scales have been limited to a T score of 30, so it is not possible to plot a lower score.

The reader is reminded that for the basic clinical Scales 1, 2, 3, 4, 6, 7, 8, and 9, uniform T scores are used in plotting a profile, whereas Scales 5 and 0 still use the linear T -score conversions from the original MMPI. Describing various elevations on the scales as "high," "very high," and so on is a subjective process that varies across different interpretative manuals and clinical situations. This text uses the K -corrected T -score ranges in Table 2.1 for describing standard clinical scale elevations on the MMPI-2. These elevation descriptions are approximations for the clinical scales and relatively rough, sometimes very rough, approximations for all of the other scales. Scores on the border between classifications are particularly open to judgment.

Once a profile has been scored and plotted onto a profile sheet, it can be coded. Coding is a procedure used to summarize the elevation and rank order of scales using a notation system. Coding is provided by most computerized report services and is easy to accomplish by hand. Coding is useful for research purposes and profile classification, such as finding a similarly matched profile.

Harris-Lingoes Subscales

Elevations on certain clinical scales often can be better understood by examining the subscale components to the parent scale. To this end, Harris and Lingoes devised subscales that are used routinely in the analysis of an MMPI-2 profile. The MMPI-2 item pool is heterogeneous, and many clinical scales have diverse content. Therefore, a particular scale score can reflect different item endorsement patterns for different individuals. For example, two individuals with the exact T -score elevation of 70 on Scale 2 (Depression) could have endorsed different content areas of depression items. One person may have endorsed many items related to depressed mood, whereas the other person may have emphasized items related to vegetative symptoms, both areas having different clinical implications for the treatment and description of depression. Dissimilar endorsement patterns of items within a scale are thought to be related to particular behavioral patterns or correlates. Harris and Lingoes developed subscales for Scales 2, 3, 4, 6, 8, and 9 after inspecting the item content of each clinical scale and grouped these items into categories that appeared homogeneous. That is, items that appeared to reflect a single trait or attribute were grouped into new subscales, which Harris and Lingoes named on the basis of the item content. They did not develop subscales for Scales 1 and 7 as the items on these scales appeared to be related to single constructs. Scale 1 content is obvious in nature and relates to bodily concerns, whereas Scale 7, also obvious in content, relates to anxiety, worry, and tension. Scales 5 and 0 are multidimensional in nature, but Harris and Lingoes chose not to develop subscales for these scales, presumably because they were added later to the instrument and were not included among the original clinical scales. Scales 5 and 0 have been factor analyzed and broken down into component subscales and are discussed later in this chapter.

The Harris-Lingoes subscales for Scales 2, 3, 4, 6, 8 and 9 are described under the appropriate clinical parent scale in this chapter. The scale composition and direction of scoring for the Harris-Lingoes subscales. Linear T -score conversions for the Harris-Lingoes subscales for men and women based on the restandardization sample. It should be noted that the Harris-Lingoes subscale items are contained within the first 370 items of the MMPI-2, so a clinician wishing to administer an abbreviated test can still derive the scores for these subscales. In the restandardization of the MMPI, only one item (MMPI Item 95) was dropped that affected any of the Harris-Lingoes subscales. Specifically, the Psychomotor Retardation subscale (D2), a Depression subscale, lost 1 item, leaving D2 with 14 items instead of 15 items on the MMPI-2. Most interpretive and scoring services provide scores for all of the Harris-Lingoes subscales, but when hand scoring the test, the clinician is advised to score for the subscales when the clinical scales are between a T score of 60 and 80. Scores much higher or lower are unlikely to reveal any significant scatter between the subscales.

The 28 subscales derived from the clinical scales for the Harris-Lingoes subscales vary in their length, with 11 of the subscales possessing 10 or fewer items, resulting in low internal consistency values for several of the subscales. However, most of the subscales have a high degree of internal consistency. The reader is referred to Graham for a listing of the internal consistency (alpha) coefficients for men and women in the MMPI-2 restandardization. Graham also presented data on the temporal stability of the subscales. These data show that the subscales are generally less stable than the parent scales.

There are also considerable inter correlations between some of the subscales because the scale constructors made no effort to eliminate item overlap. Some items may overlap up to four different subscales. It is reasonable to assume that the high intercorrelations among the subscales are a result of this structural redundancy: "For example, all 10 items on the Brooding subscale also appear on the Subjective Depression subscale, and 12 of the 15 items on the Mental Dullness subscale are on the Subjective Depression subscale". Research conducted by Childs, Dahlstrom, Kemp and Panter suggest that the Harris-Lingoes subscales are also likely to be multidimensional in nature. Harris and Lingoes presented their intercorrelations in mimeographed materials, and Graham presented intercorrelations. for the subscales based on responses by the restandardization sample.

Most recently, McGrath, Powis and Pogge found that scores on the subscales covaried significantly as a function of code-pattern. The MMPI-2 profiles of 483 psychiatric inpatients were analyzed, with the results indicating that code-pattern was found to be a predictor of every Harris-Lingoes subscale. McGrath et al. provided a useful table presenting the Harris-Lingoes subscale mean values across 14 code-patterns, thereby giving the user a basis for comparing their data against a large psychiatric sample. The value in this table lies in its ability to give the reader an opportunity to compare their individual Harris-Lingoes subscale scores to normative data for a particular code-pattern, thereby indicating whether or not the subscale scores are consistent with a prototypic code-pattern. Clearly, however, more research is needed with psychiatric patients, as well as other populations, with three- and four-point code-patterns to make these data generalizable to clinical and non clinical settings.

Most interpretive guidebooks suggest 65 as the T -score value at or above which a subscale score should be interpreted, although some researchers suggest a score of 70 as more appropriate. This text suggests 65 or greater as the cutoff for interpreting most of the subscales, although there are exceptions to this recommendation.

Because the Harris-Lingoes subscales have been used to supplement, and not replace, the interpretation of the clinical scales, clinicians have generally found the Harris-Lingoes subscales to be helpful in interpreting MMPI/MMPI-2 profiles. However, there are several concerns about the reliability and validity of the subscales. The most important problems are related to the ways in which the subscales were constructed. The rational method of forming the subscales by clustering items into content areas is a subjective process, the success of which may vary. Factors contributing to this success can include the number of candidate items and the adequacy of the definition of content areas selected. However, Harris and Lingoes made no attempt to cross-validate their subscales nor to relate them to external criteria. This type of research is greatly needed. One attempt to link behavioral correlates to the subscales failed. A more recent attempt to reproduce the Harris-Lingoes subscales, by clinicians who were asked to rationally group the items, failed to duplicate more than about one third of these subscales. This suggests that the subscales' reliability is poor and that the interpretation of the subscales may be as subjective as their development.

Another recent investigation of the factor structure of various MMPI scales (including, but not limited to, the Harris-Lingoes subscales) showed that 10 factors accounted for the majority of variance. The first factor was named Depression. The three highest factor loadings on depression were D1 (Subjective Depression), D4 (Mental Dullness), and D5 (Brooding). However, D2 (Psychomotor Retardation) and D3 (Physical Malfunctioning) did not load at all on the first factor. This suggests that these subscales may not be related to the construct of depression in the specific way Harris and Lingoes assumed. For example, D2 and D3 may be more associated with the vegetative than the depressed mood aspects of depression syndromes. Likewise, the study showed that other subscales failed to appear with significant factor loadings, as would be expected from their parent scales. Therefore, this and other studies suggest that the subscales under a given parent scale may be associated with heterogeneous constructs.

Krishnamurthy suggested generally reexamining the utility of the subscales and their limitations. We agree with this suggestion and note that there is a conspicuous lack of diverse norms in different settings, which are needed to aid in the interpretation process with the subscales. Also, because many of the subscales are short (e.g., fewer than 10 items), a change in the response to even 1 item can produce a large shift in the T -score value for that particular subscale. Wrobel found support for 16 of the 28 subscales in an empirical study using clinicians' ratings of outpatient therapy clients; however, 12 subscales were not supported. Wrobel pointed out that many of the unsupported subscales consisted of subtle content, again raising the concern that subtle items may hurt, not help, certain scales. Overall, however, his study provided support for the validity of the majority of the Harris-Lingoes subscales. But until reliability and validity studies more clearly and consistently support the use of the subscales, the clinician is urged to be cautious about the practical application of the Harris-Lingoes subscales.

Subtle-Obvious Subscales

Another important component of the clinical scales are the Subtle-Obvious subscales developed by Wiener and Harmon and later published under Wiener's name. By rationally grouping items into categories obviously reflective of psychopathology, Wiener and Harman found that they could provide additional measures useful in determining the test-taking attitude of a respondent. They created Subtle and Obvious subscales for Scales 2, 3, 4, 6, and 9. For these particular scales, the addition of the Subtle raw score to the Obvious raw score should equal the non- K -corrected raw score. Scales 1, 7, and 8 consist of mostly obvious items, which made it difficult for Wiener and Harmon to create Subtle subscales. The Subtle-Obvious subscales do not contain an equal amount of items, and no efforts were made to balance them. The subscales contain 108 subtle items and 145 obvious items. Greene stated that the empirically determined deviant response for 65 (59%) of these subtle items was in the opposite direction from what would be expected by merely inspecting item content, whereas only 8 (5%) of these obvious items were scored in the opposite direction. These findings substantiate the subtle and obvious nature of these two groups of items, respectively.

In their scheme, subtle items refer to being less obvious measures of psychopathology or, said another way, items that are lacking in face validity.

Although Wiener and Harmon defined item obviousness and subtlety according to the items' relationship to psychopathology, other researchers have defined the distinction in different terms. For example, Jackson defined item subtlety as involving the respondent's ability to determine the specific trait or scale to which an item corresponds. Christian, Burkhart, and Gynther defined subtle-obvious items by having college students rate all of the MMPI items in relationship to psychopathology on a 5-point scale ranging from 1 (very subtle) to 5 (very obvious) with the midpoint termed neutral items. For example, the mean obviousness ratings for all of the MMPI scales showed that the F scale and Scale 8 had the highest ratings, indicating their items are obvious in nature. The mean obviousness ratings were lowest, thereby indicating subtlety, for the Mf and K scales. In still another attempt to classify subtle-obvious items, Wales and Seeman made the distinction using a statistical assignment method. They called items obvious or X items if a minority of the normative group's endorsements on the items were exceeded by a larger proportion of psychiatric cases. Subtle items were referred to as 0 (zero) items when items endorsed frequently by the normative participants were exceeded in endorsement frequency by the psychiatric cases. X (obvious) items were therefore scored as pathological when answered in the converse direction of the majority of the normative group, and 0 (subtle) items were scored as pathological because more psychiatric cases endorsed the items.

Clearly, many different subtle-obvious distinctions have been made, and Dubinsky, Gamble, and Rogers provided a useful overview of the subtle-obvious literature. They stated that regardless of the item sets used, participants instructed to manipulate their MMPI scores tend to increase or decrease their obvious item scores, but their scores for subtle items tend to move in the opposite direction. In other words, it is easier for participants to more effectively manipulate the obvious rather than the subtle items. This so-called paradoxical effect "is a fairly robust phenomenon and occurs with fake bad and fake good instructions with normal and psychiatric (inpatient, outpatient, and forensic) populations, and with all three of the major S/O [subtle-obvious] item sets".

Although most of the subtle-obvious research has been conducted with the MMPI, it appears safe to generalize the research findings from the MMPI to the MMPI-2, given that only 3 of the 13 items dropped from the original test were on the Subtle-Obvious subscales of Wiener and Harmon. Specifically, Scale 2 lost one item on the Obvious subscale and two items on the Subtle subscale.

The subtle-obvious distinction has been used for two main purposes. The first is to assess the test-taking attitude of the participant. This is generally done by examining the difference scores between the Subtle and Obvious subscales. Participants who over report or magnify their problems may substantially elevate their Obvious scores over their Subtle scores, whereas the converse is true for participants underreporting their problems. Greene suggested that a participant who obtains T scores of 90 or more on all five Obvious subscales, and T scores close to 40 on all five Subtle scales, may be attempting to over report, whereas the converse relationship between scores on the subscales should suggest a possible underreporting response set. By summing the differences between the Obvious and Subtle subscales, a single overall measure can be used to determine reporting styles. Greene described this simple method as follows: Subtract the Subtle and Obvious T-score values for each of the five subscales, and add them together. The mean total T-score difference in normal samples is in the range of 0 to -30, whereas in psychiatric samples it is in the range of 50 to 60. There is more variability in psychiatric samples because patients admit to more problems, thereby increasing their scores on the Obvious subscales. (Note that because the majority of MMPI-2 items are scoreable [i.e., pathological], when endorsed "true," the percentage of items marked "true" provides a gross index of psychopathology that corresponds with the sum differences between the Obvious and Subtle subscales.) As Greene noted, it is crucial that a high score suggestive of over reporting be verified so as not to overlook genuine psychopathology. The second way in which the subscales are used is to provide personality correlates associated with the subscale scores. To this end, Dahlstrom has provided correlates for each of the Subtle and Obvious subscales derived from partner ratings on the Katz Adjustment Scales for the 841 couples in the MMPI-2 restandardization sample.

The issue of Subtle-Obvious subscale effectiveness has been the focus of much controversy. Some researchers have strongly suggested that the subtle items actually diminish the efficacy of the parent scale and fail to provide valid correlates of behavior. Unfortunately, many of the studies suggesting such evidence are deeply flawed conceptually, regardless of their varying merits in terms of execution. The typical format for such studies is to select some obvious criterion such, as the Beck Depression Inventory (BDI), the Symptom Checklist 90 Depression scale, or the Profile of Mood State Depression scale, and to then compare the success of, say, the Depression-Obvious or Depression-Subtle subscale (and sometimes the full Depression scale) in predicting to this criterion. The typical finding, of course, is that the obvious component of the Depression scale best predicts such an obvious criterion, the subtle component predicts poorly if at all, and the full scale is somewhere in the middle.

Although the Subtle and Obvious subscales are known to have different, in some cases widely different, social desirability values, this factor has rarely been addressed, much less controlled, in this rather long series of studies. Each Subtle and Obvious subscale has its own unique operating characteristics and should be assessed as such. Until recently, there has not been sufficient impartial analysis of this body of obvious-subtle research. Fortunately, the situation has recently changed with the publication of Hollrah exhaustive and balanced review of the convergent and discriminant validities of the Subtle-Obvious subscales. They also raised important questions responding some of the recent contributions to the "negative" subtle items literature, such as the article by Weed. The following statements summarize Hollrah findings, which we endorse:

> *After a thorough review of the literature, some uncertainty still remains regarding the validity of the MMPI subtle items. Support for the subtle item validity varies depending on the methodology used and the particular subtle subscale investigated. Of even greater clinical relevance, addressing the empirical method of test construction, and in response to the hypothesis that the subtle*

items were included by sampling error, there is as yet no consistent evidence that removing the subtle items would result in MMPI scales with greater clinical validity.

It is likely that some of the subtle items were indeed included by sampling error. However, some of the subtle items may belong on the respective scales. Likewise, many obvious items may be on their scales due to sampling error, as some studies do not support their discriminative validity. Analyses to determine validity for specific items, or at least specific scales, seems more appropriate than declaring either all or none of the subtle items as valid measures.

Hollrah also stated that the main support in the literature for subtle-obvious items lies in their ability to detect fake-good profiles in psychiatric settings.

Overlapping Item Content

Many of the items on the clinical scales are scored on other clinical scales, whereas some items are not. The items that are unique to a particular validity or clinical scale are referred to as non overlapping items, whereas those scored on more than one scale are called overlapping items. The overlapping items within the MMPI-2 have been a source of concern to clinicians and researchers alike. The empirical criterion approach to test construction allows the total item pool to be used repeatedly with different criterion groups. An item is retained for inclusion in the scale if it discriminates a criterion group from a normal group. The number of scales that can be derived from this method is only limited by the number of available criterion groups. The concern that arose from this construction method is that although the standard MMPI scales were capable of differentiating the normal from each of the psychiatric criterion groups, the psychiatric criterion groups were not contrasted with each other. Hence, there is overlap in item content between the criterion scales. This structural redundancy, however, does not appear to be a trivial artifact of the test construction method; many of the scales share a common variance, which is reflected by the presence of overlapping items.

Considerable range exists in the amount of item overlap among the clinical scales, and there are many more overlapping items than non overlapping items on each scale. Some items (e.g., MMFI-2 Items

9 and 31) overlap as many as five and six different scales, whereas other items overlap as few as two scales (e.g., MMPI-2 Items 11 and 34). Scale 8 (Sc), which is the longest scale on the MMPI-2 with 78 items, has 62 overlapping items, the greatest number for any of the clinical scales, whereas Scales 1(Hs) and 3 (Hy) share 20 items in common, the largest number shared by any two scales. Scales 7 (Pt) and 8 overlap almost as much, with 17 items in common. The neurotic triad consisting of Scales 1, 2, and 3 has 24, 47, and 50 overlapping items, respectively, leaving only 8, 10, and 10 items, respectively, that are unique to each of these scales. The traditional psychotic tetrad, consisting of Scales 6, 7, 8, and 9, has 33, 39, 62, and 31 overlapping items, respectively, and 7, 9, 16, and 15 non overlapping items, respectively. Of the 13 items dropped from the original MMPI for the restandardization leading to the MMPI-2, none of the items were overlap items; all were unique to the particular scale on which they were scored. A perusal of the items belonging to the basic clinical scales indicates that the traditional neurotic and psychotic scales share a considerable amount of item overlap. Thirty-five items appear concurrently on at least one neurotic and one psychotic scale. Within the neurotic triad, and exclusive of other psychotic scales, there are 30 items that appear on at least two of the three scales and in some instances all three (MMPI-2 Items 2, 10, 18, 39, 45, 141, and 175). Within the psychotic tetrad of scales, there are 18 items shared by at least two of the four scales that are exclusive of the neurotic scales and one item that overlaps all four psychotic scales (MMPI-2 Item 23).

Only seven pairs of scales have no items in common: L and Hs, Hs and K, Pd and L, Hs and Mf, Hs and Ma, L and Si, and F and Si.

Scale 1: Hypochondriasis (Hs)

Scale 1 was the first scale to be published on the MMPI and measures the number of bodily complaints claimed by an individual or, said another way, the degree to which a person is denying good physical health. Hypochondriasis is a disturbance involving an unrealistic interpretation of physical signs or sensations as abnormal, which leads the person to fear that he or she has a serious disease. Hypochondriasis was a clinical syndrome studied by Hathaway and McKinley to construct Scale 1, and the criterion group consisted of 50 inpatients with only pure, uncomplicated hypochondriasis. Patients with other coexisting disorders, like a psychosis or other physical disease, were excluded from the criterion group. Hypochondriasis was selected for study because of the large numbers of patients with this disorder, and because it was a relatively easy diagnosis to establish.

Several revisions of the scale were required before it could satisfactorily make discriminations. After the criterion group was selected, the next step in the construction of the scale was to specify the normal. Various samples within the normal group used in constructing Scale 1 were also included in assembling subsequent clinical scales. The first sample consisted of 109 men and 153 women, ranging in age from 26 to 43, who were visitors at the University of Minnesota Hospitals. Participants were eliminated if they were under the care of a physician at the time. The second normal sample consisted of 265 unmarried entering freshmen who were receiving pre college guidance counseling at the University of Minnesota Testing Bureau. Unfortunately, more is known about the demographics of the normals used in constructing Scale 1 than for the criterion participants, whose proportion of gender or other information is unreported. McKinley and Hathaway, however, did state that participants "were deleted, however, to exclude the extremes of age or other obviously disturbing influences".

The empirical method was primarily used to identify items that discriminated the normals and physically ill people from the 50 patients in the hypochondriacal criterion group. An item was considered for inclusion on the scale if the normal and patients in the criterion group differed in the frequency of responding to the item by at least twice the standard error of the proportions of true-false responses of the two groups. However, McKinley and Hathaway did reject a few of the items in a nonempirical manner if they thought the item drifted too far from the construct of hypochondriasis.

An initial version of the scale consisted of 55 items, but further work was required to refine the scale because of the high numbers of psychiatric patients without clinically observed hypochondriasis who also obtained significant Scale 1 elevations. To correct for this occurrence, 50 patients without hypochondriacal complaints, but with high scores on the initial version of Scale 1, were compared with the original group of 50 hypochondriacal patients. Items that discriminated these two groups became known as the CH (Correction for Hypochondriasis) scale. The CH scale consisted of 48 items. Experimentation with the CH items by assigning them different weights failed to improve the performance of the scale. Ultimately, the maximum discrimination was achieved when CH was subtracted from the preliminary Hypochondriasis scale. As Greene described it, "for each of these correction items where an individual answers in the non-hypochondriacal direction, one point was subtracted from the total score on Scale 1". Cross-validation with the H-C scale reliably separated normals from hypochondriacal patients. The hospitalized medical sample demonstrated that the presence of physical disease did not significantly raise scores on the scale.

A final version of Scale 1 occurred when McKinley and Hathaway attempted to improve the separation between Scales 1 and 3. Many C items were dropped, as were original Scale 1 items that did not stand up on further analysis. The addition of a 0.5 K value helped to improve the ability of the scale to make accurate diagnostic discriminations, and commercially available profile sheets provide a space to add the 0.5 K value to Scale 1.

The final scale consisted of 33 items related to various aspects of bodily functions, including generalized aches and pains and concerns about different body regions. The restandardization leading to MMPI-2 prompted the omission of one objectionable item, the modification of three items for grammatical clarification (e.g., tense), the modernization of one item for idiom or usage, and the simplification of one item. Therefore, the MMPI-2 Scale 1 has 32 items. The content of the scale is considered obvious, with no subtle items, meaning that an individual wishing to deny good health can easily do so. Given the face validity of the items, Wiener and Harmon did not categorize the item content of Scale 1 into their Subtle-Obvious subscales. Because all of the items relate to physical health and sensation, Harris and Lingoes did not discover enough item heterogeneity to form different subscales. As Greene pointed out, factor analyses of the items in several different populations have consistently identified poor physical health and gastrointestinal difficulties as the two major factors in this scale.

The following items are examples of Scale 1 content, with the item number preceding the statement and the direction of scoring in parentheses:

2. *I have a good appetite. (False)*

28. *I am bothered by an upset stomach several times a week. (True)*

53. *Parts of my body often have feelings like burning, tingling, crawling, or like "going to sleep." (True)*

57. *I hardly ever feel pain in the back of my neck. (False)*

141. *During the past few years I have been well most of the time. (False)*

The deviant direction for 66% (21 of the 32 items) of the items is "false." Therefore, a false response set tends to elevate the scale. Most items on Scale 1 overlap the other neurotic scales, D and Hy. Only four items overlap Scale 8 (Schizophrenia); one item overlaps Scale 6 (Paranoia). Twenty of the 32 items on Scale 1 are also scored on Scale 3 (Hy); therefore, an elevated score on either scale tends to raise the other one. Only eight items are unique (nonoverlapping) to Scale 1.

Greene stated that the construct validity of Scale 1 is supported by the fact that both older, well-researched scales and newer scales overlap with Scale 1. Specifically, Wiggins' Poor Health and Organic Symptoms content scales from the MMPI both have 13 items, respectively, in common with MMPI-2 Scale 1. The Health Concerns content scale from the MMPI-2 shares 23 of its 36 items in common with Scale 1.

Increasing elevations on Scale 1 correspond to increasing bodily complaints. Neurotic individuals with bodily preoccupations tend to endorse a diffuse set of complaints about the body, whereas actually ill patients without psychological disturbance contain their item endorsements to the specific physical areas concerning them. Greene reported that physically ill patients usually obtain only moderate T-score elevations between 58 and 64. Patients with actual physical illness are more likely to elevate Scale 2 (Depression) than Scale 1.

The normals in the restandardization sample averaged a raw-score value of approximately 5 and 6 for men and women, respectively, on Scale 1. As normal people age, their Scale 1 scores tend only to increase slightly, approximately two to three items over the life span. Scale 1 elevations have also been noted to occur in chronic pain patients (who also elevate Scale 3) and have been associated with high post treatment pain intensity and a failure to return to normal activity levels. Generally, a high elevation on Scale 1 is a negative predictor of treatment response. If the clinician sees an excessively low Scale 1 score, such as a raw score of 0, interpretation can range from the individual simply being unusually free of bodily complaints and concerns to being pathologically unconcerned with or unaware of his or her bodily functions. The lack of psychological mindedness so often cited with high scores on this scale has been seen in a few rare cases with unusually low Hs raw scores. Such scores may also indicate the denial of any physical problems because of a counterphobic defense.

When examining Scale 1 in a profile, it is important to note the amount of K being added. Because a 0.5 K is added to Scale 1, a person may have important hypochondriacal concerns, despite a non elevated score, because of a low K value.

Although some MMPI experts consider that Scale 1 elevations may reflect transient symptoms, such as the flu or a cold, it is generally considered a stable scale, with test-retest coefficients for psychiatric cases ranging from .79 to .86 for up to a 2-week period and from .38 to .65 for a 1-year interval.

Hunsley 's large-scale meta-analysis of MMPI reliability studies using a wide variety of populations conducted between 1970 and 1981 found an average internal consistency of .79 across 70 studies. They also reported an average test-retest reliability of .78 for 16 studies, with time intervals from 1 day to 2 years. More recently, Butcher reported reliability data for a subset of the restandardization sample that included 82 normal men and 111 normal women retested at an average interval of 8.5 days (Mdn = 7 days) and found test-retest correlation coefficients for men and women of .84 and .85, respectively, again illustrating the stability or characterologic nature of this scale. Internal consistency estimates of .77 and .81 were reported for men and women, respectively.

Scale 2: Depression (D)

Scale 2 was designed to measure the presence and depth of symptomatic depression, which is a mood state characterized by low morale, feelings of hopelessness or worthlessness, slowing of thought and action, and sometimes preoccupations with death and suicide. Scale 2 is considered to be a mood scale and is, therefore, sensitive to transient and even very brief emotional states. For this reason, it is useful in measuring response to treatment. It is the most frequently elevated scale in the MMPI-2 and the most frequent high point in adult psychiatric populations. In adolescent patients, Scale 2 appears second only to Scale 4 (Psychopathic Deviate) in high-point frequency on the MMPI.

Five participant groups were used to construct the scale. However, most of the 60 items contained on the original scale were derived by comparing normal (i.e., participants without observable depression) with a group of 50 patients who were carefully diagnosed as being in the depressed phase of a manic-depressive psychosis. Because some non depressed participants obtained elevated scores, a correction factor was derived (as was done in the construction of Scale 1) by comparing item endorsement patterns of 40 normal individuals, who earned elevated depression scores on an early version of the scale, with a group of 50 patients without observable depressive signs but who scored high on the early Depression scale. Eleven items differentiating these two groups became correction items that were included in the final scale. A depressed normal group was also used in the derivation of the scale "to help establish the meaning of more intermediate scale values between the normal and criterion groups, which would have been impossible if only the two extreme groups were contrasted" Hathaway and McKinley described the final selection of scale items in the following way:

First, each depressive item had to show a progressive increase in frequency from the normal groups through the depressed normal group to the criterion group since it was assumed that the depressed normal would be less than the criterion cases but more than the general normal. In all items primarily indicating depression, the difference in percentage between the normal and the criterion was 2.5 or more times its standard error. Second, the non-depressed group percentage for the item was required to approach that for normal. After careful analysis of all percentages for each of the 504 items, 60 items were chosen as the final depression scale.

Although the criterion group for Scale 2 consisted of individuals afflicted with a severe depressive illness characterized as psychotic, Hathaway and McKinley considered depression to be the cardinal feature of their disturbance. Dahlstrom stated that "although the scale was devised on a largely psychotic group of patients, it became clear in the early research that the items reflected depressive mood changes on a neurotic basis in fact, any depressive reaction, no matter what the underlying character structure or adjustment status of a patient might be".

The original MMPI Depression scale had 60 items, but the revision leading to the MMPI-2 deleted 3 items pertaining to religious matters (e.g., "I go to church almost every week"). The resulting 57-item MMPI-2 scale also underwent modifications on two items, one that eliminated sexist wording and one that modernized its usage (MMPI-2 Item 57; "I am a good mixer" became I am a very sociable person"). Approximately two thirds of the 57 items (37 false; 20 true) on Scale 2 are keyed in the "false" direction. Therefore, all false-response sets will inflate Scale 2 scores, as well as the other scales in the neurotic triad (Scales 1, 2, and 3). Scale 2 shares 47 of its 57 items fairly evenly with the other clinical scales. Only 10 items are unique to the scale. The MMPI-2 Depression scale shares only nine items in common with MMPI-2 DEP content scale. These two scales measure different aspects of depressive symptoms, so they should not be used interchangeably. The overlapping item content of Scale 2 is presented.

Test-retest reliability data for Scale 2, as reported in the MMPI-2 manual, were based on 82 normal men and 111 normal women, retested at about 1 week, which yielded correlation coefficients of .75 and .77, respectively. Dahlstrom reported lower test-retest stability data on clinical groups, which is expected, given the greater emotional instability of clinical patients. In Hunsley large-scale meta-analysis of MMPI reliability studies using a wide variety of populations conducted between 1970 and 1981, an average test-retest reliability of .78 was reported for 16 studies, with time intervals from 1 day to 2 years. Hunsley also reported an average internal consistency of .81 across 74 studies of Scale 2. More recently, internal consistency estimates for Scale 2 were derived from the MMPI-2 restandardization sample and yielded correlation coefficients of .77 and .81 for men and women, respectively.

The items in the scale reflect a number of concerns related to depression, including a lack of interest in things, denial of happiness or personal worth, and physical symptoms (e.g., sleep disturbance and gastrointestinal complaints). The following are examples of items from Scale 2, with the item number preceding the statement and the direction of scoring following the items in parentheses:

2. *I have a good appetite. (False)*

5. *I am easily awakened by noise. (True)*

18. *I am troubled by attacks of nausea and vomiting. (True)*

31. *I find it hard to keep my mind on a task or job. (True)*

75. *I usually feel that life is worthwhile. (False)*

95. *I'm happy most of the time. (False)*

109. *I seem to be about as capable and as smart as others around me. (False)*

In general, as Scale 2 scores elevate into the clinically significant range (T ? 65), the greater the probability the person is suffering depressive symptoms. Severity is often a function of scale elevation, but it is also reflected in other clinical scale elevations. Rarely is Scale 2 elevated in isolation. Analysis of other clinical scale elevations, as well as subscales and supplementary scales, helps to determine the nature of the depression. Scale 2 not only reflects the presence and degree of various forms of symptomatic depression but also reflects the basic personality features of hyper responsibility, high personal standards, and intropunitiveness, which can predispose an individual to experience depression. Individuals scoring in the extremely high range (T ? 91) likely have endorsed a wide range of depressive content that most likely reflects severe withdrawal, a dependent state, and serious suicidal risk.

Although several studies have provided correlates for high-scoring psychiatric patients on Scale 2, very low scores (T > 40) should not be interpreted in psychiatric patients as reflecting the converse of depression, such as an active, enthusiastic, optimistic, socially outgoing person. These very-low-score descriptors are more likely to apply to normals than psychiatric patients. However, Venn reported pathological correlates in a sample of low-scoring adult men on Scales 2 and 0 (Social Introversion) who took the MMPI as part of an employment screening process. Low-scoring participants on Scale 2, with concurrent low scores on Scale 0, had indications of probable character pathology (e.g., impulsive behavior and arrest record). As stated earlier, Keiller and Graham suggested that low scores may have different meanings for psychiatric outpatients and inpatients and that low scores may be more likely associated with unfavorable characteristics in psychiatric samples. Further research on low scores in different samples across settings (e.g., forensic, medical, and employment) is called for in order to understand the generalizability of their findings.

Harris-Lingoes Subscales

Harris and Lingoes developed five subscales for the Depression scale on the MMPI, which are identical on the MMPI-2. The five subscales for the Depression scale are: Subjective Depression (D1), Psychomotor Retardation (D2), Physical Malfunctioning (D3), Mental Dullness (D4), and Brooding (D5).

D1: Subjective Depression (32 Items)

The longest of the subscales, this subscale indicates obvious distress, such as feeling unhappy, suicidal, joyless, worrying, having sleeping and concentration difficulties, and generally not feeling worthwhile. Other descriptors include feeling easily hurt by criticism and a lack of energy for coping with problems. Dysphoria is the mood state typified by this subscale and diagnoses of depression or dysthymia often accompany elevations on this subscale as well as the other depression subscales. Caldwell stated that this subscale captures the "general misery of depression". The worrying aspect of the scale is found in the fact that all 10 of the items on the brooding subscale (D5) are contained within D1. Wrobel reported the following correlates to be applicable to high D1 scorers: pessimism, poor morale, low self-esteem, lack of energy for coping, feelings of psychological inertia, and a lack of joy in doing things. Graham also reported that high D1 scorers feel overwhelmed and unable to cope with stress.

Low scorers on this subscale tend not to report a loss of interest or general depressive feelings. The following items are examples from D1 with the MMPI-2 item numbers and direction of scoring in parentheses. Seventeen of the items are scored in the "false" direction, and 15 items are scored in the "true" direction:

2. *I have a good appetite. (False)*

39. *My sleep is fitful and disturbed. (True)*

43. *My judgment is better than it ever was. (False)*

56. *I wish I could be as happy as others seem to be. (True)*

75. *I usually feel that life is worthwhile. (False)*

D2: Psychomotor Retardation (14 Items)

The items on this subscale reflect inhibited aggression and a lack of energy, vigor, and initiative. Wrobel found a low but significant correlation with a lack of participation in social interactions. Psychiatric outpatient women in the Graham study sample were also described as not being very competitive. Nichols and Greene suggested that D2 emphasizes social withdrawal and rigid controls against hostile or aggressive expressions. In essence, this subscale is tapping a dimension of passivity and submissiveness. Caldwell asserted that elevations on this subscale may reflect indecisiveness at least as much as physiologic slowing. This is consistent with the moderate correlation Nichols and Greene reported between the Mental Dullness (D4) subscale and D2.

Levitt suggested that a low D2 score, when other depression indexes are high, may point to a suicide potential, presumably because the person has the energy to act on his or her suicidal feelings. However, Graham also found that females with high scores on the D2 subscale were described by their therapists as having suicidal ideation.

Four of the items on this subscale are scored in the "true" direction, and 10 items are scored in the "false" direction. The following items illustrate the content of this subscale, with the MMPI-2 item numbers and direction of scoring in parentheses:

9. My daily life is full of things that keep me interested. (False)

29. At times I feel like swearing. (False)

37. At times I feel like smashing things. (False)

170. I am afraid of losing my mind. (True)

233. I have difficulty in starting to do things. (True)

D3: Physical Malfunctioning (11 Items)

Seven of the 11 items overlap Scales 1 and 3, reflecting feelings of weakness, loss of appetite, weight changes, and constipation. High scores most likely reflect a preoccupation with oneself. A sense of feeling unrelieved from one's discomforts and pessimistic about ever feeling well is suggested. D3 is probably the most specific indicator of depressive somatization. It is not surprising that the Lassitude-Malaise subscale (Hy3) and D3 correlate strongly in a group of psychiatric inpatients and outpatients.

Graham reported that women psychiatric outpatients were described by their therapists as lacking energy and having a low sex drive. Furthermore, they were described as lacking interest and aspirations. Both men and women who score high on D3 were seen as having difficulty with concentration although it is interesting to note that concentration difficulties were not generally reported by Graham for patients scoring high on the Mental Dullness (D4) subscale.

Low D3 scores most likely reflect that the individual does not feel physically handicapped and may, in fact, feel very good.

Four of the 11 items on this subscale are scored in the "true" direction, and 7 items are scored in the "false" direction. The following items illustrate the content of this subscale:

18. I am troubled by attacks of nausea and vomiting. (True)

20. I am very seldom troubled by constipation. (False)

45. I am in just as good physical health as most of my friends. (False)

175. I feel weak all over much of the time. (True)

D4: Mental Dullness (15 Items)

Caldwell referred to this scale as the "mental fog" of depression. The themes he reported in the subscale consist of (a) "losing one's mind", that is, being easily distracted, unable to comprehend what one reads, and suffering memory and judgment problems. However, it is of interest to note that the Graham investigation of psychiatric outpatients did not reveal any marked concentration difficulties in high D4 scorers; (b) trouble getting started on tasks, reduced energy, and a lack of confidence; (c) a feeling of diminished interest and involvement in life (this is consistent with Wrobel's findings of feelings of unresponsiveness and distrust of one's psychological functioning being associated with high D4 scores). D4 and D2 share five items in common. D4 also shares four items with the Lack of Ego Mastery, Cognitive subscale (Sc3) and 5 items with the Lack of Ego Mastery, Conative subscale (Sc4), both reflecting mental insufficiency. Graham reported that for high D4 scorers both men and women outpatients reported a history of physical abuse, while men reported being sexually abused. Women outpatients were also described as suspicious and as being overly sensitive to criticism.

According to Caldwell, low D4 scorers do not complain that their judgment is impaired or that they are unable to be as cognitively efficient as others.

Eight of the items on this subscale are scored in the "true" direction, and seven items are scored in the "false" direction. The following items illustrate the item content of D4:

10. I am about as able to work as I ever was. (False)

31. I find it hard to keep my mind on a task or job. (True)

43. My judgment is better than it ever was. (False)

73. I am certainly lacking in self-confidence. (True)

147. I cannot understand what I read as well as I used to. (True)

D5: Brooding (10 Items)

All 10 of these items overlap with D1. The content suggests that one feels unworthy while and useless and, when elevated in conjunction with a high Scale 2 score, adds to the hopelessness of the depression. Irritability and a proneness to rumination are likely correlates. Interestingly, men but not women in the Graham study of psychiatric outpatients were described as worriers. D5 and the DEP content scale for the MMPI-2 share eight items in common. Nichols and Greene stated that D5 is a measure of general distress and is sensitive to anhedonia. They also stated that D5 can predict the intensity and pervasiveness of guilt, which may be reflected in the Self-Alienation subscale (Pd5). Specifically, guilt will be more clearly identifiable when D5 and Pd5 are both elevated above the OBS content scale, as well as above the level of other distress scales, such as Anxiety (A) and the following content scales: Anxiety (ANX), Fears (FRS), Depression (DEP), Work Interference (WRK), and Negative Treatment Indicators (TRT). Nichols and Greene underscored the fact that D5 is saturated with first-factor variance (i.e., general maladjustment), which places an emphasis on feeling miserable and upset.

Caldwell indicated that a low D5 score, especially with an accompanying low T score on Scale 2, may indicate a capacity to respond resiliently to life's stresses.

Eight of the items are scored in the "true" direction, and two items are scored in the "false" direction. The following items illustrate the item content of D5.

56. I wish I could be as happy as others seem to be. (True)

92. I don't seem to care what happens to me. (True)

130. I certainly feel useless at times. (True)

146. I cry easily. (True)

170. I am afraid of losing my mind. (True)

Scale 2: Subtle-Obvious Subscales

The Wiener-Harmon Depression-Obvious subscale (D-O) for the MMPI-2 has 39 items, of which 17 are scored in the "true" direction and 22 items are keyed in the "false" direction. The Depression-

Subtle subscale (D-S) has 18 items, of which 3 items are scored in the "true" direction and 15 are scored in the "false" direction. The following items are examples of subtle-obvious items on Scale 2, with the scoring direction and obvious or subtle distinction in parentheses. The items are preceded by the MMPI-2 number. The item composition and scoring key for the Subtle-Obvious subscales. The linear T- score conversions for the Wiener-Harmon subscales for men and women.

15. I work under a great deal of tension. (True-Obvious)

31. I find it hard to keep my mind on a task or a job. (True-Obvious)

33. I seldom worry about my health. (False-Obvious)

37. At times I feel like smashing things. (False-Obvious)

55. I sometimes keep on at a thing until others lose their patience with me. (False-Obvious)

181. I do not have spells of hayfever or asthma. (True-Obvious)

Caldwell described the 39 D-O subscale items of Wiener and Harmon as covering a "broad depressive spectrum", including feeling unhappy, worried, and useless; crying easily; and having sleep and appetite problems. The 18 subtle items include a cluster pertaining to the inhibition of anger, aggression, and self-assertion. Nichols and Greene reported a similar description, adding that the D-S subscale reflects an inhibition or suppression of irritability and sadism in emotional life and fantasy. Other subtle items report lacking perseverance and "never feeling euphoria or even unusually good". W. G. Dahlstrom suggested that the subtle items may reflect a predisposition to develop the disorder that the parent scale is measuring. For example, an individual scoring low on the D-O items but high on the D-S items may have a tendency to develop depression. In general, individuals with greater levels of maladjustment tend to endorse more obvious items, whereas defensive responders or persons with milder forms of psychopathology tend to endorse primarily subtle items in describing their feelings.

Hollrah 's review of the subtle-obvious convergent validity literature led them to caution that the D-S subscale is not a valid measure of depression. They stated, however, that the decision to use only the D-O subscale should be evaluated with caution. They found the D-O subscale to be better than the full D scale when measuring obvious depression symptoms. They also reviewed studies that show support for both the full D scale and the discriminant validity of the D-S subscale.

Dahlstrom reported several correlates for men and women for each of the Subtle-Obvious subscales derived from partner ratings in the MMPI-2 restandardization sample. For the D-O subscale, trouble sleeping, unrealistic attitude about abilities, worries about health, a lack of energy, multiple fears, a tendency to get sad, a lack of confidence, and complaints of body aches all characterize male and female participants. For women scoring high on the D-O subscale, the following descriptors were generated: nervous, not cheerful, not pleasant or relaxed, cries easily, concerned about death, and avoiding contact with others.

D-S subscale elevations were associated with the following descriptors for both men and women: does not swear or curse, dislikes flirting, cooperative, thoughtful of others, pleasant and relaxed, and attends religious functions. Specific to women only, the following descriptions were given: self-confident, few fears and bad dreams, does not break things when angry, not lacking in emotional control, not stubborn, does not worry about the future and gets along well with others. Men were described as follows: not moody or bossy, friendly, does not take prescription drugs, not argumentative or critical of others, and does not get angry and yell.

Caldwell reported that low D-O scores reflect an individual who has ample self-confidence and feels that life is worthwhile. Low D-S scores reflect willfulness and assertion and the capacity to feel anger as it is situationally appropriate.

Scale 3: Hysteria (Hy)

The diagnosis of hysteria, although common in the 1930s, was difficult to establish because clear-cut criteria in the clinical concept were lacking, hysterical phenomenon were concurrent with other neurotic symptoms in the same individual, and there was diagnostic uncertainty of hysterical reactions in individuals who were suspected of having organic disease. Thus, the 60-item Hy scale was originally developed to aid in the diagnosis of hysteria and to measure the degree to which a patient is likely to develop symptoms of conversion. The restandardization of the MMPI-2 left the scale composition intact with no item deletions, although nine items were modified regarding modernization of idioms and usage, grammatical clarifications, and simplifications.

The participants in the criterion group were taken primarily from the inpatient service of the psychiatric unit at the University of Minnesota Hospitals. McKinley and Hathaway described the criterion participants as follows:

They had each received the diagnosis psychoneurosis, hysteria, or had been especially noted as having characteristic hysterical components in the personality disturbance. In the assignment of these diagnostic terms, the neuropsychiatric staff followed, as closely as possible, current clinical practice. Where cases showed a simple conversion symptom such as aphonia, an occupational cramp, or a neurologically irrational anesthetic area, the diagnosis was usually well agreed upon. In some cases, there remained a doubt as to whether there was a true organic illness such as multiple sclerosis present or whether the syndrome reflected hypochondriasis or an early schizophrenic reaction.

Participants with less dramatic symptornatology made psychodiagnosis a more difficult and less certain task. After several attempts, a final criterion group consisting of 50 cases was selected. Although no modal description or demographic data for the Scale 3 criterion hysteric patients were provided, the 50 patients included in the criterion group did manifest the "neurotic defenses of the conversion form of hysteria" or hysteric personality features. In individuals who had developed an involuntary psychogenic loss or disorder of function, the physical symptoms allowed them to evade responsibilities and to escape from stressful and unpleasant situations. It was thought that patients whose personality organization revolves around hysterical defenses tend to function adequately or even well under ordinary circumstances, but when faced with difficult situations the tenuous nature of their personality organization is taxed beyond its capacity to cope and symptoms emerge reflecting an overburdened self (e.g., emotional lability, emotional intensity, and modulation difficulties). Dahlstrom noted that a need to detect such a predisposition for breakdown was necessary and was in part the motivation for the development of Scale 3. It was immediately apparent to McKinley and Hathaway that two major categories of items existed within the scale. One group referred to somatic complaints; the other group referred to an extraverted social style. The bodily complaint items related to such symptoms as headaches, dizzy spells, and hand tremor. As McKinley and Hathaway pointed out, the declaration of social well-being was illustrated by the frequent endorsement of "false" to items such as "I frequently have to fight against showing that I am bashful" (MMPI-2 Item 161), "I get mad easily and get over it soon" (MMPI-2, Item 213), and "Some people are so bossy that I feel like doing the opposite of what they request even though I know they are right" (MMPI-2, Item 98). Despite the predominance of these two types of items, several other items referred to feelings of dysphoria ("blue" or "unhappy"). Specifically, MMPI-2 Item 65, "Most of the time, I feel blue," is keyed in the "true" direction, whereas MMPI-2 Item 95, "I'm happy most of the time," is keyed in the "false" direction. The subsets of items describing somatic complaints and feelings of well-being and comfort are usually independent of each other or negatively correlated in normal, but tend to be positively correlated in patients whose personality functioning is organized around hysteric psychodynamics. Generally, the more elevated and prominent the role of Scale 3 in a code type, the less insightful the individual tends to be and the more likely it is that physical symptoms will emerge when the individual experiences stress.

Greene reviewed the relation of Scale 3 item content to other scales and underscored the correspondence of its content to the independent clusters of items reported by K. B. Little and Fischer. The two clusters, admission of physiologic symptoms and denial of symptoms, were used to construct the Admission (Ad) and Denial (Dn) scales. Greene stated that:

> *The Ad scale correlates positively (.89-90) with Scale 1, which is logical since the two scales have 18 items in common. The Dn scale correlates positively (.78-.88) with the K scale, with which it has 9 items in common. Clients who score high on the Ad scale complain about their somatic functioning and have poor interpersonal relationships. High scorers on the Dn scale are*

described as lacking insight into their own behavior and are morally virtuous. Little and Fischer believe that when both of these scales are elevated, the person should have conversion reaction dynamics.

Note that the Ad and Dn scales virtually overlap the obvious and subtle components of Scale 3, respectively.

The normal group used in the construction of Scale 3 consisted of 200 women and 139 men, all married and between the ages of 26 and 43, who typically had 8 years of schooling, with few being educated beyond high school. The second group of normals consisted of 114 women and 151 men who were entering college students and were included to control for age and intelligence.

McKinley and Hathaway viewed the Hy scale as measuring a variable trait closely related to the construct measured by Scale 1 (Hypochondriasis). There is considerable overlap between Scales 1 and 3, 20 items to be precise, representing the most item overlap shared by any two clinical scales. The positive correlation between Scales 1 and 3 motivated McKinley and Hathaway to attempt to decrease this correlation by eliminating as many of the overlapping somatic items as possible. The results of this effort are best summarized by McKinley and Hathaway, who stated that:

> *Elimination of the somatic items resulted in a marked drop in the number of test cases identified and introduced another disturbing difficulty; if only the nonsomatic items were used, there was a strong relation with age and education. The mean score was more than a half sigma higher for the college group than for older persons. These results forced the inclusion of some somatic items in the final scale with consequent high correlation (r = .52 normals and r = .71 clinic cases) between Hs (hypochondriasis) and Hy (hysteria). Some relation still remains between age and intelligence and the Hy score. The relation seems valid clinically.*

It appears that the positive correlation that exists between Scales 1 and 3 is not a simple artifact of the item overlap but reflects a common psychological dimension in the elevation of these two scales, apparently somatization. It is important to note that McKinley and Hathaway distinguished clinical differences between individuals when both scales were elevated but with one score higher than the other. Specifically, they identified a different prognosis and treatment for these patterns of scores:

Where Hs was higher, the physical complaints were diffuse and frequently required much less study to establish the presence of an important psychological factor in the disability. On the other hand, when Hy was dominant, the person frequently appeared normal psychologically and his physical complaints were likely to mimic closely or be accompanied by some common physical syndrome of the type now called "psychosomatic".

More generally, Duckworth and Anderson pointed out that denial and repression are the primary mechanisms of defense being tapped by Scale 3. Therefore, although symptoms associated with scale scores above Scale 3 may be acknowledged by the individual, those indicated by scales with T scores below Scale 3 may not be acknowledged and the person may show a distinct absence of insight. Greene suggested that this rule should be used cautiously, given the lack of research to support it.

The scoring direction for the majority of the items on Scale 3 is "false." Forty-seven (78%) of the items are scored as "false," with 13 items (22%) scored as "true." As with Scales 1 and 2 in the neurotic triad, a tendency to endorse the items in the "false" direction will also elevate Scale 3. Scale 3 has fairly evenly distributed overlap with the other clinical scales. Although there is no K correction added to Scale 3, there is, in effect, a built-in K correction factor since Scale 3 has 10 items in common with the K scale. The following items illustrate the varied content in Scale 3. The scoring direction for each item is in parentheses, with the MMPI-2 item number preceding the item. For a complete listing of items on Scale 3, with the direction of scoring.

2. *I have a good appetite. (False)*

3. *I wake up fresh and rested most mornings. (False)*

11. *There seems to be a lump in my throat much of the time. (True)*

18. *I am troubled by attacks of nausea and vomiting. (True)*

29. *At times I feel like swearing. (False)*

95. *I am happy most of the time. (False)*

High scores on Scale 3 are obtained by individuals often described as childishly self-centered with a high need for approval and affection. They will seek reassurance that they are likeable and will try to elicit it by flattering, rewarding, and complimenting others. Conformity and naivete are characteristic, along with the absence of insight due to the predominance of denial and repression in their personality organization. Fearful of emotional and physical pain, they tend to limit their awareness, which can result in impaired reality testing under stressful circumstances. Lewak suggested that it is helpful to look for what these individuals explicitly deny because that is often at the center of their conflict. Sociable, but shallow in their relationships, high Scale 3 scorers can become resentful of perceived demands and develop somatic concerns to remove themselves from responsibilities they resent or fear being unable to handle. It is rare for high scorers to develop psychotic symptoms, although their symptom pictures can be quite pronounced when they feel overwhelmed. Although the behaviors measured by Scale 3 are trait like in appearance, the item content reflects behaviors that can change over time. The phrasing of the items in the present tense also allows test takers to interpret the items according to their current circumstances. For these reasons, Dahlstrom stated that the scale may show less test-retest agreement relative to other scales and that split-half estimates of reliability are inappropriate or misleading for Scale 3.

The test-retest correlation coefficients for psychiatric patients on Scale 3 ranged between .66 and .80 for intervals between 1 and 2 weeks and between .36 and .72 for a 1-year interval between tests. More recently, Butcher provided test-retest reliability coefficients for 82 normal men and 111 normal women retested at an average interval of about 1 week, with the men and women obtaining coefficients of .72 and .75, respectively. Hunsley 's large-scale meta-analysis of reliability studies using a wide variety of populations conducted between 1970 and 1981 reported an average internal consistency of .78 across 70 studies of Scale 3 and also reported an average test-retest reliability of .74 for 15 studies with time intervals from 1 day to 2 years. In contrast to the Hunsley internal consistency findings, Butcher reported much lower estimates of internal consistency; specifically, they reported coefficient alpha values of .58 and 56 for men and women, respectively, in their restandardization sample. The much lower values reported by Butcher et al. is most likely due to the greater diversity in participants used in the Hunsley meta-analysis, which included college students, psychiatric patients, medical patients, alcohol and/or drug abusers, and incarcerated criminals.

Although various correlates for Scale 3 are reported in the literature, it is important that the clinician be selective in choosing the descriptors to be applied to any one individual. Some correlates, for example, although reported to be valid, may not have the validity always ascribed to them. Hedlund, in comparing the results of seven independent studies that attempted to empirically identify the behavioral or symptom correlates of individual MMPI clinical scales for psychiatric patients, found that Scale 3 did not always correlate with specific items of dissociation, amnesia, or conversion symptoms, items that might be assumed to be relevant to the construct of hysteria. He did find, however, that Scale 3 was regularly related to a number of somatic complaints (e.g., diarrhea, loss of appetite, and sleep disturbance) and significantly correlated with a number of depression related complaints. It is recommended that the clinician assess individuals on a case-by-case basis that includes an understanding of their psychosocial history and context in which they are being evaluated, as well as carefully inspect the various subscales and supplementary scales to better understand the meaning of the particular clinical scale elevation.

Harris-Lingoes Subscales

Harris and Lingoes developed the following five subscales for Scale 3: Denial of Social Anxiety (Hy1), Need for Affection (Hy2), Lassitude-Malaise (Hy3), Somatic Complaints (Hy4), and Inhibition of Aggression (Hy5).

The Harris-Lingoes subscales for the MMPI are identical in the MMPI-2. No items were deleted in Scale 3 for the restandardization, so the composition of the Harris-Lingoes subscales has remained intact.

Hy1: Denial of Social Anxiety (6 Items)

This short, 6-item subscale is keyed entirely in the "false" direction. The items on Hyl are contained completely in K. B. Little and Fischer's Dn scale and the Hy-S subscale. The subscale appears to reflect the denial of social shyness and inhibition and never tends to be elevated when Scale 0 (Si) is elevated. Caldwell described high scorers as manifesting an "over-socialized friendliness" toward unfamiliar others. Nichols and Greene described high Hyl individuals as seeking attention, approval, support, and affection in the context of their interactions with others. Levitt described low scorers as socially maladjusted and anxious, shy, and easily embarrassed. It appears that Hyl taps the personality dimension of social extraversion (when elevated) and social introversion (when submerged). Nichols and Greene suggested examining Hyl in the context of its relation to other measures of introversion to determine if the introversion is situational or long term. Specifically, when Pd3 (Social Imperturbability), Hy1, and Hy-S are all low, they should be examined in relation to the SOD content scale, Scale 0, and Sil (Shyness/Self-Consciousness). Nichols and Greene (1995) stated the following configural guidelines for interpreting introversion as a state versus a trait:

> *High scores on SOD, Si and Si 1 when in the context of low scores on Pd3, Hy 1 and Hy-S, suggest long term or congenital trends toward shyness and social withdrawal.*

When SOD, Si, and Si l are high, but Pd3, Hy 1 and Hy-S are in an average range, an acute or temporary withdrawal secondary to loss or distress is suggested.

It should be noted that Wrobel did not find that social introversion was linked to Hyl per therapist ratings of clients in psychotherapy. He suggested that the short length of the subscale or the nature of the outpatient sample may have attenuated his results.

The following 6 items represent the entire scale content for Hyl. The MMPI-2 item number precedes the item with the scoring direction in parentheses following each item:

> *129. My conduct is largely controlled by the behavior of those around me. (False)*
>
> *161. I frequently have to fight against showing that I am bashful. (False)*
>
> *167. I find it hard to make talk when I meet new people. (False)*
>
> *185. I wish I were not so shy. (False)*

243. When in a group of people, I have trouble thinking of the right things to talk about. (False)

265. I am likely not to speak to people until they speak to me. (False)

Hy2: Need for Affection (12 Items)

The items in this subscale appear to emphasize a faith and trust in others and reflect a denial of resentment or suspicion toward others. It appears that high scorers prefer to avoid interpersonal conflicts. Graham found high scoring Hy2 psychiatric men and women outpatients to be more empathic than low scorers and this correlate was unique to Hy2 among the Hy subscales. They also reported that high scoring women were seen as moralistic by their therapists. There is a strong element of unconflicted passivity and submissiveness in Hy2 which reflects a "go along to get along" social spirit according to Nichols and Greene, high scorers believe that the consequences of self-assertion are generally not socially constructive:

> *High scorers seem to believe that, if one thinks the best of others, others will oblige by behaving in accordance with a benign and benevolent set of expectations, and that argument, disagreement, challenge, and confrontation are to be rejected because they can only serve to make social relations unpleasant, create hurt feelings, and foster alienation.*

They also view Hy2 as related to an aspect of cynicism, with low scorers "disclaiming self-traits of trustworthiness and social constructiveness". Caldwell described low scorers as perceiving the world as "combative" where one has to take care of oneself and fight for what one wants and believes.

The following items represent examples of the subscale, with the scoring direction following the item and the MMPI-2 item number preceding the item. Eleven of the 12 items are scored in the "false" direction with only 1 item scored as "true":

58. I think a great many people exaggerate their misfortunes in order to gain the sympathy and help of others. (False)

76. It takes a lot of argument to convince most people of the truth. (False)

81. I think most people would lie to get ahead. (False)

124. I often wonder what hidden reason another person may have for doing something nice for me. (False)

213. I get mad easily and then get over it soon. (False)

230. I can be friendly with people who do things which I consider wrong. (True)

Hy3: Lassitude-Malaise (15 Items)

Although 10 of the 15 items on this scale overlap with Scale 2, Caldwell suggested that the scale taps less of the generalized devaluation of the self that is seen in depression and is more of a measure of having been made to feel weak, tired, sleepless and less interested in life by life's aggravations or one's own poor health. High scorers report not feeling like themselves physically and mentally. Nichols and Greene described Hy3 as reflecting some depressive somatization, like D3 (Physical Malfunctioning), but having a greater emphasis on moods than on somatic difficulty. In a sample of psychotherapy patients, Wrobel found that complaints about physical and mental functioning, and feelings of needing attention and reassurance, positively correlated with elevated Hy3 scores, whereas efforts to keep up a good front negatively correlated with Hy3 scores. Graham found high scoring Hy3 psychiatric men and women outpatients to have suicidal ideation.

Prokop investigated the Harris-Lingoes subscale patterns for Scale 3 in a low-back pain sample. Prokop recommended that if Hy3 and Hy4 are elevated (but not Hyl, Hy2, and Hy5), in a low-back pain population, it may be appropriate to describe the individual as abnormally focusing on his or her physical symptoms. It should be noted that Hyl, Hy2, and Hy5 all overlap with the K. B. Little and Fischer's Dn scale (except that Hy5 has one item not appearing on the Dn scale according to Greene. Prokop cautioned against inferring the presence of conversion dynamics when only Hy3 and Hy4 are elevated in low-back pain patients, stating that the patient may be attempting to express his or her distress about confusing or frightening symptoms. Such patients are often diagnosed with a non conversion-based somatoform disorder. Consistent with

Prokop's contention of an abnormal focus on one's bodily functioning is Greene's description of Hy3 having 14 of its 15 items in common with the Little and Fischer' Ad scale. As noted earlier, Little and Fischer suggested that conversion reaction dynamics should be suspected if both the Dn and Ad scales are elevated.

Five of the items on this subscale are scored in the "true" direction, and 10 items are scored in the "false" direction. The following items are examples of the Hy3 content, with the scoring direction in parentheses following the item. The MMPI-2 item number precedes the item:

2. *I have a good appetite. (False)*

3. *I wake up fresh and rested most mornings. (False)*

9. *My daily life is full of things that keep me interested. (False)*

31. *I find it hard to keep my mind on a task or job. (True)*

65. *Most of the time, I feel blue. (True)*

175. *I feel weak all over much of the time. (True)*

Hy4: Somatic Complaints (17 Items)

Caldwell described this subscale as generally characterizing the "somatic conversion" (p. 19) component of Scale 3. Twelve of the 17 items are also scored on Scale 1 (Hs). The five items that are not scored on Scale 1 have elements of anxiety (e.g., fainting spells and "lump in my throat") that are in noteworthy contrast to the reporting of somatic dysfunction, without the explicit anxiety that characterizes Scale 1. Graham reported that 17% of 305 psychiatric women outpatients who scored above T = 65 on Hy4 reported current anxiolytic medication usage. Greene pointed out that 16 of the 17 items in this scale overlap with K. B. Little and Fischer's Ad scale and that the Ad scale correlates positively (r = .89-.90) with Scale 1. The only items missing from Hy4 (and Scale 3) that are Scale 1 items relate to gastrointestinal complaints. The single exception is MMPI-2 Item 18, which reports attacks of nausea and vomiting. Whereas Scale 1 and the HEA content scale represent general physical complaints, Hy4 (and Hy-O) emphasize specific, as opposed to vague, symptoms. Low scores should be interpreted as reflecting a person free of excessive somatic concerns.

The following items are examples of Hy4 content. The scoring direction follows each item in parentheses with the MMPI-2 item number preceding the item. Six of the items in this subscale are scored in the "true" direction, and 11 items are scored in the "false" direction:

11. *There seems to be a lump in my throat much of the time. (True)*

18. *I am troubled by attacks of nausea and vomiting. (True)*

40. *Much of the time my head seems to hurt all over. (True)*

47. *I am almost never bothered by pains over my heart or in my chest. (False)*

91. *I have little or no trouble with my muscles twitching or jumping. (False)*

159. *I have never had a fainting spell. (False)*

224. *I have few or no pains. (False)*

Hy5: Inhibition of Aggression (7 Items)

The seven items in this scale appear to reflect the inhibition or suppression of aggression, irritability, and anger in emotional life and fantasy. Caldwell reported that high scorers "get upset" by aggression in others and have a "hysteroid abhorrence of violence" that is likely to be quite prominent if Hy5 is elevated with a high Scale 5 score in the "feminine" direction by men or women. Nichols and Greene pointed out that although Hy5 moderately correlates with measures of denial of anger or hostility, it "appears to operate more as a disgust with anger and hostility than a denial scale per se". Low scores suggest an ability to experience anger directly; in fact, very low scores (e.g., raw score of 0 or 1) suggest an interest or fascination with anger or violence with its potential consequences, as well as a lowered threshold for experiencing morbid or violent fantasies. Very low Hy5 scores may particularly indicate hostility when accompanied by elevations on ANG2 (Irritability), TPA1 (Impatience), and TPA2. It is important to carefully note other indicators of impaired empathy when Hy5 is very low, such as the particular code pattern and other measures (e.g., ASP1 and CYN). Inspection of the item content of Hy5 shows it to be subtle in nature, with six of its seven items overlapping with the Hy-S subscale.

The following items represent the entire scale membership for Hy5. The MMPI-2 item number is provided, with the direction of scoring in parentheses. All of the items on Hy5 are keyed in the "false" direction:

7. *I like to read newspaper articles on crime. (False)*

14. *I enjoy detective or mystery stories. (False)*

29. *At times I feel like swearing. (False)*

115. *The sight of blood doesn't frighten me or make me sick. (False)*

116. *Often I can't understand why I have been so irritable and grouchy. (False)*

135. *I have often lost out on things because I couldn't make up my mind soon enough. (False)*

157. *What others think of me does not bother me. (False)*

Scale 3: Subtle-Obvious Subscales

Wiener and Harmon developed Subtle and Obvious subscales for Scale 3. The MMPI-2 Hysteria-Obvious subscale (Hy-O) has 32 items, of which 12 items are keyed in the "true" direction and 20 are, scored in the "false" direction. The Hysteria-Subtle subscale (Hy-S) has 28 items, of which 27 items are scored in the "false" direction and 1 item is keyed in the "true" direction. The following items are examples of these subscale items, with the direction of scoring and subtle-obvious distinction in parentheses. The MMPI-2 item number precedes the item.

11. *There seems to be a lump in my throat much of the time. (True-Obvious)*

31. *I find it hard to keep my mind on a task or job. (True-Obvious)*

45. *I am in just as good physical health as most of my friends. (False-Subtle)*

58. *I think a great many people exaggerate their misfortunes in order to gain the sympathy and help of others. (False-Subtle)*

76. *It takes a lot of argument to convince most people of the truth. (False-Subtle)*

230. I can be friendly with people who do things I consider wrong. (True-Obvious)

The Hy-O items appear to emphasize specific, as opposed to vague, symptoms. In fact, as Caldwell indicated, the composition of the Hy-O subscale is almost identical to HY3 and Hy4, as well as K. B. Little and Fischer's Ad scale. The numerous physical concerns reflected in this subscale include some items related to the construct of hysteria, such as fainting spells and hand tremors. The Hy-O subscale appears to reflect somatic problems and discomforts that may also antagonize normal sleep. A low score contraindicates depleted energies due to physical discomfort and distress.

Dahlstrom derived correlates for the Hy-O subscale from partner ratings on the Katz Adjustment Scales in the MMPI-2 restandardization sample. Men and women with high Hy-O scores were described as having trouble sleeping; worrying about their health; lacking energy and appearing worn out; lacking an interest in things; not appearing self-confident, cheerful, or pleasant; and complaining about body aches and ailments. Women in particular were seen as restless, self-blaming, worried about the future, and feeling like others do not care about them. Men in particular were seen as having a poor sense of humor; getting easily upset by small, unexpected events; having difficulty making decisions; lacking ambition; and not willing to try new things.

Caldwell pointed out that the Hy-S subscale is very similar in item content to the Hyl, Hy2, and Hy5 subscales, as well as virtually identical to K. B. Little and Fischer's Dn scale. Nichols and Greene viewed the Hy-S subscale as measuring a subtle and complex disposition to claim freedom from problems in adaptation, hostile feelings and impulses, cynicism and distrust, and social discomfort. An elevated Hy-S score usually is not the result of an intentional effort to mislead the psychologist. Nichols and Greene generated several hypotheses for an elevated Hy-S score (as well as an elevated K score): These elevations may be the product of honest but erroneous self-appraisal (self-deception); above-average adjustment, resourcefulness and resiliency; or a social advantage that confers protection or insulation from major stresses or challenges to adjustment such as great wealth, high socioeconomic status, or a close, active, and committed circle of friends or family.

They also pointed out that the full Hy scale is a somewhat less satisfactory measure of the repression construct than Hy - S, mostly because of the dysphoric content in Hy3.

Low Hy - S scores are likely to indicate mild cynicism. Admission to feeling somewhat beleaguered, uncomfortable with strangers, and having a view of the world as antagonistic would also characteristic low scorers.

Dahlstrom provided the following correlates for the Hy - S subscales. Both men and women are perceived as being self-confident, lacking shyness, willing to try new things, getting along well with others, not being suspicious of or avoiding others, friendly, and not lacking in emotional control. Women in particular were rated as not getting very sad or bored, not lacking in energy or having many fears, being able to laugh with others, not worrying about the future, and not getting their feelings easily hurt. Men were described as not arguing about minor things, being constructive or helpful, affectionate, generous, not bossy, cooperative, and not demanding attention.

Scale 4: Psychopathic Deviate (Pd)

Scale 4 was developed to measure the "personality characteristics of the amoral and asocial subgroup of persons with psychopathic personality disorders". The scale is named Psychopathic Deviate because McKinley and Hathaway did not expect it to differentiate all the cases of psychopathic personalities; rather, the scale was successful in identifying half or somewhat more of the cases repeatedly classed as clinical psychopathic personalities. The scale name implies "a variation in the direction of psychopathy", in keeping with the psychopathic personality classification of the American Psychiatric Association in use at that time, which was broad and included pathological emotionality and sexuality as well as asocial or amoral trends.

The criterion group consisted of more women than men ranging in age from 17 to 22, but the sample size was not reported. The criterion participants were referred by the courts for study in a psychiatric setting. McKinely and Hathaway provided the following description of these participants:

> *The symptomatic backgrounds of the criterion cases were highly varied but can be characterized in several ways. Most often the complaint was stealing, lying, truancy, sexual promiscuity, alcoholic over-indulgence, forgery, and similar delinquencies. There were no major criminal types. Most of the behavior was poorly motivated and poorly concealed. All the criterion cases had long histories of minor delinquency. Although many of them came from broken homes or otherwise disturbed social backgrounds, there were many in whom such factors could not be seen as particularly present.*

The common denominator across the participants seemed to be that they had low anticipation of the consequences of their behavior and could not seem to "learn those anticipatory anxieties which operate to deter most people from committing antisocial behavior". Essentially, individuals with psychopathic traits were seen as lacking in their ability to form warm and stable bonds to others, to appreciate social customs and abide by societal rules, and to profit from experiences that had negative consequences. They were, in essence, psychologically immature. These individuals may appear free from disabling anxiety and not be perceived as particularly troubled or disturbed until found in a situation demanding the use of inner resources that the psychopathic individual lacks. The general social maladjustment that characterizes these individuals leads to dissatisfaction with the self and others and often results in strong feelings of social and self-alienation.

The normal comparison participants (294 men and 397 women) used to construct the 50-item Pd scale consisted of college freshmen receiving guidance counseling at the University of Minnesota and married Minnesota residents who were considerably older. The average age of these latter participants was 35, so the college sample introduced some balance. Cross-validation procedures involved 100 prisoners and 78 psychiatric inpatients diagnosed with "psychopathic personality." The scale was expected to identify only the asocial individuals. McKinley and Hathaway reported that among the prisoners, 59% obtained T scores at or above 70 on the Pd scale, whereas 45% of the psychiatric cases obtained scores above that level.

Five preliminary scales were developed before the final items were selected for inclusion on the Pd scale. The MMPI-2 Pd scale did not lose any items in the recent revision, although four items were changed (two items were modernized in language, one item was grammatically clarified, and the wording of one item was simplified).

The item content of Scale 4 is diverse. McKinley and Hathaway initially identified the following three general groupings of item content: (a) social maladjustment items, (b) depression items, and (c) paranoid-trend items. The mixed factor content of the scale is reflected in factor analytic studies of the scale. For example, Dahlstrom described the results of Comrey 's and Astin 's factor analytic investigations. They reported that hypersensitivity, poor impulse control, social maladjustment, and emotional deprivation were four of the many factors emerging from their work. Nichols and Greene captured these factors in their poignant description of how the high Pd scorer tends to manifest his or her psychopathology in the environment:

In Pd, an impoverished emotional life and feelings of emptiness lead the individual to make his/her mark on the social environment and to force others to acknowledge an autonomy that the individual experiences internally as incomplete and poorly consolidated. The usual result is a series of scrapes, broken promises, underachievement, lost employment, ephemeral relationships, and legal difficulties.

Harris and Lingoes also identified different sub groupings of items on Scale 4, which we describe shortly.

The critical scoring direction is about evenly split between true and false responses (24 true, 26 false) for this 50-item scale. A K-correction factor of 0.4 added to the Pd scale improved its ability to make diagnostic discriminations, and this value is generally added to the raw score on the Pd scale. Ten out of 50 items are non-overlapping or unique to Scale 4, with the remaining 40 overlapping items being distributed over the clinical scales and the F and K scales. Scale 4 shares five and seven items with the F and K scales, respectively, and only one overlapping item with Scale 1 (Hs). It shares 1 or 2 items with Scale 5 (Mf), depending on whether male or female norms are being used. Scales 3 (Hy) and 8 (Sc) both share 10 items with Scale 4, and Scale 2 shares 7 items with Scale 4. The fact that there are 7 Scale 4 items overlapping with Scale 2 (D) may be consistent with the situational or state condition of the criterion participants at the time of testing. Greene noted that because all the members of the criterion group were involved in legal proceedings and/or incarcerated, it is likely that they may have manifested depressive moods more reflective of their situation rather than an inherent tendency to feel depressed.

McKinley and Hathaway originally reported a test-retest correlation coefficient of .71 for Scale 4 obtained on a normal sample of 47 cases, with a time interval of a few days to more than a year. Butcher reported test-retest reliability data for their community (normal) sample of 82 men ($r = .81$) and 111 women ($r = .79$) retested at an average interval of 8.6 days (Mdn = 7 days).

In psychiatric cases on the MMPI Scale 4, test-retest correlation coefficients for 1-to 2-day intervals ranged between .69 and .75 and between .48 and .49 for 1-year intervals between tests. Hunsley large-scale meta-analysis of MMPI reliability studies using diverse populations conducted between 1970 and 1981, reported an average test-retest reliability of .71 for 16 studies, with time intervals from 1 day to 2 years.

Internal consistency estimates for Scale 4 were derived from the MMPI-2 restandardization sample and yielded coefficients of .60 and .62 for men and women, respectively. Hunsley reported higher internal consistency values for Scale 4, but used a wider variety of populations (abnormal and normal) in their meta-analysis. They reported an average internal consistency value of .81 across 71 studies for Scale 4.

The following items from Scale 4 illustrate the broad content of the scale. The MMPI-2 item numbers precede the item, with the direction of scoring in parentheses. It provides the item composition of Scale 4 with the direction of scoring):

9. My daily life is full of things that keep me interested. (False) 21. At times I have very much wanted to leave home. (True) 22. No one seems to understand me. (True) 32. I have had very peculiar and strange experiences. (True)

35. Sometimes when I was young, I stole things. (True) 95. I am happy most of the time. (False) 264. I have used alcohol excessively. (True) 266. I have never been in trouble with the law. (False)

Individuals with high Scale 4 scores, especially when it is the highest or second highest scale elevation in the profile, typically have shallow emotional lives that may go undetected by others until the "situation demands evidence of a sense of responsibility, appreciation of social patterns, or personal and emotional loyalties". These individuals can be described as having feeling deficits as they have developed the coping mechanism of numbing out their vulnerable feelings. Prolonged exposure to abusive or neglectful caregivers in early life often sets the stage for the development of a constellation of personality traits that include poor frustration tolerance, impulsiveness, antisocial attitudes, and a reduced capacity for empathy toward others. Traumatogenic experiences, such as dysfunctional childrearing, could often lead to the development of a cognitive style that allows these individuals to recognize and intellectually understand their experiences but feel emotionally cut off from their own vital resources, thereby limiting or handicapping their ability to have genuine reciprocal exchanges with others. In fact, Rathvon and Holmstrom recently found that Scale 4 showed a significant positive correlation with a narcissistic depletion factor. Even in so-called normal populations, such as police applicants, or among sensation seekers, such as sky divers, where the Pd score is the highest score but still within the normal limit range, some of the Pd characteristics or trends are still observed. For example, instead of being overtly antisocial, an individual may be somewhat cynical or immature in relation to authority figures.

In the normative sample for the restandardized MMPI-2, partner ratings revelaed that Scale 4 appears sensitive to distress and recent life changes. Participants from this sample who scored high on the Pd scale were perceived by their partners to be dysphoric, antisocial, hostile, impulsive, and nonconforming. Hathaway and Meehl, reported a large number of adjectives characteristic of normals with high Pd scores that were generated by friends of the normal participants. Overall, these high Scale 4 scorers tended to be quite socially visible. Typical descriptors applied to these normals obtaining normal range Pd scores included extraverted, adventurous, enthusiastic, sarcastic, exhibitionistic, talkative, high-strung, assertive, active, energetic, immature, and irritable.

Several normal groups score in the high-normal and low-moderate range on Scale 4, including social activists, mental health professionals, and adolescents. Although a high Scale 4 score is often associated with a personality disorder diagnosis, such as narcissistic, passive-aggressive, borderline, or antisocial, the presence of a high Scale 4 elevation does not always indicate that an individual will manifest antisocial behaviors, especially if there is not a history of such actions. If Scale 9 is elevated, along with Scale 4, as a primary high point, then the probability is increased for overt expression of antisocial behavior. The reader is cautioned to be aware that negative emotionality as reflected in feelings of alienation is often more prominent in high Scale 4 scorers than is antisocial behavior, especially if the individual is not being assessed in the context of the correctional system. Butcher and Williams underscored this point by stating that the ASP content scale is only modestly correlated (.37) with the Pd scale. Scale 4 is a mixed content scale that includes, but is not limited to, measuring antisocial behavior; the ASP scale is a more direct measure of that construct.

Duckworth and Anderson viewed "fighting something" as a cardinal feature of an elevated Scale 4. They suggested that the individual may be in conflict with his or her parents, friends, spouse, society, or school and that it is essential to examine the context in which the person is being assessed in order to better understand the significance of the Scale 4 elevation. Lower elevations on the scale suggest that the "fighting out" may not be expressed directly but may reflect instead a covert attitude or feeling that something or someone other than the client needs to be changed. Duckworth and Anderson also emphasized the importance of recognizing that moderate Pd elevations may reflect situational stress, such as marital difficulties rather than a personality trait disturbance.

Alcohol, drug, and polydrug abuse and addiction are often associated with high Scale 4 scores and can be conceptualized as a remedial stimulant for the feeling deficits that these individuals experience. Greene and Garvin for a comprehensive review of the

MMPI in relation to drug and alcohol abuse. Although additional diagnoses, such as depression, are often given to drug and alcohol dependent individuals, it should be pointed out that if indicators in the MMPI-2 (e.g., DEP content scale and Scale 2) do not support such a diagnosis, a high Scale 4 scorer may not be experiencing a typical depressive feeling state, such as a sense of sadness and loss, but rather may be experiencing feelings of emptiness and alienation.

It appears that scores on Scale 4 decrease with age in men and women in all populations. Greene suggested that this pattern most likely reflects the slow maturational changes that occur in persons with elevated scores. Archer noted that there is also clear evidence that Scale 4 scores also differ as a function of adolescence versus adulthood in both normal and clinical populations. He pointed out that adolescents tend to endorse more Scale 4 items than do adults and that the normal adolescents in the MMPI-A sample would produce a mean T-score value of approximately 55 if scored using MMPI-2 norms. It is, therefore, not surprising that adolescent code types typically include prominent Scale 4 elevations.

Harris-Lingoes Subscales

As previously noted, the Harris-Lingoes subscales can help identify the particular pattern of item content that characterizes a high score on the MMPI-2 parent scale. Scale 4 is particularly well served by a subscale pattern analysis as the scale is rich and varied in its content. Several Pd subscales assess very different aspects of psychopathy; consideration of these differences may have significant implications for clinical practice and assessment. Harris and Lingoes developed five subscales for Scale 4: Familial Discord (Pd1), Authority Problems (Pd2), Social Imperturbability (Pd3), Social Alienation (Pd4), and Self-Alienation (Pd5). Unlike the majority of Harris-Lingoes subscales that were unaffected by the MMPI-2 revision, several item changes and deletions on the Pd subscales called into question the consistency between the MMPI and the MMPI-2 for these subscales. In the original construction of their subscales, Harris and Lingoes, for unexplained reasons, added from two to six items to each of the Pd subscales taken from an unpublished earlier version of Scale 4. For reasons that are also unclear, the MMPI-2 revision deleted these items from the Pd subscales. The only rationale provided was that these items were not included in the final version of Scale 4 and questions about the possible advantages of retaining these "off-scale" items on the basis of their content or their contribution to enhanced subscale reliability were not addressed. The MMPI-2 manual provides normative data for the reduced Pd subscales.

In examining the consistency between the original MMPI and the MMPI-2, Chojnacki and Walsh concluded that the shortened Pd subscales do not materially affect the T scores for these subscales. On the revision of the MMPI-2, Pd1, Pd2, Pd3, Pd4, and Pd5 lost two, three, six, five, and three items, respectively.

Familial Discord. Pdl (9 Items)

The items in this subscale reflect current and historical problems with one's family and the accompanying feeling that one wishes to escape a loveless home. Levitt reported that high scorers reject a family situation that they consider affectionless, stressful, and lacking in emotional support. Wrobel 's study of clinician descriptions for Pd1 elevations showed feelings of struggle against family control to be significant. Graham reported that high scoring psychiatric outpatient women on Pd1 tended to blame their families for their difficulties, demanded much attention, and appeared argumentative. Given the item content for this subscale, it is not surprising that Pancoast and Archer found that adolescents, in contrast to adults, are particularly likely to endorse items on this subscale. Nichols and Greene report that Pd1 is biased toward conflict and alienation in the family of origin and viewed it as a general measure of family alienation. In fact, when F, Sc1 (Social Alienation), and Pd1 are all elevated, there is a good likelihood of the respondent making explicit statements concerning hatred toward one or both parents. Caldwell reported that low scores reflect a supportive family with genuine compatibility and strong ties or possibly a need to minimize and deny family problems.

The following items are examples of Pd1 content, with the scoring direction in parentheses and the MMPI-2 item number preceding the item. Five items in this subscale are scored in the "true" direction, and four items are scored in the "false" direction:

21. At times I have very much wanted to leave home. (True) 83. I have very few quarrels with members of my family. (False) 125. I believe that my home life is as pleasant as that of most people I know. (False) 202. My parents often objected to the kind of people I went around with. (True) 214. I have been quite independent and free from family rule. (False) 288. My parents and family find more fault with me than they should. (True)

Authority Problems: Pd2 (8 Items)

The content of Pd2 reflects an opposition to authority figures, dislike of school, and a lack of constraint. The items have a strong historical bias, with an emphasis on past delinquent behavior, legal involvement, and trouble with authority. This may account for why they seem not to be suppressed by elevated K scores. Lilienfeld found Pd2 to be more highly correlated than other Pd subscales with most indexes of antisocial behavior, a finding that is not surprising, given that several items refer explicitly to illegal actions. He also reported that Pd2 may be the better marker of primary psychopathy as compared with the other Pd subscales, a finding generally consistent with those of Meloy and Gacono and Graham. High scores reflect a lack of behavioral control or impulsivity, either in the form of "clear violations of social norms and rules or attitudes that clearly suggest a lower threshold for behavior that violates rules and brings one into conflict with others, especially those in authority". Wrobel found the descriptor "resents demands and convention of parent and/or society" to apply to his sample of outpatients scoring high on Pd2. Levitt described high Pd scorers as rebellious and having difficulty accepting standards of behavior that impose responsibilities and interfere with personal gratification. The clinician should take careful note of elevated Pd2 scores, especially if elevated with other indicators of social disinhibition, such as the ASP content scale or its component subscale, Antisocial Behavior (ASP2). Pd2 and ASP2 imply the direct expression of antisocial conduct, but the prediction of antisocial behavior is higher when ASP2 is greater than Pd2, Pd2 is greater than ASP, and ASP is greater than CYN. It should be noted that Pd2 and the MMPI-2 ASP content scale share three items.

Graham found that psychiatric men and women outpatients who scored high on the Pd2 subscale reported recent alcohol and substance abuse and dependence problems. This finding is consistent with the above description of impulsive individuals with low frustration tolerance.

Low Pd2 scorers do not admit having difficulties with authority and tend to be socially conforming. They have a capacity for constraint that high scorers lack, and this may reflect a "mature submission to the rules and regulations that make for a sense of community with orderly and harmonious social relations among citizens".

The following items are examples of the Pd2 content, with the scoring direction in parentheses and the MMPI-2 item number preceding the item. Two items on this subscale are scored in the "true" direction, and six items are scored in the "false" direction:

34. I have been in trouble because of my sex behavior. (False) 105. In school, I was sometimes sent to the principal for bad behavior. (True) 129. My conduct is largely controlled by the behavior of those around me. (False) 160. I liked school. (False) 266. I have never been in trouble with the law. (False)

Social Imperturbability: Pd3 (6 Items)

Originally a 12-item subscale, the removal of 6 items from the MMPI-2 version of the subscale left it with 6 items, ali of which overlap the Pd-S subscale. This subscale appears to reflect a strong extraversion tendency but without the need for affection and approval from others. Nichols and Greene stated that "Pd 3 reflects a highly aggressive and insouciant sociability consistent with a desire to use interpersonal relationships to manipulate, intimidate, exploit, and otherwise extract goods and services from others. There is little emphasis on social approval". There is a socially aggressive or impervious nature to high Pd3 scorers that is especially pronounced if signs of cynicism, hostility, and antisocial trends are present in the MMPI-2 profile. High Pd3 scorers (raw scores of 5 or greater on the MMPI-2) tend to be pushy and insensitive in their social interactions or even aggressive or overbearing. The Denial of Social Anxiety subscale (Hy1) and Pd3 now share 67% of their item content, making their interpretation similar. The elimination of the earlier mentioned six items in the MMPI-2 version of the Pd3 (because the items were not part of the final Pd scale) accounts for this increased proportion of item overlap. In effect, these two subscales reflect a social insensitivity that may constitute part of a narcissistic syndrome.

Low Pd3 scorers are likely to feel uncomfortable in social situations and experience difficulty taking social initiative. When Pd3, Hy1, and Hy-S are all low, and there are high scores on the SOD content scale, Si, and Si2 (Social Avoidance), there may be long-term or congenital (temperamental) trends toward shyness and social withdrawal. If, however, Pd3, Hy1, and Hy-S are within normal limits, but SOD, Si, and Si1 are significantly elevated, the individual may be experiencing a temporary social withdrawal in reaction to a loss or other distress.

The following items represent the Pd3 subscale in its entirety. The MMPI-2 item number precedes the item, with the scoring direction in parentheses. All of the items are scored in the "false" direction:

> *70. I am easily downed in an argument. (False) 129. My conduct is largely controlled by the behavior of those around me. (False) 158. It makes me uncomfortable to put on a stunt at a party even if others are doing the same sort of thing. (False) 167. I find it hard to make talk when I meet new people. (False) 185. I wish I were not so shy. (False) 243. When in a group of people, I have trouble thinking of the right things to talk about. (False).*

Social Alienation: Pd4 (13 Items)

This subscale has six items that overlap with Scale 6 (Pa) and reflects a general feeling of "paranoid flavored resentments". Nichols and Greene classified Pd4 under their paranoid thought process category in their structural summary as it reflects severe alienation from others and a sense of felt deprivation and of being given a "bum deal." There is an element of residual sadness and longing in Pd4 that indicates a vulnerable, lonely, and unhappy self. High Pd4 scorers have a pervasive mistrust of others, who are viewed as more depriving than hostile. Consequently, they feel that others are uncaring and cannot be counted on. This sense of emotional deprivation is supported by Wrobel 's findings that anchored clinician ratings to patient characteristics associated with elevated Pd4 scores. Those characteristics consisted of feeling socially isolated, a lack of gratification in social relationships, a lack of feeling of belongingness, and externalizing blame. The finding of sadness from the Graham study for psychiatric men outpatients is consistent with the lonely and unhappy individual just described. Levitt suggested examining Pd1 when Pd4 is elevated to ascertain if family members and intimates are the source of failed support. To this end, the clinician would want to also examine other measures, such as the FAM content scale. If only Pd4 and Pd5 (Self-Alienation) are elevated relative to the other Pd subscales, particularly Pd2, the individual may prove to be more likely to benefit from psychotherapy. However, research is needed to substantiate this conjecture.

Low Pd4 scorers feel understood, fairly treated, and enjoy a sense of belongingness in their social environments.

The following items are examples of Pd4 content, with the direction of scoring in parentheses and the MMPI-2 item number preceding the item. Ten of the items on this subscale are scored in the "true" direction, and 3 items are scored in the "false" direction:

> *12. My sex life is satisfactory. (False) 22. No one seems to understand me. (True) 42. If people had not had it in for me, I would have been much more successful. (True) 56. I wish I could be as happy as others seem to be. (True) 157. What others think of me does not bother me. (False) 225. My way of doing things is apt to be misunderstood by others. (True)*

Self-Alienation: Pd5 (12 Items)

Wrobel described feelings of despondency as a correlate of the high Pd5 scorer, and Caldwell and Graham described a similar feeling state underscoring the guilt and self-blame, regretful feelings, and feelings of hopelessness and unhappiness so typical of these individuals. The subscale appears sensitive to the anhedonia elements inherent in Scale 4 that McKinley and Hathaway viewed as an important component of the parent scale.

Nichols and Greene believed that guilt, which can negatively effect one's capacity to enjoy life in a spontaneous and fluent fashion, is best assessed using Pd5. They pointed out that the level or intensity of guilt as measured by Pd5 can be estimated from scores on D5 (Brooding) and the LSE content scale. Nichols and Greene elaborated by stating that it is important to discriminate guilt as a specific emotional state from states of more general upset in which guilt is only a component of distress and dysphoria. Many individuals experience guilt, regret, and remorse in the context of other, mostly unpleasant, emotions such as anxiety, fearfulness, apathy, depression, worry, and so forth. Such experiences often so obscure or obstruct the assessment of guilt per se that this emotional state and its role in the individual's psychic life are left uncertain. Guilt is most readily identified when Pd5 and D5 are elevated above OBS, as well as above the level of other distress scales such as A, ANX, FRS, DEP, WRK, and TRT.

The level or severity of the expressed guilt in high Pd5 scorers approximates a theme of self-flagellation (with elevated LSE) with "exaggerated culpability and ostentatious remorse". Caldwell and Nichols and Greene agreed that Pd5 may also reflect the characteristic remorse seen in some alcoholic patterns (e.g., MMPI-2 code-patterns 247/274, 427/472, and 724/742).

Low Pd5 scorers do not report feeling unhappy, can in fact experience pleasures in life, find daily life stimulating and rewarding, do not express guilt or remorse about past misdeeds, and deny excessive use of alcohol.

The following items are examples of Pd5 content, with the scoring direction in parentheses and the MMPI-2 item number preceding the item. Ten of the items on this subscale are scored in the "true" direction, and 2 items are scored in the "false" direction:

9. My daily life is full of things that keep me interested. (False) 31. I find it hard to keep my mind on a task or job. (True) 52. I have not lived the right kind of life. (True)

56. I wish I could be as happy as others seem to be. (True) 82. I do many things which I regret afterwards. (I regret things more than others seem to) (True) 89. My hardest battles are with myself. (True)

Scale 4: Subtle-Obvious Subscales

Wienerand Harmon developed Subtle and Obvious subscales for Scale 4 of the MMPI. The MMPI-2 Psychopathic Deviate-Obvious subscale (Pd-O) has 28 items, of which 20 are scored in the "true" direction and 8 items are keyed in the "false" direction. The Psychopathic Deviate-Subtle subscale (Pd-S) consists of 22 items, of which 4 are keyed in the "true" direction and the remaining 18 items keyed in the "false" direction. The following items are examples of subtle-obvious items on Scale 4, with the scoring direction and obvious or subtle distinction in parentheses.

9. My daily life is full of things that keep me interested. (False-Obvious) 17. I am sure I get a raw deal from life. (True-Obvious) 35. Sometimes when I was young, I stole things. (True-Obvious) 95. I am happy most of the time. (False-Obvicus) 113. I know who is responsible for most of my troubles. (True-Subtle) 129. My conduct is largely controlled by the behavior of those around me. (False-Subtle) 157. What others think of me does not bother me. (False-Subtle) 219. I have been disappointed in love. (True-Subtle)

The Pd-O items reflect various subjective discomforts that include feeling misunderstood, feeling unhappy, and feeling unfairly treated, and having gotten into trouble. Examining the convergent validity literature, Hollrah concluded that methodological problems with the MMPI subtle-obvious studies make it difficult to summarize the validity of the Subtle and Obvious subscales as the results of their research reveals different findings for different scales. They reported, however, that in isolated studies, the Pd-O subscale does correlate with discomfort and the admission of social nonconformity. The content of the Pd-O subscale suggests feeling unhappy and at odds with others and with life. Low scores suggest a closeness and warmth with others and social conformity.

Dahlstrom examined the correlates of the Subtle and Obvious subscales derived from partner ratings on the Katz Adjustment Scales used in the MMPI-2 restandardization. For both men and women, the following descriptions emerged as significant for high Pd-O scorers: lacks interest in things, feels others do not care about him or her, gets very sad or blue, has many fears, moody, worries about the future, takes nonprescription drugs, has been arrested or had legal difficulties, lacks social judgment, and whines and demands attention.

For women only, the following represents a partial list of significant findings: poor sense of humor, restless, not affectionate, lacks energy, feelings easily hurt, easily annoyed, lacks self-confidence, lacks emotional control, argues about minor things, suspicious of others, has difficulty making decisions, and does not get along well with others. There were no significant descriptors derived for men only.

Caldwell pointed out that some subtle items on the Pd-S subscale appear nearly as obvious as the Pd-O items. These items report family quarrels, getting little sympathy, and wanting to leave home. The more subtle items are those that report an absence of social anxieties, ease in talking to others, and a denial of manipulation.

Dahlstrom derived the following correlates for the Pd-S subscale for men and women from the partner ratings made in the MMPI-2 restandardization sample: moody, stubborn, easily annoyed, swears or curses, not passive and obedient, talks too much, makes big plans, and has conflicts over sex. For men only, the following correlates were derived: trouble sleeping, not shy, lacks energy, gets very sad, and has been arrested or had legal troubles. For women only, the following correlates were derived: temper tantrums, resents being told what to do, argues about minor things, nags, feels others do not care about her, gets bossy, is uncooperative, lacks emotional control, and drinks excessively.

Low Pd-s scores suggest self-confidence, a sense of inner calmness, and a restraint or shyness with strangers.

In reviewing the literature on the Subtle subscales, Hollrah were unable to find studies that supported the discriminative validity of the Pd-S subscale. Therefore, appropriate caution is warranted.

Scale 5: Masculinity-femininity

The exact motivation of Hathaway and McKinley for developing Scale 5 could be somewhat unclear to readers consulting different texts, given that various accounts are given to explain this scale's origins. For example, Dahlstrom, generally considered the most reliable historical chroniclers of the MMPI, stated that

Scale 5 was designed to identify the personality features related to the disorder of male sexual inversion. Persons with this personality pattern often engage in homoerotic practices as part of their feminine emotional makeup; however, many of these men are too inhibited or full of conflict to make any overt expression of their sexual preferences.

As Colligan indicated, the 1943 MMPI manual describes the Mf scale as intending to measure "the tendency toward masculinity or femininity of interest pattern in the direction of the opposite sex". Clearly, the original manual's description differs from the more psychopathological account given by Dahlstrom in describing the origins and intent of Scale 5. Hathaway and McKinley discovered that it was too difficult then to obtain a large enough group of homosexual men and women possessing enough similar qualities to classify into a single criterion group. At least three subgroups of homosexuals were identified with different etiologies for their homosexuality. One subgroup was a pseudo homosexual type with neurotic features related to inferiority; another subgroup was a psychopathic type who tended to elevate Scale 4 (Pd,) and a third subgroup became the final reference criterion group. This group consisted of 13 homosexual inverted men. Although no demographic data were reported for these participants, they were screened for gross psychological abnormalities, like psychosis, and any clear-cut neurotic tendencies. They were also considered free of psychopathy. These individuals were seen as having a feminine emotional makeup; however, many were considered too inhibited or conflicted to express their homoerotic sexual preferences. Their feminine disposition was believed to be apparent in their expressive styles, interests, and attitudes, as well as in their sexual relationships. Greene stated that "such persons were thought to engage in homoerotic behavior as a part of their feminine (i.e. inverted) personality characteristics".

Many items used to develop Scale 5 were added after the original Minnesota normative group had already participated in the various scale constructions; consequently, newly formed normal groups were selected for comparison purposes. These groups consisted of 67 female airline employees and 54 soldiers. Three basic comparisons resulted in the addition of 55 new items in the MMPI pool. When an item differentiated a soldier from a criterion group participant (homosexual inverted men), the item was said to be a trend in the direction of femininity on the part of homosexual inverted men. A second comparison step in item selection involved identifying a group of men scoring in the "feminine" direction on an Invert scale derived by Terman and Miles. The item endorsements of these inverted men were then compared with a group of normals. The use of the invert scale from Terman and Miles' Attitude Interest Analysis Test "represents the first time that items from one diagnostic test were used to select a contrast group that was employed as an additional criterion group used for selecting items on an MMPI scale". A third comparison step, which appears to have been conducted initially but is considered the least important by Hathaway involved comparing the normal men (soldiers) with normal women (airline employees) to determine their response frequencies by gender.

The 60 items that persevered through all three comparison steps became Scale 5. Twenty-three of the Scale 5 items are borrowed from Terman and Miles, whereas the other 37 items came from the MMPI item pool.

Despite some preliminary efforts, Hathaway and McKinley were unable to successfully construct an independent scale measuring female homosexual inversion. A number of subsequent studies have demonstrated that despite the efforts of the scale constructors, Scale 5 does not adequately discriminate male homosexuals from male non homosexuals, which was the original intent of the scale. Therefore, it is important not to infer homosexuality based solely on an elevated Scale 5 score. In fact, it is difficult to predict homosexuality from MMPI or MMPI-2 data. The final Mf scale was believed to measure masculinity at one pole and femininity at the opposite pole; therefore, this scale was seen as being bipolar. However, as other researchers suggested, masculinity and femininity may be more accurately assessed using separate scales for each dimension. They may each represent a different construct. On the other hand, Bem 's measures of gender role are not independent of masculinity versus femininity scales, such as Scale 5 of the MMPI. Also, the psychometric adequacy of Bem's Femininity scale has been criticized. Recent studies suggest that bipolar masculinity-femininity scales have not yet been, and may not be, replaceable with separate masculine and feminine factors. However, the MMPI-2 Manual describes two recently developed gender-role scales developed by

Peterson and Dahlstrom. These scales, named GM (Gender Role -- Masculine) and GF (Gender Role -- Feminine), were designed as independent measures of the masculine and feminine factors in Scale 5. Developed on data provided by the normative sample for the MMPI-2, these new scales can be useful adjuncts to aid in the interpretation of Scale 5.

Factor analytic studies of Scale 5 indicate that the scale is composed of multiple factors. Given its multidimensional character, inferences about masculinity and femininity drawn from Scale 5 elevations should be made cautiously. The item content of the scale is varied and, to a degree, does seem to reflect, among other things, stereotypic masculine and feminine interest patterns. Items reflecting masculine-feminine interests appear to have the highest correlation with overall scale scores and are therefore considered the most differentiating items on the scale. Although the interest-type items are obvious or face valid in nature, there are other items on the scale with more subtle meaning. For example, MMPI-2 Item 193, "In walking, I am very careful to step over sidewalk cracks," is keyed in the "false" direction for both men and women. A "true" response would earn both men and women a point in the "masculine" direction. Apparently, this item empirically differentiated the criterion groups and no obvious theoretical explanation (except perhaps post hoc) can be offered.

Because Scales 5 and 0 were added after the publication of the MMPI, it took time for their assimilation into the mainstream of research and clinical practice. It was soon recognized that Scale 5 (and Scale 0) was an important measure, and research attention was eventually paid to the scale, although Harris and Lingoes and Wiener and Harmon did not develop subscales for Scale 5 (or Scale 0). As mentioned previously, the content of Scale 5 is diverse and has been studied fairly extensively. The item content covers "a range of emotional reactions, interest, attitudes, and feelings about work, social relationships, and hobbies on which men and women in general differ". Graham factor analyzed the responses to MMPI Scale 5 (and Scale 0) from 422 psychiatric inpatients, outpatients, and normals. Their six factors were then used by Serkownek to develop subscales in order to provide additional content information for the interpretation of Scale 5: Narcissism-Hypersensitivity (Mfl), Stereotypic Feminine Interest (Mf2), Denial of Stereotypic Masculine

Interests (Mf3), Heterosexual Discomfort-Passivity (Mf4), Introspective-Critical (Mf5), and Socially Retiring (Mf6). Graham reported test-retest reliability coefficients for men and women (over a 6-week interval) provided by Moreland. For men on the Mf subscales, test-retest reliability coefficients range from .67 to .83, with an average of .78. For women, test-retest reliability coefficients range from .69 to .83, with an average of .76.

In a large-scale study, Foerstner investigated the interrelationships among the 63 MMPI subscales developed by Serkownek, Harris and Lingoes, Wiggins, and Wiener and Harmon. The stability of her factor structure was also studied across different populations. Nine hundred MMPIs for male and female psychiatric inpatients, chemical-dependent residents, and private practice outpatients were analyzed. Ten factors were identified that accounted for 75.5% of the total variance. The 10 factors were named (a) Depression, (b) Agitated Hostility, (c) Social Introversion, (d) Cynical Distress, (e) Health Concerns, (f) Ideas of Reference, (g) Traditional Feminine Interests, (h) Family Conflict, (i) Inner Directedness, and (j) Qvetch Vague Dysphoria or Hypersensitivity. Most of the factor structures were similar for the samples, although a difference existed between the factor structure of psychiatric inpatient samples and private practice outpatients. Of interest in this discussion of Scale 5 are Foerstner 's findings for the Serkownek subscales. Mf1 loaded positively on the depression factor (.57), with Mf4 loading negatively on the Social Introversion factor (-.50). Mf2 loaded on the expected Traditional Feminine Interest factor.

It is clear from the data reported in Foerstner's study that Scale 5 (and Scale 0) is multifactorial in nature; therefore, its composition is not limited to masculine-feminine factors. Scale 5 scores, whether high or low, may be achieved by item endorsements affecting any of a combination of at least six factors. Schuerger, Foerstner, Serkownek and Ritz pointed out that the subscale correlates for Scale 5 are generally personological and non pathological in nature. That is, the only subscale for Scale 5 that suggests psychopathology is Mf1. This is in contrast to the findings for the Scale 0 subscales, described under the Scale 0 heading in this chapter. Most of the Serkownek subscales for Scale 0 are psychopathological in nature.

A new set of seven Mf subscales has been developed for the MMPI-2 by Martin and Finn using factor analytic procedures. The normative sample used in constructing these subscales was the MMPI-2 community participants. These subscales are free of item overlap and have internal consistency coefficients high enough to suggest that these subscales are cohesive measures. The first subscale, Denial of Stereotypical Masculine Interests, is a measure of lack of interest in activities typically considered male or masculine. The second subscale, Hypersensitivity-Anxiety, is a measure of self-focused worry and sensitivity. Stereotypical Feminine Interests is the third subscale and is a measure of activities typically considered female of feminine. Low Cynicism, the fourth subscale, is a measure of the lack of cynicism and suspiciousness about human motivations. Aesthetic Interest is the fifth subscale and is a measure of interest in the arts and written expression. The sixth subscale, Feminine Gender Identity, measures the wish to be female and to have interests traditionally associated with women. Restraint is the seventh subscale and is a measure of restraint from loud and aggressive interests and behaviors. Martin and Finn also provided a composite bipolar femininity-masculinity scale that is a combination of the three subscales that they believe to be the most central to the construct of masculinity-femininity. These subscales are: Denial of Stereotypical Masculine Interests, Stereotypical Feminine Interests, and Feminine Gender Identity.

In the MMPI-2, Scale 5 lost four items in the revision, leaving it with 56 items. The four dropped items (MMPI Items 69, 70, 249, and 295) were either outdated or often considered offensive on a religious or sexual bases. Fifty-two of the items on this scale are scored in the same direction for men and women. An endorsement of any of these items in the keyed direction gives the respondent a point in the direction of femininity. Four of the items in the scale deal with clear sexual concerns and represent a scoring exception in that they are keyed in the opposite direction for women and men. For example, Item 121, "I have never indulged in any unusual sexual practice," is keyed "true" for women and "false" for men. The other three items dealing with sexual concerns are keyed "true" for men and "false" for women (MMPI-2 Items 166, 209, and 268.) Because of the obvious nature of these four Mf items dealing with sexual concerns, someone wishing to conceal his or her sexual interests could easily do so. If using hand-scoring templates, it is important to use the appropriate male or female template for scoring the record sheet. For men, 25 of the items on the Mf scale are keyed in the "true" direction, whereas 31 items are keyed in the "false" direction. For women, 23 of the items are keyed in the "true" direction, whereas 33 items are scored in the "false" direction.

Scale 5 uses linear T scores rather than uniform T -score conversions. This is also the case for Scale 0 and the L, F, and K scales as well. For women, high T scores on the profile sheet are associated with low raw scores, indicating a response to the items in a "masculine" direction. For men, the converse is true, with high raw scores associated with high T scores. Therefore, a man with a high raw score or high T score is said to be endorsing Scale 5 items the way in which women stereotypically respond. Low T scores in men reflect a low endorsement of feminine-type items and indicates a more masculine interest pattern. The reason for reversing the raw scores on the profile sheet is to maintain uniformity with the other scales, in that high scores represent a form of deviation. In the case of Scale 5, elevated T scores represent endorsement patterns similar to the opposite gender.

The following items are examples of Scale 5, with the scoring direction in parentheses and the item numbers preceding the item. It presents the item composition for Scale 5, with the direction of scoring for the items.

> *1. I like mechanics magazines. (False) 4. I think I would like the work of a librarian. (True) 19. When I take a new job, I like to find out who it is important to be nice to. (False) 26. I feel that it is certainly best to keep my mouth shut when I' m in trouble. (False) 64. I enjoy reading love stories. (True) 137. I used to keep a diary. (True) 271. I think that I feel more intensely than most people do. (True)*

For Scale 5 on the MMPI, test-retest correlation coefficients for psychiatric cases range between .79 and .83 for a 1-to 2-day interval and between .77 and .99 for college students. The correlation coefficients for 1-to 2-week intervals between test administrations in psychiatric cases range between .76 and .79; the corresponding correlation coefficient for male college students is .72.

In Hunsley's large-scale meta-analysis of MMPI reliability studies using a wide variety of populations conducted between 1970 and 1981, an average internal consistency of .73 across 39 studies of Scale 5 was reported. They also reported an average test-retest reliability of .69 for 10 studies, with time intervals from 1 day to 2 years. For MMPI-2 Scale 5, the MMPI -2 Manual reports reliability data for a subset of the recent normative sample (82 men and 111 women). An average interval of about 1 week shows Scale 5 to have a test-retest correlation of .82 and .73 for men and women, respectively. Internal consistency estimates (coefficient alpha) for Scale 5 for men and women were .58 and .37, respectively.

Scale 5 is one of the scales most affected by the revision of the MMPI. It appears that men in the new normative group have answered more items in the "feminine" direction as compared with the original fixed reference group. This has resulted in the lowering of most men's T scores on the Mf scale by about 10 T -score points. For women, there is much less change in the endorsement frequencies of the items and women's T scores are less dramatically affected. Another factor that influences MMPI-2 elevations on Scale 5 is education level. In the MMPI-2 normative sample, less educated men earned lower T -score means on Scale 5 and less educated women obtained higher average T -score values.

Investigations of the correlates for high and low Scale 5 scores in normals have been conducted by Hathaway and Meehl and Gough, McKee and Yandell. Hathaway and Meehl found that high Scale 5 normal men were described by their peers as sensitive and prone to worry, idealistic and peaceable, sociable and curious, and having general aesthetic interests. Women with high Mf scores did not have corresponding similar descriptors, although they were described as adventurous. Low-scoring men on the Mf scale were described by their peers as practical, balanced, cheerful, self-confident, and independent, whereas low-scoring women on the Mf scale were seen as sensitive, responsive, modest, grateful, and wise.

Gough described the high Scale 5 man as inner-directed and intellectually curious. Work and achievements provided these men significant gratification, and they were seen as mature, self-aware individuals. They had good judgment and common sense. They could communicate effectively and were quite verbal. Some of the adjectives typical of these high Scale 5 men included ambitious, clear-thinking, effeminate, imaginative, nervous, organized, sensitive, and submissive. Low-scoring men on Scale 5 were seen as lacking insight into their motives, preferring action to thought, and having narrow interests. They did not appear to have the psychological complexity or inner-directedness that the high Scale 5 men had. Nichols and Greene provided a good summary of high Mf scores in men (low scores in women). They stated that the Mf scale emphasizes passivity, sensitivity, and aesthetic and/or intellectual interests: "Sedentary activities and pastimes are preferred over those involving movement, competition, and the out-of-doors. Mf seems to reflect intellectualization over rationalization".

More recently, Long and Graham, using ratings provided by significant others, studied the descriptions of normal men with various levels of scores on Scale 5. The participants were 819 heterosexual couples who were included in the normative samples of the MMPI-2. In contrast to previous literature indicating high Scale 5 men to be passive, dependent, and submissive, they found that men with higher Scale 5 scores actually tended to be less passive and obedient. They found that level of education was a better predictor of certain behaviors and personality characteristics than Mf scores in normal men.

The correlates for high and low Mf scale scores vary as a function of the type of individuals being assessed. For example, high Scale 5 scores are frequently obtained by normal married men, although not for women. Although relatively frequent among normal men, Scale 5 is not often a high point among psychiatric patients. Given that much of the Mf item content suggests mild maladjustment, Ward and Dillon investigated whether emotional distress is a correlate of the Mf scale in clinical populations. In studying the Mfraw scores and symptom ratings obtained on psychiatric patients, emotional distress correlates for Scale 5 were identified. Anxiety, depressed mood, guilt feelings, and tension were associated with high raw scores ("feminine" direction) in both men and women. It is interesting to note that Ward and Dillon found these correlates to be largely independent of other MMPI clinical scales.

It is clear that high Scale 5 scorers, particularly men, vary in their behavioral descriptions or diagnoses as a function of their normal versus psychiatric status. High Mf scores in men (low Mf scores in women) in a normal population may indicate sensitivity, as well as aesthetic or intellectual interests, particularly if the person is college educated. Traditionally, the literature has emphasized the passivity or submissiveness often noted in high Scale 5 men, although Long and Graham found opposite trends. An underlying dimension of Scale 5 has been hypothesized to be role flexibility. The high Scale 5 man is able to appreciate a diversity of interests and show tolerance for differences in others. Traditional masculine interests are likely to be expressed by men who score in the T = 46-55 range. Scores below 46 begin to suggest "macho" orientations, with very low scores (T < 40) strongly suggestive of an activity-oriented, nonverbally expressive type of individual who may be perceived as insensitive, competitive, aggressive, independent, and possibly crude, with traditional masculine-feminine views and possible underlying doubts about his own masculinity. High Scale 5 women are likely to be seen in many ways similar to low Scale 5 men, that is, as aggressive, competitive, dominating, energetic, and confident. The low Scale 5 woman may be described as hyper feminine if her score is below a T score of 40 and if she is not lege educated. Between a T score of 40 and 55, she is likely to be described as having stereotypically feminine interests.

Scale 6: Paranoia (Pa)

There is no available information describing the exact way the paranoid criterion group was selected, nor do data exist about the demographic characteristics of the participants used in the construction of this 40-item scale. It is assumed that the usual item selection procedures were used as with the other MMPI scales. The criterion patients, according to Hathaway, had a diagnosis of paranoid state, paranoid condition, or paranoid schizophrenia, and the scale was developed to assess paranoid symptoms and features. The patients studied in the criterion group manifested various signs of paranoia, including ideas of reference, feelings of persecution, grandiose self-concepts, hypersensitivity, rigid thinking, and suspiciousness. There were attempts to improve the operating characteristics of the scale, but Hathaway stated that the results were disappointing:

As with other scales, several different scales were derived and tested by cross-validation. This cross-validation was always disappointing and the published scale was considered weak although it was the best that could be developed. One factor that seemed to justify at least temporary use of the scale was that there were few false positives. When a person had a high score, he tended to be diagnosed as paranoid or at least he was felt to be sensitive and rigid in personal relationships.

Hathaway went on to state that, as was true with Scale 8, the hope that Scale 6 could be improved was not realized. "Even the K variable failed to sharpen the differentiation. It was felt that the K correction did not help because more than 20% of the Scale 6 items were already subtle in character" Consequently, there is no added fraction of K to Scale 6 on the profile sheet as there is for other clinical scales.

Scale 6 measures a range of chronic and acute paranoid mentation and attitudes that include frank psychotic ideation, over sensitivity, and rigid denials of cynicism. The scale also taps externalizing processes, such as projection, hyper vigilance, and scanning for "evidence" of hostile intentions or actions. According to Nichols and Greene, Scale 6 is "the most general measure of projection and is sensitive to both implicit and explicit operations to place or locate motives, responsibility, and other, especially undesirable, personal attributes outside the self". This is consistent with Ihilevich and Gleser 's definition of projection, which involves the attribution of negative intent or characteristic to others without substantiating evidence.

To help determine the nature of the psychopathology, it is critical to examine the Harris-Lingoes subscales from this scale when a score is elevated. For example, an individual with no clear-cut thought disorder (e.g., ideas of reference or feelings of persecution) may in fact be clinically paranoid if he or she is pathologically oversensitive to others' slights or failures of consideration. Often these individuals may be diagnosed with paranoid character traits or a paranoid personality disorder. However, Morey and Smith, in their comprehensive review of personality disorders, pointed out the rarity of a diagnosis of paranoid personality disorder in clinical populations with base-rate ranges between 0.9% and 1.4%. They stated that it has not been conclusively demonstrated that increasing elevations on Scale 6 are associated with a paranoid personality disorder. Because individuals with this disorder are characterized as mistrustful and suspicious, it may be that they are unlikely to endorse the face-valid (obvious) items reflecting paranoia. For this reason, the K+ profile described by Marks may reflect paranoid symptomatology in psychiatric inpatients. In this K+ code pattern, all of the clinical scales are below a T score of 70, with six or more scales below a T score of 60. The only prominent scale is an elevated K. Marks et al. found in their psychiatric inpatient sample that 18% of the participants with the 86/68 code pattern were diagnosed with paranoid personality disorder, whereas 68% were diagnosed with paranoid schizophrenia. Another code pattern that may include paranoid personality disorder features is the 248 profile, with elevated L and K scales suggesting guardedness. It is important to note that Scale 6 may not always be elevated in paranoid-personality disordered patients, and other scales should be examined for indications of blame, anger, and mistrust.

Nichols and Greene described the cognitive operations of the high Scale 6 scorer. They stated that:

> *Pa emphasizes the rationalization of anger, resentment, and the loss of control. One sees rigid self-justification, the accumulation and hostile or self-justifying use of "evidence" or authorization for accusation, suspicion, and attack. Pa seems to reflect rationalization over intellectualization.*

Typically, high scorers on Scale 6 fear moral and/or physical attacks, feel easily misunderstood, and unfairly criticized and treated, as well as self-righteous, opinionated, suspicious, and self-dissatisfied. Additionally, they are seen as argumentative, stubborn, self-centered and lacking in social skills. Normal men with high MMPI Scale 6 elevations in their profile have been described as sensitive, sentimental, loyal, trustful, cooperative, kind, and submissive, whereas normal women have been described as emotional, soft-hearted, and sensitive. Individuals scoring in the normal range on Scale 6 (T = 46-57) may either lack paranoid symptoms or have well-ingrained paranoid traits with sufficient reality testing to avoid endorsing the obvious items on the scale.

The recent MMPI-2 restandardization project examined the meaning of elevated Pa scores for normals. Women in the MMPI-2 normative sample who scored high on Scale 6 were described by their husbands as moody with a tendency to get sad and blue, lacking emotional control, having a tendency to cry easily, and being susceptible to bad dreams. Men were not clearly differentiated in the way their partners described them, and no significant correlates were reported for men.

There is mixed information on the meaning of low scores on Scale 6. Some authors contend that low scores actually reveal the hidden presence of paranoia, as a respondent who is trying to conceal his vulnerabilities may deny any suspiciousness or hypersensitivity whatsoever. Other researchers failed to find a consistent relationship between Scale 6 scores and paranoid symptomatology. In our experience, we have observed clinically paranoid individuals attempting to look good to obtain very low scores on Scale 6. A very low score on this scale should alert the clinician to look for other measures of suspiciousness or cynicism, such as a low score on the Pa3 (Moral Virtue) subscale and/or high scores on the CYN (Cynicism) content scales, especially CYN 2 (Interpersonal Suspiciousness).

Dahlstrom reported the descriptions of Hathaway and Meehl 's low-scoring normals on Scale 6. Men were described by their acquaintances as cheerful, balanced, and decisive but also as conscienceless. These men perceived themselves as orderly and as good social mixers. Women were seen by others as serious, mature, reasonable, and trusting. They saw themselves as self-controlled, persevering, wise, loyal, and modest. W. Anderson found that college students in counseling with MMPI Scale 6 scores below a T score of 40 tended to be underachievers with low grades and reported difficulties with their parents.

All 40 of the original items in Scale 6 have been retained in the MMPI-2. However, two items were modified to eliminate sexist wording and to simplify the item meaning. The following items illustrate the range of content in Scale 6. The MMPI-2 item numbers precede the item, with the direction of scoring in parentheses.

16. Once in a while I think of things too bad to talk about. (True) 22. No one seems to understand me. (True) 24. Evil spirits possess me at times. (True) 42. If people had not had it in for me, I would have been much more successful. (True) 95. I am happy most of the time. (False) 314. I have no enemies who really wish to harm me. (False)

Twenty-five of the items on Scale 6 are scored in the "true" direction, and 15 items are scored in the "false" direction. Because more items are endorsed in the "true" direction, as is the case with the other psychotic clinical scales, an all-true response set will tend to elevate this scale. Thirty-three of the items on Scale 6 overlap other scales, with the F scale and Scales 4 and 8 sharing 9, 8, and 13 items, respectively, with Scale 6. Seven items on Scale 6 do not overlap with other scales. Dahlstrom reported early itemetric research of J. W. Little examining which Scale 6 items were the most discriminating with the highest item-total scale (biserial) correlations. The frankly paranoid item "I believe I'm being plotted against" (MMPI-2 Item 138) was the most differentiating item for his college-level participants with a biserial correlation of .77. Other items tended to be less related to the total scale scores.

For MMPI Scale 6, the test-retest correlation coefficients for psychiatric cases ranged between .61 and .71 for a 1-to 2-day interval between testing and between .59 and .65 for a 1-year interval between testing. In Hunsley 's large-scale meta-analysis of MMPI reliability studies using various populations conducted between 1970 and 1981, an average internal consistency of .73 across 70 studies of Scale 6 was reported. They also reported an average test-retest reliability of .69 for 15 studies for time intervals of 1 day to 2 years. On the MMPI-2, Butcher reported test-retest reliability data on Scale 6 for their community (normal) sample of 82 men (r = .67) and 111 women (r = .58) retested at an average interval of 8.6 days (Mdn = 7 days). Scale 6 has the lowest test-retest values for the clinical scales as well as the lowest internal consistency estimates for the clinical scales (excluding the Mf scale for women) with alpha coefficients of .34 and .39 for men and women, respectively.

Harris-Lingoes Subscales

Harris and Lingoes developed three subscales for Scale 6: Ideas of External Influence (Pa1), Poignancy (Pa2), and Moral Virtue (Pa3).

Ideas of External Influence: Pa1 (17 Items)

Sixteen of the 17 items on Pa1 (formerly Persecutory Ideas) are scored in the "true" direction and mostly reflect the open persecutory content of Scale 6. Ward, Kersh and Waxmonsky suggested that Pa1 is the only MMPI-2 scale or subscale that measures uniquely paranoid ideas. These researchers derived a three-factor structure for the Scale 6 using substance abuse patients and found that Pa1 and the Paranoid factor had 14 of 16 items in common, thereby supporting the construct of validity of this subscale. It should be noted that although Pa1 "does have substantial item overlap with the Bizarre Mentation content scale, Bizarre Mentation intermixes explicitly paranoid items with more general psychotic symptoms". Wrobel found projection to be a defense associated with patients having high Pa1 scores. Nichols and Greene stated that their paranoid thought process category is best represented by Pa1 "which emphasizes persecutory ideas, resentment, and convictions of having been unfairly treated, and delusional ideas of being attacked, influenced, subverted, or undermined". They also noted that the Pa-O subscale is highly redundant with Pa1. High Pa1 scorers tend to feel that the world is an unsafe or hostile place and that others are not to be trusted. It is not surprising that Pa1 and Pd4 (Social Alienation) share six items in common and are highly inter correlated in a sample of psychiatric inpatients and outpatients. Caldwell stated that raw scores as low as 5 or 6 may point to a paranoid process. High scorers tend to blame others for their problems, feel that others have unfairly blamed or punished them, and feel misunderstood. High Scores never except their problems and always blames others for injustice. It is not surprising to learn that high male Pa1 scorers in the Graham investigation of psychiatric outpatients tended to report a history of being physically abused as well as reporting a history of committing domestic violence, a finding generally supportive of the clinical lore and empirical data linking the two.

Low scorers do not endorse items suggesting externalization of their problems or the use of projection as their main mechanism of defense and tend not to externalize their problems.

The following items represent the Pa1 content, with the direction of scoring in parentheses and the MMPI-2 item number preceding the item. Only one item is scored in the "false" direction:

17. I am sure I get a raw deal from life. (True) 22. No one seems to understand me. (True) 42. If people had not had it in for me, I would have been much more successful. (True) 113. I know who is responsible for most of my troubles. (True) 138. I believe I am being plotted against. (True) 314. I have no enemies who really wish to harm me. (False)

Poignancy: Pa2 (9 Items)

This subscale appears to measure how sensitive or thin-skinned an individual is in reaction to others. It reflects a facet of the mood or feeling aspect of depression. Individuals with high scores report an unusual intensity of feelings, angry resentment, a painful sensitivity to criticism, cry easily, feel misunderstood, and feel lonely even in the presence of others. These individuals tend to see themselves as taking a longer time to heal from emotional hurts compared to others and they recognize that they are easily wounded. Feeling more high-strung than others, high scorers may tend to look for risky or exciting activities to make them feel better.

Low scorers feel understood and accepted and do not experience themselves as more sensitive than others.

Seven of the nine items in this subscale are scored in the "true" direction. The following items are example of the Pa2 content, with the MMPI-2 item number preceding the item and the direction of scoring is in parentheses:

22. No one seems to understand me. (True) 100. I have never done anything dangerous for the thrill of it. (False) 146. I cry easily. (True) 271. I think I feel more intensely than most people do. (True) 285. I am more sensitive than most other people. (True)

Moral Virtue: PA3 (9 Items)

This subscale primarily measures how one perceives other people in terms of their trustworthiness. High scorers tend to have optimistic and naive attitudes about others and themselves and may have difficulty experiencing forgiveness when they feel they have been deceived or treated unfairly. There appears to be an underlying rigidity of opinions and attitudes that translates into a judgmental orientation toward others' behavior (e.g., good/bad; right/wrong, and moral/immoral). For this reason, Caldwell thought that the scale is better named as Moral Righteousness. High scorers endorse items reflecting firm expectations regarding the honesty and trustworthiness of others. Endorsement of Pa3 items could also "represent a tendency by some paranoid patients to deny cynical attitudes". Meehl and Hathaway speculated that "paranoid deviates are characterized by a tendency to give two sorts of responses, one of which is obviously paranoid, the other 'obviously' not".

Low scorers view others as untrustworthy and motivated by self-interest and are likely to be suspicious of their motives. Nichols and Greene suggested that a low Pa3 score coupled with a high Hy2 (Need for Affection) score reflects cynicism of a competitive, narcissistic, or suspicious variety.

All of the items except one are scored in the "false" direction for this subscale. The following items are examples of Pa3 contents with the MMPI-2 item number preceding the item, and the direction of scoring in parentheses.

16. Once in a while I think of things too bad to talk about. (True) 81. I think most people would lie to get ahead. (False) 104. Most people are honest chiefly because they are afraid of being caught. (False) 286. Most people inwardly dislike putting themselves out to help other people. (False) 315. I tend to be on my guard with people who are somewhat more friendly than I had expected. (False)

Scale 6: Subtle-Obvious Subscales

Wiener and Harmon developed Subtle and Obvious subscales for Scale 6 on the MMPI. The MMPI-2 Paranoia-Obvious subscale (Pa-O) has 23 items, of which 20 items are keyed in the "true" direction and 3 items are keyed in the "false" direction. The Paranoia-Subtle subscale (Pa-S) has 17 items, of which 5 items are keyed in the "true" direction and 12 items are keyed in the "false" direction. The following items are examples of subtle-obvious items on Scale

6, with the MMPI-2 item number preceding the item and the scoring direction and obvious or subtle distinction in parentheses.

> *17. I am sure I get a raw deal from life. (True-Obvious) 24. Evil spirits possess me at times. (True-Obvious) 113. I know who is responsible for most of my troubles. (True-Subtle) 145. I feel that I have been often punished without cause. (True-Subtle) 244. Something exciting will almost always pull me out of it when I'm feeling low. (False-Subtle) 314. I have no enemies who really wish to harm me. (False-Obvious)*

Caldwell categorized the 23 items in the Pa-O subscale into three categories: (a) persecutory paranoid items (e.g., feeling personally mistreated and knowing who your enemies are), (b) feelings of loneliness and social isolation, and (c) self-awareness of a distressingly low threshold for emotional reactions (e.g., hypersensitivity). Pa1 overlaps greatly with Pa-O, sharing 15 of its 17 items with Pa-O. Not surprisingly, Nichols and Greene reported a high correlation r = .94) between Pa1 and Pa-O in a sample of psychiatric inpatients and outpatients. Overall, Pa-O appears to emphasize the operation of blaming and attributing hostility to others, as well as including a few oversensitive/depressive items from Pa2. Hollrah reviewed Wrobel and Lachar 's results and reported that Pa-O correlated positively with measures of discomfort and reality distortion. Dahlstrom reported that Wiener and Harmon found that the original Minnesota normal men endorsed the Pa-O items much less frequently than they did those of the other Obvious subscales. A perusal of the mean number of item endorsements for the Obvious subscales in the recent MMPI-2 restandardization sample shows that both men and women again endorse the Pa-O items much less frequently than those of the other Obvious subscales, although Pa-O has significantly fewer items than the other Obvious subscales. An elevated Pa-O score in a "normal" participant warrants a careful assessment of potential paranoid symptoms or paranoid character traits.

Dahlstrom examined the correlates of the Subtle and Obvious subscales derived from partner ratings on the Katz Adjustment Scales used in the MMPI-2 restandardization. For both men and women, the following descriptions emerged as significant for high Pa-O scorers: suspicious of others, poor sense of humor, lacks interest in things, feels others do not care about him or her, has many fears, experiences bad dreams, frets over little things, moody, not cheerful, complains of body aches, overly sensitive to rejection, does not show sound judgment, and gives up too easily. For men, some of the descriptions included the following: whines and demands attention, lacks affection, bossy, unpleasant, hostile, and unfriendly. For women, some of the descriptors included the following: gets very sad, thinks others are talking about her, cries easily, lacks energy, appears worn out, lacks emotional control, worries about the future, does not get along with others, and acts helpless.

Caldwell suggested that low Pa-O scores may reflect an absence of resentments, successful social engagement, a comfort with one's own feelings, and possibly a high threshold for aggravation.

The Pa-S items, although classified as subtle, appear to have some obvious items (e.g., "I know who is responsible for most of my troubles"). Nine of the 17 items on this subscale overlap with Pa3, moral virtue, and therefore there may be some interpretive redundancy between high scores on these two subscales. The male and female normal participants in the restandardization sample tended to obtain a lower mean score on Pa-S versus the other Subtle subscales. Although this could be due in part to the relatively shorter length of Pa-S, or to particular features of the restandardization sample, among psychiatric patients a high score on Pa-S, like Pa-O, warrants a careful assessment of potential paranoid symptoms or paranoid character traits.

Dahlstrom found that both men and women in the MMPI-2 restandardization sample who had elevated Pa-S scores were described by their partners as not being nervous, passive, or obedient. Women were described as not suspicious of others, showing sound judgment, not overeating, and thoughtful of others. Men were described as not lying, having a good sense of humor, not lacking an interest in things, not worrying over small things, being cooperative, and not overly sensitive to rejection.

Scale 7: Psychasthenia (Pt)

Scale 7 was designed to measure a neurotic pattern called psychasthenia, a term introduced by Pierre Janet but which is no longer generally used. Psychasthenia involves an inability to resist undesired, maladaptive behaviors, which McKinley and Hathaway described as deriving from the concept of a "weakened will". Preceding this concept of a weakened will was the idea of a weakened (asthenic) nervous system that was commonly referred to as neurasthenia. The catch-all diagnosis of neurasthenia applied to a syndrome with vague and variable symptoms, "particularly manifesting as extreme fatigue, insomnia, depression, headaches, dyspepsia, and a variety of non-verifiable physical complaints". This diagnosis, one of the most common diagnoses in the late 19th and early 20th centuries, was given to individuals unable to keep up their former pace of life and, in fact, appeared in the second edition of the DSM as neurasthenic neurosis but was subsequently dropped from the third edition of the DSM. The emphasis in this syndrome was on physical manifestations, with exhaustion, easy fatigability, and chronic weakness as the cardinal features, although proponents of the syndrome were unable to discover the pathological basis of the so-called disease (Gosling, 1987).

Rather than emphasizing physical problems, individuals classified as having psychasthenic tendencies in the initial MMPI development were described as having excessive self-doubts and worries, leading to tension, difficulty in making choices, various fears, obsessive preoccupations, compulsive urges and acts (e.g., hand washing), vague anxieties, and feelings of low self-confidence and insecurity. These individuals might find themselves ruminating about meaningless facts (like repeatedly counting unimportant objects) in an attempt to control their high anxiety levels. In the past, psychasthenic conditions were often referred to as compulsion neuroses, obsessive-compulsive states, or obsessive-ruminative tension states.

Scale 7 does not contain items reflecting specific phobias and compulsions because individual differences between participants probably failed to permit an item to be endorsed with sufficient frequency to survive an item analysis. It is believed, therefore, that the underlying personality structure of psychasthenia, rather than specific fears and/or phobias, is reflected in the content of Scale 7. Marks stated that "although the specific fears, preoccupations, and compulsive acts are different from individual to individual and are potentially innumerable, the personality makeup of such persons has sufficient homogeneity to comprise a recognizable common pattern".

Scale 7 consists of 48 items that were derived by using the usual empirical method of contrasting the criterion group to a mixed group of normals. Because the resultant number of items selected in this fashion was small, the scale was augmented by selecting additional items that correlated with the total scale score. In the revision of the MMPI, Scale 7 did not lose any items but did have two of its items slightly rewritten (e.g., grammatical clarification).

In constructing the original scale, 20 psychiatric inpatients with a diagnosis of psychasthenia were selected as criterion participants, a relatively small sample. It was apparently very difficult to locate outpatients with this syndrome, and few patients were so severely handicapped by their condition as to require hospitalization. McKinley and Hathaway admitted that even with the small group of carefully examined inpatients, there was at least one, and possibly more, incorrectly diagnosed participants. The item endorsements of the 20 criterion cases were compared with a group of 139 normal married men ranging in age from 26 to 43 and 200 normal married women ranging in age from 26 to 43. Additionally, 265 college students were included in a separate comparison to ascertain the effects of age on item endorsements. Once items were identified as differentiating the criterion group from the two normal groups, an additional item analysis was performed correlating each item with the total scale score in a sample of 100 randomly selected psychiatric patients and 100 normal persons. Because of the small number of criterion cases studied, the scale was not cross-validated at the time it was published. However, the scale is internally consistent with split-half values that are almost as high as the test-retest coefficients. The content of the scale seems to indicate a trait underlying the various psychasthenic symptoms it is measuring. For example, as cited in Duckworth and Anderson, Kunce and Anderson have hypothesized an underlying dimension of organization for this scale that in the normal individual with moderate elevations is shown as the ability to organize and to be punctual and methodical".

Because the items on Scale 7 clearly reflect maladjustment, the lack of item subtlety did not permit Wiener and Harmon to construct Subtle and Obvious subscales. Similarly, Harris and Lingoes did not categorize the items on this scale as the items cannot be easily separated into subcategories. "True" is the scoring direction for 81% of the 48 items on Scale 7, and therefore an all-true response set would tend to elevate this scale. The addition of a full K value (the entire raw K score) to Scale 7 helps to correct for a defensive response set affecting Scale 7 scores, and a space is provided on the profile sheet to add 1.0 K to the Pt raw score. Scale 7 has 9 non overlapping items, with most of its overlapping content being shared with Scales 8 (17 items) and 2 (13 items). The following items illustrate the content of Scale 7. The MMPI-2 item number is presented before the item, and the scoring direction is in parenthesis.

> *3. I wa ke up fresh and rested most mornings. (False) 11. There seems to be a lump in my throat much of the time. (True) 31. I find it hard to keep my mind on a task or job. (True) 56. I wish I could be as happy as others seem to be. (True) 73. I am certainly lacking in self-confidence. (True) 140. Most nights I go to sleep without thoughts or ideas bothering me. (False)*

Scale 7 measures many of the tendencies and traits of the obsessive-compulsive and anxiety disorder. High scores reflect negative emotionality characterized by feelings of low self-confidence and self-doubts about one's abilities, self-blame, heightened sensitivity, rigid efforts to control impulses, moodiness, and general maladjustment or Subjective distress. In fact, Scale 7 on the MMPI/MMPI-2 is the best marker for the first factor among the basic scales that is usually identified in factor analytic studies. This first factor is typically named general maladjustment or subjective distress. Scale 7 is highly correlated with Welsh's A scale (.90 for non- K -corrected T scores and .55 for K -corrected T scores), which is the classic marker for the first factor. It is for this reason that Scale 7 (and Scale 2) is often referred to as a distress scale (e.g., Lachar, 1974). In general, Scale 7 is sensitive to a general dimension of cognitive inefficiency and worrying that leads to tension and the inability to relax. It appears that Scale 7 emphasizes a fear or dread of some external catastrophe against which an individual might try to prepare or insulate him- or herself by rumination, obsession, and worry. It is, therefore, not surprising that high Scale 7 scores can be associated with sleep disturbances. Duckworth and Anderson viewed Scale 7 as a measure of long-term distress (trait anxiety) rather than as situational stress (state anxiety). McKinley stated that the symptoms of psychasthenia become ingrained into the individual's personality, and thus they tend to last for years, although periods of acute discomfort commonly occur. Although high Scale 7 scorers are often seen as agitated, the specific clinical manifestation will depend on other scale elevations. For example, Scale 7 is frequently elevated in the profiles of psychiatric patients (e.g., 278/728 and 87/78 profiles). When significantly elevated with Scale 2, depression and indecision are often observed, and when coupled with Scale 8 (e.g., 78/87), confusion, disorganized thinking, and feelings of depletion are manifested. In psychiatric inpatient settings, Scale 7 elevations reflect severe guilt, low energy, depressed mood, and sometimes hallucinations.

There is no single source of variance in Scale 7; thus, individuals scoring high on this scale can manifest any number of aspects of maladjustment, ranging from poor concentration and agitation to psychotic tendencies. High-scoring normals are generally described in more favorable terms than psychiatric patients, although women have more neurotic features typically than men. Dahlstrom described peer ratings reported by Hathaway and Meehl using MMPI Scale 7. High Scale 7 men were described as sentimental, peaceable, good-tempered, verbal, and dissatisfied whereas women were rated as sensitive, prone to worry, emotional, and high-strung. More recently, the restandardization participants with high Scale 7 scores were rated by their spouses as having many fears, being nervous, being indecisive, lacking in self-confidence, and having sleep problems.

Low-scoring individuals on Scale 7 are often seen as relaxed and able to handle their responsibilities without distress. They appear self-controlled, realistic, and able to organize themselves.

Test-retest coefficients for psychiatric patients on MMPI Scale 7 range from .83 to .86 for 1-to 2-week intervals between administrations and from .49 to .58 for 1-year intervals between tests. In Hunsley 's large-scale meta-analysis of MMPI reliability studies using several diverse populations conducted between 1970 and 1981, an average internal consistency of .84 across 70 studies of Scale 7 was reported. They also reported an average test-retest reliability of .82 for 16 studies for time intervals of 1 day to 2 years. More recently, Butcher reported test-retest reliability data for their community (normal) sample of 82 men (r = .89) and 111 women (r = .88) retested at an average interval of 8.6 days (Mdn = 7 days). Internal consistency estimates for Scale 7 were also derived from the restandardization sample and yielded coefficients of .85 and .87 for men and women, respectively.

Scale 8: Schizophrenia (Sc)

Schizophrenia, first identified as a syndrome by Kraepelin and later named schizophrenia by Bleuler in 1911, is currently recognized as a group of disorders with a biogenic etiological basis. Diagnostic criteria for a schizophrenic disorder, according to the fourth edition of the DSM, include impairment in various psychological processes involving thinking, perceiving, feeling, and behaving, with no specific feature considered pathognomonic of the disorder. Often a deterioration from a previous level of functioning is observed, with continuous signs of the disorder necessary for at least 6 months during the individual's life. Various symptoms precede the illness (prodromal phase) or remain (residual) after the active phase of the disorder. These symptoms often vary between individuals and include social withdrawal; inappropriate affect; bizarre ideation; odd behavior; and digressive, vague, circumstantial speech, which, according to Marks and Seeman, can lead the clinician talking to a schizophrenic patient to often wonder "How did we get to this?" because logical thought is so circuitous and frequently interrupted.

It is not surprising that the development of Scale 8 was the most difficult of all the clinical scales to construct because schizophrenia involves diverse behavioral, emotional, and cognitive symptoms. Although more research time was devoted to this scale than the others, it is still considered one of the weaker diagnostic scales. Despite many efforts at refinement, the ability of the Sc scale to separate the criterion schizophrenic participants from the normals (hit rate) could not be made to exceed 60%. As many as a dozen variations of the scale were attempted from four preliminary scales before the final version of the Sc scale was accepted and cross-validated. These preliminary scales were derived from two partly overlapping groups of 50 patients with varying subtypes of schizophrenia (catatonic, paranoid, simple, and hebephrenic). About

60% of the participants were women and 40% were men. Hathaway did not offer more specific definitional features of the criterion participants, but Dahlstrom gave the following description of schizophrenic individuals:

Most commonly, persons showing this psychiatric reaction are characterized as constrained, cold, and apathetic or indifferent. Other people see them as remote and inaccessible, often seeming sufficient unto themselves. Delusions of varying degrees of organization, hallucinations, either fleeting or persistent and compelling, and disorientation may appear in various combinations. Inactivity or endless stereotypy, may accompany the withdrawal of interest from other people or external objects and relationships. These persons frequently perform below the levels expected of them on the basis of their training and ability.

Nichols pointed out that the criterion schizophrenic group very likely was contaminated, with a large minority of affectively disordered participants. Historically, schizophrenia had been grossly over diagnosed in this country, whereas affective disorders had been under diagnosed, especially in relation to each other. Because there is much symptom overlap between the two syndromes, many affectively disordered participants were probably inaccurately classified as schizophrenic. In contrast, few false-positive classifications were likely made in constructing the criterion group for Scale 9, as manic patients with schizophrenic-like symptoms were excluded. Therefore, Nichols stated that Scale 9 was probably rendered an "unusually valid measure of the core features of the manic syndrome".

Despite the many efforts to improve the detection ability of Scale 8, it was not until the K scale was developed by Meehl and Hathaway and used as a device to improve the discriminative ability of Scale 8 that it was considered complete. As indicated earlier, about 60% of the cross-validation cases could be correctly identified with the scale when 1 full K value was added to Scale 8. The addition of 1 full K value helped to reduce the number of false positives or high-scoring normals from 15% to 2%. Hathaway pointed out, however, that even with the correction, a considerable number of the 91 cross-validation cases (all of which were psychiatric patients diagnosed as schizophrenic) remained below a T score of 61 on NMPI Scale 8.

The K value appears to work in improving the operation of Scale 8 in the following way. By adding K to the raw score on Scale 8, the T scores for the criterion participants (schizophrenics) and normals were both raised, but the T scores of the criterion group increased more relative to the normals. Presumably, the reason the schizophrenic participants failed initially to be identified was due to the denial or minimizing of psychopathology associated with K. Adding K to their scores is intended to correct for this minimizing tendency, which is less pronounced in the normals, who presumably have less psychopathology to minimize.

It is now customary to add the value of 1.0 raw K to the raw score of Scale 8 before plotting the standard score on the profile sheet. It is recommended that clinicians continue to use the K correction factor for Scale 8, especially with psychiatric patients, as the vast majority of research conducted on Scale 8 has used K - corrected rather than non- K -corrected scores. Note that because 1 full K value is added to Scale 8, it is possible to obtain an elevated Scale 8 score (T ? 65), with approximately 20 Scale 8 items endorsed in the deviant direction and an average score on the K scale. Therefore, it is important to examine the raw score on

Scale 8 as well as the endorsed item content before inferring a diagnosis of psychosis from a high score on Scale 8 considered in isolation. A diagnostic conclusion of schizophrenia cannot be made solely on the basis of a Scale 8 elevation. The relationship of other scale elevations and patterns must be examined, as well as special indexes, in the context of the referral question and other clinical information in order to accurately identify an individual with schizophrenia or schizophrenic-like symptoms. Many individuals with elevated Scale 8 scores as the most prominent high point in a profile are not psychotic; in some cases, an individual may be suffering from severe depression, perhaps with psychotic features and acute distress, a severe personality disorder, an organic brain disorder, or some extreme sensory impairment, or have an unconventional, rebellious orientation toward society.

Scale 8 does appear to operate in a differentiating fashion in psychiatric settings. Walters found that Scale 8 elevations differentiated schizophrenic and schizophrenic-spectrum disorders in general psychiatric patients. In a nonpsychiatric setting, a moderately elevated Scale 8 score should be interpreted with attenuated descriptors as many individuals will not present psychopathology suggestive of a schizophrenic disorder. For example, Anderson and Kunce found that in a sample of university counseling center clients with Scale 8 as their highest score and a T score above 70, the majority of clients tended to feel socially isolated and had interpersonal difficulties, but only a minority were assessed as having bizarre thoughts. The case notes in the files of all of these participants indicated that the significantly elevated Sc scale reflected stressful identity or personal crises rather than chronic or severe psychopathological conditions. Although this study demonstrates the lack of expected psychopathology associated with a Scale 8 elevation, other research has shown that although "normal" or noripsychiatric participants with high Scale 8 scores may not carry a diagnosis of schizophrenia, they often share certain characteristics with the schizophrenic participants, thereby providing construct validity for the scale. For example, S. P. Keane and Gibbs tested the hypothesis that participants (university students) with elevated Scale 8 scores would exhibit qualitatively different word associations from those with normal MMPI profiles. Students with elevated profiles exhibited associations similar to those frequently observed in hospitalized schizophrenic patients, such as preservations, self-references, and blocking. Although the students were not described as manifesting any form of a severe disturbance, Keane and Gibbs hypothesized that their associational deficits, as detected by Scale 8 elevations, could exhibit themselves in a subtle way on tasks that tap organizational ability, grammatical structure, and conventional associative linkages.

In general, researchers have found that prominent Scale 8 elevations, especially in psychiatric settings, do predict a schizophrenic diagnosis, especially if there is a concurrent elevation on Scale 6 (Pa) or on scores in the psychotic/schizophrenic direction on certain MMPI indexes. Marks found that 68% of their 86/68 code pattern participants were diagnosed as psychotic (schizophrenic/paranoid), whereas 18% were diagnosed as having paranoid personality disorders. Seventy percent of their 89/98 code pattern participants were described as psychotic (schizophrenic/mixed), whereas 58% of their 278/872 participants and 70% of their 28/82 participants were diagnosed as schizophrenic and schizophrenic/

schizo affective, respectively. Greene reported the frequency of MMPI code patterns in a large sample (N = 8,727) of psychiatric inpatients and outpatients collected by Hedlund and Won Cho in the 1970s. For women, some of the most frequently occurring codes were the 86,48, and 84 code patterns (Spike 4 was the most frequent code pattern); for men, the 86 was one of the most frequently occurring code patterns. Greene provided detailed data on the frequency with which each MMPI-2 code pattern occurred in the sample of patients collected by Hedlund and Won Cho. This comparison was accomplished by eliminating the omitted 13 items from the MMPI-2 and rescoring the data using uniform T scores. Many changes in the frequency of scale elevations and code patterns resulted, but in general Scale 8 occurred less frequently in both the male and female patients. Greene pointed out that there is considerable heterogeneity in psychiatric diagnoses within a given code pattern as the Marks data indicate. However, it does appear that Scale 8 is useful in describing the behavior of and, to a certain extent, deriving a diagnosis for individuals scoring high on this scale. Studies (e.g., Walters, 1984) consistently show that schizophrenic patients earn higher mean scores on Scale 8 relative to normals and other non schizophrenic psychiatric patients.

As with certain other clinical scales, it is important to examine the Harris-Lingoes subscales to help determine the meaning of a particular scale elevation. Wiener and Harmon did not develop Subtle and Obvious subscales for Scale 8.

Disorganized thinking, impaired reality testing, and communication problems appear to be cardinal features of high Scale 8 scorers. As scores increase, the individual's logic appears less coherent, and at markedly high levels, individuals tend to have impaired communications between themselves and others. Duckworth and Anderson also indicated that at increasing levels of Scale 8 individuals are likely to manifest poor judgment that lands them into difficulties. Extremely high elevations (T > 100) usually reflect situational stress rather than chronic disorganization and typically individuals with identity crises ("Who am I?") score in this range. Coupled with an elevated Scale 0, the person tends to show even greater communication disturbance because of a lack of social contact with others. Nichols and Greene viewed Scale 8 as a measure of a tendency to withdraw into fantasy and, at high levels (T =85), to prefer the world of fantasy to real-world relationships. They provided detailed and useful information on the relation of Scale 8 to the F scale and to the BIZ content scale stating that when BIZ (especially BIZ I [Psychotic Symptomatology]) is elevated along with Sc, the fantasy tends toward the psychotic and bizarre, with a significant breach in reality testing and in the ability to discriminate external from internal events. When Sc is not accompanied by elevations on BIZ, fantasy tends to be of a compensatory, wish fulfillment type, in which reality adherence is relatively well preserved. These inferences may be fortified with reference to the difference between F and BIZ scores: F substantially greater than BIZ suggests social deviance and poor reality testing without bizarre aspects; a large negative difference suggests bizarre fantasy but with relatively less impaired reality contact. A similar relationship between F and Sc scales also bears upon the expression of psychoticism. When the elevation of both scales is nearly equivalent or F is slightly higher than Sc, psychotic manifestations are apt to be public, including interpersonal bizarreness with evident emotional and motivational dyscontrol. When Sc is elevated, to the extent that it exceeds F, psychotic manifestations are apt to be of an internalized kind, such as bizarre fantasies and autism, with interpersonal detachment and withdrawal.

Individuals with significant Scale 8 elevations tend to feel mistrustful toward others and think that people will dislike them. Lewak and Caldwell hypothesized that Scale 8 elevations are associated with a childhood of being despised and rejected by a person on whom life and security depended:

Perhaps in some instances the child expressed some peculiar habit or eccentricities or was physically inept which led others to express anger, hatred, and resentment towards him or her. The assumption is that the child, in an act of self-protection, would shut down, that is, not think or not pay attention, which would lead in turn to faulty cognitive and emotional functioning.

With high Scale 8 elevations, individuals might experience hallucinations, confusion, panic, or anxiety and possibly be delusional. Scale 8 is associated with feeling unhappy, moody, inferior, and alienated, as well as with immaturity, impulsivity, and reclusion. High Scale 8 scorers are viewed by others as odd or peculiar and shy, even schizoid at times. Low Scale 8 scorers are seen as friendly, responsible, cautious, and unimaginative in their approach to problem solving and as practical and concrete in their thinking.

Hathaway and Meehl found that the normal men in their study who had elevated scores on this scale were not seen by their peers as withdrawn or deviant. Social difficulties were not perceived, although these men were seen as self-dissatisfied and prone to worry. Overall, they were described as good-tempered, verbal, enthusiastic, and having wide aesthetic interests. Peaceable, kind, and sentimental were emotional descriptors given to them. Women were described as sensitive and high-strung, as well as frank, kind, and modest. Other descriptors for normal men in a different sample provided by Gough are much more negative. Terms like hostile and irritable suggest difficulties in handling aggression and imply a certain lack of control in modulating emotions.

Scale 8 on the MMPI-2 lost no items in the restandardization project, but 13 of the scale's 78 items were modified, with mostly grammatical clarifications and simplifications. As the longest clinical scale, there is considerable item overlap with other scales. Scale 8 shares the most items with Scales 7 (17 items) and the F scale (15 items) and has more items in common with the other psychotic scales that it does with the neurotic scales. There are only 16 items unique (non overlapping) to Scale 8. As is the case for other psychotic scales, the deviant direction of endorsement for the majority of Scale 8 items is "true;" specifically, 59 (76%) of the 78 items are scored as "true" and 19 (24%) items are scored as "false." J. W. Little found that the item "I hear strange things when I am alone" has the highest correlation (r = .70) to the total scale, with the next highest item having a value of .67 ("I cannot keep my mind on one thing"). The following items demonstrate the diversity of content on Scale 8. The MMPI-2 item number precedes the item, and the scoring direction is in parentheses.

9. My daily life is full of things that keep me interested. (False) 12. My sex life is satisfactory. (False) 17. I am sure I get a raw deal from life. (True) 21. At times I very much wanted to leave home.

(True) 22. No one seems to understand me. (True) 32. I have had very peculiar and strange experiences. (True) 138. I believe I am being plotted against. (True)

MMPI Scale 8 test-retest coefficients for psychiatric cases ranged from.75 to .82 for a 1- to 2-day interval between tests and from .56 to .64 for a 1-year interval between tests. Test-retest correlation coefficients for a sub sample of the MMPI-2 restandardization group (82 men and 111 women) retested at about a 1-week interval were .87 and .80 for men and women, respectively. In Hunsley large-scale meta-analysis of MMPI reliability studies using a wide variety of populations conducted between 1970 and 1981, an average test-retest reliability of .78 for 17 studies was reported for time intervals for 1 day to 2 years. They also reported an average internal consistency of 82 across 73 studies of Scale 8. More recently, Butcher et al. reported internal consistency estimates for Scale 8 on the MMPI-2 of .85 and .87 for men and women, respectively. Scales 8 and 7 had almost identical alpha coefficients, the highest for all of the validity and clinical scales. Clearly, Scale 8 appears to be an internally consistent scale with good test-retest reliability.

Harris-Lingoes Subscales

Harris and Lingoes developed the following subscales for Scale 8: Social Alienation (Sc1); Emotional Alienation (Sc2); Lack of Ego Mastery, Cognitive (Sc3); Lack of Ego Mastery, Conative (Sc4); Lack of Ego Mastery, Defective Inhibition (Sc5); and Sensorimotor Dissociation (Sc6).

Social Alienation: Scl (21 Items)

This subscale consists of items reflecting emotional deprivation. Specifically, the items reflect feeling misunderstood, insulted, punished unfairly, plotted against, and detached from one's own family and others and a sense of loneliness around others. High Scl scorers tend to lack a viable support system. Graham reported that the men in their outpatient psychiatric sample tended to report that their families lacked love and that there was a history of physical abuse. Women, in particular, admitted to more suicide attempts if they were a high versus a low scorer on Scl. Although an individual may also concurrently score high on Pd1 (Familial Discord) and Pd4 (Social Alienation), it is important to assess these and other subscale scores separately as the clinical implications can vary. For example, a high Sc1 score, coupled with relatively low Sc2 (Emotional Alienation) and Pd5 (Self-Alienation) scores, suggests that the person's sense of pessimism and hopelessness may be confined to other people, although he or she is still able to derive gratification from activities of nonsocial interests. High Scl scorers feel they have been given a "bum deal" but do not feel the residual sadness or longing that appears in Pd4. To a large extent, high Sc1 individuals prefer noninvolvement with others. Scl also measures an element of paranoia in that high scorers are generally mistrustful of others. When the F scale and/or Pdl are also elevated, the person may express hatred toward one or both parents.

Low Scl scorers tend to like others, feel attached to them, feel understood, respected, well treated, and deny feelings of hatred/ resentment toward family members.

Sixteen of the items on this subscale are scored in the "true" direction, and 5 items are scored in the "false" direction. The following items illustrate the content of Sc1. Preceding the item is the MMPI-2 item number, with the direction of scoring in parentheses:

17. I'm sure I get a raw deal from life. (True) 21. At times I have very much wanted to leave home. (True) 22. No one seems to understand me. (True) 138. I believe I am being plotted against. (True) 278. I get all the sympathy I should. (False) 280. I seem to make friends about as quickly as others do. (False)

Emotional Alienation: Sc2 (11 Items)

This subscale consists of items reflecting an existence devoid of interests, engagement, or aspiration. Levitt thought the scale basically measured depression, and in fact, the scale does appear to measure an emotional withdrawal from life. Graham reported a similar description of the high Sc2 scorer suggesting a greater likelihood of depression as well as having few or no friends. Caldwell described high scorers as experiencing life as an "ungratifying strain" and as taking pleasure in hurting loved ones or being hurt by them. Graham also described high scorers as feeling apathetic and frightened. Wrobel provided correlates for Sc2 that included feeling a lack of rapport with oneself, a flat or distorted affect, and a feeling of oneself as strange. Nichols and Greene described emotional alienation as reflecting a "pathological disengagement from life that discounts future interests, prospects, and engagements to the extent that they can no longer serve as incentives for continuing to live". In this regard, the high Sc2 scorer is seen as lacking an investment in the future, which raises the possibility of suicidal behavior and thoughts, which should be further evaluated by examining critical items (MMPI-2 Items 150, 303, 506, 520, and 524) and the suicidal ideation component DEP4 of the DEP content scale. Although Sc2 does have items reflective of unconventional thought processes, the items tend not to be as strongly suggestive of psychosis as other measures, such as Psychotic Symptoniatology (BIZI) or Sensorimotor Dissociation.

Low Sc2 scorers deny feelings of depression and despair, feel that life is worthwhile, and deny sadistic or masochistic needs.

Eight of the 11 items on this subscale are scored in the "true" direction, whereas 3 items are scored in the "false" direction. The following items illustrate the content of Sc2, with the MMPI-2 item number preceding the item and the scoring direction in parentheses:

> *9. My daily life is full of things that keep me interested. (False7) 65. Most of the time I feel blue. (True) 92. I don't seem to care what happens to me. (True) 273. Life is a strain for me much of the time. (True) 303. Most of the time I wish I were dead. (True) 323. Sometimes I enjoy hurting persons I love. (True) Lack of Ego Mastery, Cognitive: Sc3 (10 Items)*

This short subscale contains items that reflect cognitive deficits in the areas of memory, attention, and concentration. Although similar to D4 (Mental Dullness), Sc3 emphasizes a disruption of thought processes by the intrusion of troubling thoughts, whereas the D4 content emphasizes disability that interferes with the completion of mental work. The MMPI-2 HEA content scale contains items sensitive to cognitive deficits, such as confusion and impaired judgment, but Sc3 should exceed the score on the HEA scale before giving an interpretation specific to Sc3. The high Sc3 scorer tends to have a sense of disability where thinking is concerned. High Sc3 scorers tend to experience more distress or discomfort by their cognitive deficits than high D4 scorers although the two scales frequently elevate as a pair. High Sc3 scores generally indicate individuals who feel they are losing their minds, report strange thought processes and feelings of unreality, and have trouble with concentration and memory functions. Graham reported in their outpatient psychiatric sample, that the high Sc3 scorer was described by their therapist as suffering acute psychological turmoil and as not coping well with stress.

Low scorers generally deny any difficulty with their thinking processes. Nine of the 10 items on this subscale are scored in the "true" direction, with 1 item scored as "false." The following items illustrate the content of Sc3, with the MMPI-2 item number preceding the item and the scoring direction in parentheses:

> *31. I find it hard to keep my mind on a task or job. (True) 32. I have had very peculiar and strange experiences. (True) 165. My memory seems to be all right. (False) 170. I'm afraid of losing my mind. (True) 180. There's something wrong with my mind. (True) 299. I cannot keep my mind on one thing. (True)*

Lack of Ego Mastery, Conative: Sc4 (14 Items)

Conation means an inclination to act purposively, which is exactly what high Sc4 scorers lack. This subscale consists of items that reflect the degree of lost motivation to behave in a constructive and productive fashion. High scorers have a sense of malfunction in their cognitive operations, such as attention, concentration, judgment, and memory, along with a withdrawal of interest, that leads to a lack of pleasure and interest in daily life. Caldwell stated that the items reflect an inability to mobilize one's energy, that it is tough to get going and focus one's mental energy. Indeed, this subscale appears to measure the psychic equivalent of psychomotor retardation (D2); in fact, Nichols and Greene viewed this subscale as being sensitive to a "general psychic disability". Wrobel found that clinician raters found feelings of psychological weakness to be a significant correlate for high Sc4 scorers. Typically, high scorers feel that life is a strain and may be experiencing depression, in that they have given up hope of things ever getting better. Some items reflect a tendency to withdraw into fantasy and daydreaming as an escape from stress, and one item (MMPI-2 Item 303, "Most of the time I wish I were dead") raises the question of suicidal apathy or despair. The inertia and lack of initiative high scorers experience lead to severe emotional alienation, in fact Sc4 overlaps heavily (eight items) with Sc2. High Sc4 scorers, however, can differ from the pure emotional alienation that high Sc2 scorers experience, in that Sc4 measures a lack of sustained mental focus and passive distractibility, which proceeds more from anergy and indifference than from the cognitive disruption that is often seen in the case of Sc3.

Sc4 may capture much of the essence of the Sc parent scale, as the two measures correlate highly ($r = .84$) in a sample of psychiatric inpatients and outpatients. Low Sc4 scores reflect a feeling that life is worthwhile, a denial of depression and suicidal ideation, and the feeling that one has enough energy for spontaneously initiating actions. Generally, the person is happy to be alive and does not complain of cognitive deficits.

The following items are examples of Sc4 content, with the MMPI-2 item number preceding the item and direction of scoring in parentheses. Eleven of the items are scored in the "true" direction, and 3 items are scored in the "false" direction:

> *9. My daily life is full of things that keep me interested. (False) 31. I find it hard to keep my mind on a task or job. (True) 32. I've had very peculiar and strange experiences. (True) 48. Most any time I would rather sit and daydream than do anything else. (True) 65. Most of the time I feel blue. (True) 210. I like to visit places where I have never been before. (False) 290. I worry over money and business. (False)*

Lack of Ego Mastery, Defective Inhibition: Sc5 (11 Items)

This subscale consists of items that emphasize a fear or dread of internal disintegration or loss of control. Graham reported that high scorers may feel restless, hyperactive, and irritable and may have periods of laughing/crying that they cannot control, as well as have episodes during which they did not know what they were doing.

Caldwell noted that Sc5 shares six items with Scale 9 (Ma) and that Sc5 is often elevated when Scales 8 and 9 are both elevated. Therefore, the potential for eruptions of uncontrollable rage are high when Sc5 is elevated. When Sc5 is elevated, the person may be vulnerable to being overwhelmed with rage affect and other scales should be examined in relation to this subscale to assess the potential for range full expressions of emotions. Nichols and Greene addressed this issue and made the following statement about how content scales in relation to Sc5 can be useful in this assessment:

Relative to ANG, TPA and Sc5 reflect a more chronic condition, one closer to concepts of hostility, rage, and resentment. Thus, ANG scores well above scores on TPA and Sc5 imply amore state-like anger. When elevations on TPA andSc5 equal or exceed the ANG score, however, anger is likely to operate in a trait-like fashion, with the respondent appearing to seek opportunities for discharge or to anticipate situations in which anger in one or more of the parties involved will be stimulated, if not expressed. The relations among the three scales (ANG, TPA, and SO) provide some basis for predicting the degree of focus that will characterize angry feelings and expressions: If ANG is greater than TPA and TPA is greater than Sc5, anger is likely to be tightly focused on specific issues, perceived offenses, or persons. The reverse pattern (Sc5 > TPA > ANG) implies blind or diffuse rage with appropriate targets determined largely by opportunity and convenience.

Graham findings of women clients with high Sc5 scores having a higher likelihood of a borderline personality disorder diagnosis is consistent with the rage and hostility associated with elevated Sc5 scores.

Low Sc5 scores reflect the self-perception that it takes a lot to get oneself excited, that one is well controlled and not restless or irritable. In essence, a low Sc5 score may indicate good control over one's impulses.

The following items are examples of Sc5 content with the scoring direction in parentheses and the MMPI-2 item number preceding the item. All 11 items on this subscale are scored in the "true" direction and are obvious (vs. subtle) making Sc5 vulnerable to response-style distortions (e.g., all true or all false response sets or fake-good or fake-bad response sets).

At times I have fits of laughing and crying that I cannot control. (True) 85. At times I have a strong urge to do something harmful or shocking. (True) 168. I have had periods in which I carried on activities without knowing later what I had been doing. (True) 218. I have periods of such great restlessness that I cannot sit long in a chair. (True) 274. I am so touchy on some participants that I can't talk about them. (True) 322. I am afraid of using a knife or anything very sharp or pointed. (True)

Sensorimotor Dissociation: Sc6 (20 Items)

This subscale covers a range of content that includes unexplainable bodily changes, like twitching, unusual weakness or numbness, blank spells, voice changes, loss of taste, ringing in the ears, feelings of depersonalization, and fits of laughing and crying. Sc6 is primarily focused on motor, sensory, and dissociative symptoms, and it is recommended that the content component scales, such as Gastrointestinal Symptoms (HEM), Neurological Symptoms (HEA2), and General Health Concerns (HEM), be examined to determine both the range of symptoms claimed and their level of intensity. It appears that high Sc6 scores reflect a deterioration of control in the way impulses are inhibited; the items reflect a certain loosening of ties to reality. However, the original name of the scale Bizarre Sensory Experiences does not appear to represent the scale content in its entirety. For this reason, the scale has been renamed Sensorimotor Dissociation, which appears to more accurately capture the nature of the subscale items. Nichols and Greene provided some much-needed clarification of this issue, stating that in the 1955 edition of their subscale manuscript, Harris and Lingoes designated Sc6 (Sc3 at that time) "bizarre sensory experiences." In their 1968 revision, however, the authors renamed this subscale "sensorimotor dissociation." The revised designation corresponds far more closely to the actual content of the items comprising Sc6. While many of the items on this subscale are unusual and a few reflect psychoticism (311, 319, 355), only one item (355) has possible bizarre connotations. The remaining items mostly reflect soft neurologic signs: sensory (252, 247, 255, 298), motor (23, 91, 106, 177, 179, 182, 295), and possible dissociation (168, 182, 229, 296, 311). (p. 31)

In general, high Sc6 scorers feel their bodies are changing in strange and unusual ways. They may report skin sensitivities, voice changes, muscle twitching, clumsiness, balance difficulties, ringing in their ears, and feelings of weakness and paralysis. Wrobel reported that a feeling of depersonalization was a significant correlate for the high Sc6 scorer in his sample of clients in therapy in a private outpatient facility. Low scorers tend to not report the occurrence of these symptoms and experiences.

The following items are examples of the Sc6 content, with the direction of scoring in parentheses and the MMPI-2 item number preceding the item. Fourteen of the items are scored in the "true" direction and 6 items are scored in the "false" direction:

23. *At times I have fits of laughing and crying that I cannot control. (True)*

32. *I've had very peculiar and strange experiences. (True)*

44. *Once a week or oftener I suddenly feel hot all over for no real reason. (True)*

91. *I have little or no trouble with my muscles twitching or jumping. (False)*

168. *I have had periods in which I carried on activities without knowing later what I had been doing. (True)*

177. *My hands have not become clumsy or awkward. (False)*

255. *I do not often notice my ears ringing or buzzing. (False)*

Scale 9: Hypomania (Ma)

Scale 9 consists of 46 items measuring the aspects of a mildly elevated mood that often is accompanied by a flight of ideas, affective lability, and psychornotor excitement. The personality pattern the scale reflects is the affective disorder termed hypomania. Hypomania indicates heightened activity levels with accompanying symptoms or traits such as easy distractibility, insomnia, over optimism, occasional grandiosity, suspiciousness, and irascibility. McKinley and Hathaway selected a group of 24 inpatients at the University of Minnesota Hospital as their criterion participants for constructing this scale. Unfortunately, no available demographic data are reported on the criterion participants. According to McKinley and Hathaway, only patients with less than a full-blown manic syndrome were usable, because the more severe cases could not participate fully in the task of sorting inventory items into the appropriate true, false, and Cannot Say categories: "The clinical diagnoses were either hypomania or mild acute mania, depending on the severity of the case". Hence, the scale name Hyponiania reflects this measure of a less than full-blown manic condition. It was important to derive a measure of more subtle or moderate cases of mania so that the condition could be identified early on to improve the prognosis and treatment options for the patient. Patients were excluded from study if they were delirious, confused, schizophrenic, or depressed with agitation. McKinley and Hathaway recognized the small number of cases in their criterion group and conceded that "in spite of the small number of criterion and test cases available, a scale for Hypomania is presented. It is the best that we could derive from the patients seen over a 5-year period".

Scale 9 is sensitive to expansive, elated, and euphoric mood states. Additionally, Nichols and Greene stated that "Ma reflects the ease of access that thoughts, feelings, and impulses have to the motor system. When Ma is elevated, motor readiness is high". The higher the elevation on Scale 9, the more energetic a person tends to be and the more compelled the individual feels to act in using that energy. In fact, as scale elevations increase, the more likely the person is to get over committed or over involved in activities. Nichols provided an excellent description of manic affect that can be useful in understanding Scale 9 elevations:

Affect is characteristically elated, euphoric, enthusiastic, expansive, triumphant, and disinhibited. The patient may present as playful, jocular, quick-witted, and high-spirited, free of all normal cares and concerns, in tip-top shape, and ready for action. This picture is unstable, however, and may change suddenly into one of anger and hostility if the patient is blocked in the pursuit of some goal, has his or her self-esteem challenged, experiences a rebuff, or in some other way feels thwarted. The patient often feels highly vulnerable to real or implied personal criticism even though he or she may be quite imperturbable regarding other matters. For a large minority of patients the dominant mood is one of irritability rather than elation and affect may be somewhat dysphoric. The patient may seem cantankerous and constantly in transit between flare-ups of litigiousness, contentiousness, and antagonism. Fear may emerge in some cases, usually relatively late in the manic episode, and may be related to reverses, rejections, and alienation, secondary to the reactions of friends, family, or staff to the patient's obnoxiousness. Major lapses in judgment, including sexual or financial indiscretions occurring early in the episode, which become clear to the patient, may also stimulate a fearful response. Finally, fear may be a reaction to the realization that the manic flight will soon expire and be supplanted by depression. Not uncommonly, such fears may reach delusional proportions and involve themes of retribution or of being poisoned (by medication, i.e., being slowed down to the point that depression may catch up).

High scores on Scale 9 tend to reflect a proclivity to distance oneself from personal distress either by running away or by acting out. There is a tendency to deny emotional distress and to shift these feelings to the motor sphere. Lewak hypothesized that the high Scale 9 scorer is protecting him- or herself against frustration and unhappiness associated with failure. They hypothesized that these individuals may have had parents with excessively high expectations, which led to internalized, anxious strivings. A significant Scale 9 elevation energizes behaviors, particularly those associated with other clinical scale elevations. For example, when the Ma scale is elevated with the Pd scale, acting out will occur with a possible antisocial focus. However, other scales, such as the Hy scale, need to be considered as the Ma scale "appears to play a role in determining both the frequency of acting out and the extent to which it will take an antisocial direction". Specifically, the Hy scale, when elevated with the Ma scale, tends to augment the expression of social interest such as through the observance of social propriety and approval seeking.

Caldwell viewed Scale 9 elevations as reflecting the degree of fear of future frustrations, which leads to a diminished capacity to enjoy the here and now. The person cannot relax as his or her future depends on Maintaining an increasing activity level in attempt to Maintain his or her reward schedule or avoid deprivation or failure.

The Ma scale content is heterogeneous and covers the classic features of a hypo Ma nic syndrome, such as excitement, heightened activity levels, expansiveness, and over ambitiousness or high aspirations. Other items describe extraversion, moral attitudes, family relationships, and bodily concerns. The following items illustrate the content of Scale 9. The MMPI-2 item number precedes the item, and the scoring direction is in parentheses.

15. *I work under a great deal of tension. (True)*

21. *At times I have very much wanted to leave home. (True)*

23. *At times I have fits of laughing and crying that I cannot control. (True)*

55. *I sometimes keep on at a thing until others lose their patience with me. (True)*

85. *At times I have a strong urge to do something harmful or shocking. (True)*

100. *I have never done anything dangerous for the thrill of it. (False)*

154. *I am afraid when I look down from a high place. (False)*

169. *When I get bored I like to stir up some excitement. (True)*

263. *I am always disgusted with the law when a criminal is freed through the arguments of a smart lawyer. (False)*

Patients with only mild affective symptoms may be difficult to distinguish from ambitious, energetic normal. Therefore, it is important to observe periods of euphoria, increased irritability, and unproductive activity to assist in making an accurate diagnosis. Nichols pointed out the importance of retesting individuals suspected of having an affective disorder as the variability in their mood state will influence their MMPI-2 profile. For example, a psychiatric inpatient may initially test without a Scale 9 elevation if he or she is depressed but, on later retesting, may show an elevated Scale 9 score suggestive of mood instability. Scale 9 does in fact figure prominently in code patterns associated with mood disorders, especially those with Manic correlates. Code patterns 49/94, 69/96, and 89/98 all contribute to a diagnosis of Mania. The setting can often determine the diagnoses associated with MMPI-2 profiles. For example, Marks classified approximately 70% of their female psychiatric inpatients with the 89/98 code pattern as psychotic (schizophrenic/mixed) and 17% of them were diagnosed as psychoneurotic (depressive reaction). Raskin and Novacek administered MMPIs and the Narcissistic Personality Inventory to undergraduate students. The highest scorers on the measure of narcissism were best represented by the 98/89 code pattern (with an average elevated F score of T = 65). This code pattern in a normal population appears to reflect narcissism and Manic defenses rather than Mania per se.

Low scores on Scale 9 reflect a low energy or activity level. Kunce and Anderson viewed zest as an underlying dimension of Scale 9. Therefore, low Scale 9 scores reflect a lack of vitality or even depression. Low Scale 9 scorers May feel chronically tired, have trouble performing their work, or even be temporarily ill. Low Scale 9 scorers are not likely to stir up excitement or be too talkative. They may feel empty or depleted, and lack self-confidence and motivation.

Dahlstrom reported the correlates of Hathaway and Meehl 's investigation of normal men and women. Sociability, energy, and openness appeared to be the major theme characterizing men, which is consistent with the optimism factor that McKinley and Hathaway described as a stable factor in normals. These men were further described as talkative, impulsive, adventurous, curious, generous, affectionate, and sentimental. Women were described similarly and were also seen as frank, courageous, idealistic, and possessing high energy as reflected by the adjectives talkative, enthusiastic, and versatile.

Butcher and Williams reported data from the couples rating study in the MMPI restandardization project. Husbands of high Scale 9 scorers viewed their wives as wearing unusual clothes, talking too much, stirring up excitement, taking many risks, getting excited or happy for little reason, and telling people off. Wives viewed their high Scale 9 husbands as acting bossy, talking too much, whining and demanding attention, and taking drugs other than those prescribed by a doctor.

As Duckworth and Anderson noted, it is common to see peak Scale 9 (and Scale 5 in men) scores in college students. It is important to examine the elevation of Scale 9 in Making an appropriate interpretation. When a person with a high score is generally well-adjusted, the appropriate descriptors for Scale 9 would be enthusiastic, eager, talkative, versatile, driven to be successful and involved, and friendly and happy. As scores increase, however, expect to see Maladaptive hyperactivity and agitation.

Scores on Scale 9 tend to be related to age, with older individuals obtaining lower scores (reflecting lower energy and activity levels and more body concerns) and late-adolescent or younger participants, such as teenagers, tending to score in the upper normal to moderate range, which could be considered indicative of impulse control problems. Age should, therefore, be considered when examining Scale 9. Consistent results have not emerged regarding the effects of race on scale scores. But Gynther described various demographic effects on MMPI scales, and African Americans do appear to score higher than Whites, although not dramatically so.

Scale 9 did not lose any items in the restandardization project. However, seven items were changed; four items had sexist wording modified, two items were modernized, and one item had a grammatical clarification. Thirty-five of the 46 items are scored in the "true" direction, and 11 items are scored in the "false" direction. As the predominant deviant response to the items is "true," as it is for the other psychotic scales, an all true-response set would elevate Scale 9 with the other scales in the psychotic tetrad. Other than Scale 8, with which it shares 11 overlap items, Scale 9 shares few overlapping items relative to the other scales. Fifteen of the 46 items are unique to the scale. According to J. W. Little, the highest bi serial correlation for any item was .48 on the item "At times I have very much wanted to leave home" (NIMPI-2 Item 21), with two other items tied with similar correlations of .45. These items were "I don't blame anyone for trying to grab everything they can get in this world" (MMPI-2 Item 227) and "I do not blame a person for taking advantage of people who leave themselves open to it" (MMPI-2 Item 248). It is likely that these low correlations reflect the heterogeneity of the scale.

It should be noted that an examination of the mean lexile values (lexile is a special index of reading difficulty and comprehension) for the basic scales shows Scale 9 to have the most difficult items to read and understand of all the clinical scales. For example, the Harris-Lingoes subscale Amorality (Ma1) has a reading level of about the ninth grade. Reading level requirements, but in general the MMPI-2 manual recommends an eighth grade reading level for taking the MUTI-2. According to Paolo, Ryan and Smith, for clinicians who are working with populations whose members possess average reading skills of eighth or ninth grade, the Hypomania (Ma) subscales, and possibly the Hypomania clinical scale itself, should be interpreted cautiously. At the very least, clinicians should determine whether individual patients are able to read and comprehend adequately the more difficult items on these scales.

Commercially available profile sheets provide for adding 0.2 K to Scale 9 as this value has been shown to increase the ability of the scale to make accurate diagnostic discriminations.

Internal consistency estimates (alphas) for MMPI-2 Scale 9 based on the restandardization sample are .58 for men and .60 for women. Test-retest correlation coefficients for Scale 9 in the restandardization sample over an interval of about 1 week were .83 for men and .68 for women. Test-retest correlation coefficients for MMPI Scale 9 for psychiatric cases with a 1- to 2-day interval between tests ranged from .71 to .81 and from .43 to .52 with a 1-year interval between tests. Hunsley 's large-scale meta-analysis of MMPI reliability studies using a diversity of populations conducted between 1970 and 1981 reported an average internal consistency of .71 across 73 studies of Scale 9.

They also reported an average test-retest reliability of .65 for 17 studies with time intervals from 1 day to 2 years.

Harris-Lingoes Subscales

Harris and Lingoes developed four subscales for Scale 9: Amorality (Ma1), Psychomotor Acceleration (Ma2), Imperturbability (Ma3), and Ego Inflation (Ma4).

Amorality: Mal (6 Items)

This short six-item subscale has five items scored in the "true" direction. Caldwell believed that the scale is better named as Opportunism, given that high scorers on this subscale see others as selfish, dishonest, and opportunistic and feel justified to behave in a similar fashion. They also tend to derive vicarious gratification from the exploitative ways of others. Nichols and Greene viewed Mal as reflecting a kind of "thoughtless expediency" that can put others at a disadvantage and as a somewhat subtle measure of cynicism. According to Levitt, high scorers believe that a person is foolish not to take every possible advantage of every situation and, as selfish people, see life as an endless series of minor skirmishes in which the person who is not overburdened with scruples is usually victorious.

Graham reported the following information for high scorers (T ? 65) on Mal in their sample of psychiatric outpatients. Both men and women reported a history of alcohol abuse within the last 6 months preceding their intake interview; women patients were more likely to have an Axis I diagnosis (DSM III-R) of substance abuse or dependence and an Axis I diagnosis of antisocial personality disorder. During intake interviews, men with high scores were described as having an angry mood and their therapists indicated that they had tendencies to act out. This is consistent with their higher frequency of being physically abusive, committing domestic violence, and the greater likelihood of having a domestic violence conviction.

Low Mal scorers (0 or a raw score of 1) may have moral values emphasizing individual responsibility and control over oneself and may also reflect a lack of cynicism in the individual.

The following six items represent the entire Mal content. The MNVI-2 item number precedes the item, with the scoring direction in parentheses:

131. When I was a child, I belonged to a group of friends that tried to be loyal through all kinds of trouble. (True)

227. I don't blame people for trying to grab everything they can get in this world. (True)

248. I do not blame a person for taking advantage of people who leave themselves open to it. (True)

250. At times I have been so entertained by the cleverness of some criminals that I have hoped that they would get away with it. (True)

263. I am always disgusted with the law when a criminal is freed through the arguments of a smart lawyer. (False)

269. If several people find themselves in trouble, the best thing for them to do is to agree upon a story and stick to it. (True)

Psychomotor Acceleration: ma2 (11 Items)

Although the items in this subscale are manic in nature, they do not appear to reflect a negative tension state or unwanted arousal. The Wiggins HYP content scale is a better measure of excessive or undesired excitability. Although the behaviors implied by the items in this subscale are unusual in nature, the item content is not strongly suggestive of psychosis. Generally, high scorers report accelerated speech, thought processes, and motor activities and may report tension, restlessness, and excitement. High scorers are easily bored and may look for stimulation in order to change their mood state. Wrobel reported hyperactivity as a significant correlate for this subscale. Levitt viewed Ma2 as a sensation-seeking measure, with high scorers having a high optimal stimulation level. These individuals may have a significant need for a variety of experiences. If Scale 9 is significantly elevated, it is likely that Ma2 will also be elevated.

Graham found in their sample of psychiatric outpatients that high scoring women on Ma2 (T ? 65) were more likely to have a diagnosis of borderline personality disorder. Male patients were more likely to report a history of being physically abusive and to have a history of committing domestic violence.

Low Ma2 scores may reflect a slow, cautious pace or tempo and may be indicative of a low general level of excitement in one's life. Nichols and Greene suggested that a low Ma2 score may indicate psychomotor retardation, whereas a low Scale 9 score, with an elevated Ma2 score, may not report a loss of energy. Low Ma2 scorers may also deny any tension or hyperactivity and not desire excitement. In fact, they may altogether avoid situations or activities involving risk or danger.

The following items illustrate the item content of Ma2. Nine of the 11 items are scored in the "true" direction, and 2 items are scored in the "false" direction:

15. I work under a great deal of tension. (True)

85. At times I have a strong urge to do something harmful or shocking. (True)

100. I have never done anything dangerous for the thrill of it. (False)

106. My speech is the same as always (not faster or slower, no slurring or hoarseness). (False)

122. At times my thoughts have raced ahead faster than I could speak them. (False)

169. When I get bored I like to stir up some excitement. (True)

Imperturbability: Ma3 (8 Items)

The items on this subscale suggest that one is not bothered by interruptions, distractions, and tensions and a certain quality of imperviousness is reflected in the items. Ma3 could be considered as subtle in nature as seven of the eight items are scored on the Ma-S subscale. Five of the eight items are scored in the "false" direction. High Ma3 scorers deny social anxiety in a manner similar to high Hy1 (Denial of Social Anxiety) scorers. High Ma3 scores reflect a socially comfortable person who feels secure interacting with others with little concern about the opinions, values, and attitudes of others. Extraversion appears to be related to high Ma3 scores, although Ma3 is not a direct measure of this factor. Nichols and Greene described the high Ma3 scorer as not being afraid to be socially visible. They also saw Ma3 as reflecting dispassion ("cool") and composure under difficult social stresses. Successful individuals may elevate this scale. Caldwell said that " Ma3 is often the predominant subscale in controlled striving and performance-oriented patterns such as a relatively unelevated code 39/93 with K up". Likewise, the Graham investigation of MMPI-2 correlates in a psychiatric outpatient population failed to identify pathological correlates for elevated Ma3 scores.

Low scores may reflect an impatience at being interrupted or distracted and a self-conscious hesitation in groups. Low scorers often feel uncomfortable in the presence of others and are easily influenced by people's opinions, values, and attitudes. Levitt viewed low scores as reflecting anxious, shy, easy-to-embarrass individuals who are uncomfortable in social situations.

The following items illustrate the item content of Ma3. The MMPI-2 item number precedes the item, and the scoring direction is in parentheses:

93. Sometimes when I am not feeling well I am irritable. (False)

136. It makes me impatient to have people ask my advice or otherwise interrupt me when I am on something important. (False)

167. I find it hard to make talk when I meet new people. (False)

220. I never worry about my looks. (True)

Ego Inflation: ma4 (9 Items)

The nine items of this relatively short subscale are all scored in the "true" direction; therefore, a "true" response bias could inflate this subscale. This subscale reflects the grandiosity so typical of the manic or hypomanic individual, and high scorers usually have unrealistic appraisals of their own abilities and self-worth. They tend to become resentful when people make demands on them or are bossy toward them. The items on this subscale appear to suggest anger when one's importance is not appreciated and there is an underlying theme of "willful stubbornness". Nichols and Greene reported that Ma4 reflects a quality of willfulness and bravado and often the individual appears to be defending him- or herself against passivity and dependency by behaving in a counter dependent or counter submissive fashion (e.g., asserting dominance in an overt fashion). High Ma4 scores also connote a sense of superiority and contempt for others. Graham found that female psychiatric outpatients with high scores on Ma4 (T 565) were viewed as sociopathic by their therapists with narcissistic and histrionic features. Difficult to motivate, they were described as easily bored and impatient.

Low scores reflect interpersonal submissiveness with a willingness to accept arbitrary treatment from others. A low Ma4 score, coupled with an elevated Sc2 (Emotional Alienation) score, suggests apathy and psychological impotence. The low scorer is more likely to show a willingness to tolerate domineering behavior in others. There is also a certain modesty regarding their self-importance, making it easier for them to accept orders without objection. Low Ma4 scores may reflect an individual who is also very self-critical.

The following items are examples of the Ma4 content. The MMPI-2 item number precedes the item, and the scoring direction is in parentheses.

50. I have often had to take orders from someone who did not know as much as I did. (True)

55. I sometimes keep on at things until others lose their patience with me. (True)

61. I am an important person. (True)

98. Some people are so bossy that I feel like doing the opposite of what they request, even though I know they are right. (True)

190. My people treat me more like a child than a grownup. (True)

211. I have been inspired to a program of life based on duty which I have since carefully followed. (True)

Scale 9: Subtle-Obvious Subscales

Wiener and Harmon developed Subtle and Obvious subscales for Scale 9 in the MMPI. The MMPI-2 Hypornania-Obvious subscale (Ma-O) has 23 items, of which 20 items are scored in the "true" direction and 3 items are scored in the "false" direction. The Hypomania-Subtle subscale (Ma-S) also consists of 23 items, of which 15 items are scored in the "true" direction and 8 items are scored in the "false" direction. The following items are examples of the subtle-obvious items on Scale 9, with the scoring direction and obvious or subtle distinction in parentheses; the MMPI-2 item number precedes the item.

15. I work under a great deal of tension. (True-Obvious)

23. At times I have fits of laughing and crying that I cannot control. (True-Obvious)

100. I have never done anything dangerous for the thrill of it. (False-Obvious)

106. My speech is the same as always (not faster or slower, no slurring or hoarseness). (False-Subtle)

113. I know who is responsible for most of my troubles. (True-Subtle)

169. When I get bored I like to stir up some excitement. (True-Subtle)

263. I am always disgusted with the law when a criminal is freed through the arguments of a smart lawyer. (False-Subtle)

The majority of obvious items on the Ma-O subscale pertain to episodes of intense excitement and periods of great restlessness, with excitement, impulse pressures, and vigilance predominating. Hollrah reviewed the research of Wrobel and Lachar, which examined the correlates for the Subtle and Obvious subscales. The Ma-O subscale correlated positively with the factors labeled Discomfort and Sociopathy, although discomfort was a less than optimal scale descriptor, as it correlated with all of the obvious subscales. Nevertheless, the description of the Ma-O item content given by Caldwell is consistent with the finding of Discomfort and, to a lesser extent, with Sociopathy. Clearly, other MMPI-2 measures, such as Antisocial Practices (ASP), Cynicism (CYN) and Antisocial Attitudes should be examined to help establish the presence of sociopathy.

Dahlstrom examined the correlates of the Subtle and Obvious subscales derived from partner ratings on the Katz Adjustment Scales used in the MMPI-2 restandardization. For both men and women, the following descriptors emerged as significant for high Ma-O scorers: nervous, does not go to religious functions, moody, and does not show sound judgment. For men only, the following descriptors were given: takes nonprescription drugs, whines and demands attention, prone to temper tantrums, suspicious of others, swears and curses, not pleasant and relaxed, upset by small unexpected events, talks back, acts without thinking, and is not thoughtful of others. For women only, the following descriptors were given: restless, has many fears, does strange things, has bad dreams, lacks emotional control, gets excited or happy for no reason, worries about the future, not helpful or constructive, talks too much, bored and restless, takes too many risks, cries easily, wears strange clothes, gives up too easily, and tells others off about their faults.

Low Ma-O scorers suggest a constrained sense of self-importance, an absence or careful avoidance of intense excitement in one's life, and possibly a strict but integrated individual conscience.

Although some of the Ma-S items clearly reflect hypomania (e.g., "When I get bored I like to stir up some excitement"), other items indicating a denial of anxiety (mostly occurring on Ma3) appear to be more subtle in nature (Caldwell, 1988). Examples of such items include "I never worry about my looks" (scored as "true"), and "I find it hard to make talk when I meet new people" (scored as "false"). The variety in the content of the Ma-S subscale makes it difficult to summarize, but Caldwell stated that much of the content relates to a "heightened level of arousability and interpersonal assertiveness that is similar to but less disruptive than Ma-O ".

Hollrah in a thorough review of the validity of the subtle items in the MMPI, stated that of all the subtle subscales the Ma-S subscale showed the best validity: " Ma-S was consistently related to scale-appropriate external measures and occasionally had more validity than ma-full and Ma-O ". He suggested that the convergent validity of the ma-S subscale is due to the subtle items obvious relationship to hypomania.

Dahlstrom derived the following correlates for the Ma-S subscale for both men and women from the partner ratings made in the MMPI-2 restandardization sample: not shy, talks too much, makes big plans, talks back, tells others off about their faults, stubborn, gets excited or happy for no reason, takes too many risks, and gives advice too freely. For men only, the following correlates were derived: bossy, craves attention, does not lack energy, does strange things, has temper tantrums, reports bad dreams, resents being told what to do, apathetic about others' feelings, does the opposite of what is asked, takes nonprescription drugs, has been arrested or had trouble with the law, likes to flirt, acts without thinking, stirs up excitement, expresses a belief in strange things, whines and demands attention, laughs and jokes with others, volunteers for projects, and enjoys parties and friends. For women only, the following correlates were derived: wears strange clothes, tries too hard, resents being told what to do, does not avoid contact with others, does not show sound judgment, stirs up excitement, brags too much, threatens to harm others, and takes advantage of others.

A low Ma-S score suggests a high level of interpersonal constraint and social caution consistent with a slow personal pace.

Scale 0: Social Introversion (SI)

The original 70-item Social Introversion scale was designed to evaluate an individual's degree of introversion-extraversion. The Si scale is the only clinical scale in the MWI for which the criterion group was composed of a non psychiatric (normal) sample. Its construction was motivated by the use of a test being routinely administered in the guidance program at the University of Wisconsin. This test, developed by C. Evans and McConnell, was designated as the Minnesota T-S-E (Thinking-Social-Emotional) Inventory. Evans and McConnell separated the character traits of introversion-extraversion into areas of thinking, social activity, and emotional expression. An individual could be considered as introverted or extraverted in any of these three areas. Because the MMPI was also part of the standard battery of tests being administered to students, Drake decided to devise a scale measuring social introversion from the MMPI that would produce data similar to the T-S-E Inventory. Two criterion groups were selected. The first group consisted of 50 female students ranking at the

65th percentile or higher on the social introversion-extraversion dimension of the T-S-E Inventory; the second group consisted of 50 female students who scored below the 35th percentile. Three participants scoring high on the L scale of the MMPI were excluded from the criterion groups. Although the scale was constructed with all of the female students, it was later validated with men. Because men and women scored so similarly, Drake combined them as a single group for purposes of establishing the norms. The items in the MMPI pool that differentiated these two groups (after removing items with very high or very low endorsement frequencies in either or both groups) became the 70-item Social I.E. scale, later known as Scale 0 on the MMPI.

After the 70 items were identified that discriminated the two criterion groups, a new group of MMPI record sheets were scored with the new scoring key for social introversion-extraversion. As Drake noted, "these MMPI record sheets contain the responses of a group of students who had cleared through the testing office after the group of students who provided the data for the item analyses". The scores were then correlated with the Social I.E. scores obtained on the T-S-E Inventory and yielded a correlation coefficient of -.72 for a sample of 87 female students and -.71 for a sample of 81 male students. The correlation coefficients yielded negative values because a low score on the T-S-E Inventory indicates introversion, whereas a high score on the MMPI/MWI-2 indicates introversion.

Norms were reported in terms of linear T scores and were based on the test records of 193 male students and 350 female students. As stated previously, men's and women's scores were so similar that the norms were combined for both genders. In a subsequent study, Drake and Thiede obtained additional cross-validation for Scale 0 by examining the level of high school and college activity participation in a sample of 594 female college students. Students tending to participate in more activities scored higher on extraversion, whereas those with lower activity participation scored higher on introversion. The developers of the Minnesota T-S-E Inventory conceptualized social introversion as indicating a withdrawal from social responsibilities and contacts, with little real interest in people, and social extraversion as involving an interest in social contact, with a strong interest in others. The final Si scale may be limited by any of the biases inherent in the T-S-E Inventory because the criterion groups of social introverts and extraverts were derived from scores on the Social I.E. scale.

Elevated scores on Scale 0 (T > 50) indicate introversion tendencies, whereas scores below a T score of 50 indicate extraversion tendencies. The item content of the scale broadly reflects a dimension of introversion-extraversion that emerges as a primary dimension from statistical studies of the MMPI. The items reflect uneasiness in social situations; feelings of inferiority and discomfort; unhappiness, shyness, and hypersensitivity. Two broad content domains of Scale 0 have been identified as shyness and self-consciousness, which is the Subjective aspect of introversion, and social avoidance, the objective or socially visible part of introversion. As described in the Scale 5 section of this chapter, Graham factor analyzed the responses to Scale 0 (and Scale 5) from 422 psychiatric inpatients, outpatients, and normals. They identified seven Scale 0 factors, of which six were used by Serkownek to construct subscales for Scale 0 (and Scale 5). The seventh factor, Demographic Variables, was not used to construct a subscale. The Scale 0 subscales were named Inferiority-Personal Discomfort (Sil,) Discomfort With Others (Si2), Staid-Personal Rigidity (Si3,) Hypersensitivity (Si4), Distrust (Si5), and Physical-Somatic Concerns (Si6). As Greene pointed out, clinicians can continue to use the Serkownek subscales on the MMPI-2 as only 1 item has been dropped from Scale 0, which reduced Si2 from 14 to 13 items. Graham reported test-retest reliability coefficients for men and women (over a 6-week interval) provided by Moreland (1985). For men, on all of the Serkownek subscales, the coefficients range from .68 to .89, with an average of .77. For women, the range is from .63 to .87, with an average of .76. C. L. Williams (1983) reported 1-week test-retest reliabilities for Si subscales averaging .84 for women and .68 for men.

In a large-scale study, Foerstner investigated the interrelationships among the 63 MMPI subscales developed by Serkownek, Harris and Lingoes, Wiggins and Wiener and Harmon. (Note that neither Harris and Lingoes, nor Wiener and Harmon developed subscales for Scale 0 or Scale 5.) Nine hundred MMPIs from male and female psychiatric inpatients, chemical-dependent residents, and private practice outpatients were analyzed by Foerstner. Ten factors were identified that accounted for 75.5% of the total variance. SN (Hypersensitivity) loaded on the first factor, Depression (.67), as did Sil (Inferiority-Personal Discomfort; .65) and Si5 (Distrust; .44). Si3 (Staid-Personal Rigidity) loaded negatively on the factor named Social Introversion. Sil also loaded on the third factor, Agitated Hostility (.64). Si5 loaded on the factor Cynical Distrust (.63). It is clear from the data in Foerstner's investigation that Scale 0 (like Scale 5) is multi factorial and that maladjustment is a major component of the scale. A Scale 0 score, whether high or low, may be achieved by item endorsements affecting any of a combination of at least six factors. In contrast to the nonpathological correlates for the Serkownek Mf subscales, the Si subscales, with the exception of Si3, appear pathology related.

More recently, Ben-Porath, Hostetler, Butcher and Graham developed three new content-homogeneous subscales for the

MMPI-2 Si scale. They used a multistage approach involving a series of empirical and rational procedures to develop the subscales. These subscales -- named Shyness/Self-Consciousness (Sil,) Social Avoidance (Si2), and Self-Other Alienation (Si3) were developed with data provided by college students. Data analysis with this and the MMPI-2 normative sample demonstrated that these new measures combined to contribute to the assessment of nearly 90% of the variance in the full Si scale. Validation of these MMPI-2 Si subscales was provided by the results of Sieber and Meyers. These investigators compared results on the Si subscales against self-report measures of constructs that were believed to be differentially related to the three subscales. They stated that:

> *specifically, measures of self-esteem, public self-consciousness, social anxiety, and slyness were expected to correlate with Sil; measures of self-esteem, public self-consciousness, social anxiety, and social avoidance were expected to correlate with Si2; finally, measures of self-esteem, alienation, anornia, loss of control, and personal and social identity were expected to correlate with Si3.*

These hypotheses were generally supported by the data. It appears that elevated Sil scores reflect shyness around others, uneasiness in social surroundings, and discomfort in unfamiliar situations. High Si2 scores appear to reflect an active avoidance of others, a dislike of group situations, and an aversion to social events. High Si3 scorers appear to have low self-esteem, a lack of interest in activities, low self-confidence, and to not feel in control of their life outcomes.

Most recently, Ward and Perry investigated the Si subscales and found that, as in previous research, the three Si subscales accounted well for variance in Si scores in clinical samples. Si3 items were found to be less obvious indicators of social introversion as compared with Sil and Si2 items; Si3 appears to be more of a measure of the general maladjustment factor of the MMPI-2. Ward and Perry cautioned users of the Si subscales to recognize that Sil and Si2 are purer measurements of the social introversion construct and are not reflective of negative emotionality. In fact, they pointed out that the item content of Sil and Si2 is virtually the same as that from the SOD content scale.

Although Scale 0 lost only one item in the revision of the MMPI-2, six items were modified to modernize idioms and usage of words, improve grammatical clarification, simplify wording in the items. There is a fairly even balance of "true" and "false" scoring for this scale, with 34 of the 69 items scored in the "true" direction and 35 items scored in the "false" direction. For both men and women the assignment of 1 raw point increases a person's score in the direction of introversion. In other words, the higher one's raw score, the more introverted one tends to be.

The following items represent the broad content of Scale 0. The MMPI-2 item number precedes each item, and the scoring direction is in parentheses.

> *25. I would like to be a singer. (False) 49. I am a very sociable person. (False) 56. I wish I could be as happy as others seem to be. (True) 79. I do not mind being made fun of. (False) 100. I have never done anything dangerous for the thrill of it. (True) 135. I have often lost out on things because I couldn't make up my mind soon enough. (True) 161. I frequently have to fight against showing that I am bashful. (True) 207. I would like to belong to several clubs. (False)*

Scale 0 has proportionately fewer overlapping items than any other validity or clinical scale. Forty-three of the items on the scale overlap other scales, with the Pd and Mf scales sharing the most items with the Si scale (11 and 9 items, respectively). The L and F scales share no items in common with Scale 0. Twenty-six of the items are non-overlapping items. It should be noted that, like Scale 5, Scale 0 uses linear, rather than uniform, T scores.

Many researchers and clinicians believe strong constitutional and biological factors contribute to the introversion-extraversion dimension of personality. The stability of scores on this scale over time seem to reflect this biological and/or constitutional component. Test-retest correlation coefficients support this contention, with generally high test-retest coefficients for the scale. For psychiatric patients, the coefficients range from .80 to .88 for a 1- to 2-week interval between MMPI administrations and from .63 to .64 for a 1-year interval between tests. In Hunsley 's large-scale meta-analysis of MMPI reliability studies using a wide variety of populations conducted between 1970 and 1981, an average test-retest reliability of .86 for 16 studies with time intervals from 1 day to 2 years was reported. More recently test-retest reliability data were reported for the MMTI-2 scales over about a 1-week interval. Scale 0 test-retest correlation coefficients were .92 for men and .91 for women, and were the highest correlation coefficients reported for any of the validity or clinical scales.

In the Hunsley meta-analysis study of the MMPI, an average internal consistency of. .81 across 41 studies of Scale 0 was reported. The MMPI-2 Manual reports internal consistency estimates (coefficient alpha) of .82 and .84 for men and women, respectively, on Scale 0.

Scale 0 reflects how comfortable an individual is around other people. High scores (introversion) reflect a preference for being alone, whereas low scores (extraversion) reveal a preference for being with others. It is important to examine other clinical scales when Scale 0 is high or low because Scale 0 can operate as an activator or inhibitor for certain behaviors. For example, a high Scale 8 score will indicate more social isolation and communication problems when Scale 0 is also elevated. A very low Scale 0 score will accentuate the impulsivity often seen in high Scale 4 scorers and indicate a superficiality and shallowness in relationships. Individuals with impoverished social relations, as is often seen in schizoid or certain other personality disorders, tend to elevate Scale 0. Lewak stated that elevated Si scores may reflect a childhood characterized by an absence of warmth and physical contact from others. Elevated scores suggest that these people have extinguished their feeling response to physical touch and affection. They suffer from a form of "affect hunger" and yet, they feel conflicted about close, intimate relationships.

Lewak also suggested that low Si scores reflect more than just social extraversion. Rather, a low score (T > 40) suggests an intense need for social stimulation driven more by insecurity than a proclivity for intense social experiences.

Hathaway and Meehl examined the descriptions of high Scale 0 scorers. Men were described by their acquaintances with only one typical adjective, modest. Dahlstrom suggested that perhaps the introverted personality style of these men made it difficult for others to get to know them and, therefore, characterize them more fully. In contrast, women scoring high on the Si scale were described as modest, shy, self-effacing, and sensitive. They showed emotional warmth and had home and family interests. Dahlstrom made the important point that the personality styles of these individuals appear to reflect the basic preference for a style of life in keeping with their emotional needs, rather than individuals who are inhibited or thwarted in their efforts to have broader social contacts.

Dahlstrom also presented the research descriptions of high-and low-scoring men on Scale 0 provided by Gough More maladjustment appears inherent in the following description as compared with the Hathaway and Meehl depiction of the introvert:

> *The high 0 men were described as slow in personal tempo, stereotyped, and lacking originality in approach to problems. The implication seems to be that these men showed such qualities as part of a general insecurity. They were also described as unable to make decisions without vacillation, hesitation, or delay. They were seen as rigid and inflexible in thought and action, as overly controlled and inhibited, and as lacking confidence in their own abilities. They were conforming and followed prescribed methods in the things they did. They became fussy and pedantic in even minor matters.*

In their relations with others, they were seen as lacking poise and social presence, as becoming rattled and upset in a social situation. Perhaps as a consequence, these men were rated as cold and distant. They were not affected in this aloofness, but appeared free of pretense and conscientiousness and dependable in their responsibilities. They seemed to derive personal reward and pleasure from their work and placed a high value on productive achievement for its own sake. Toward authority, these men were submissive, compliant, and overly accepting. They tended to sidestep as a way of handling troublesome situations. They either made concessions to avoid unpleasantness or passively resisted pressures by not getting involved in things. They were generally permissive and accepting, however, in their relations with others, respecting other people, and not making judgments. As a result, these high 0 men kept out of trouble and showed socially appropriate behavior. They get along well in the world as it is.

Low-scoring men (extraverts) in the normal group examined by Hathaway and Meehl were described as versatile and sociable, whereas low-scoring women, also described as mixing well with others, were also seen as enthusiastic, talkative, assertive, and adventurous. Gough described men scoring low on Scale 0 in more unfavorable terms than did Hathaway and Meehl. Although male low scorers were seen as expressive and colorful, they were also described as ostentatious and exhibitionistic. They focused on success as a means for achieving status and power. Competitive and vigorous, they were dominant in relation to others. They could be opportunistic in that they viewed others only in terms of what they could get from them, rather than being sensitive to their feelings. Self-indulgent and unable to delay gratification, they were often impulsive, acting without sufficient deliberation. Their actions could easily stimulate hostility and resentment around them.

3

Screening Psychiatric Disorder in Primary Care

Introduction

Estimates of occurrence in medical populations place prevalence rates substantially higher than community estimates. Barrett, Barrett, Oxman, and Gerber reported rates of between 25% and 30% in their research, whereas Derogatis and Wise in their review summarized overall rates at between 22% and 33%. Similar rates were reported more recently by Hansson, Nettelbladt, Borgquist, and Nordstrom and Olfson. The large majority of these conditions are comprised of anxiety and depressive disorders, which can be difficult to identify and diagnose.

Psychiatric disorders represent a significant and serious public health problem in their own right; however, when they exist in a comorbid fashion with primary medical disorders, the health care liability associated with them grows dramatically. Such comorbid conditions have a long list of undesirable features associated with them, including atypical responses to treatment, high side effects rates, increased numbers of medical events, longer durations of hospital stay, failure to adhere to treatment regimens, increased utilization rates, and significantly higher costs. In addition, because patients with comorbid conditions, when identified, are undergoing multiple treatment regimens simultaneously, the possibility of undesirable drug interactions is increased.

The latter issue, concerning complications arising from multiple treatment regimens, logically rests on the assumption that comorbid psychiatric disorders are routinely identified, an assumption that is not supported by the facts. A vexing feature of these comorbid disorders is that this assumption is only sometimes met, because the identification of psychiatric disorders in primary care is extremely problematic, often hampering their effective treatment and disposition.

Psychiatric Disorders In Primary Care

The incentive for the development and systematic implementation of effective psychiatric screening in primary care derives not only from the increases in morbidity and mortality associated with undetected psychiatric disorders, but also from several additional considerations. First, it is well established that between two-thirds and three-quarters of individuals with psychiatric disorders either go completely untreated or are treated by nonpsychiatric physicians; these individuals are never seen by a mental health professional. Second, although a significant comorbidity exists between physical illness and psychiatric disorder, the detection by primary care physicians of the most prevalent psychiatric disorders (i.e., anxiety and depressive disorders) is far less than comprehensive. It is not rare to find recognition rates in medical cohorts falling below 50%. Third, given the documented increases in rates of health care utilization and health care costs attendant on undetected cases of psychiatric disorder, the implementation of systematic psychiatric screening in primary care would almost certainly result in a significant savings in health care expenditures. Finally, and perhaps most importantly, those individuals in our communities who are currently afflicted with undetected psychiatric disorders would be identified earlier in the course of their illnesses, enabling the initiation of effective treatment before the pervasive morbidity associated with chronicity sets in.

Problems Unique to Psychiatric Disorders

The prototypic psychiatric disorder is a hypothetical construct, with few if any pathognomonic clinical or laboratory signs and a pathophysiology and etiology that are only vaguely discernible. For these reasons, unique problems arise in the detection of psychiatric disorders, particularly in medical patients. The most prominent confound arises from the fact that the highly prevalent anxiety and depressive disorders often present with complaints of multiple somatic symptoms, which are difficult to differentiate from those arising from verifiable physical causes. Schurman, Kramer, and Mitchell indicated that 72% of visits to primary care doctors resulting in a psychiatric diagnosis present with somatic symptoms as the primary complaint. Katon and Bridges and Goldberg both indicated that presentation with somatic symptoms as primary complaints is a key reason for misdiagnosis of psychiatric disorders in primary care. In their study of high health care utilizers, Katon reported that the high health care utilization group had elevated SCL-90-R scores of almost a standard deviation, not only on the anxiety and depression subscales, but on the somatization subscale as well.

A second problem has to do with the misperception of clinical depressions as demoralization reactions. The courses of many chronic illnesses, particularly those that inevitably result in mortality, are characterized by a period of disaffection and demoralization. These negative affective responses are a natural reaction to the loss of vitality and well-being associated with being chronically ill and, in some instances, with the anticipated loss of life itself. Physicians familiar with caring for such patients (e.g., cancer, emphysema, renal diseases) can often misperceive true clinical depressions (for which effective treatments are available) as reactive states of demoralization that are a natural part of the illness. They subsequently fail to initiate a therapeutic regimen because they view such mood states as an aspect of the primary medical condition. There is good evidence that such reactive states can be reliably distinguished from major clinical depressions, and patients suffering such painful comorbid conditions are done a substantial disservice by our failure to diagnose and treat them adequately.

Because most physicians have limited training in psychiatric nosology and diagnosis, a third impediment to the accurate identification of these cases is an incomplete diagnostic workup. Already responsible for an immense amount of information concerning the diagnosis and effective treatment of the patient's principal medical condition, it is not surprising that many primary care physicians do not feel highly confident about their skills in diagnosing comorbid psychiatric disorders. Also, although not readily prone to admit to such attitudes, some primary care physicians tend to minimize the importance of concomitant psychiatric problems relative to the primary medical disorder. Table 3.1 lists a series of factors found to often underlie the failure to detect anxiety and depressive disorders in primary care patients.

Physician Recognition of Psychiatric Disorder

There is no longer much debate concerning the fact that primary care physicians represent a de facto mental health care system in the United States. Evidence suggests that one-fifth to one-third of the primary care population suffer from at least one psychiatric condition (typically an anxiety or depressive disorder), underscoring the fact that primary care physicians' proficiency in recognizing psychiatric disorders is an significant health care issue. Current evidence suggests that only a fraction of prevalent psychiatric disorders are detected in primary care, a deficiency that unfortunately has considerable implications for the physical and psychological health of our patients.

Table 3.1. Factors Responsible for Physicians' Failure to Detect Anxiety and Depressive Disorders in Primary Care

1. Affective syndrome masked by predominantly somatic symptoms.
2. Affective syndrome judged to be a demoralization reaction.
3. Affective syndrome missed because of incomplete diagnostic workup.
4. Affective syndrome minimized relative to medical disorder.
5. Affective syndrome misdiagnosed as dementia in elderly patient.
6. Affective syndrome misunderstood as negativistic attitude.

Unaided Physician Recognition. In recent years, a substantial number of studies documented both the magnitude and nature of the problem of undetected psychiatric disorder in primary care. The data from these studies establish rates of accurate physician diagnosis of psychiatric conditions that range from a low of 8% to a high of 53% observed by Shapiro. In a more recent primary care study, Yelin observed that 44% of over 2,000 primary care patients who screened positive for clinical anxiety on the SCL-90-R, had been previously assigned a mental health diagnosis. Although this is an improvement, these data also underscore the fact that 56% of these patients went undiagnosed. Although the methodology and precision of studies of this phenomenon continue to improve, rates of accurate physician diagnosis have remained for the most part unacceptably low. A summary of these investigations along with their characteristics and accurate detection rates appear in Table 3.2.

Aided Physician Recognition. The data from the investigations outlined previously highlight the need to intervene proactively to facilitate the recognition of psychiatric conditions among primary care doctors. This is particularly so in light of the strong consensus that in the future, primary care physicians will be playing even more of a gatekeeper role. If these health care professionals cannot accurately identify psychiatric conditions, they can neither adequately treat them personally nor refer them to appropriate mental health professionals. Such a situation will ultimately serve to degrade the quality of our health care systems further, and will act to deny effective treatment to those who in many ways need it most.

There is some evidence that primary care physicians can accurately identify both the prevalence of psychiatric disorders and the nature of these conditions. They estimate prevalence to be between 20% and 25% in their patient populations, and perceive anxiety and depressive disorders to be the most prevalent conditions they encounter. In an effort to identify and overcome the psychiatric diagnosis problem in primary care, a number of investigators have studied the effects of introducing a diagnostic aid in the primary care setting, in the form of results from a psychological screening test. Although far from unanimous, the studies to date have concluded that in the appropriate situation, screening tests can significantly improve physician detection of psychiatric conditions.

Table 3.2. Recent Research on Rates of Accurate Identification of Psychiatric Morbidity in Primary Care

Investigator	Study Sample	Criterion	Correct Diagnosis
Andersen and Harthorn	120 Physicians, primary care	DKI	33% - Affective disorder 48% - Anxiety disorder
Davis	377 Family practice patients	Zung SDS	15% - Mild symptoms 30% - Severe symptoms
Jones	20 Family physicians/51 patients	DIS	21%
Rand	36 Family practice residents/520 patients	GHQ	16%
Kessler	1,452 Primary care patients	GHQ	19.7%
Linn and Yager	150 Patients in a general medical clinic	Zung	8%
Schulberg	294 Primary care patients	DIS	44%
Shapiro	1,242 Patients at university internal medical clinic	GHQ	53%
Zung	41 Family medicine patients	Zung SDS	15%

Linn and Yager used the Zung Self-rating Depression Scale (SDS) and found an increase of from only 8% correct diagnosis to 25% in a cohort of 150 general medical patients. Similarly, Zung, Magill, Moore and George reported an increase in correct identification rising from 15% to 68% in family medicine outpatients with depression using a similar intervention. Likewise, Moore, Silimperi and Bobula observed an increase in correct diagnostic identification from 22% to 56% working with family practice residents. Not all studies have shown such dramatic improvements in diagnostic accuracy, however. Hoeper, Nyczi, and Cleary found essentially no improvement in diagnosis associated with making General Health Questionnaire (GHQ) results available to doctors and Shapiro reported only a 7% increase in accuracy when GHQ scores were made accessible. The issue of aided recognition of psychiatric disorders is a complicated one, with numerous patient and doctor variables having an effect. Nonetheless, the results of the studies on aided recognition appear promising, and an excellent contemporary review of the issues involved has been published by Anderson and Harthorn.

To summarize this issue, the complex of problems inherent in identifying psychiatric cases in primary care is having a highly regressive impact on our overall health care system. As it is now structured, the preponderance of psychiatric disorders are seen by primary care physicians, who leave a majority of these conditions undiagnosed. Of the cases correctly identified, only a small minority are ever referred to mental health specialists, even though such conditions are known to be of a chronic and recurrent nature, and primary care "gatekeepers" admit that they feel less than fully competent to treat them. Undetected or improperly treated, anxiety and depressive disorders are frequently associated with substance abuse, alcoholism, suicide, excessive utilization of the health care system, and spiraling health care costs. Faced with these data, we should make a concerted effort to facilitate the proficiency of primary care physicians in the detection of psychiatric disorders.

Overview of Screening

Screening has been defined traditionally as "the presumptive identification of unrecognized disease or defect by the application of tests, examinations or other procedures which can be applied rapidly to sort out apparently well persons who probably have a disease from those who probably do not". Screening is a procedure conducted in an ostensibly well population in order to identify occult instances of the disease or disorder in question. Some authorities make a distinction between screening and case finding, which is defined as the ascertainment of disease in populations comprised of patients with other disorders.

Under such a distinction, the detection of psychiatric disorders among primary care patients would more precisely fit the criteria for case finding than for screening. In actual implementation, there appears to be little real difference between the two processes, so we have chosen to use the term screening for both methods. Regardless of its specific manifestation, the screening process represents a relatively unrefined sieve, designed to segregate the cohort under assessment into "positives," who presumptively have the condition, and "negatives," who are ostensively free of the disorder. Screening is not a diagnostic procedure per se. Rather, it represents a preliminary filtering technique that identifies those individuals with the highest probability of having the index disorder for subsequent specific diagnostic evaluation. Typically, those screened "negative" are usually not involved in further evaluation. The conceptual foundation for screening rests on the premise that the early detection of unrecognized disease in apparently healthy individuals carries with it a discernable advantage in achieving effective treatment and/or cure of the condition. Although logical, this assumption is not always justified. In certain conditions, early detection does not measurably improve our capacity to alter morbidity or mortality, either because diagnostic procedures are unreliable, or because effective treatments for the condition are not yet available.In an attempt to facilitate a better appreciation of the particular health problems that lend themselves to effective screening systems, the World Health Organization (WHO) has published guidelines for effective health screening programs. A version of these criteria is listed here.

1. The condition should represent an important health problem that carries with it notable morbidity and mortality.
2. Screening programs must be cost-effective; that is, the incidence/significance of the disorder must be sufficient to justify the costs of screening.
3. Effective methods of treatment must be available for the disorder.
4. The test(s) for the disorder should be reliable and valid, so that detection errors (i.e., false positives or false negatives) are minimized.
5. The test(s) should have high cost-benefit; that is, the time, effort and personal inconvenience to the patient associated with taking the test should be substantially outweighed by its potential benefits.
6. The condition should be characterized by an asymptomatic or benign period, during which detection will significantly reduce morbidity and/or mortality.
7. Treatment administered during the asymptomatic phase should demonstrate significantly greater efficacy than that dispensed during the symptomatic phase.

Some authorities do not believe that psychiatric disorders, and the screening systems designed to detect them, conclusively meet all of these criteria. For example, the efficacy of our treatments for certain psychiatric conditions (e.g., schizophrenia) is arguable, and in some conditions we have not definitively demonstrated that treatments initiated during asymptomatic phases (e.g., "maintenance" period of antidepressant treatment) are more efficacious than treatment initiated during acute episodes of the disorder. Nevertheless, it is generally accepted that psychiatric conditions and the screening models designed to identify them do meet the WHO criteria in the large majority of instances, and that the consistent implementation of screening systems in primary care populations can substantially improve the quality and cost-efficiency of our health care.

Epidemiologic Screening Model

Because many readers do not possess detailed familiarity with screening paradigms, we briefly review the basic epidemiologic screening model. Essentially, a cohort of individuals who are apparently well, or, in the instance of case finding, who present with a condition distinct from the index disorder, are evaluated by a "test" to determine if they are at high risk for the particular disorder or disease. As outlined earlier, the disorder must have sufficient incidence or consequence to be considered a significant public health problem, and be characterized by a distinct early or asymptomatic phase during which it is anticipated that detection will substantially improve the results of treatment.

The screening test itself (e.g., Pap smear, Western blot) should be both reliable, that is, consistent in its performance from one administration to the next, and valid, that is, capable of identifying those with the index disorder and eliminating individuals who do not have the condition. In psychometric terms this form of validity has been traditionally referred to as predictive or criterion-oriented validity. In epidemiologic models, the predictive validity of the test is apportioned into two distinct partitions: the degree to which the test correctly identifies those individuals who actually have the disorder, termed its sensitivity, and the extent to which those free of the condition are correctly identified as such, its specificity. Correctly identified individuals with the index disorder are referred to as true positives, and those accurately identified as being free of the disorder are termed true negatives. Misidentifications of healthy individuals as affected are labeled false positives, and affected individuals missed by the test are referred to as false negatives. It should be noted that each type of prediction error carries with it a socially determined value or significance, termed its utility, and that utilities need not be equal. The basic fourfold epidemiologic table and the algebraic definitions of each of these validity indices are given in Table 3.3.

Sensitivity and specificity are a screening test's most fundamental validity indices; however, they are not the only parameters that can markedly affect a test's performance. In particular, the prevalence or base rate of the disorder in the population under evaluation can have a powerful effect on the results of screening. Two other indicators of test performance, predictive value of a positive and predictive value of a negative, reflect the interactive effects of test validity and prevalence. These indices are also defined in Table 3.1.

Table 3.3. Epidemiologic Screening Model

	Actual	
Screening Test	**Cases**	**Noncases**
Test positive	a	b
Test negative	c	d

Note. Sensitivity (Se) = a/(a + c)
False negative rate (1 - Se) c/(a + c)
Specificity (Sp) = d/(b + d)
False positive rate (1 - Sp) b/(b + d)
Positive predictive value (PPV) = a/(a + b)
Negative predictive value (NPV) = d/(c + d)

Psychometric and Evaluative Principles in Screening

Basic to a realistic appreciation of the psychometrics underlying psychiatric screening is the realization that we are involved in psychological measurement. The principles underlying psychological assessment are no different from those that govern any other form of scientific measurement; however, a major distinction that characterizes psychological measurement concerns the fact that the object of measurement is usually a hypothetical construct. In contrast, measurement in the physical sciences usually involves tangible entities, which are measured via ratio scales with true zeros and equal intervals and ratios throughout the scale continuum (e.g.,. weight, distance, velocity). In quantifying hypothetical constructs (e.g., anxiety, depression, impulsivity), measurement occurs on ordinal-approaching interval scales, which by their nature are less sophisticated and have substantially larger errors of measurement. Psychological measurement is no less scientific due to this fact; however, it is less precise than measurement in the physical sciences.

Reliability. All scientific measurement is based on consistency or replicability. Reliability concerns the degree of replicability inherent in measurement. To what degree would a screening test provide the same results upon re-administration? To what extent do two clinicians agree on a psychiatric rating scale? Conceived differently, reliability can be thought of as the converse of measurement error. It represents that proportion of variation in measurement that is due to true variation in the attribute under study, as opposed to random or systematic error variance. Reliability can be conceptualized as the ratio of true score variation to the total measurement variance. It specifies the precision of measurement and thereby sets the theoretical limit of measurement validity.

Validity. Just as reliability indicates the consistency of measurement, validity reflects the essence of measurement: the degree to which an instrument measures what it is designed to measure. In the context of screening, it specifies how well an instrument discriminates those who possess the attribute being screened from those in whom it is absent. Establishing the validity of a screening instrument is more complex and programmatic than determining its reliability, and rests on more elaborate theory. Although the validation process involves many types of validity experiments, the most explicitly applicable to the screening process is predictive validity.

The predictive validity of an assessment device pivots on its degree of correlation with an external reference criterion some sort of gold standard. In the case of screening tests, the external criterion usually takes the form of a comprehensive laboratory and/or clinical diagnostic evaluation that definitively establishes the presence or absence of the index disorder. Central to a genuine appreciation of the concept of predictive validity is the realization that it is highly specific in nature. To say that a particular screening test is "valid" has little or no scientific meaning; tests are valid only for specific purposes. Psychological tests employed in screening for psychiatric disorder(s) must be validated empirically in terms of the diagnostic assignments they are designed to predict. For example, a particular unidimensional test for depression should be validated specifically in terms of its ability to accurately predict clinical depressions. The fact that it may also be valid for other purposes extends the overall utility of the test, but does not contribute to its validation as a screening measure.

Generalizability. Like reliability and validity, generalizability is a fundamental psychometric characteristic of test instruments used in psychiatric screening paradigms. Many clinical disorders and manifestations of disease are systematically altered as a function of characteristics such as age, sex, race, and the presence or absence of a comorbid medical illness. When validity coefficients (i.e., sensitivity and specificity) for a screening test are established relative to a specific diagnostic condition, they may vary considerably if the demographic and health characteristics of the cohort on which they were established are altered significantly. To the extent that the test's validity is sustained across such shifts, its validity is considered highly generalizable, or robust.

For example, it is well established that men are more constrained than women in reporting emotional distress. Well-constructed tests measuring symptomatic distress develop distinct sets of norms for the two genders to deal with this effect. Another illustration resides in the change of the phenomenologic characteristics of depression across age: Depression in the very young tends toward less dramatic affective display, and progresses through the classic clinical delineations of young and middle adult years, to the geriatric depressions of the elderly, which are more likely to be characterized by dementia-like cognitive dysfunctions. Any single test is unlikely to perform with the same degree of validity across shifts in relevant parameters; therefore, generalizability must be established empirically and cannot merely be assumed. In a recent treatise on modernizing our conceptualization of validity in psychological assessment, Messick explicitly integrated generalizability, along with external criterion validity, as one of six discriminable aspects of construct validity.

The Problem of Low Base Rates

Over 40 years ago, psychologists were sensitized to the problem of low base rates and their dramatic impact on the predictive validity of psychological tests through the publication of a now classic paper by Meehl and Rosen. The authors demonstrated that attempts to predict rare attributes or events, even with highly valid tests, would result in substantially more misclassifications than correct classifications if the prevalence of the event was sufficiently low. Unfortunately, knowledge and understanding of this important but obscure fact remained limited to a few specialists at that time. However, 11 years later, Vecchio published a report in the medical literature dealing with essentially the same phenomenon. In Vecchio's paper, the substantive aspects of the report focused on screening tests in medicine, and the information reached a much wider audience. As a result, knowledge of the special relationship between low base rates and the predictive validity of screening tests has since become well recognized.

To be precise, low prevalence does not affect all aspects of a test's validity equally; its impact is felt primarily in the validity partition that deals with correctly classifying positives or "cases." Predictive validity concerning negatives, or "noncases," is minimally impaired because with extremely low prevalence, even a test with moderate validity will perform adequately in this regard. This relationship is summarized in Table 3.4, which is a synopsis of data originally given by Vecchio.

In the example developed by Vecchio, the sensitivity and specificity of the screening test are given as .95, values that, although characteristic of laboratory-based screening tests, do not represent realistic validity coefficients for psychological screening tests. Table 3.5 provides a more realistic example of the relationship between prevalence and positive predictive value, based on a hypothetical cohort of N = 1,000, with validity coefficients (i.e., sensitivity and specificity) more consistent with those that might be genuinely anticipated for such tests.

Table 3.4. Predictive Values of Positive and Negative Tests at Varying Prevalence (Base) Rates (Sensitivity and Specificity = 95%)

Prevalence or Base Rate (%)	Predictive Value of a + (%)	Predictive Value of a - (%)
1	16.1	99.9
2	27.9	99.9
5	50.0	99.7
10	67.9	99.4
20	82.6	98.7
50	95.0	95.0
75	98.3	83.7
100	100	-

The data of Tables 3.4 and 3.5 make it clear that as prevalence drops below 10%, the predictive value of a positive declines precipitously. In the first example, when prevalence reaches 1%, the predictive value of a positive is only 16%, which means in practical terms that in such situations five out of six positives will be false positives. The predictive value of a negative remains extremely high throughout the range of base rates shown and is essentially unaffected by low-prevalence situations. The example from Table 3.5 is more realistic in that the validity coefficients are more analogous to those commonly reported for psychological screening tests. In the screening situation depicted here, the predictive value of a positive drops from 77% when prevalence is 30% (e.g., the approximate rate of psychiatric disorders among medical cohorts) to 7.5% when prevalence falls to 1%. In the latter instance, 12 out of 13 positives would be false positives.

Sequential Screening: A Technique for Low Base Rates

Although screening for psychiatric disorders in general is not usually affected by problems of low base rates, there are specific mental health problems (e.g., suicide) and certain diagnostic categories (e.g., panic disorder) that have low community prevalence rates. In addition, as Baldessarini, Finklestein and Arana noted, the nature of the population being screened can markedly affect the quality of screening outcomes. A good example of this distinction is provided by the dexamethasone suppression test (DST) when used as a screen for major depressive disorder (MDD). The DST functions as a relatively effective screen for MDD on inpatient affective disorders units where the prevalence of the disorder is quite high. In general medical practice, however, where the prevalence of MDD is estimated to be about 5% to 6%, the DST results in unacceptable rates of misclassification. The validity of the DST is insufficient to support effective screening performance in populations with low base rates of MDD.

Table 3.5. Relationship of Prevalence (Base Rate) and Positive Predictive Value

Assumed Test Sensitivity = 0.80 Assumed Test Specificity = 0.90											
Prevalence = 0.30 **Actual Disorder**				**Prevalence = 0.05** **Actual Disorder**				**Prevalence = 0.01** **Actual Disorder**			
Test	**Pos.**	**Neg.**		**Test**	**Pos.**	**Neg.**		**Test**	**Pos.**	**Neg.**	
+	240	70	310	+	40	95	135	+	8	99	107
-	60	630	690	-	10	855	865	-	2	891	893
Sum	300	700		Sum	50	950		Sum	10	990	
Pos. predict value = 240/310 = 77%				Pos. predict. value = 40/135 = 30%				Pos. predict. value = 8/107 = 7.5%			

A method designed to help overcome low base rate problems is commonly referred to as sequential screening. In a sequential screening paradigm, there are two phases to screening and two screening tests. Phase I involves an initial screen, whose primary purpose is to correctly identify individuals without the condition and eliminate them from consideration in Phase II evaluation. The initial screening also has the important effect of raising the prevalence of the index condition in the remaining cohort. Subsequently, in Phase II, a separate test of equal or superior sensitivity is then utilized. Because the base rate of the index condition has been significantly raised by Phase I screening, the performance of the Phase II screen will involve much lower levels of false positive misclassification. A hypothetical example of sequential screening is given in Table 3.6.

In Phase I of the hypothetical screening, a highly valid instrument with sensitivity and specificity equal to .90 is used in a large population cohort (N = 10,000) with a prevalence of 4% for the index condition. Because of the low base rate, the predictive value of a positive is only 27.2%, meaning essentially that less than one out of every three positives will be true positives.

Table 3.6. Hypothetical Example of Sequential Screening as a Strategy for Dealing With Low Base Rates

Phase 1
N = 10,000; Sensitivity = .90; Specificity = .90
Prevalence (Base Rate) = 4%
Phase II
N = 1,320; Sensitivity = .90; Specificity = .90
Prevalence (Base Rate) = 27.2%

The 1,320 individuals screened positive from the original cohort of 10,000 subsequently become the cohort for Phase II screening. With an equally valid, independent test (sensitivity and specificity = .90) and a base rate of 27.2%, the predictive value of a positive in Phase II rises to 77%, representing a substantial increase in the level of screening efficiency.

Sequential screening evaluates a high-risk subgroup of the population of interest by virtue of a series of consecutive sieves. These have the effect of eliminating from consideration individuals with low likelihood of having the disorder, and simultaneously raising the base rate of the condition in the remaining sample. Sequential screening can become costly because of the increased number of screening tests that must be administered. However, in specific circumstances where prevalence is low (e.g., HIV screening in the general population) and the validity of the screening test is already at a maximum, it may be the only method available to minimize errors in classification.

ROC Analysis

Although some screening tests operate in a qualitative mode, depending on the presence or absence of a key indicator, psychological screening tests function, as do many others, along a quantitative continuum. The individual being screened must obtain a probability or "score" above a criterion threshold or "cutoff" to be considered a "positive" or a "case." The cutoff value is usually determined to be that value that will maximize correct classification and minimize misclassification of the index disorder. If the relative consequences of one type of error are considered more costly than the other (i.e., the consequences have dramatically different utilities; e.g., false negative = missed fatal but potentially curable disease), the cutoff value will often be adjusted to take the differential utility into account. Although quantitative methods exist to estimate optimal threshold values, conventionally, they have simply been selected by inspection of cutoff tables and their associated sensitivities and specificities.

The selection of a cutoff value automatically determines both the sensitivity and specificity of the test because it defines the rates of correct identification and misclassification. Actually, for any given population, an entire distribution of cutoffs exists, with corresponding sensitivities and specificities. Further, as mentioned in the previous section, test performance (i.e., the error rates associated with a particular cutoff value) is highly affected by the prevalence or base rate of the disorder under study. Viewed from this perspective, a test should not be characterized by a sensitivity and specificity; rather it should be perceived as possessing distributions of sensitivities and specificities associated with the distribution of possible threshold values and the distribution of prevalences.

Receiver operating characteristic (ROC) analysis is a method that enables the visualization of the entire distribution of sensitivity / specificity combinations for all possible cutoff values and prevalences. As such, it enables the selection of a criterion threshold based on substantially more information and represents a much more sophisticated clinical decision process. ROC analysis was first developed by Swets in the context of signal detection paradigms in psychophysics. Subsequently, applications of the technique were developed in the areas of radiology and medical imaging. Madri and Williams and Murphy introduced and applied ROC analysis to the task of screening for psychiatric disorders. More recently, Somoza and his colleagues published an extensive series of in-depth reports integrating ROC analysis with information theory to optimize the performance of diagnostic and screening tests. In their comprehensive series, these investigators reviewed the topics of test construction, the effects of prevalence, optimization of information yield and maximization of expected utility relative to ROC analysis and optimal screening strategies.

Typically, an ROC curve is generated by plotting corresponding values of a test's sensitivity (true positive rate) on the vertical axis, against the compliment of its specificity (false positive rate) on the horizontal axis, for the entire range f possible cutting scores from lowest to highest. A number of computer programs are available to generate and plot ROC curves. The ROC curve demonstrates the discriminative capacity of the test at each possible definition of threshold (cutoff score) for psychiatric disorder. If the discriminative capacity of the test is no better than chance, the curve will follow a diagonal straight line from the origin of the graph (lower left) to its uppermost right corner. This line is termed the line of no information. The ROC curve rises from the origin (point 0,0) to its termination point (1,1) on a plane defined as already described. To the extent that a test possesses discriminative validity, the curve will bow in a convex manner toward the upper left corner of the graph. The greater the deviation in this manner, the greater discriminative capacity the test has for the application at hand. Examples of ROC curves are presented in Fig. 3.1.

An ROC summary statistic describing the discriminative capacity of a test is referred to as the area under the curve (AUC). The AUC may be thought of as a probability estimate that at each cutoff score a randomly chosen positive (or "case") will demonstrate a higher score than a randomly chosen negative. When the ROC curve follows the line of no information, the AUC = .50. In the situation of an optimal discrimination, the ROC curve would follow the outline of the ordinate of the graph from point 0,0 to point 1,0, and then move at right angles to point 1,1. In this situation the AUC would equal 1.0.

Although ROC analysis has been implemented in the area of psychiatric screening only within the past decade, investigators have found numerous imaginative applications for the technique. In addition to simply describing the distribution of validity coefficients for a single test, ROC analysis has been used to compare screening tests performances, aid in the validation of new tests, compare different scoring methods for a given test, contrast the screening performance of a test in different populations and assist in validating a foreign-language version of a standard test. ROC analysis has also been effectively integrated with paradigms from information theory to maximize information yield in screening, and with decision-making models to optimize expected utilities of screening outcomes. Although ROC analysis does not represent a definitive solution for the complex problems of psychiatric screening, it does significantly increase the information available to the decision maker and provides a relatively precise and sophisticated method for making decisions.

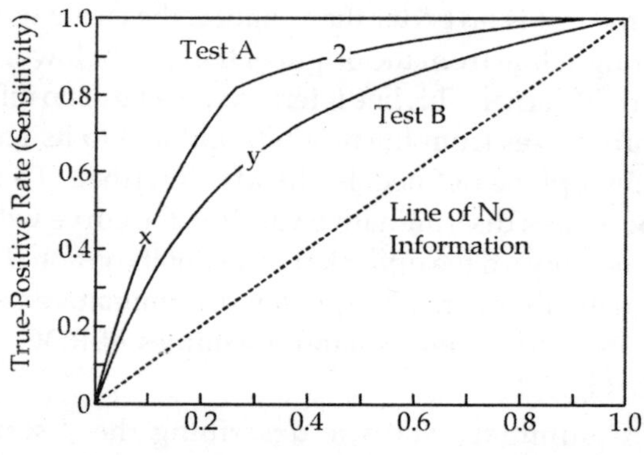

Fig. 3.1. ROC curves for two hypothetical psychiatric screening tests. From "Performance of Screening and Diagnostic Tests"

Screening Tests for Psychiatric Disorders

The predecessors of modern psychological screening instruments date back to the late 19th and early 20th centuries. Sir Francis Galton created the prototype psychological questionnaire as part of an exposition for the World's Fair. The first self-report symptom inventory, the Personal Data Sheet, was developed by

Robert Woodworth as part of the effort to screen American soldiers entering World War I for psychiatric disorders. At approximately the same time, the psychiatrist Adolph Meyer constructed the first psychiatric rating scale, the Phipps Behavior Chart, at Johns Hopkins University. Since these pioneering efforts, hundreds of psychological tests and rating scales have been developed, and a number of the well-validated instruments have become widely used. In the current chapter we briefly review a small number of these instruments in an effort to familiarize the reader with the nature of screening measures available. This chapter is not the appropriate place for a comprehensive review of psychological screening tests, particularly given the number of excellent detailed reviews presented in the accompanying chapters of this book.

Assessment Modality: Self-Report Versus Clinician Rating

Although advocates and adherents argue the differential merits of self-report versus clinician ratings, a great deal of evidence suggests that the two techniques have strengths and weaknesses of roughly the same magnitude. Neither approach can be said to function more effectively overall in screening for psychiatric disorder. Each screening situation must be assessed independently, and the circumstances of each must be objectively weighed to determine which modality is best suited for any particular screening implementation.

Traditionally, self-report inventories have been more frequently used as screening tests than clinical rating scales, probably because the self-report modality has much to recommend it to the task of screening. Self-report measures tend to be brief, inexpensive, and are tolerated well by individuals being screened. These features lend the important attributes of cost efficiency and cost benefit to self-report. Self-report scales are also transportable; they may be used in a variety of settings, and minimize professional time and effort. In addition, their administration, scoring, and evaluation require little or no professional input. Recently, self-report tests have been adapted for use on personal computers, enabling test administration, scoring, evaluation, and storage of results entirely by computer, reducing both professional and technical time. Finally, perhaps the most significant advantage of self-report resides in the fact that in this modality, the test is being completed by the only person experiencing the phenomena the respondent him- or herself. A clinician, no matter how skilled, can never know the actual experience of the respondent; rather, he or she must be satisfied with an apparent or deduced representation of the experience.

This last feature of self-report tests can also represent their greatest potential source of error that is, patient bias in reporting. Because the test respondent is providing the test data, there exists the opportunity to consciously or unconsciously distort the responses given. Although patient bias does represent a potential difficulty for self-report, empirical studies have indicated that such distortions represent a problem only in situations where obvious personal gain is associated with response distortions. Otherwise, this problem usually does not represent a major source of bias. There is also the possibility that response sets such as acquiescence or attempts at impression management may result in systematic response distortions, but such effects tend to add little error variance in most realistic clinical screening situations.

Probably the greatest limitation of most self-report arises from the inflexibility of the format: A line of questioning cannot be altered or modified depending on how the individual responds to previous questions. In addition, only denotative responses can be appreciated; facial expressions, tones of voice, attitudes and postures, and cognitive / emotional status of the respondent are not integral aspects of the test data. This inflexibility extends to the fact that the respondent must also be literate in order to read the questions.

The psychiatric rating scale or interview is a viable alternative to self-report instruments in designing a screening paradigm. The clinical rating scale introduces professional judgement into the screening process, and is inherently more flexible than self-report. The clinician has both the expertise and freedom to delve in more detail into any area of history, thought, or behavior that will deliver relevant information on the respondent's mental status. The clinician also carries the capacity to clarify ambiguous answers and probe areas of apparent contradiction. In addition, because of the clinician's sophistication in psychopathology and human behavior, there is the theoretical possibility that more complex and sophisticated instrument designs may be utilized in developing psychiatric rating scales.

On the negative side, just as self-report is subject to patient bias, clinical rating scales are subject to equally powerful interviewer biases. Training sessions and videotaped interviews may be utilized in an attempt to reduce systematic errors of this type; however, interviewer bias can never be completely eliminated. Furthermore, the very fact that a professional clinician is required to make the ratings significantly increases the costs of screening. Lay interviewers have been trained to do such evaluations in some instances, but they are rarely as skilled as professionals, and the costs of their training and participation must be weighed into the equation as well. Finally, the more flexibility designed into the interview, the more time it is likely to take for the clinician to complete the ratings. At some point, the "test" will no longer resemble a screening instrument, but begin to take on the characteristics of a comprehensive diagnostic interview.

Both self-report and clinical interview modalities are designed to quantify the respondent's status in such a way as to facilitate a valid evaluation of his or her "caseness." Both approaches lend themselves to actuarial quantitative methods, which allow for a normative framework to be established within which to evaluate individuals. Most importantly, both approaches "work." The nature of the screening task, the resources at hand, and the experience of the clinicians or investigators involved determine which method will work best in any particular situation.

Table 3.7 provides summary data on seven such instruments frequently employed as screening tests: SCL-90-R, BSI, GHQ, BDI, BASIS-32, CES-D, HAS, and HRDS. Five of the screening tests mentioned here are self-report, and the remaining two are clinician rated. Because many of the chapters in this book are devoted to detailed reviews of these tests, and a test overview would be highly redundant, Table 3.7 provides only a very brief summary of instrument characteristics.

Widely Used Psychological Screening Instruments

SCL-90-R/BSI. The SCL-90-R is a 90-item, multidimensional, self-report symptom inventory, derived from the Hopkins Symptom

Checklist and first published in 1975. The inventory measures symptomatic distress in terms of nine primary dimensions and three global indices of distress. The dimensions include somatization, obsessive-compulsive, interpersonal sensitivity, depression, anxiety, hostility, phobic anxiety, paranoid ideation, and psychoticism. Several matching clinician rating scales, such as the Derogatis Psychiatric Rating Scale and the SCL-90 Analogue Scale, which measure the same nine dimensions, are also available.

Norms for the SCL-90-R have been developed for adult community nonpatients, psychiatric outpatients, psychiatric inpatients, and adolescent nonpatients. The Brief Symptom Inventory (BSI) is the brief form of the SCL-90-R. The BSI measures the same nine symptom dimensions and three global indices using only 53 items. Dimension scores on the BSI correlate highly with comparable SCL-90-R scores and the brief form shares most psychometric characteristics of the longer scale. Most recently, an 18-item version of the BSI has been developed and normed.

Both the SCL-90-R and the BSI have been used as outcome measures in an extensive array of research studies, among them a number of investigations focusing specifically on screening. To date, the SCL-90-R has been utilized in over 1,000 published research studies, with over 500 available in a published bibliography. The BSI has also demonstrated sensitivity to psychological distress in a numerous clinical and research contexts. Both the SCL-90-R and the BSI have been translated into over two dozen languages.

General Health Questionnaire (GHQ). The GHQ was originally developed as a 60-item, multidimensional, self-report symptom inventory by Goldberg. Subsequent to its publication four subscales were factor-analytically derived: somatic symptoms, anxiety and insomnia, social dysfunction, and severe depression. The GHQ is one of the most widely used screening tests for psychiatric disorder internationally, with its popularity arising in part from the fact that several brief forms of the test are available (e.g., the GHQ30 and GHQ12). The more recent brief forms retain the basic four-subscale format of the longer parent scale, but avoid including physical symptoms as indicators of distress. The GHQ has been validated for use in screening and outcome assessment in numerous populations, including the traumatically injured, cancer patients, geriatric populations, and many community samples.

Table 3.7. Psychiatric Screening Tests in Common Use With Medical and Primary Care Populations

Instrument	Author and Date	Mode	Description	Time	Application	Sensitivity (Se)/ Specificity (Sp)
BASIS-32	Eisen 1965	Self	32 Items Multidimensional	5-20 min	3, 5, 7	Se NA Sp NA
BDI	Beck 1961	Self	21 Items Unidimensional	5-10 min	2, 3, 4	Se .76-.92 Sp .64-.80
BSI	Derogatis 1975	Self	53 Items Multidimensional	10-15 min	1, 2, 3, 4, 7	Se .72 Sp .90
CES-D	Radloff 1977	Self	20 Items Unidimensional	10 min	1, 2, 3, 4	Se .83-.97 Sp .61-.90
GHQ	Goldberg 1972	Self	60, 30, 12 Items Multidimensional	5-15 min	1, 2, 3, 4, 5	Se .69-1.0 Sp .75-.92
HAS	Hamilton 1959	Clin. Rat.	14 Items Bidimensional	20 min	1, 2, 3, 4, 6	Se .91 Sp .94
HRDS	Hamilton 1960	Clin. Rat.	21 Items Unidimensional	30+ min	1, 2, 3, 4, 5, 7	Se .94-1.0 Sp 1.0
SCL-90-R	Derogatis 1975	Self	90 Items Multidimensional	15-20 min	1, 2, 3, 4, 7	Se .73 Sp .91

Note. Applications are (1) community adults, (2) community adolescents, (3) inpatient / outpatient, (4) medical patients, (5) elderly, (6) children, and (7) college students.

Center for Epidemiologic Studies-Depression Scale. The Center for Epidemiological Studies Depression Scale (CES-D) was developed by Radloff and her colleagues. It is a brief, unidimensional self-report depression scale comprised of 20 items that assess the respondent's perceived mood and level of functioning within the past 7 days. Four fundamental dimensions depressed affect, positive affect, somatic problems, and interpersonal problems have been identified as basic to the CES-D. The CES-D also has a total aggregate score.

The CES-D has been used effectively as a screening test with a number of community samples, as well as medical and clinic populations. Recently, Shrout and Yager demonstrated that the CES-D could be shortened to 5 items and still maintain adequate sensitivity and specificity, under the constraint that prediction be limited to traditional two-class categorizations. Generally, an overall score of 16 has been used as a cutoff score for depression, with approximately 15% to 20% of community populations scoring ?16.

Beck Depression Inventory (BDI). The BDI is a unidimensional, self-report, depression inventory that employs 21 items to measure the severity of depression. Pessimism, guilt, depressed mood, self-deprecation, suicidal thoughts, insomnia, somatization, and loss of libido are some of the symptom areas covered by the BDI. The BDI was developed by Beck and his colleagues in 1961. A short (13-item) version of the BDI was introduced in 1972, with additional psychometric evaluation accomplished subsequently. Recently, a revised version of the BDI has been published.

The BDI is characterized by the author as being most appropriate for measuring severity of depression in patients who have been clinically diagnosed with depression. It has been utilized to assess depression worldwide, with numerous community and clinical populations. Each of the items represents a characteristic symptom of depression on which the respondent is to rate him- or herself on a 4-point (i.e., 0-3) scale. These scores are then summed to yield a total depression score. Beck's rationale for this system is that the frequency of depressive symptoms is distributed along a continuum, from "nondepressed" to "severely depressed." In addition, number of symptoms is viewed as correlating with intensity of distress and severity of depression.

The BDI has been used as a screening device with renal dialysis patients, as well as with medical inpatients and outpatients. More recently, Whitaker used the BDI with a group of 5,108 community adolescents and noted that it performed validly in screening for major depression in this previously undiagnosed population. In screening community populations, scores in the range of 17-20 are generally considered suggestive of dysphoria, whereas scores greater than 20 are felt to indicate the presence of clinical depression.

Behavior and Symptom Identification Scale (BASIS-32). The BASIS-32, otherwise known as the Behavior and Symptom Identification Scale, was designed and developed by Eisen, Grob and Klein to evaluate the outcome of mental health interventions from the perspective of the patient. It is a 32-item, self-report inventory that assesses current "difficulty in the major symptom and functioning domains that lead to the need for inpatient psychiatric treatment". A 1-week time window is typically utilized with the BASIS-32, and respondents rate the degree of difficulty they have been experiencing on each item via 5-point (0-4) scales. The BASIS-32 contains five cluster analysis-derived subscales: relation to self and others, daily living and role functioning, anxiety and depression, impulsive and addictive behavior, and psychosis. The five domains are not consonant with diagnostic entities, but reflect problems and manifestations of mental illness that are central aspects of the majority of psychiatric illnesses.

The BASIS-32 has been utilized primarily with psychiatric hospital inpatients, and to a lesser degree with psychiatric outpatients and day-hospital patients. Fundamental psychometric characteristics of the scale are quite respectable and its sensitivity to change has been demonstrated in large sample improvement profiles. Although developed and validated within psychiatric inpatient populations, research on the use of the BASIS-32 with outpatient cohorts is in progress, and may confirm its utility for psychiatric populations in general. By integrating items reflecting problems in daily living and functional status with those representing formal psychiatric symptoms, the BASIS-32 could fulfill a long-standing need for a brief outcomes measure focused on psychosocial integration.

Hamilton Anxiety Scale (HAS). The HAS is a 14-item clinician rating scale published in 1959 by Hamilton. Each item represents a clinical feature of anxiety, requiring the clinician to rate the client on a 5-point scale from 0 (not present) to 4 (very severe). The items reflect both somatic (e.g., cardiovascular, respiratory, gastrointestinal, and genitourinary), and psychic / cognitive (e.g., memory and concentration impairment) manifestations of anxiety. The HAS was designed to yield two separate subscores for "psychic anxiety" and "somatic anxiety." The HAS has been used with children as well as adults, coronary artery bypass patients, general medical / surgical patients, psychiatric outpatients and many other groups. In addition to these applications, the HAS has become accepted as a standard outcome measure in clinical anxiolytic drug trials.

Hamilton Rating Scale for Depression (HRDS)/(HAM-D). The HRDS is similar to the HAS in that both provide quantitative assessments of the severity of a clinical disorder. The HRDS was developed in 1960 by Hamilton, and later was revised in 1967. It consists of 21 items, each measuring a depressive symptom. Hamilton recommended using only 17 items when scoring because of the uncommon nature of the remaining items (e.g., depersonalization).

Hedlung and Vieweg reviewed the psychometric and substantive properties of the HRDS in two dozen studies and gave it a very favorable evaluation. More recently, Bech completed a similar review and concluded that the HRDS is an extremely useful scale for measuring depression. A Structured Interview Guide for the HRDS (SIGH-D) also is available. It provides standardized instructions for administration, and has been shown to improve interrater reliability. Like the HAS with anxiety, the HRDS has also become a standard outcome measure in antidepressant drug trials.

Special Screening Issues

As mentioned previously, there is a high comorbidity between medical and psychiatric disorders, and physicians often have difficulty identifying the latter. Anfinson and Kathol go as far as to recommend laboratory screening for psychiatric patients because of a high prevalence of untreated medical disorders, and suggest that physicians are likely to miss both physical and psychiatric diagnoses in patients who need psychiatric hospitalization. Because of limited diagnostic training, physicians will probably continue to have difficulty with psychiatric disorders, and could greatly benefit from the introduction of efficient psychiatric screening methods.

Examples of psychiatric screening for a variety of the most prevalent medical conditions are reviewed next. The emphasis here is on sensitive and efficient screening methods that will help enable the identification of comorbid psychiatric disorders in a variety of primary care settings.

Psychiatric Screening in Cancer Patients

Psychological distress is common among cancer patients due to the effects that the disease has on the patient, the patient's family, and the inherent difficulty in coping with a life-threatening illness. The initial diagnostic phase can be very stressful and can cause a great deal of psychological turmoil, including feelings of depression, anxiety, anger, and denial. Other difficult issues arise from the fact that cancer is potentially a terminal disease that often requires invasive treatment and has a high rate of recurrence. Zabora noted that there is about a 30% prevalence of elevated psychological distress at diagnosis of cancer and at recurrence. There is mixed evidence concerning whether patients who experience recurrence of symptoms may be less distressed and cope better with future treatment. Some may react more favorably because they have a familiarity with the medical system, whereas others may experience greater distress due to the symptom recurrence. Many experts suggest that psychological treatment should be available for highly distressed individuals first diagnosed with cancer, noting that patients' levels of preexisting distress may be exacerbated by the diagnosis and become progressively worse if left unchecked.

Recently, Gotay and Stern published a review of the Journal of Psychosocial Oncology for the years 1986 to 1993 with a focus on the most common measures used to screen for patient psychological status. The authors further reviewed how these measures were applied with cancer patients. Seven instruments measuring depression, anxiety, mood, or other indices of psychological integration were found to be used most frequently. They included the Beck Depression Inventory (BDI), Center for Epidemiological Studies-Depression Scale (CES-D), State-Trait Anxiety Inventory (STAI), Symptom Checklist-90-R (SCL-90-R), Brief Symptom Inventory (BSI), Profile of Mood States, and Psychological Adjustment to Illness Scale (PAIS / PAIS-SR).

Psychiatric Screening in Patients With Coronary Artery Disease

Psychological distress is also a common experience of individuals with coronary artery disease and can adversely affect outcomes in these patients. More profound psychological conditions such as formal psychiatric disorders, particularly depressions, carry with them an even greater risk for adversely affecting cardiac morbidity and mortality. In this situation, screening systems can efficiently and effectively distinguish individuals who are at risk for comorbid psychopathology and, having identified such patients, possibly point the way toward effective interventions.

An outstanding example of the potential utility associated with screening in this patient population is provided in a report by Allison. These investigators studied 381 cardiac rehabilitation patients who were partitioned into "distressed" and "nondistressed" categories on the basis of scores on the SCL-90-R. Evaluation across a 6-month postdischarge interval disclosed that the distressed group had dramatically higher rates of cardiovascular rehospitalization and recurrent cardiac problems than the nondistressed patients. In addition, the mean rehospitalization costs for the distressed patients were approximately five times those for the low-distress group. The authors concluded that high levels of psychological distress not only increase the morbidity and risk of mortality of cardiac patients, but also substantially increase the costs of treating these patients.

Screening for Alcoholism

Alcoholism is a disease that many physicians feel unprepared to diagnose and treat. Israel noted that 30% to 40% of physicians feel unprepared to diagnose alcoholism, whereas Chang reported that only 19% of physicians felt they had adequate preparation for treating alcohol-related disorders. Physicians often lack knowledge about the disorder and its symptoms, which often impedes treatment and may contribute to further medical problems. Hopkins, Zarro, and McCarter observed that physicians identified only 37% of problem drinkers appropriately. These authors believe that it is necessary to increase awareness about referral and screening procedures in medical school curricula and through the continuing education of practicing physicians. In these instances, the routine use of alcohol screens would help primary care doctors identify these conditions quickly and accurately so that they can initiate appropriate treatment or referrals. Although there are a number of alcohol screening tests available, one of the simplest tools physicians can use is the CAGE questionnaire. This instrument consists of four questions that have sensitivity and specificity that range from 60% to 95% in identifying problem drinking. The four questions of the CAGE are:

1. Have you ever felt the need to Cut down on your drinking?
2. Have you ever felt Annoyed by someone criticizing your drinking?
3. Have you ever felt Guilty about your drinking?
4. Have you ever felt the need of an Eye opener (a drink first thing in the morning)?

Ford, Klag, Whelton, Goldsmith and Levine noted that although 45% of physicians had heard of the CAGE, only 14% could recite all four questions needed. This research suggests that general knowledge about screening for alcoholism requires some enhancement in the training curricula for primary care physicians.

Several studies have addressed the differences in presentation, identification, and treatment needs for women with alcoholism. Alcoholism research has predominately focused on male treatment approaches, and few studies have addressed the distinct drinking behavior of women. Cyr and Moulton noted that problem drinking in women often goes unrecognized and untreated by primary care physicians. The authors feel there is a further need to educate physicians about female drinking problems so that they can educate their female patients about dysfunctional drinking behavior. Differential metabolism, higher blood alcohol levels, and higher alcohol-related morbidity and mortality are characteristic of females with an alcohol problem.

Screening for Depression

Depression is the most common psychological disorder seen in primary care and is the underlying basis for many symptoms reported to primary care doctors. Obviously, an accurate diagnosis of depression is needed for effective treatment, an ac- complishment that often proves difficult due to the high overlap of depressive symptoms with the symptoms of concomitant medical disorders. Primary care physicians are most likely to see depressed patients who present with a variety of somatic complaints as well as fatigue and irritability. The addition of one of the many well-validated depression screening measures can make a significant contribution to the physician's ability to recognize clinical depressions in his/her patients.

As an example of effective screening, Callahan implemented a screening program for depression using the Centers for Epidemiologic Studies Depression Scale (CES-D) and the Hamilton Depression Rating Scale (HAM-D) along with physician training that included education on depression. The investigators found that physicians who were educated about depression, had access to the screening instruments data, and were encouraged to make a diagnosis of depression were significantly more likely to diagnose depression and prescribe antidepressant medication. Rapp, Smith and Britt also noted that use of the Extracted Hamilton Depression Rating Scale (XHDRS) substantially helped to correctly identify depression in an elderly cohort. The authors concluded that the XHDRS is a reliable and valid instrument with substantial utility for detecting depression in the elderly, and provides primary care physicians with a quick assessment tool that can aid the diagnosis of depression in their patients.

On a related issue, Wyshak and Barsky evaluated a subset of depressed and anxious clinic patients concerning the effectiveness of their medical care. In general, patients appeared satisfied, but there was little correlation between physician ratings of treatment effectiveness and patient satisfaction ratings. Patients who reported significant depressive symptoms were more likely to be dissatisfied with their medical care. Physicians tended to rate themselves as more effective with older, male patients who were not significantly depressed.

Screening in elderly patients is addressed more fully in a later section. However, the need for effective screening for depression in the elderly cannot be overemphasized. Depression is often mistaken for dementia or delirium in elderly patients, and multiple medical problems, typical of older patients, also decrease the likelihood of recognition of a depressive disorder.

Screening for Suicidal Behavior

Chiles and Strosahl defined suicidal behavior as a "broad spectrum of thoughts, communications, and acts ranging from the least common completed suicide to the more frequent suicidal communications and the most frequent suicidal ideations and verbalizations". They report that the rate of suicide has remained stable in the United States for the past 20 years at approximately 12.7 deaths per 100,000 and ranks as the eighth leading cause of death in the general population. Suicide ranks as the third leading cause of death for individuals 18-24 years old, and the suicide rate in the elderly is approximately double the rate of suicide in the population 18-24 years old.

Lish noted that 82% of the people who commit suicide have visited primary care physicians within the past 6 months, 53% within 1 month, and 40% within 1 week prior to the suicide. This realization makes it imperative for primary care physicians to recognize the risk factors involved in suicidal behavior. As noted previously, one risk factor for suicide is the presence of a medical illness, which makes primary care physicians more likely to see cases of suicidal behavior earlier, as opposed to other professionals such as psychologists or psychiatrists. Unfortunately, it is likely that practitioners may miss the warning signs associated with imminent suicide.

Chiles and Strosahl noted that suicidal behavior can be broken down into three subtypes. The first type is suicidal ideation, which involves thoughts about suicidal behavior. Little is known about the predictive value of suicidal ideation, or how often it is followed by legitimate suicide attempts. The second subtype involves a suicide attempt, which tends to be more common in females and younger individuals. It is enlightening to note that 50% of those individuals who attempt suicide have no formal mental health diagnosis. The final category of suicidal behavior is completed suicide, which is more common in males and older individuals who often have diagnoses of depression, schizophrenia, alcoholism, or panic disorder. Lish also reported that Whites and divorced or separated individuals are at increased risk for suicide. In contrast to suicide "attempters," between 50% and 90% of those who complete suicide do have some form of psychiatric diagnosis. Other risk factors include loss of a spouse (increased risk for up to 4 years), unemployment, physical illness, bereavement, and physical abuse. Certain personality traits have also been associated with an increased risk for suicide.

Clearly, a clinical interview with a detailed medical history that includes any psychiatric history and previous suicidal behavior is currently the most effective method for identifying suicide risk. Unfortunately, such interviews are quite time-consuming and not cost-effective, given the low base rate of completed suicide. This being the case, the most frequently utilized measures in screening for suicide are self-report inventories. Several inventories have been found useful in screening for suicidal behavior, including the Beck Hopelessness Scale and the Beck Depression Inventory. Westefeld and Liddel noted that the 21-item Beck Depression Inventory is often used for screening in college students, and has been found to be very useful. Derogatis and Derogatis reported that the SCL-90-R and the BSI also showed utility in screening for suicidal behavior. Several investigators have reported that both the primary symptom dimensions and the their global scores were able to distinguish suicidal positives versus negatives, in a cohort diagnosed with depression and panic disorder. In addition, Swedo found that all SCL-90-R subscales distinguished suicide attempters in an adolescent population. Throughout these studies, investigators observed that both adolescents and adult suicide attempters perceived themselves as more distressed and hopeless than individuals designated "at risk."

Another instrument that has been used to screen for suicidal behavior is the SCREENER. Lish used this brief self-report inventory to screen for psychiatric disorders in a group of possibility suicidal individuals. The SCREENER screens for DSM-IV Axis I conditions and is available in a 96-item long form and a 44-item short form. Three questions address death or suicide, and an additional item addresses suicidal ideation directly. The authors recommend that clinicians should screen for substance abuse, panic disorders, and major depression, because these disorders all increase the risk of suicidal behavior in primary care settings.

Screening for Cognitive Impairment

Screening for cognitive impairment, particularly in geriatric populations, is extremely important because it is estimated that up to 70% of patients with an organic mental disorder (OMD) go undetected. Because some OMDs are reversible if discovered early enough, screening programs in high-risk populations (such as the elderly) can have a very high utility. Even in conditions found to be irreversible, early detection and diagnosis can help in the development of a treatment plan and the education of family members. Although the prevalence of cognitive disorders in the general population is fairly high, it is even more dramatic in the elderly. Furher and Ritchie noted a 6% prevalence of dementia in the general population, but indicated that the rate may rise to as much as 14% to 18% in the elderly. In terms of a specific cognitive impairment such as delirium, Hart noted a prevalence of 10% to 13% in the general medical population, with a rate between 15% and 30% among elderly patients. Because the prevalence of cognitive disorders is so high in the elderly, it is necessary to have effective screening tools to facilitate early detection and timely treatment. Because cognitive decline is manifest disproportionately in this group, we limit our current review to work associated with elderly or geriatric patients.

Screening the geriatric patient can often be a challenging enterprise for a number of diverse reasons. First, these patients often present with sensory, perceptual, and motor problems that seriously constrain the use of standardized tests. Poor vision, diminished hearing, and other physical handicaps can undermine the appropriateness of tests that are dependent upon these skills. Similarly, required medications can cause drowsiness or inalertness, or in other ways interfere with optimal cognitive functioning. Illnesses such as heart disease and hypertension, common in the elderly, have also been shown to affect cognitive functioning. These limitations require screening instruments that are flexible enough to be adapted to the patient with handicaps or illnesses, and yet sufficiently standardized to allow normative comparisons.

Another difficulty in assessing cognitive impairment in this population is distinguishing cognitive impairment from aging-associated memory loss. This distinction requires a highly sensitive screening instrument, because the differences between these conditions are often subtle. Normal aging and dementia can be differentiated through their differential effects on language, memory, perception, attention, information-processing speed, and intelligence. An example of an instrument designed specifically for this purpose is the Global Deterioration Scale (GDS). The GDS is a screening test that has the capacity to describe the magnitude of cognitive decline, and to predict functional disability.

An additional important issue encountered in screening geriatric populations involves comorbid depression. Depression is one of a number of disorders in the elderly that may imitate dementia, resulting in a syndrome referred to as "pseudodementia." These patients lack a discernable degenerative organic process underlying their conditions, and their dementia-like symptoms usually remit once the underlying affective disorder is effectively treated. Variability of task performance quality can often distinguish these patients from truly-demented patients, who tend to have an overall lowered performance level on all tasks. If depression is suspected, it should be the focus of a distinct diagnostic work-up.

One of the most demanding diagnostic discriminations in this population is often that between dementia and the patient with acute confusional states, or delirium. This is particularly important, not only because of the increased occurrence of delirium in elderly medical patients, but because if left untreated delirium can progress to an irreversible condition. Delirium can have multiple etiologies, such as drug intoxication, metabolic disorders, fever, cardiovascular disorders, or effects of anesthesia. The elderly are particularly susceptible to misuse or overuse of prescription drugs, as well as metabolic or nutritional imbalances. Hypothyroidism, hyperparathyroidism, and diabetes are some of the medical conditions that can be mistaken for dementia. Fortunately, three cardinal characteristics enable us to distinguish dementia from delirium. The first of these is rate of onset of symptoms. Delirium is marked by acute or abrupt onset of symptoms, while dementia is a more gradual progression. Second is impairment of attention. Delirious patients have special difficulty sustaining attention on tasks such as serial sevens, and digit span. Finally, nocturnal worsening is a frequent feature characteristic of delirium, but not dementia. Collectively, these three cognitive markers usually enable an competent and accurate discrimination.

Recently, a number of measures were designed specifically to aid in the differentiation of delirium from dementia and depression in the elderly. One of these instruments is the Cognitive Test for Delirium (CTD), which is a nine-item examiner-administered scale that evaluates the cognitive components of orientation, attention span, memory, comprehension, and vigilance. The CTD is completely nonverbal and can be administered in 10 to 15 minutes. Using ROC analysis the authors found an optimal cutoff of <19 to distinguish delirium from other disorders. Overall, the CTD achieved 100% sensitivity and 95% specificity when the optimum cutoff score was used with demented ICU patients.

It is not uncommon for cases of cognitive impairment go undetected. This may be due to the fact that the early stages of cognitive dysfunction are often quite subtle, and that many cases first present to primary care physicians who have their principal focus on other systems. Also, many physicians are unfamiliar with the available procedures for detecting cognitive impairment, whereas others are reluctant to add a formal cognitive screening to their schedule of procedures. Although relatively brief, the 10 to 30 minutes required by screening instruments may remain a formidable impediment, considering that, on average, family practice physicians spend 7 to 10 minutes with each patient. The solution to this problem may rest in training nurses and other health care professionals to administer cognitive screening instruments. Such an approach would not increase the time burden on the physician, and would enable him or her to evaluate the screening data in an abbreviated format.

Instruments With a General Versus Specific Focus

There are now quite a few instruments available that provide quick and efficient screening of cognitive functioning. Most of these address the general categories of cognitive functioning covered in the standard mental status examination, including attention, concentration, intelligence, judgment, learning ability, memory, orientation, perception, problem solving, psychomotor ability, reaction time, and social intactness. However, not all instruments include items from all of these categories. These general instruments can be contrasted with another class of cognitive screening measures characterized by a more specific focus. For example, the Stroke Unit Mental Status Examination (SUMSE) was designed specifically to identify cognitive deficits and plan rehabilitation programs for stroke patients. Another example of an instrument with a specific focus is the Dementia of Alzheimer's Type Inventory (DAT), designed to distinguish Alzheimer's disease from other dementias. A more recent example of a specific measure is the Cognitive Test for Delirium (CTD), which screens specifically for delirium in intensive care units. In recent years, use of specific types of measures in combination with broader measures, has become more common.

Unlike other screening tests, the great majority of cognitive impairment scales are administered by an examiner. Of the instruments to be reviewed in this chapter, none are self-report measures. There are no pencil-and-paper inventories that can be completed by the respondent alone. Instead, these screening measures are designed to be administered by a professional and require a combination of oral and written responses. Most of the tests are highly transportable, however, and can be administered by a wide variety of health care workers.

Cognitive Screening Instruments

This section provides a brief summary of nine popular cognitive impairment screening measures. This is not intended to be an exhaustive review, but rather to provide some data on the nature of each measure and its psychometric properties.

Mini-Mental State Examination (MMSE). The MMSE was developed by Folstein, Folstein, and McHugh to determine the level of cognitive impairment. It is an 11-item scale measuring six aspects of cognitive function: orientation, registration, attention and calculation, recall, language, and praxis. Scores can range from 0 to 30, with lower scores indicating greater impairment.

The MMSE has proved successful at assessing levels of cognitive impairment in many populations, including community residents, hospital patients, residents of long-term care facilities and neurological patients. Escobar suggested using another instrument with Spanish-speaking individuals, as the MMSE may overestimate dementia in this population. Roca also recommended other instruments for patients with less than 8 years of schooling for similar reasons. In contrast, the MMSE may underestimate cognitive impairment in psychiatric populations.

Table 3.8. Screening Instruments for Cognitive Impairment

Instrument	Author	Description	Application	Sensitivity/ Specificity
MMSE	Folstein	11 Items; designed to determine level of cognitive impairment	1,3,4	.83/ .89
CCSE	Jacobs	30 Items; designed to detect presence of organic mental disorder	2,3,4,5	.73/ .90
SPMS	Pfeiffer	10 Items; designed to detect presence of cognitive impairment	1	.55-.88/ .72-.96
HSCS	Faust and Fogel	15 Items; designed to estimate presence, scope, and severity of cognitive impairment	2	.94/ .92
MSQ	Kahn	10 Items; designed to quantify dementia	1,4,5,6	.55-.96/NA

Note. Applications are as follows: 1, community populations; 2, cognitively intact, 3, hospital inpatients; 4, medical patients; 5, geriatric; 6, long-term care patients.

Finally, the MMSE has lower sensitivity with mildly impaired individuals, who are more likely to be labeled as demented. As such, the MMSE is most useful for patients with moderate to moderately severe dementia. Fuhrer and Ritchie also found that the MMSE was more discriminating for moderate dementia rather than mild dementia, but they did not find a significant difference between those who had less than 8 years of education versus those who had more than 8 years of education. The authors noted, however, that cutoff scores for the MMSE need to be adjusted when comparing clinical samples of dementia with higher prevalence than the 6% prevalence in the general population. Furher and Ritchie disagreed with cutoff points (18/19 for moderate dementia and 22/23 for mild dementia) presented by Jagger, Clark and Anderson because they believe the latter's prevalence numbers were inflated due to the increased age of their sample. Both groups of authors supported the use of ROC analysis as a means for assessing the utility and cutoff scores for screening instruments.

Cognitive Capacity Screening Examination (CCSE). The CCSE is a 30-item scale designed to detect diffuse organic disorders, especially delirium, in medical populations. The instrument was developed by Jacobs, Berhard, Delgado, and Strain and is recommended if delirium is suspected. The items include questions of orientation, digit recall, serial sevens, verbal short-term memory, abstractions, and arithmetic, all of which are helpful in detecting delirium.

The CCSE has been used with geriatric patients, as well as hospitalized medical-surgical patients. In comparisons of the MMSE, SPMSQ (discussed later), and CCSE, the CCSE was shown to be the most reliable and valid. Like the MMSE, the CCSE is also influenced by the educational level of the subject. However, unlike the MMSE, the CCSE cannot differentiate levels of cognitive impairment or types of dementias and is most appropriate for cognitively intact patients.

Short Portable Mental Status Questionnaire (SPMSQ). The SPMSQ is a 10-item scale for use with community and/or institutional residents. This scale is unique in that it has been used with rural and less educated populations. The items assess orientation, and recent and remote memory; however, visuospatial skills are not tested. The SPMSQ is a reliable detector of organicity but should not be used to predict the progression or course of the disorder.

High Sensitivity Cognitive Screen (HSCS). This scale was designed to be as sensitive and comprehensive as lengthier instruments while still being clinically convenient. It was developed by Faust and Fogel for use with native English-speaking subjects 16-65 years old with at least an eighth-grade education who are free from gross cognitive dysfunction. The 15 items include reading, writing, immediate and delayed recall, and sentence construction, among others. The HSCS has shown adequate reliability and validity and is best used to estimate presence, scope, and severity of cognitive impairment. The HSCS cannot pinpoint specific areas of involvement, and, as for most of these scales, should represent a first step toward cognitive evaluation, not a substitute for a standard neuropsychological assessment.

Mental Status Questionnaire (MSQ). The MSQ is a 10-item scale developed by Kahn, Goldfarb, Pollock and Peck. It has been used successfully with medical geriatric patients, community residents and long-term care patients. Disadvantages of this measure include its sensitivity to education and ethnicity of the subject, its reduced sensitivity with mildly impaired individuals, and its omission of tests of retention, registration, and cognitive processing.

Other Instruments. Four additional measures have been developed that are particularly appropriate for primary care use because their main function is to simply rule out or detect the presence of dementia. FROMAJE classifies individuals into normal, mild, moderate, and severe dementia groups and has been used successfully with long-term care patients. The Blessed Dementia Scale measures changes in activities and habits, personality, interests, and drives, and is useful for determining presence of dementia, though not its progression. The Global Deterioration Scale can be used to distinguish between normal aging, age-associated memory impairment, and primary degenerative disorder. The GDS is useful for assessing the magnitude and progression of cognitive decline. In terms of diagnosing Alzheimer's disease, Steffens have proposed using the Telephone Interview for Cognitive Status along with a videotaped mental status exam to improve diagnostic accuracy. The authors state that gathering information over the phone from Alzheimer's patients shows some promise and may limit physician time constraints.

A final instrument worth mentioning is the Chula Mental Test (CMT), developed by Jitapunkul, Lailert, Worakul, Srikiatkhachorn and Ebrahim for use with the elderly in underdeveloped countries. The CMT was developed in response to a major problem with standard screening measures, which arises from the fact that they are based on Western concepts of cognitive dysfunction and may not be culturally or linguistically relevant in other countries. The

CMT is a 13-item test that is less biased toward education and literacy, in order to minimize the number of false positives when screening in underdeveloped countries. The 13 items on the CMT test for remote memory, orientation, attention, language, abstract thinking, judgment, and general knowledge. The recommended cutoff score is 80% of the maximum score attainable. When this score is used, the CMT achieves a sensitivity of 100% and specificity of 90%, values that are quite good in this context.

Monitoring Psychiatric Disorders in Primary Care

Once a diagnosis has been made and a treatment regimen implemented, the next major consideration involves establishing a mechanism to evaluate the effectiveness of treatment. What degree of symptom control has been achieved? What is the patient's subjective sense of well-being? How are family relations? Is the patient adjusting well at work? These questions all address major dimensions of response to treatment. Without becoming involved in formal outcomes studies, the practitioner can nonetheless introduce a systematic program of treatment monitoring to establish the nature and extent of the patient's treatment response.

As indicated elsewhere, the cardinal characteristic of a psychological monitoring measure is that it be sensitive to treatment-induced change. The latter may be thought of as a central effect that is imbedded in an array of diverse alternative effects, which requires separation and elucidation. An instrument selected to achieve treatment monitoring must have the capacity to represent response to treatment as "figure" against the collective "ground" of alternative effects. This means that in addition to having high discriminative potential (i.e., the ability to distinguish "functional" from "dysfunctional" individuals), instruments chosen for treatment monitoring must also possess powerful evaluative capacities that enable them to accurately represent changes in patient's status across time.

Time of Monitoring

The time frame for monitoring is obviously an important parameter that must be considered in designing a treatment monitoring system. Fundamentally, the nature of the condition being monitored and the characteristics of treatment response are major determinants of the optimal assessment schedule (i.e., days, weeks, months). Monitoring acute conditions calls for a different schedule of assessments than does the assessment of chronic disease states. Likewise, the variables or attributes being assessed (e.g., drug side effects, patient's mood, services utilization) also play a role in determining the most effective monitoring schedule. Initially, a baseline assessment must be done; however, "baseline" can be defined in myriad ways. Ideally, baseline measurement is established prior to the introduction of the treatment(s) under evaluation, but in close temporal contiguity to treatment initiation. Subsequently, additional follow-up assessments should be routinely done (monthly, semiannually, annually), with scheduling depending on the configuration of the parameters just discussed. Typically, a follow-up evaluation at 6 months post baseline enables an evaluation of the success of both acute treatment and continuation treatment phases. A further evaluation at 12 months enables an assessment of any maintenance treatment regimens initiated, and also serves to determine any signs of relapse or recurence. Familiarity with the nature and course of the condition under assessment, along with an understanding of typical patterns of episodes of illness and episodes of care, usually serves as the most useful guide for establishing a monitoring schedule.

Domains of Monitoring

Treatment effects can be measured via a multitude of potential outcomes variables, from various indicators of clinical status (symptoms, side effects, complications) and measures of functional health status (e.g., physical capacity, cognitive functioning), to global well-being (e.g., affects balance) and measures of services utilization. At present, there are numerous well-validated psychological tests, rating scales, and standardized interviews to accurately quantify and assess the majority of these characteristics.

First and foremost, measures of morbidity should be integrated into the monitoring system. Evaluations of symptomatic distress, side effects of treatment, and concurrent medical events should be primary components of the monitoring package. The system must also be designed to register signs of relapse or recurrence should they occur, and to effectively communicate them to the treating physician.

Quality-of-life variables, including measures of functional health status, have become increasingly important, as we progress from traditional biomedical approaches to a more biopsychosocial model in viewing illness and treatment outcomes. Cognitive functioning, physical capacity, interpersonal and social relations, and vocational performance require assessment periodically to determine the effects treatment(s) are having on these important expressions of health status. Subjectively perceived well-being is also frequently included within the broad rubric of quality of life, and refers essentially to how the patient currently "feels" about the quality of his or her life experience. For measurement purposes, well-being is often construed as the nature and degree of balance between positive and negative emotional experiences (i.e., affects balance), with a positive affects balance being associated with good health and constructive engagement with the environment, and a negative affects balance being associated with psychological distress and loss of vitality. Measures of well-being are brief and simple to administer and have been shown to have strong empirical relationships with health status, in medical as well as in psychiatric populations. A number of well-designed instruments of this type are currently available.

Monitoring Change

Although seemingly rudimentary, the assessment and evaluation of changes in health status is often exceedingly complex. The answer to the fundamental question, "Did the patient improve as the result of treatment?" is frequently confounded by multiple mitigating issues. First, psychiatric disorders (e.g., anxiety, depression) are hypothetical constructs, which means that they must be operationally defined to be measured. Because the scales used to conduct such measurement possess no "ostensive" characteristics (e.g., distance, weight), the resulting measurements are relatively crude compared to those of the physical sciences. Although magnitude and direction of change are the most basic parameters of treatment efficacy, in the case of psychiatric conditions the magnitude of change required to define clinical improvement is a relative rather than an absolute number. Depending on where in the distribution (on the outcomes test) the patient scored at baseline, a 10-point score reduction could be interpreted as anywhere from "dramatic" to "minor" clinical change. This difficulty is due in part to the fact that overlap almost always exists between "normal" and "patient" score distributions, which means there is no definitive score or value at which clinical status ends and normal status begins.

In spite of these problem, well-designed instruments, with standardized norms possessing actuarial properties, do provide sufficient information to make reasonable clinical judgments comfortably. Such test instruments usually publish norms for both "patient" and "community" groups, which enable comparisons of where in each distribution treatment induced change places the patient. Recently, relatively elegant models have been proposed to ascertain the "clinical significance" of change. However, a simple examination of the patient's pre-post treatment movement in the context of well-established norm sets will usually provide a satisfactory answer to the question, "Did the patient improve significantly?"

Conclusion

Currently, there is little doubt that psychiatric disorders qualify as conditions appropriate for the development of effective health screening programs. The magnitude of the health problem they represent is extensive, and the morbidity, mortality, and costs associated with these conditions are imposing. We currently possess valid, cost-efficient mechanisms to effectively identify these conditions in medical and community settings, and the efficacy of our treatment regimens for most psychiatric conditions has improved substantially. It is unquestionably time to systematically implement psychiatric screening systems in primary care. This is particularly so when one considers the alternative, where compelling evidence exists that left to their natural courses, such conditions will result in chronic, compound morbidities of both a physical and psychological nature. Ultimately, it is of little consequence to develop effective systems of treatment planning and outcomes monitoring, if the majority of individuals who would benefit from these exercise are lost to the health care system.

4

Integration of Behavioral Health Care

Introduction

Health care providers working alongside physicians and other medical personnel in primary health care settings to more thoroughly address the complex interaction between physical illness and psychological factors. This chapter addresses these developments in the area of children's health care, specifically in pediatric primary care settings. Several topics will be addressed: the justifications for integrating behavioral health care into pediatric primary care settings, current trends in identifying behavioral issues in these settings, and the issues and concerns that are important to consider in providing integrated care in pediatric primary care settings.

Integrating Behavioral Health Care into Pediatric Primary Care Settings

The challenges facing U.S. children and families in the 1990s are alarming. About 20% of children live in poverty, and that number increases to about 25% for children under 6 years of age. The infant mortality rate in this country is higher than in 19 other developed nations. There has been a resurgence of preventable childhood diseases, due in part to inadequate rates of immunizations for infants and toddlers in urban areas. Families are under stress from a high divorce rate, difficulties finding adequate child care, and large numbers who lack health insurance and access to appropriate medical care.

Recently the American Psychological Association (APA) Task Force on Comprehensive and Coordinated Psychological Services for Children 0-10 released a call for service integration to better meet the needs of children. Members of the task force reported that there is an increasing consensus that the current service delivery system is not meeting the needs of children and families and that it will be necessary to make fundamental changes in how the system operates to ensure that services are comprehensive, responsive, and integrated. They encouraged psychologists to broaden their role in these systems to provide advocacy, prevention, consultation, assessment, and treatment for children and families. An emphasis on promoting psychological competence and self-sufficiency rather than focusing on dysfunction and pathology was also recommended. This would, of course, require a balance between prevention, early intervention, and treatment modalities. Finally, the task force members identified pediatric primary health care settings as a natural entry point for providing integrated care to address children's mental health needs.

Marketplace issues are also creating a move toward integrated systems of care, particulary the tendency for private insurers to eliminate or severely restrict mental health benefits. In addition to pressures from private insurers, many states have converted their Medicaid programs into managed care systems and many of these have also added a behavioral health "carve-out". As financial resources shrink, integrated systems are likely to present the most efficient means of meeting the increasingly serious needs of children and families.

The high frequency with which children present with behavioral needs in pediatric primary care settings provides another justification for integrating psychological care into them. Pediatricians have long recognized the importance of psychological issues in medical care, and the field has expanded its boundaries to include addressing emotional, educational, and social aspects of children and their development. Prevalence studies have found that children can present with developmental, emotional, and behavioral problems throughout their developing years and that the incidence of these problems increases over time. Zill and Schoenborn reported that 5.3% of 3- to 5-year-olds, 12.7% of 6- to 11-year-olds, and 18.5% of 12- to 17-year-olds have these kinds of problems. It also has been estimated that 20% of pediatric primary care patients have biosocial or developmental problems. This prevalence rate is similar to other community studies. It is no surprise, then, that care for behavioral and psychological problems has been referred to as "the new morbidity" in pediatrics and pediatricians tend to be the first professionals parents talk to about their children's behavior and development.

Problems in Traditional Pediatric Service Delivery

Although there are clearly demands for addressing biopsychosocial and developmental problems in pediatric primary care settings, it is increasingly difficult for pediatricians and other medical health care providers to meet them. For example, the demand to see increasing numbers of patients has had a dramatic effect on the time they can spend with each child. If pediatricians are asked to see four to six children each hour, they simply have very little time available to address developmental anticipatory guidance or to identify and manage psychological problems. For example, one observational study of pediatricians found that the time spent on anticipatory guidance averaged a high of 97 seconds for babies under 5 months of age and a low of 7 seconds for adolescents.

There are also concerns about pediatricians' training to meet these needs. In 1978 a survey conducted by the American Academy of Pediatrics Task Force on Pediatric Education found that large numbers of pediatricians thought that biosocial and developmental issues had been under emphasized in their training. It is unclear how much improvement has been made in this area since the Task Force's report. Weinberger and Oski surveyed 29 pediatric residency training programs and found no trend indicating an increased emphasis in training on biopsychosocial issues. In a more recent study, Wender and her colleagues did a follow-up survey of pediatricians trained after 1978 and found that many still rated their training in these areas as insufficient, although Wender et al.

noted less dissatisfaction among those trained after 1984 and an increased interest in developmental and behavioral pediatrics as subspecialties.

Pediatricians' concerns about their abilities to identify behavioral and developmental concerns appear to be well founded. Costello and her colleagues found that while pediatricians seldom misdiagnosed children as having a significant psychiatric disturbance (84% of those they identified as nondisturbed had no psychiatric disorder), they often failed to identify children with psychiatric disorders (only 17% of the children with significant problems were identified). One difficulty in identifying problems may be parents' apparent tendency to not talk to their pediatricians about these issues. Various studies have found that 40% to 80% of parents have questions or concerns about their children's behavior and development but few discuss these issues during office visits.

Even when problems are identified, they are often not adequately addressed by the provider. Sharp found that 60% of psychosocial concerns expressed by parents resulted in no response or only a passive response (acknowledgment of the problem by asking more questions, but no information or reassurance offered) from pediatric and family medicine residents. Although parents may fail to report their concerns about psychological issues, they appear to expect that pediatricians will address behavioral issues when they are raised. One study found that 41.3% of parents who had changed or were strongly considering changing their pediatrician cited the doctor's lack of interest in the child's behavior as a primary reason for dissatisfaction. Another study found that 37% of all well child visits to pediatricians involved support and counseling for issues related to parenting and behavior management, with an additional 19% of questions concerning school performance.

Pediatricians also express concern about parents' compliance with recommendations to obtain mental health services for their children. One study found that pediatricians referred 16% of the children they identified as having significant problems to specialty services, whereas another study found that only 53% of children referred for counseling received the prescribed therapy. Tuma estimated that 70% to 80% of children needing mental health services do not receive them. Having behavioral health care providers available in pediatric primary care settings would certainly help to ensure that more children in need of services would be identified and that the appropriate services would be more likely to be obtained.

Integration as a Solution to the Problems

Some evidence also suggests that parents like this model of care and are very comfortable using mental health care services provided in this way. Hurley, McIntire, and Evers-Szostak surveyed 320 parents to study parent satisfaction with the pediatric psychology services provided within two private pediatric offices -- one in Fort Worth, Texas, and the other in Durham, North Carolina. They found that parents who had seen the psychologist in the pediatrics office were overwhelmingly positive about their experience. Even parents who had not seen the psychologist responded very positively. Although only 16% of the parents had actually used the psychologists' services, 94% of those responding thought that it was a good or excellent idea to provide these services within the pediatric office. Most parents (75%) thought there were no disadvantages to having a pediatric psychologist in the office. Of those who indicated at least one disadvantage, 42% thought parents might feel pressured to use the psychologist in the practice rather than one of their own choosing, 36% were concerned about confidentiality with the front office staff, and 27% were concerned about confidentiality with the pediatrician. The general impression held by parents was that having a pediatric psychologist in the primary care pediatric setting was beneficial, and most stated that they would use this service if they ever needed it. Most (84%) felt their child would be more comfortable in the familiar setting, and 80% felt there would be better communication between the psychologist and pediatrician. Another 63% stated that parents would be more comfortable in the familiar setting, 56% felt the psychologist would be child-oriented in that setting, and 45% would trust the psychologist if their pediatrician trusted him or her. Parents especially appreciated the opportunity to get some input about their children's development or minor concerns with a free phone call. Finney, Riley, and Cataldo also measured a high level of parental satisfaction with behaviorally oriented psychological services in a primary care setting.

Pediatricians and child psychologists certainly seem to be likely to collaborate well because both disciplines share interests in children's health and development. In fact, Lightner Witmer wrote about these common interests a hundred years ago. Wilson recognized the potential benefits of including pediatric psychologists in primary care settings more than thirty years ago in his presidential address to the American Academy of Pediatrics. He said, "One of the things I would do if I could control the practice of pediatrics would be to encourage groups of pediatricians to employ their own clinical psychologists." Not long after Wilson made his remarks, Logan Wright began describing a new breed of psychologists pediatric psychologists -- who would have the skills necessary to work in pediatric medical settings rather than traditional psychiatric settings. An early description of collaboration in pediatric primary care settings also appeared at about the same time. LeBaron and Zeltzer also argued that pediatrician-psychologist collaboration can result in significant improvements in children's primary health care.

Although the initial interest in this collaboration may have included some emphasis on primary care, pediatric psychology has developed since the late 1960s, largely as a specialty area focusing on psychological issues related to chronic physical illnesses mainly treated in tertiary care settings, usually large university medical centers. During this period, pediatric psychology developed a unique set of characteristics, including clinical practice based in medical settings, a medically based referral mechanism, an orientation toward health promotion and prevention to enhance normal development, an emphasis on developmental considerations, familiarity with consultation to physicians and parents, and a practical orientation to treatment techniques that are effective, time-efficient, and economical. Given current changes in the health care system, it seems likely that pediatric psychologists will begin to become more involved in primary care settings. This is particulary true when one considers that most children receive their medical care in some sort of primary care setting (frequently a pediatric office or clinic) and that many children access the behavioral health care system in these settings. This also will likely prove to be a "natural fit" because the types of problems seen by pediatric psychologists tend to involve primary and preventive mental health care and often involve collaboration with pediatric medical care providers.

Identifying Behavioral Issues in Pediatric Primary Care

Although pediatricians clearly struggle to identify children with psychiatric disorders, there has been some evidence to suggest that they may be better suited to identify subthreshold problems that do not meet the criteria for a formal psychiatric diagnosis. For example, Horwitz found that the pediatricians in their study identified 27.3% of 4- to 8-year-old children with problems that could be identified using a 13-point checklist of psychosocial and developmental problems based on a triaxial classification system developed by Bums, Burke, and Regier. Although this represented an improvement over identification rates for psychiatric diagnoses, it must be noted that this classification system included social problems, which are usually viewed as risk factors in other prevalence and identification studies.

Pediatricians have also reported that large numbers of children present with mental health problems that cause distress but fail to reach the level of severity required for a diagnosis using the rules in the American Psychiatric Association's Diagnostic and Statistical Manual of Mental Disorders-IV. Their concerns about children with subthreshold problems have not been heavily studied, but have received some support in research findings. Costello and Shugart found that 42% of children seen in a pediatric primary care setting had these kinds of problems. They also found that most disruptive behavior problems of this severity were associated with significant functional impairment and concluded that intervention for these problems may be needed to avoid more serious levels of impairment.

Pediatricians' efforts to treat children with psychological problems have also been thwarted by a reimbursement system that has often arbitrarily reserved DSM-IV diagnostic codes and psychiatric current procedural terminology (CPT) codes for use only by mental health providers. The organizational structure of managed care, in particular its emphasis on mental health "carve-outs," has also led to a separation of mental disorders from medical disorders at a time when research findings have increased our understanding of the interplay between mind and body. The current classification system clearly needs some additional work to make it possible for pediatricians to provide care for psychological concerns and to enhance communications between primary care providers and mental health clinicians. To better meet the needs of children, an addition to the classification system would have to include information about the common, but less severe psychosocial problems that primary care pediatricians frequently manage.

Development of a Useful Classification Scheme

In 1989 the National Institute of Mental Health sponsored two meetings between primary care practitioners in internal medicine, family practice, pediatrics, and obstetrics/gynecology and representatives of the American Psychiatric Association. Those meetings concluded that primary care providers did not find the DSM-IV useful and ended with a recommendation to develop a more appropriate system for use in primary care. Although the American Psychiatric Association assumed responsibility for development of a system to be used with adults, pediatricians expressed a need for a system that would not only address disorders but would also emphasize developmental changes and environmental factors. A collaborative effort led by the American Academy of Pediatrics and including the American Psychiatric Association, the American Psychological Association (primarily the Society for Pediatric Psychology), the Society for Developmental and Behavioral Pediatrics, the American Academy of Child and Adolescent Psychiatry, the American Academy of Family Physicians, the Canadian Pediatric Society, the Zero to Three/National Center for Clinical Infant Programs, the Matemal and Child Health Bureau, and the National Institute of Mental Health then began to develop a classification system for use with children in primary care settings.This effort resulted in the development of the Diagnostic and Statistical Manual for Primary Care (DSM-PC) Child and Adolescent Version. Several assumptions were made in constructing the system:

1. Children demonstrate symptoms that vary along a continuum from normal variations to mental disorders, and this continuum can be grouped into normal developmental variations, problems, and disorders.

2. Environment has an important impact on the mental health of children, and if stressful situations are addressed, more severe mental health problems can be prevented later.
3. Children vary in how they manifest symptoms or respond to situations, depending on their age and development.
4. A useful system must remain compatible with existing systems such as DSM-IV.
5. The system must be clear, concise, and user-friendly for primary care physicians.
6. The system must be based on objective information as much as possible, with consensus when this is not possible, and organized so that it can be verified or revised by subsequent research.

The DSM-PC is divided into two major sections. The first section addresses the issue of the child's environment and allows the clinician to consider the impact of situations and stressors on the child's mental health. This section also includes information about potentially adverse situations and key risk and protective factors. A summary of common behavioral responses to stressful events for children of various ages is also provided.

The second section describes child manifestations that are organized into behavioral clusters. A clinician can begin by using an index of presenting complaints. Each cluster was developed to help the clinician evaluate the spectrum of the child's symptoms, common developmental presentations, and the differential diagnosis. The classification system is based on the assumption that most behavioral manifestations reflect a spectrum from normal to disordered behavior and each cluster has three categories: developmental variations, problems, and disorders. Developmental variations are behaviors that may raise some concern, but are within the range of expected behaviors for the child's age. Problems reflect behavioral manifestations that are serious enough to disrupt the child's functioning with peers, in school, and/or in the family but are not severe enough to warrant the diagnosis of a mental disorder. The disorders are those defined in the DSM-IV. Although pediatricians may often manage developmental variations and problems, most children presenting with disorders would be referred to mental health clinicians. In a primary care setting that includes the integration of a pediatric psychologist, the psychologist or the pediatrician might manage developmental variations and problems. The psychologist would likely manage the care for children with disorders either directly or by referral to another mental health clinician in the community.

The section on childhood manifestations also includes developmental guidelines broken into four age periods: infancy (birth to 2 years of age), early childhood (3 to 5 years of age), middle childhood (6 to 12 years of age), and adolescence (13 years of age and older). These guidelines are designed to help the clinician recognize the differences in presentation of various problems or disorders in various age groups. The system is also designed to allow for the identification of alternative causes and differential diagnoses. Moreover, it addresses the issue of comorbidity of disorders. Finally, the manual provides general guidelines to determine the severity of a child's condition by considering symptoms, functioning, burden of suffering, and risk/protective factors. It suggests using the three categories of mild, moderate, and severe to describe severity.

Although the DSM-PC is certainly a welcome addition to the tools available to primary care pediatricians, it remains to be seen whether it will, in fact, see much use. Widespread utilization of this manual will certainly depend on its usefulness in securing reimbursement for services. Most insurers have confined reimbursement for mental health services to a short list of psychiatric CPT codes linked to DSM-IV diagnoses. Rappo provided a list of current medical CPT codes that could be used along with DSM-PC diagnoses. Although pediatricians may find these codes useful, they have generally not been recognized for use by mental health clinicians. Therefore, it will also be necessary for third-party reimbursement to allow mental health clinicians working in pediatric primary care settings to link DSM-PC diagnoses with Rappo's list of CPT codes. Finally, mental health clinicians in other settings will need to become familiar with the DSM-PC if it is to help improve communication with pediatricians regarding children's mental health conditions.

Aids to Pediatric Classification

If pediatricians are to efficiently identify children with significant psychosocial problems, it seems likely that they will need good instruments to assist in the process. Although the development of behavior rating scales like the Child Behavior Checklist (CBCL) and structured interviews like the Diagnostic Interview Schedule for Children have helped with the identification of children with psychiatric diagnoses, there is some question about their utility in primary care settings. This is a particular concern when children with subthreshold problems are considered because psychiatric measures are unlikely to identify children with less severe but still significant problems. Psychiatric measures also tend to be more lengthy and could prove cumbersome for primary care clinicians to use. For example, the CBCL has 113 questions and is scored on eight clinical subscales. Structured interviews like the DISC are even more labor-intensive. Primary care clinicians clearly need simpler instruments that can be used quickly and are best described as screening tools.

Pediatricians should probably also remain flexible about screening. Some children are in obvious need of mental health care services and screening would be of little help to them. Children who are clearly developing normally probably also do not require much screening. To solve these problems, it has been suggested that screening be done in two stages. The first stage is done in the pediatrician's office and involves quick, simple testing that would preferably overestimate the number of children in need of further screening, thus resulting in a relatively high number of false positives. The second stage of screening would utilize instruments that take longer to administer but would yield more information for the clinician. It would likely be most efficient for this screening to be done by a pediatric psychologist in the office. Children could also be referred to other mental health care providers who do not operate with the same time pressures as do pediatricians.

Screening questionnaires to be used in the first stage should be valid, reliable, and select the correct children for further evaluation. They should also be brief, understandable, easily completed, and scored quickly. Finally, they should require a minimum of professional time unless the results indicate a problem. Eisert, Sturner and Mabe have provided a helpful review of the issues involved in selecting screening tools for pediatricians. Their guidelines are also applied to several behavioral questionnaires.

Some instruments have been developed that are appropriate for use in the first stage of screening and two will be reviewed here. The Eyberg Child Behavior Inventory has been used widely in research and is well validated. It is a 36-item questionnaire that parents can complete in about 5 minutes and that pediatricians can review quickly. It includes questions about child behavior during bedtime and mealtime and is particularly helpful in identifying children at risk for disruptive behavior problems. It yields two scores that reflect the number of problems a child is having and their intensity.

Another instrument that has been used widely in research is the Pediatric Symptom Checklist (PSC). The PSC was designed specifically for psychosocial screening in pediatric office settings. It is a 35-item questionnaire that measures the presence of behavioral and/or emotional symptoms. Scoring is quick and yields a single total score. Cutoff scores of 24 for 4and 5-year-old children and 28 for children 6-12 years of age have been empirically established.

It should be noted that several other questionnaires are available to screen for psychosocial concerns in younger children. These include the Behavior Checklist, Behar's Pre-school Behavior Questionnaire and the Toddler Behavior Screening Inventory.

Although there has been increasing interest in first-stage screening among pediatricians, several problems have been identified. First, it appears that many primary care physicians are interested in screening but only a small percentage actually implement these procedures. One study followed up on 201 pediatricians and family practitioners who had requested information about the PSC and found that only 23% of those who responded reported that they had used the measure. Second, a recent review of the current status of behavior screening methods concluded that it is unclear whether screening will cause a significant change in physician behaviors necessary to improve child functional outcomes. Jellinek and Murphy noted that screening is just one step in a process that raises additional questions about the pediatrician's ability to follow up on the results of the screening, family acceptance of referral to mental health clinicians, time devoted to psychosocial issues in light of time constraints and problems with reimbursements, and the effectiveness of interventions. Finally, most of the efforts to develop screening tools have focused on identifying children with psychiatric disorders. Although this is certainly necessary, use of these tools fails to identify many of the more common problems that pediatricians are likely to encounter and manage.

Integrated Care in Pediatric Primary Care Settings

Pediatricians will continue to be called on for anticipatory guidance, advice about common behavior problems, early detection of problems, and referral for more serious disorders. Interested pediatricians can find a good deal of helpful information in the behavioral pediatrics literature. In fact, behavioral pediatricians have assumed a good deal of the responsibility for training current pediatric residents in the management of the "new morbidity." Several techniques for managing common behavior problems can be found in an article by Christophersen. These ideas have been further expanded to address behavioral problems, medical/behavioral problems, educational intervention strategies, advanced intervention techniques, and office management strategies. Both of these publications include numerous examples of handouts that can be given to parents during office visits.

Additional attention has also recently been given to the idea of including behavioral health care professionals in the pediatric primary care office. Pediatric psychologists already have a strong history of successful collaboration with pediatricians in tertiary care settings and are probably extremely well suited to making the transition into working in pediatric primary care settings. In particular, the emphasis within pediatric psychology on preventive care and a focus away from psychopathology matches well with the issues to be managed in primary care settings.

Models of Integrated Pediatric Care

Several qualities of successful collaboration between pediatricians and pediatric psychologists have been identified. Psychologists who practice effectively in tertiary care hospitals or in primary care do not just transfer their training in traditional clinical psychology to these medical settings. They take the time to understand and adapt to the special characteristics of the settings, populations, and providers. Most effective psychologists in medical settings have a strong personal and professional identity. A high level of professional commitment is common in this group, and they tend to be thorough, work hard, and go beyond minimal expectations. They are also flexible and know when to stick up for things and when to let things go. They know how to advocate for themselves without being overly aggressive or demanding. This comes in handy when one is dealing with the competing expectations that can go along with any collaboration. Most are comfortable developing plans and taking action. The best ones easily make psychological knowledge very user-friendly. It is important to remember that the psychologist's relationship with the pediatricians will be a long-term one. Therefore, appreciation and respect for pediatricians are important. The successful psychologist will understand the demands that pediatricians face, respect their expertise, and understand and tolerate their limits. This appreciation for colleagues is particularly important for pediatric psychologists working in primary care settings, because their frequent interactions with the pediatricians are likely to have an effect on the setting as well as on all the professionals involved. In other words, the pediatrician is likely to learn from the psychologist and the psychologist is likely to learn from the pediatrician throughout the course of their collaboration. Hamlett and Stabler described a developmental process that takes place in these collaborations that moves in higher degrees of complexity from clinical case management to long-term collaboration, and eventually on to program and policy development.

The model for integrated care in pediatric primary care settings is generally a collaborative one. The partners in this collaboration are the pediatricians, pediatric psychologists, nurses, lab personnel, and support staff within the office or clinic. Community contacts are also important and can include school personnel, developmental therapists, public sector providers, psychiatrists, and other therapists. There are some disadvantages to this approach, such as the need to negotiate with colleagues, some loss of control, and additional demands on the psychologist's time. The advantages are the input from colleagues with different areas of expertise, a broader range of activities, and not having to carry the entire load alone.

This type of collaboration is well known to pediatric psychologists because they have often functioned in tertiary care settings as behavioral health care consultants to their medical colleagues. Several conceptual models of pediatric consultation have been advanced. Roberts and Wright discussed a three-part model of consultation. Effective psychology practice in pediatric primary care settings features aspects of all three parts.

In the independent functions model, the consultant provides independent diagnosis and treatment of the patient. This model has also been called noncollaborative, the resource consultation model and the client-centered model. The main information exchanges between the pediatrician and the consultant happen at the point of the referral and at the completion of care. The pediatrician and the consultant have very little contact with each other and do not work collaboratively. This model is very familiar to most pediatricians because it characterizes the majority of consultation they receive from their medical colleagues. An example for a pediatric psychologist in a pediatric primary care setting would be if the pediatrician referred a child with a learning disability for an evaluation and family support for appropriate educational planning. In that case, the psychologist would take over the responsibility for helping the child and family and would keep the pediatrician informed of plans and important developments.

The second type of consultation is the indirect functions model, which has also been called the process-educative model. In this model, the consultant functions as a teacher or informed colleague, providing advice, teaching, or protocols for patient management. The pediatrician retains responsibility for patient care. In this model, the consultant has little or no direct contact with the patient. An example would be if a pediatrician were managing stimulant medication for attention deficit hyperactivity disorder (ADHD) and asked the psychologist for help in interpreting feedback from parents and teachers in determining whether the medication was helpful for a child.

The collaborative team model is similar to process consultation and collaboration as defined by Burns and Cromer. In this model the consultant and the pediatrician truly collaborate and share responsibility and decision making for patient care. This model is employed more often in teaching/research centers and less in private practice settings because it is time-intensive and often requires team meetings. An example in a primary care setting would be if the psychologist and the pediatrician were collaborating in the care of a child with complicated encopresis that required medical management as well as behavioral interventions.

Effective integrated care models involve more than just providing traditional mental health services in primary care settings. This level of integration relies on using the indirect functions model and the collaborative teams model when appropriate and requires frequent communication between the pediatricians and the pediatric psychologist. This kind of collaboration allows the pediatric psychologist to have some input into a child's medical care as well as for the pediatrician to influence the child's behavioral health care. As such, it provides a more holistic approach to children's health care.

Although interest in integrating pediatric psychologists into primary care settings has increased recently, several earlier works described some of the aspects of this work. It may now be more common for pediatric offices and clinics to include a pediatric psychologist, but the trend has been slow to develop. One reason for this has been psychologists' lack of familiarity with the characteristics and demands of pediatric primary care settings. Students are not usually exposed to these settings during their training, and relatively few publications are available to guide psychologists interested in entering this area of practice. Another reason is that many pediatric primary care offices are private practices, and psychologists moving into these areas must take on many business issues. Most pediatric psychologists are better prepared to confront practice in more academic settings, like university medical centers. Finally, private practice pediatricians are often so busy with patient care and their own business issues that it is difficult for them to take on the additional job of recruiting pediatric psychologists to work with them. There is some suggestion that the effort necessary to integrate a pediatric psychologist into a pediatric primary care office or clinic results in a positive experience for the psychologist. A recent survey of 261 pediatric psychologists found that 21% of them were working in private practice or outpatient pediatric settings and also found that the group in private practice reported the highest levels of job satisfaction.

Although some information is available for pediatric psychologists working in these settings, it must be recognized that a shift in the focus of research and training will be necessary if more of them are going to be integrated into this kind of care. Although the clinical areas of psychology have emphasized pathology and dysfunction, truly integrated work in primary care settings requires a shift toward normal development and common, less severe problems. Pediatric psychologists working in primary care will be in a unique position to demonstrate treatments and management techniques that work with normally developing children in much the same way that many psychologists working in traditional mental health specialties have moved toward empirically validating treatments for psychiatric disorders. Holden and Schumann pointed out that little research has been done to evaluate the integration of pediatric psychology services into primary care, but it seems likely that more pediatric psychologists will have to move into these settings before this research can be done. Because many of these practices are not affiliated with university departments and rely heavily on fee-for-service work, it may prove difficult to complete these studies unless pediatric psychologists in academic departments and those working in these practices collaborate on this work. There are some indications that these studies would find positive results. Finney found that 74% of the children served in an outpatient health care setting improved. They also noted some medical cost offset for some diagnoses with outpatient psychological interventions.

If psychologists are to be effective members of primary care teams, it is critical that they have a good understanding of these settings as well as the ways in which pediatricians approach their own work. In other words, psychologists must adapt their own thinking and approaches to be successful. Drotar identified ways in which pediatricians' and psychologists' expectations about how the other should perform their duties may differ. For example, pediatricians' familiarity with medical consultation may lead them to expect that a psychologist will provide prompt and specific feedback following a referral, as well as any necessary follow-up care for a patient. Psychologists who are more familiar with traditional mental health care settings may expect that pediatricians will supply them with comprehensive information about each patient they refer and be available to discuss the results of an evaluation in great detail. Because pediatric psychologists are trained in medical settings and are familiar with their demands and expectations, it should be expected that these kinds of conflicts are less likely to occur when they collaborate with pediatricians in primary care settings.

Pediatric psychologists accustomed to the work in tertiary care settings will have to become familiar with the demands of primary care. Pediatric primary care practices are very busy and are results oriented. A fast pace and a heavy workload are the norm. Work in these settings requires the quick recognition of problems and their solutions as well as the timely implementation of effective plans. The pace for pediatricians in primary care settings is much faster than that of their medical colleagues working in specialty clinics and tertiary care settings. In short, there is no time for the discussion of interesting diagnostic dilemmas or power struggles over psychological treatment plans. The focus is more likely to be on what the psychologist plans to do to solve a child's problems. Because pediatricians are often the first providers to identify developmental and psychological problems but may not have the time and skills to fully address them, a pediatric psychologist can play a valuable role in providing necessary patient care. Pediatricians can also be quite helpful to the pediatric psychologist. For example, they can frequently provide useful background information about children and families because they often have very long-term relationships with them. They may know things about children and families that it may be difficult for the psychologist to find out early in an evaluation.

At any given time, the pediatrics office is mostly full of babies and young children. These age groups have more frequent visits for preventive care and also are the ones more likely to be sick. It is important that a psychologist working in primary care pediatrics be comfortable working with infants, toddlers, preschoolers, and their parents. Most of the children seen in primary care settings are also developing normally, so it is necessary for the psychologist to become familiar with the problems common to most children. It also helps to be comfortable working with seasonal demands. The increased demand for medical care for acute illness in the winter means that the pace around the office or clinic is much more hectic at that time of year.

Finally, parents rely heavily on telephone contact with pediatricians and nurses, and it is important for the psychologist to develop strategies to be available this way as well. For example, it can be helpful to have a parent hotline that allows parents to call for advice on handling common behavior problems their children might be having that do not warrant an office visit. Work by Schroeder and her colleagues provides some guidance about parental concerns that are likely to be encountered in telephone calls and advice that parents find helpful. These studies have found that parents called most frequently with concerns in the following areas: negative behavior, toileting, personality or emotional problems, school problems, sleeping problems, developmental delays, sibling/peer problems, and divorce/separation. Parents who used a come-in/call-in service expressed high degrees of confidence in the counselors they talked with, and the vast majority of them rated the service as good.

The heavy workloads and quick pace of these settings require that psychologists manage stress well. Managing the workload can be difficult because it is unpredictable, so it is important to help the pediatricians, patients, and parents develop realistic expectations for the psychologist. It is also important that psychologists in these settings have realistic expectations for themselves. For example, it is critical for a pediatric psychologist working in a primary care setting to be absolutely clear about how many patients can be seen in a week and stick to that limit, particularly when things are more hectic in the office. It is also important to be clear about the types of problems the pediatric psychologist will manage. Although it may be tempting to become the mental health care provider for all the children in a pediatrics practice, doing so will quickly interfere with the psychologist's ability to take care of the more common, less severe problems that are more frequently the focus of the pediatrician's care.

Characteristics of Pediatric Psychology Practice

It is clear that the emphasis on prevention, intervention, and care for normally developing children in pediatric primary care has an effect on the practice of psychology in these settings. Much of the discussion here is based on experiences in the author's practice in Durham, North Carolina. This pediatrics practice has seven full-time pediatricians and one full-time pediatric nurse practitioner, who care for about 35,000 patients. The pediatric psychology practice was started in 1988. A full-time pediatric psychologist and a half-time pediatric psychologist have now seen about 1,900 children. The average is about five new referrals per week, and the pattern of referral sources has remained very stable. Some parents in the pediatric practice view pediatric psychology as another part of their health care services, so 58% of referrals come from parents themselves. The pediatricians refer 31% of the psychologists' patients, and other physicians in the community refer an additional 2%. The remaining 9% of referrals come from a number of other sources. Many come from the nursing staff and sometimes from the receptionists. Other referrals come from teachers, school counselors, attorneys, and managed care companies.

As in most clinical situations, more boys than girls (63% vs. 37%) are seen. Because most of the children seen in the pediatrics office are younger, the psychologists' patients also tend to be younger, with 76% of them being 10 years old or younger. The age groups are as follows: 29% are 1-5 years of age, 47% are 6-10 years old, 20% are 11-15 years old, and 4% are 16 or older.

Presenting complaints have been tracked over the years. It should be noted that the percentages reported here reflect the fact that some children present with multiple complaints. The most common presenting problems (73%) involve negative behavior, attention deficit hyperactivity disorder (ADHD), and school concerns. Anxiety, divorce/separation, and depression are concerns for another 25% of the patients. Concerns that are quite familiar to pediatric psychologists (developmental delays, chronic illness, physical complaints, toileting problems, sleep disturbances, and grief issues) are involved in 14% of the presenting complaints. Other frequent concerns include child abuse/sex abuse (3%), peer problems/self-esteem (3%), fears/phobias (2%), and parent-child conflict (2%). When the data are examined further, some other patterns emerge. Boys tend to be seen more often for negative behavior and ADHD, and girls are more evenly spread out among the various categories of presenting complaints. Younger children are seen most frequently for negative behavior, and children in elementary school are frequently seen for ADHD. Adolescents continue to be seen for negative behavior and ADHD, but also begin to present with complaints about depression.

As can be seen, the psychologist in a pediatric primary care setting is confronted with the demand to address the needs of a very large number of children. This volume requires that the psychologist maintain a constant availability to new patients. This is critical to ensure that parents and children make appointments and keep them. Pediatricians in these settings value the increased likelihood of parents' following through on referrals to the psychologist in the office, but long waits to be seen can create problems with compliance and the timeliness of interventions. This demand leads to the necessity of referring children with certain types of problems out to other providers. These include complicated child abuse cases, eating disorders, major conduct disorders, substance abuse, and severe psychopathology. Children with these problems tend to slow down the flow of patients for the pediatric psychologist because they require a very large number of visits and the services of teams of providers that are not available in the pediatrics office. Thus, it is clearly necessary for pediatric psychologists practicing in pediatric primary care settings to maintain relationships with other mental health care clinicians in the local community who can be available to care for children and adolescents with more complicated and severe problems. It is particularly important to identify child psychiatrists who can be helpful in managing the pharmacological care for these patients and who may also have admitting privileges at local psychiatric units. Finally, these patients may also require referral to therapists who are more familiar with severe psychopathology.

As in most pediatric settings, the workload in primary care can be quite heavy and requires that the pediatric psychologist play several roles, including consultant, educator, clinician, and case-manager/advocate. A full-time pediatric psychologist can expect to average 25 patient hours per week with a range throughout the year of 15 to 35 patient hours per week. Typical clinical services include interviewing, testing, and psychotherapy. This is in addition to administrative time, consultation time, and phone calls. The emphasis on collaboration and integration of services means that the psychologist must be prepared to give away some services, such as consultations with the pediatricians and phone calls with parents. The advantage of providing these services is an increase in the visibility and perceived value of pediatric psychology in the practice.

Most children (60%) are seen for treatment only, and 29% are seen for evaluation only. The additional 11% are seen for evaluation and treatment. The number of visits in the author's practice ranges from 1 to 112, but the heaviest emphasis is on brief treatment. The modal number of visits is 1 and the median is 3 visits. Twenty-six percent of the children are seen for 1 visit, 75% are seen for 5 visits or less, and 86% are seen for 10 visits or less. Children seen for more visits tend to come for evaluation and treatment. Many of them also present with multiple problems.

This information easily leads to conclusions about the types of services that are effective in pediatric primary care settings. First, evaluations that quickly lead to appropriate developmental and educational interventions are important. These should mesh well with the efforts of special educators, speech/language therapists, occupational therapists, and physical therapists. Second, interventions must be problem-focused and brief. As a result, short-term behavioral approaches combined with long-term intermittent work are most effective. The psychologist in these settings must be also be comfortable with behavior management/parent training techniques, psychoeducational approaches, and early intervention. Third, because this is primary care, the psychologist must also be familiar with many community resources in order to be prepared to provide appropriate referrals for children and their parents. This work can include referrals to developmental therapists, school personnel, and other mental health professionals.

In a broad sense, services also include the psychologist's communication with the pediatricians and community physicians. They place a very high value on prompt feedback about their patients and often complain that mental health professionals frequently fall short in this regard. In the author's practice, parents are informed that the pediatric psychologists will be working collaboratively with the pediatricians and are told that this might limit their confidentiality. Parents' reactions to this approach tend to be very positive, and only a handful have expressed any concerns about it. In addition to providing prompt feedback, psychologists in these settings must communicate in the style of medical settings. This means that the message must be brief, accurate, and thorough. Good psychological consultants can take complicated concepts and present them in ways that are clear and seem sensible and pragmatic to physicians. It is critical in primary care to think from healthy, normal models rather than from pathology-oriented models.

Several methods of communication can be helpful. Within the office the pediatric psychologists and pediatricians rely most heavily on short curb-side consults, informal notes, and chart notes. Written feedback tends to be very brief and emphasizes conclusions and recommendations. There is usually little need to include much historical information because the pediatricians already know this. Recommendations for things the pediatricians should do in caring for a patient are particularly important and must be communicated clearly. It is also helpful to include something about how the psychologist plans to intervene. Communications outside the office are more variable. For example, the local schools want only full psychological reports. Local physicians tend to prefer letters they can use for chart documentation and sometimes request that these be faxed to improve the speed of response. A few physicians also ask for brief e-mail messages to keep them updated on progress.

Setting Up a Pediatric Primary Care Office

Truly integrated care requires that the psychologist be available in the pediatrics practice on a full-time basis. There are certainly other models that allow for close cooperation between pediatricians and pediatric psychologists, including part-time practice in the pediatrics office and strong referral relationships between pediatricians and pediatric psychologists in the community. This section provides information on setting up a full-time practice within a primary care pediatrics office to achieve a model of truly integrated care.

A good background in clinical child psychology is absolutely critical and a strong background in pediatric psychology is even better. Familiarity with interdisciplinary care models is also helpful. Pediatric psychologists have an advantage in these settings because of their skills in diagnosis and treatment, their familiarity with medical consultation-liaison models, their commitment to prevention and early intervention, and the emphasis in their training on working with physicians and medical patients. Experience in psychiatric settings or mental health centers is not as valuable to the psychologist in a pediatric primary care setting as is experience in a tertiary medical hospital or developmental disabilities center. A successful primary care pediatric psychologist must know how to work with infants, preschoolers, and elementary age children. Experience working with adolescents is helpful, particularly if it has emphasized normal adolescents rather than those with more severe psychological problems. The author's experience suggests that severely disturbed adolescents access the mental health system somewhere other than the private pediatrics office. In general, it is critical to have a good grounding in normal child development and common childhood problems. A strong understanding of ADHD, learning disabilities (LD), and developmental disabilities is also necessary.

Finally, the psychologist must have a firm grasp of behavioral and cognitive-behavioral treatments that are effective in individual work with children and in parent training. Long-term insight-oriented approaches are not appropriate in these settings, and children requiring them should be referred to other providers in the community. Although some of the children and parents seen in primary care might benefit from family therapy, formal training in this area is not necessary for the pediatric psychologist in these settings, because these needs can be addressed by other providers in the community.

The first step in the process of establishing a practice is, of course, identifying a pediatrics practice interested in having a psychologist in the office or clinic. In some instances, the pediatricians might approach a psychologist to join them. If this happens, the psychologist should listen carefully to what they are asking for. Once they have explained their reasons for looking for a psychologist, it will be possible to add to the list of things they could expect by describing other skills and interests that would mesh well with their practice.

It is more likely that a psychologist wishing to work in a primary care pediatric setting will have to actively look for a group of pediatricians to join and that it Will be necessary to contact several groups before finding one that seems truly interested. In looking, it is important to first determine the pediatricians' general level of interest in mental health issues and their tendency to refer to mental health professionals. The psychologist's chances of joining a pediatrics practice obviously increase when the pediatricians themselves are psychologically minded. Although the pediatrics group is likely to be a private practice, possibilities also include ambulatory clinics at medical centers and public health clinics. The author's experience suggests that a pediatrics practice should have at least 10,000 and preferably at least 15,000 patients to support a full-time psychologist. That probably means three or four full-time pediatricians. It will also be important to be aware of changes in the local health care market. Many pediatric primary care practices are being considered for mergers and buyouts, and this could mean that a psychologist looking to join them could end up left out in the end.

There are two models for finding a group to join. First, the psychologist could approach a group he or she already knows. When doing this, it will be helpful to talk to the member of the group most likely to be open to the idea and to be willing to help sell the other members of the group on it. If possible, try to do a brief (10-15 minutes) presentation on having a psychologist in the office for all the pediatricians in the group at a convenient time. Follow up mainly with one member of the group, and keep in mind that it could take several months to convince the group to add a psychologist. Another way to find a pediatrics practice to join is to contact groups unfamiliar with the psychologist but possibly interested in having a psychologist in the office. To do this, begin by sending out an introductory letter and a curriculum vitae. The psychologist can then follow-up in much the same way as for a group he or she knows.

To establish a strong practice, the psychologist must be clear on setting up the appropriate business arrangements. It may be best to first be an independent contractor with the pediatricians, because they may not be interested in hiring the psychologist as an employee or as a partner. If there is more than one psychologist involved, it may be necessary to incorporate. Unless the pediatricians have a collection rate in excess of 95%, the psychologist will do better financially to handle his or her own billing. The financial arrangements between the psychologist and the pediatricians genrally follow one of two patterns either the psychologist pays a fixed cost for overhead, or the pediatricians collect a set percentage of the psychologist's collections.

Negotiating for space will be another critical area. Medical practices tend to be squeezed for space, so the psychologist will probably have to take whatever space the pediatricians can offer, provided that patients can be reasonably comfortable there and privacy can be assured. At a minimum, this means a door and enough room to seat a few people. These are busy settings, so expect this space to be noisy. It will be necessary sometimes to protect this space, and the psychologist should probably not expect to be able to get more space later unless the practice or clinic moves to a bigger building. When calculating overhead, the psychologist should include something for the use of the waiting room, but not for space like the lab and the nurses' station, which are not used for psychological services.

The psychologist will need access to telephones. It may be best at first to use the same phones as the pediatricians do and to ask for the receptionists to answer calls for the psychologist. Phone messages can be a problem, so a voice-mail system is good to add. The psychologist will also need to have a pager for emergency coverage. A computer to handle billing, word processing, and Internet access will also be necessary. Office furniture will be required, including a desk, chairs, a small table and chairs, a larger table for testing, and locked filing cabinets. The psychologist will also have to provide the appropriate tests and equipment.

It is important that the psychologist establish an appropriate niche in the office. The power structure of a medical office basically has two levels the physicians and the support staff. To ensure an effective collaborative relationship, the psychologist should function at the level of the physicians. Several strategies are helpful in this regard. First, settle the issue of names. Call the physicians by their first names. In many settings, it will also be necessary for the psychologist to ask that the support staff address him or her as "Doctor." Second, follow the dress code of the office. For most pediatric primary care settings, this is fairly comfortable and informal. Third, if possible, the psychologist should ask for his or her name to be on the door and on the pediatricians' letterhead. Arrangements should also be made to do minimal but effective charting in the medical charts. Fourth, the psychologist should attend physician meetings and some staff meetings. It will be necessary to push for this in some instances. Finally, joining informal conversations around the office is also important, but remember to keep it short. At first, when the practice is getting established, it is vital for the psychologist to be in the office even when there are no patients to see. In general, times without patients are good for the psychologist to use to increase the visibility of psychological services in the office. Marketing efforts should focus most heavily on the pediatrics practice, because most referrals will come from parents in the practice and from the pediatricians.

It is probably necessary for pediatric psychologists in pediatric primary care settings to be prepared to work with managed care. Families with young children tend to favor this type of health insurance, and these settings are highly penetrated by managed care. Because the psychologist's availability to see the pediatricians' patients is critical to the functioning of this model of practice, it may be very difficult to avoid being on panels. If there is any good news in this, it is that the focus on brief treatment in these settings can be compatible with the demands of managed care. The bad news is the same as it is for other psychologists more work in return for reduced reimbursements.

In closing, it is important to point out why a pediatric psychologist wants to practice psychology in a pediatric primary care setting and confront the various demands and complications involved with it. First, the collaboration between the psychologist and the pediatricians can be very supportive. Second, this model allows for very effective patient care that really can include prevention and early intervention. Third, the children are in these settings and it just makes sense to go to them. Fourth, the pediatrics office provides instant credibility and a steady referral base if the collaboration works well. Finally, this kind of work can be interesting and fun. Because things are so child focused, there are very few dull moments. No two days are quite alike in these settings, and new challenges constantly present themselves.

5

Assessing Process in Psychological Assessment

Introduction

The word "process" is derived from the Latin procedure, meaning to advance, to progress, to move onward. Individualized assessment directly addresses progressing. From the point of view of a human-science psychology, tests are simplified and specialized versions of challenges that also face clients elsewhere. They are challenges to clients' progress--to their continuing the courses of their lives. Clients cope with the challenge, whether defensively, offensively, or routinely, as they cope with similar events in similar situations.

For certain other forms of evaluation, it is sufficient and appropriate to address only the milestones that have been passed, the achievements left behind. Sometimes such data are used to predict what other milestones and achievements might be reached in the future. Some evaluations regard test profiles as products of various cognitive styles or psychodynamics, and thereby attend to process, albeit indirectly. Assessors can, of course, look to test scores and patterns for clues to process, which then can be pursued directly with clients.

Witnessing and Exploring Process

Whether studied in clients' environments or in an assessor's office, the process through which a person approaches, goes through, influences, and is changed by situations, is most accessible when the person is directly observed coping with challenges and then discusses what it was like, and how it was similar to and different from other situations. Clients, however, may offer explanations for what has happened rather than describing events directly and holistically. A major part of the assessor's task is to encourage the client to present events phenomenally--as they were lived at the time. A person progresses, after all, through a simultaneously affective/cognitive/actional engagement with the world.

To begin to explore process, the assessor first must be present to it. In particular, one does not ask "why," but instead asks, who is this person? Where is she or he going? What is her or his world like? Within that world, which things are seen as obstacles and which as invitations? What assumptions are made? What futures are possible from such positions? Process may seem to be internal to the client, but his or her travels are inextricably engaged with the worlds we share--the physical world, the world of past common experience, and the world in which our respective projects touch, clash, or cooperate. We know each other by what we do and where we go. Process becomes visible as style through first-hand encounters with the client's pathways, sequences, strategies.

Explicit anticipations of where the client will go next allow the assessor to be surprised, to direct well-grounded requests for clarification to the client, and to reformulate. Throughout, the purpose is to continue reformulating, reunderstanding, until the referral can be answered in terms of this individual's life and until recommendations can be tailored. There is no need to search for absolute categories or explanations. It may be appropriate to judge, for example, whether one person is brain-damaged or whether another person fits the Borderline Personality Disorder designation. But to the extent that the assessment is to be individualized, greater priority is given to how the person lives her or his life-what the person's world looks like, and how the person perpetuates problems and perhaps could modify them.

An assessment is not intended to be a total portrait; the assessor does not look for themes or categories that would explain a person completely. The assessor remains open to complexity and to the diverse meanings that co-exist. Early confusion should be allowed to continue until the assessor discovers that a certain sense of things has begun to evolve. Actually, the assessor's presence, or attention, moves through many vicissitudes: openness to impressions, reflection, calculation, recollection, back to openness, and so on. The point is that unless the assessor becomes an access to the lived world of the client, calculations and deductions cannot lead to an individualized assessment.

During the assessment, meanings may occur to the assessor before their source is identified. For example, one may experience a client as evasive even though she or he is providing immediate, enthusiastic, elaborated answers to inquiries. The assessor should trust the impression long enough to search for its source and appraise its significance. In one case, the assessor recognized that the "evasiveness" of his client was his own impatience with the client's lengthy answers, which were tangential to the assessor's unspoken concerns. It was he who had not yet come to the point.

Another assessor experienced a client as haughty. He located that impression, after a while, in her turning away and tilting her head upward when he expressed concern for her. Then he noticed that the client's knuckles were white as she clutched the books in her lap. He realized that although she appeared to be haughty, she was also feeling tense and uncertain. He could now share both impressions with the client, pointing to their sources in what was visible and in his own differing reactions. This is another important reason for locating the source of impressions: The client can then "see" what others see, and can discuss what the observed event was like from the actor's perspective.

At other times, the assessor notices details that seem somehow meaningful even though the specific meaning is not clear. A lapel stickpin worn at an odd angle may be noticed early, only to gestalt much later with other "off center" ways that the client establishes independence. During discussions and in the report, a concrete example such as the stickpin can serve to collect or to recollect other instances of referral-relevant themes.

Ambiguity should be regarded as possibly inherent to phenomena rather than necessarily a deficient or confused form of knowing. This approach helps the assessor to accept both sides of apparently contradictory observations. The haughty woman was both disdainful of the assessor's solicitude and anxious about what they might discover. Apparent contradictions are in fact the dynamics of a person's moving toward goals.

While observing two graduate students making a class presentation, I noted that Pat directed Kevin and that she waited for Kevin's agreement. Upon reflection I saw that her way of taking charge considered others' perspectives and desires; but this solicitude occurred in a context of being the leader. That Pat is experienced by most acquaintances as both pleasantly serious and quietly dynamic has to do with the tension of her living toward both goals (directing and waiting) concomitantly.

There are many ways to be present to process. In general, one should remain open, not interpret too readily, not reach closure prematurely, not explain away what one has witnessed. To keep myself attuned to process, rather than becoming sidetracked in a search for explanations, I ask, "How could this event have come into being?" I ponder the evolution of a completed Bender (the task that asks the client to copy freehand nine geometric patterns) much as one ponders footprints along a beach. One might guess the owner's height, weight, and gender fairly accurately. But where was this person going? Perhaps just for a walk; the prints follow the tide's edge as though the goal were to follow the tide line rather than to reach some particular destination. Yes, the prints are relatively flat--unlike those where the hurried walker's heels have struck the wet sand sharply. Perhaps the walker was on a nature stroll. But look at all these intriguing shells that the stroller left unturned and the huge horseshoe crab he did not investigate. How could a nature lover ignore these things? Perhaps they are familiar; maybe he was just walking home along an habitual route. Perhaps he ignored these marvels because he was preoccupied--I wonder about what? Here, the tracks veer to avoid walking through a child's small, crumbling moat. Although preoccupied, the stroller noticed it and cared. This form of presence to process enriches perception and helps one to address meaningful questions to the client.

Other queries that I pose to myself and later address to the client include: Where does this experiaction bring the client? How and when does it work for him or her? When not? What is the short-term outcome? Long-term? Is the person winding up at places that were not intended? Where else is the person going? And coming away from? And avoiding? Because people often are not focally aware of all these facets of their travels, the assessor must be all the more alert to those moments when the client is in touch with a pertinent aspect of his or her movement. Those moments are entry points for joint exploration.

In general, the assessor accepts a client's account as the client's account, and then suggests additions and modifications as they become apparent. Even these revisions are revised as the session goes on. When the client resists a line of inquiry, the assessor has failed to begin that inquiry within areas of the client's world that he or she experiences as familiar and traversable. Common ground was not adequately established. Sometimes, however, clients for their own reasons or because of severe disability do not allow the assessor access to more than end-product data. In all cases, as long as one's impressions can be documented with primary data, they should be retained and reported, even if the client does not agree, or does not understand. The client is an expert about what he or she remembers, and about what he or she is now concerned about and believes; but the assessor's differing impressions may be just as valid in a broader sense. Both views are important for understanding and planning, and both should be reported.

Table 5.1 illustrates the collaborative exploration of process. Many of the excerpts forerun activities illustrated in Table 5.2, on developing viable options. In actuality the activities of exploration and option-development are not so distinct.

Table 5.1. Witnessing and Exploring Process: Excerpts

The client is a 28-year-old program monitor, a woman, self-referred for career guidance.

Assessor: Sandy, what was your turning the paper horizontally about? [The client's Bender drawing paper is placed vertically, but was repositioned twice by the assessor after Sandy moved it.]

Client: I don't know. It just seemed better that way.

Assessor: Most people just leave it the way it's placed. You moved it to suit your preference. Is that like anything you've done at work that Mr. O'Pake might have seen as "going off on your own [part of the referral issue]"?

Client: No. It's just that the cards run this way [horizontal], so I thought the drawings would fit better if my paper were running the same way.

Assessor: Oh! So perhaps what Mr. O 'Pake and I have seen as persistent individuality may be instead your effort to be even more conscientious than other monitors have been? [Sandy then describes how her work has been demonstrably more thorough and more timely than that of all others in her office, but superiors in her present and prior jobs have criticized her for unorthodox, sometimes defiant, sometimes lackadaisical work habits.] Well, you know we already talked about how surprised I was when your copies of the designs turned out to be so precise. As I was watching you, taking your time but not erasing or otherwise appearing to me to be concerned about accuracy you were chatting with me most of the time I expected the copies to be haphazard. At the end I still had that feeling, even though each design had turned out just fine. I think I'm beginning to see what Mr. O 'Pake may be responding to.

Client: [Long pause] Well, that's it in a nutshell. I guess I've just got to find ways of letting my supervisors see that I am in fact doing exactly the job they want done. I'd hate to do it, but maybe I should ask them to check my work en route so they can see it instead of me. At least that would be easier than changing careers!

The client is a 19-year-old college junior, male, referred to the Guidance Center by a business law professor for trouble in attending classes regularly.

Assessor: You seem to enjoy the challenge of these test items. I have trouble imagining you being bored with Dr. Pressinger 's course?

Client: That's why he said I should see somebody. When I'm in class, I enjoy it and I participate. And like I said, I write the papers. On other days I get up early, but on business law days I often just sleep in. I know I ought to, but . . .

Assessor: Ought to? Who says people should go to early classes? [Client: You just should.] What happens to people who go to their early classes?

(Contd.)

Client: [Laughingly] They get good grades, get elected to offices, and grow up to be responsible executives.

Assessor: And who wants you to grow up to be an executive?

Client: I do. Well, I mean it's expected, and I do have the skills and the opportunity.

Assessor: Who's doing this expecting? [Discussion continues, as the client discovers that he feels as though he has been pushed into his father's career line. An appointment is made for career advisement assessment, through which the client could make some informed choices, including possibly his present business major.]

The client is a 41-year-old marketing manager in a corporation-sponsored manager- development assessment.

Assessor: Many people who score as high as you did on these two scales have been described as stubborn. [Personality Research Form, high dominance and endurance scales].

Client: Well, it's sure right about that! My wife would tell you that!

Assessor: Yes? What would she say?

Client: Well, that I'm not satisfied until something is finished, till it's done right. [Assessor: Like?] Like putting up the dry wall for our driveway; took me all summer a couple years back, but ours is the only one that didn't buckle during these severe winters we've had recently.

Assessor: Your approach certainly paid off. But what do people call your being stubborn when they don't like it?

Client: What do you mean?

Assessor: What do your kids, or your subordinates at work, say about your being persistent?

Client: Oh, I see what you mean. I'd say the boy and my daughter don't much notice unless I'm after them to do something right. Then they say I'm picky. [Assessor: And at work?] Perfectionistic. [Long pause] I guess we're onto something. This seems to relate to what we were saying before--about my having trouble delegating authority. Like you said, it's not a question of my knowing how to analyze a problem and break it out into assignments. I just don't like to let go until I know it is done right. Lord, I just remembered [smiling]: my house painter told me he was going to increase his charges if I didn't get out from underfoot!

Assessor: Okay. Tell me some times when you do get out from underfoot.

Client: Do you mean like at home? [Assessor: Okay--whenever.] Well, it would never occur to me to interfere with my wife's cooking. And of course I don't insert myself into the sales manager's side of things. If anything goes wrong there, everyone knows it's got nothing to do with me.

Assessor: Is that similar to when you were copying the designs [Bender-Gestalt]? You said you hadn't been "assiduously careful" since you didn't see what they had to do with your intelligence or your management competence? [Client nods.] Then so far it seems that being persistent and proud of a job done right has been an asset except in those situations when you're afraid that someone else's work will reflect badly on you? Is that a key to when you haven't "let go"?

Client: I guess that's fair to say, although I'd never thought of it that way before.

Assessor: As we go along, let's keep an eye out for what else might be involved.

The client is an 18-year-old college freshman, woman, self-referred for academic problems.

Assessor: I noticed just now [on the Bender-Gestalt] that you started out very carefully--checking the card several times, making small drawings. Then toward the end you only glanced at the cards, and the drawings became bigger and somehow more casual. Do you recognize that as something you've done before?

Client: I've never done this before [the Bender].

Assessor: I meant have you done other things in the same way? For example, if you're cooking with a recipe, do you start out double-checking the instructions, and then toward the end just trust your inclinations?

Client: [Laughs] That's exactly what I do! Unless it's a recipe I've done several times. Then I just review it once.

Assessor: What was it like while you were doing the drawings? How did it become different when you began to draw them on your own? Somehow you looked both more confident and more impatient at this juncture [pointing to the Bender- Gestalt reproductions].

Client: I wouldn't say "confident." I just decided it was pretty silly to take something so simple so seriously.

Assessor: Okay. Is that what has happened on your English term papers? Maybe your instructor was partly right--perhaps

(Contd.)

you didn't follow the instructions carefully, especially if you've already done other papers. And I'll bet since you did study the instructions very carefully at first, you assumed you remembered them.

Client: Oh my!

The client is a 60-year-old male stroke (CVA) victim, a lawyer, assessed for recovery of function.

Assessor: This graph [WAIS-R profile] shows how well you did on each of the sections. Here's Vocabulary and here's the section with the items about the mailbox and getting out of the forest. You earned about the same score on each of them, and I think it's probably at your pre stroke level. Does that square with your experience? You didn't feel as though you were at a disadvantage on these, did you?

Client: No. Do they [scores] compare favorably with other lawyers'? [Assessor: Yes] Except the one with copying of the figures [Digit Symbol]?

Assessor: Yes, you're right, your score on it is way below where it probably used to be. This one [pointing to profile] has fallen significantly too; could you take a guess at which one it is [Digit Span]?

Client: The one with the blocks?

Assessor: Here's Block Design. That's in the middle range of your scores. I really don't know whether it was much higher before, or not. But you felt disadvantaged while working with the blocks?

Client: Toward the end I was feeling nervous--my insides knotted up.

Assessor: Okay. And how about when you repeated numbers to me?

Client: I managed to forget that. Yeah, that really scared me. Where's that one [on the profile sheet]?

Assessor: Here. Now let me ask you: How did your insides do on this [holds up Trail-Making B test sheet]?

Client: I figure I did all right. I just was careful to slow down. But I don't like that; it feels like I'm a kid in school just learning his letters and numbers.

Assessor: Again, you're right on target. You made very few mistakes, but you took as much time as a schoolboy to do it. Let me tell you what I think is involved on all these tasks where you had trouble. They all look pretty simple at first, but they're things you don't do every day, things that require you to figure out and then remember the principle. Especially when you realize that in earlier years you could have done these tasks more or less automatically, you become "scared" and tighten up.

Client: Yes, but that's preferable to faking answers--or throwing things [which he reported he had done].

Assessor: Indeed. And as we agreed before, you seem to acknowledge these new limitations and cope with them honestly when you are with somebody who knows about the stroke. We can make this recommendation to your wife and partners: Whenever you're confronted by something that's a little new for you, family or staff should be around. Another recommendation is that when you go back to work, you've got to limit yourself to things you know how to do by heart, things that don't require you to think on your feet. I imagine title searches and wills wouldn't give you trouble . . .?

Client: But what about numbers? These tests all had numbers.

Assessor: I don't think it's numbers as such that throw you. See--here's where you scored on Arithmetic; that's not at all bad. And your wife tells me that you're back to balancing the checkbook, and that you come within pennies of estimating the grocery checkout total.

Client: That's true. You know, I vacillate between extremes: One minute I'm afraid I can't do anything, that I've no business thinking about going back to the office. The next minute I'm furious about being restricted to jobs any punk law clerk could handle.

Assessor: And sometimes you worry that you're getting worse, that your brain is deteriorating? [Client looks up, surprised, and nods slowly.] The only danger of that is if you had another stroke. You've probably recovered about as much as you're going to from the damage you have, though. [Long silence] You will have to restrict your assignments. For example, you shouldn't argue trial cases in court anymore; you'd probably miss some of the abstract points or unfamiliar lines of argument, like you did on this Concept Formation Test. [Extended discussion of other tasks at work and at home that he could or should not undertake, followed by a discussion of his embarrassment at returning to what he felt was "clerk status."] You've already come a long way in coping realistically with your stroke. Frankly, I admire your courage and honesty. But

(Contd.)

as you said, there will be a lot of ups and downs as you develop ways of accommodating at work. You'll make some mistakes, but a good way to minimize them is to respect those signs that you're moving into dangerous zones. What are the signs?

Assessor: Here's Block Design. That's in the middle range of your scores. I really don't know whether it was much higher before or not. But you felt disadvantaged while working with the blocks?

Client: Toward the end I was feeling nervous--my insides knotted up.

Assessor: Okay. And how about when you repeated numbers to me?

Client: I managed to forget that. Yeah, that really scared me. Where's that one [on the profile sheet]?

Assessor: Here. Now let me ask you: How did your insides do on this [holds up Trail-Making B test sheet]?

Client: I figure I did all right. I just was careful to slow down. But I don't like that; it feels like I'm a kid in school just learning his letters and numbers.

Assessor: Again, you're right on target. You made very few mistakes, but you took as much time as a schoolboy to do it. Let me tell you what I think is involved on all these tasks where you had trouble. They all look pretty simple at first, but they're things you don't do every day, things that require you to figure out and then remember the principle. Especially when you realize that in earlier years you could have done these tasks more or less automatically, you become "scared" and tighten up.

Client: Yes, but that's preferable to faking answers--or throwing things [which he reported he had done].

Assessor: Indeed. And as we agreed before, you seem to acknowledge these new limitations and cope with them honestly when you are with somebody who knows about the stroke. We can make this recommendation to your wife and partners: Whenever you're confronted by something that's a little new for you, family or staff should be around. Another recommendation is that when you go back to work, you've got to limit yourself to things you know how to do by heart, things that don't require you to think on your feet. I imagine title searches and wills wouldn't give you trouble . . .?

Client: But what about numbers? These tests all had numbers.

Assessor: I don't think it's numbers as such that throw you. See--here's where you scored on Arithmetic; that's not at all bad. And your wife tells me that you're back to balancing the checkbook, and that you come within pennies of estimating the grocery checkout total.

Client: That's true. You know, I vacillate between extremes: One minute I'm afraid I can't do anything, that I've no business thinking about going back to the office. The next minute I'm furious about being restricted to jobs any punk law clerk could handle.

Assessor: And sometimes you worry that you're getting worse, that your brain is deteriorating? [Client looks up, surprised, and nods slowly.] The only danger of that is if you had another stroke. You've probably recovered about as much as you're going to from the damage you have, though. [Long silence] You will have to restrict your assignments. For example, you shouldn't argue trial cases in court anymore; you'd probably miss some of the abstract points or unfamiliar lines of argument, like you did on this Concept Formation Test. [Extended discussion of other tasks at work and at home that he could or should not undertake, followed by a discussion of his embarrassment at returning to what he felt was "clerk status."] You've already come a long way in coping realistically with your stroke. Frankly, I admire your courage and honesty. But as you said, there will be a lot of ups and downs as you develop ways of accommodating at work. You'll make some mistakes, but a good way to minimize them is to respect those signs that you're moving into dangerous zones. What are the signs?

Client: Knotted insides! And feeling impatient and wanting to dismiss obstacles. Or feeling like a schoolboy--that precedes impatience.

Assessor: Yes, it's important to catch yourself there, before you became impatient. And what were our suggestions in that regard?

Client: Here, I made notes on that too. (1) If there's time, just slow down as I did on "follow-the-dots" [Trail Making]; (2) if not, or if I'm not sure I'm getting it right, go to someone for consultation.

Assessor: Right. Of course, these steps are new for you, so you'll have to go slowly with them too! Seriously, it will take considerable practice. But since we'll work this out with your

(Contd.)

family, partners, and staff, they'll understand what's going on. Let's ask your wife in now, to explain our progress and then continue our discussion. All right?

The client is a 24-year-old man, arrested for car theft, referred by his lawyer.

Assessor: You mentioned that your parole officer accuses you of not planning ahead? [Client nods.] And that other people have said that too, but you disagree? [Client nods.] Well, I don't know yet whether I agree with them, but I'll bet we've got an example right here [Bender-Gestalt] of what they're talking about. You did all of these [pointing to early designs] accurately and efficiently, but look how these later ones had to be squeezed in on their sides. Could that be an example of not planning ahead? What I mean is, you could have figured out the space ahead of time, especially since I mentioned how many designs there would be.

Client: I don't waste time planning for easy things. I just know what to do without thinking. Corsky [parole officer] says that's impulse; I say it's intuition. If you don't have it, don't knock it. Besides you said yourself it [Bender copy] was pretty good.

Assessor: Yes, it is. So I guess going by intuition worked pretty well this time. Tell me some other times it worked well.

Client: like what?

Assessor: Well, I don't know. I need for you to tell me. But I would imagine that another example would be getting ready to come here today. Some guys would lie awake planning what to say. I'll bet you thought about it a little, and then figured you'd know what to do when you got here. [Client nods approvingly.] Okay; so can you think of other times when somebody else might have to do a lot of figuring, but you don't have to?

Client: Sure, all right. I did some boxing at Haywood, and everybody said I was a natural. [Assessor writes that down and nods.] Or if I'm going out drinking, the way to do that is you must flow with the tide. Have a good time. This one time I wound up on the other side of town in this executive's penthouse. To this day I don't know how I got there, but I helped myself to breakfast.

Assessor: Tell me about times you've wound up someplace by surprise, but it didn't work out so well. [Client looks startled. "You mean . . ."] Yes, go ahead.

Client: [Avoiding assessor's gaze] Well, I guess that's like how I wound up getting arrested. I mean we was all in the car, and I was driving, but I didn't mean to steal it.

Assessor: Right. So generally, going by intuition works quite well for you. But it doesn't work all the time. When it doesn't work is when people say you didn't plan?

Client: [Slowly] Yeah, I guess. But see, I plan by taking things as they come, one day at a time. [Picking up speed] See, I knew this fellow . . .

Assessor: Hey, hold on. I want you to tell me about times you have planned-- perhaps planning what to take on a trip, or calculating how many months you have left on parole.

Client: Well, yeah. What the _____ does Corsky know. I probably have planned more than he ever knew how! [Assessor: Give me some specific instances.] Once I took this shop course, and the instructor really knew his stuff. I made this wood-based lamp, and gave it to my mother. [Assessor: And that required a lot of planning?] Oh, yeah, lots. You have to use a template and measure and check. And choose a die and figure what you had to get done before the shop closed.

Assessor: Okay, so the point is that you can plan, and in fact often do so quite well. But you don't plan "when to plan": You get in trouble when a situation calls for planning, but you keep going on intuition.

Client: When you put it that way, it's true.

Assessor: Okay, as we go on here, let's keep one eye out for signs that might tell you when to shift from intuition to "planning to plan." Mr. Corsky probably could be more helpful to you if he knew those signs too.

The client is a 35-year-old self-referred graduate student in a Humanities Department, who wants to know if he is "officially paranoid" or whether his university's faculty and administration are in collusion against him.

Assessor: You know, I think I know how that woman security officer [at his university] felt when you were explaining your complaint. You knew that what you were saying made sense, but until the very end, she didn't. Just now [during copying of the Bender-Gestalt] I couldn't imagine that this design [twelve three- dot parallel slanted columns] was going to come out right. I've never seen anyone do it that way. [Client smiles.] Most people draw an entire row or column at one time. You were

(Contd.)

all over the place--a dot here and one there. I was amazed when it all came together. I think she and I were both confused [client nods, smiling broadly], and I think you thoroughly enjoyed and abetted our confusion. At this point I find this intriguing, but I'd guess that in her shoes I'd have felt used. No wonder she began avoiding you, and being short with you on those other visits. What do you think--are we onto something?

Client: Yes, that is an astute and accurate assessment. People have to learn to appreciate the internal beauty of the universe. Instead, the sheep.

Assessor: Yes, well, I see that you regard me as one of your sheep.

Client: A likely proposition, but one that remains to be proven.

Assessor: Well, if you have repeatedly told your advisor, chair, and dean, in one way and another, that they are all sheep, you thereby make it impossible for them to want to spend their time with you. I suspect that you make us into sheep by nipping at our heels, and lurking behind trees waiting for us to be caught off guard. [Client nods, smiles derisively.] Let's see what else we can learn together. [Rorschach, including inquiry, is completed.] What struck me most here is that even though you appeared to be relaxed and fairly low key, in fact you were very actively searching through each card, looking for connections, building up a story that would take everything into account. Many people just say what this part or this one looks like [pointing to areas on card] and let the rest alone if it doesn't seem at first glance to fit in. I have a better appreciation now of why you have insisted on receiving the full year's syllabus, and why you don't want anyone to interfere with any one step on your worksheets.

Client: That's correct. They don't see that there's an entire system involved. So you tell me who's schizo.

Assessor: Let's talk about that. It's clear to me that you do not match the official category that we call schizophrenic. You don't experience hallucinations, or see or understand things in bizarre ways. You're not crazy. But there are some categories that you do match and these categories do include the word paranoid. Not crazy, but paranoid. What does that word mean to you?

Client: If it doesn't mean crazy, what does it mean? It's a label for not having to deal with people who are different.

Assessor: As always, you do have a point there. But there is also some worth to this label; it refers to being suspicious, competitve, angry in a certain pattern, one in which a person tries to read other people's motives at the cost of letting them be.

Client: I let others be! What else can I do as a "mere" student?

Assessor: Let's look at this card [Rorschach] again. You put together an image that was complex, didn't leave anything out, and so on. It was quite amazing, very unusual. And you enjoyed doing that and impressing me. That's the "good news"; the "bad news" is that while doing all that, you missed what most people notice, namely that this whole thing [holds card up and out at a distance] strikes most people as a bat. Or here, this part strikes many persons as a woman.

Client: [After a moment of silence] I'm not most people! I don't give a rat's ass what they see! It's got nothing to do with me.

Assessor: They're all sheep? Look, your creative side is admirable, but your way of being creative puts others in a one-down position. You've been doing it to me ever since we started. Even though I'm trying to be objective, and even though I don't know what actually happened on your campus, I find it very easy to sympathize with the faculty and administrators. [Client starts to protest.] No, let me answer the questions you brought to me. (1) You're not schizophrenic; (2) but if you took the university to court [client's reason for consulting the assessor], the lawyers, judge, jury would all see your complaints as paranoid--they would see from the way you would treat them that you probably did the same thing with university representatives. That is, that you did not look at their side, that you ignored usual protocol, that you made it difficult for them to be sympathetic to your complaints, that you looked everywhere for evidence of their inferiority and their disregard for yourself. Whatever validity there is to your complaints, and I'm sure there must be some, the judicial system would probably find in favor of the university. You would be your own worst enemy in court. [There ensued an hour's discussion, in which the assessor stood by the above conclusion, but pursued what she felt were the client's worries about undergoing some kind of breakdown in the future, and his deep (albeit vehemently denied) longings for approval, support, and love. The assessor spoke of ways the client might moderate (not give up) his aggressive stance, just to take some pressure off himself. She also said that she felt he deserved an opportunity to explore his concerns with a therapist--somebody who would hear him out, who could be sympathetic without taking sides, and who could

(Contd.)

offer a place of refuge. About a month later, the client entered therapy with another psychologist, although he attended erratically. He backed off his threatened law suit against his university, and settled into a more or less workable relation with his professors. Of course he maintained his basic defensively competitive stance. He refused to pay for the assessment he had contracted.]

The client is a 22-year-old male, accused of attempted rape, referred by his attorney.

Client: [During Rorschach.] Jesus, you must be making something of all these insides I'm seeing. [Assessor: I am a little surprised; what do you think is going on?] Maybe you think I'm falling apart. [Long pause] Maybe you think I think women are just anatomy.

Assessor: There's probably something to both of those points, but not quite that severe. Back here [Card VI] you mentioned "muscles tautened" [sic]. Tell me what about the card helps give that appearance?

Client: The way they are. See, they're knotted and straining. This darkness shows how they're stirated [sic]. This is a larger section but it looks smaller because it's behind this section.

Assessor: I don't think you're breaking down, but I do think that you're doing a lot of struggling--trying to keep things in perspective but feeling caught, maybe held immobile, when you'd like to just do something. [Client nods incredulously but vigorously.] Okay, tell me--just let your thoughts go wherever they want to--of a time, any time, when your muscles were like that.

Client: Okay, but I don't know if this makes sense. [Assessor nods and shrugs.] I think of when my father chased my mom around the kitchen table with a butcher knife. He cut her too. She went to the hospital. [Assessor: And you were where?] In the corner. God, was I scared. I wanted to save my mother, but I was too little. My father and I, we respect each other now; but we keep our distance. He didn't come to my wedding. [Assessor: That must have hurt, and made you mad too.] Naw. Well, yeah, it did.

Assessor: I know it was different too, but were you feeling "knotted" the day you picked up that woman?

Client: Yeah, at least all afternoon. [Client tells that he was tired that day, had been teased in front of the secretarial staff, and had collected his pay check only to spend it all at a local bar on pinball machines and buying drinks for his "buddies," who left him there after his money ran out. Further discussion reveals that in his own way the client recognizes the dynamics of his having struck the woman who refused to go with him that night, but that he does not know what he could have done instead.]

Assessor: Tom, let me tell you what I'm going to say to Mr. Letterman [lawyer] in my report. I'm going to say that in fact it is possible you could threaten or hurt a woman again in similar circumstances, you know--if your manliness and competence are severely challenged as they were that day: being fired, the men laughing at you, the woman calling you a "kid." [Client nods, looking to the floor.] But I can also say that you don't want it to happen again and that there is an unusually good chance that, if you see a psychotherapist regularly to explore other ways of handling challenges, you won't show up in the judge's court again. I'll also write to Mr. Letterman about the vocational options we have discussed.

The client is a 24-year-old male arrested for reckless driving and resisting arrest, referred by his attorney.

Assessor: [After Rorschach] You know, I can see just from how you sit back, keeping your distance [assessor gestures between herself and client] as you go through these tests that most people must see you as laid back. Is that true? [Client: Yeah.] But I can also imagine that there are a lot of situations when you also feel vaguely restless, kind of tense, like you wish you were going somewhere, but you don't know where.

Client: [Wide-eyed, but slumps further back into his chair] Where did you get that?

Assessor: Well, like this card [Card VI]. It's hard for many people to see that this skin could be stretched out and pulling against the nails while it's drying, unless they know what it's like to be stretched that way.

Client: I don't let nobody push me around.

Assessor: I understand. But sometimes there's no person there, and you still feel that way, right? [Client: I guess.] Maybe, since you're already feeling held down, you're sort of ready to strike back if somebody crowds you.

Client: Yeah, I guess. But that's the way it has to be.

Assessor: Not if you had a sense that you were getting somewhere, that you were on the way somewhere.

(Contd.)

Client: I am going places. I am somebody.

Assessor: Uh-huh, [gently] you're somebody who's going to jail. You're somebody who smarts off with police officers instead of keeping cool.

Client: That's what you have to do. I'd rather do that than get pushed around.

Assessor: We have to stop in a few minutes, but we'll finish tomorrow. I want to leave a thought with you today. I think that in a vague, kind of haunting way, you long to be more of a somebody than you already are, that you long to be on your way, and that you wish people would help you instead of getting in your way. [Client: Nah, that's shrink stuff.] We'll have to agree to disagree about this. I really don't know how to be clearer about what I'm talking about. But I do know that whenever you're feeling "nailed down," you're aware that life could be different for you, that it would be nice if everybody could be more gentle with everyone, and you could take care of yourself without having to fight back. [Client sighs and sits quietly for a full minute, then leaves without a word. The next day he showed up early for his appointment.]

The client is a 31-year-old technician, being screened for employment at a nuclear facility.

Assessor: Considering the reason we're doing this evaluation, I don't think I should use the word "explode" in my report. [Both smile.] What's another term for that feeling you've had when different supervisors have given you conflicting instructions?

Client: It [the explosive feeling] only happened when it went on for a long time and when there wasn't anybody, except my wife, I could talk to about it.

Assessor: Yes, but it's happened twice, you say? [Client nods.] Anyway, how shall we describe the feeling?

Client: Torn apart. Like if I'm not going to wind up in shreds, I'd better quit the job or keep on drinking. I did each once.

Assessor: Okay. That's the language we'll use. I'm going to tell the New York office that you do meet their criteria for clearance under special supervision; that they should advise your company's personnel section of what you consider to be stressful work conditions, and that you would appreciate an early opportunity to discuss with your superiors your concerns in this regard. The idea is that you'd like to have an advance, agreed-upon strategy for handling any such conflicts.

Client: I wish I had done that on the second job. [Discussion follows of the ways the client could cope with disagreements.]

The client is a 6-year-old girl, referred for "gifted student" evaluation.

Assessor: I'm going to tell you two things you said, and you tell me what's different about them: (1) "I don't know. There's some. Is it five pennies?" and (2) "It's when there's snow. It's a season." [Client's tone is imitated.] What's different about you in those two answers?

Client: I was smart about winter. [Assessor: And what about the number of pennies in a nickel?] I was ignorant about pennies.

Assessor: Ignorant? Who says "ignorant"? [Client, giggling: Eddie, he's my brother. He's in fifth grade.] But you knew the right answer; five is correct. What's ignorant about that?

Client: I didn't know if I was sure. I didn't know ahead of time if it was right. [Assessor: If I hadn't kept at you, do you think you would have guessed by yourself?] Nope, I mighta made a mistake.

Assessor: Here's a new test [Stanford Binet]. This time the rules are that you're supposed to guess, even if you might be wrong. Okay? [Assessor continues with the S-B, documenting that client in fact has been earning misleadingly low scores because of her fear of looking ignorant.] Marie, you know what? I think you were "smart" when you guessed. I'm going to suggest to your mother and father that they tell Eddie that sometimes it's "ignorant" not to guess. What do you think about that?

Client: Eddie says you're not allowed to guess at school or kids'll make fun of you.

Assessor: Maybe they do sometimes, especially if you're being silly. Let's practice some more guessing, and see if you can tell when it's silly and when it's not.

The above clients were not unusually responsive or reflective. The transcription does, however, make the tempo seem faster than it was. At the time, there were many pauses within and between sentences and between interchanges. For the sake of economy, these excerpts do not show the gradual evolution of the dialogue. In addition, the false starts, unintelligible mumblings, and "ums" and "ahs" have been deleted. The excerpts do not show the long periods of working and observing, during which the participants do not converse.

The assessor does not mention everything that seems interesting; interjections are carefully selected and timed, are calculated to reach clients at their present state of awareness, and are all referral-relevant. (The brief identifications of clients preceding the excerpts are not the clarified referrals, but are meant only to provide the reader with a brief orientation.)

The assessor's Rorschach remarks were not mere intuitions, but were based also on empirical research, most often that reported by Exner.

This research is particularly useful in that it reports the relations of test patterns to actual life events, such as going through a divorce or waiting for the results of a gross anatomy examination. The remarks addressed to clients are not based only on a single, just-observed comportment. Rather, prior observations of similar comportment have suggested that it would be productive to share these related impressions with the client.

One does not simply "dream up" daily life parallels to clients' test comportment as one goes along. Comportment has been observed directly from the moment the client knocked on the office door. The person's knocking, greeting, and way of walking into the room and taking a chair are all life events. Comparing these to test comportment helps the assessor to look for parallels with pre assessment events.

These direct observations also provide a link for my graduate student assessors with two of their training exercises. First, each time a student encounters a distinctive production (DAP or Bender, for example) with a volunteer "client," the student later reproduces that drawing several times. The student tries different approaches and notes his or her own posture, breathing, attention, and so forth, as for instance, one draws tiny, light figures in the lower corner of the page, and later draws large, bold, one-per-page figures. This exercise attunes one to what it may be like to be the client in those moments. The light lines, for example, may be tenuous, delicate, or evasive; all are (nonexclusive) possibilities. The second exercise is to notice how people go about everyday tasks, such as short-order cooking, waiting tables, mowing a lawn, driving, carrying on a conversation, conducting a media interview, and so on. Assessment attunement develops as one has imagined how the cook, waitress, mower, driver, whatever, would approach a DAP, Bender, or Rorschach.

I have developed a stock of common tactics people employ in carrying out school and household tasks and in entering new social situations. After observing a copy Bender evolve, I might remark that "I'm reminded of a friend who cleans house by starting with windows, discovers a cobweb in the casing, begins dusting all corners, discovers fingerprints around a light switch, goes to the closet for a sponge, and is surprised to find the windows only half done." I would then indicate the step-by-step parallel with the Bender's evolution. This client might respond, "No, no. I always stick to one thing at a time till it's finished. But I do go back to wipe up streaks in the midst of washing another pane. My husband says I'm deceptively unmethodical for being such a meticulous person." It does not matter if my comparison is not accurate, so long as the client can use it as a starting point for providing actual instances similar to the Bender performance.

Finally, reading excerpts such as those in Table 5.1 often dissolves assessors' reservations about sharing written reports with clients. What makes a difference is the way the assessment was conducted. Its findings were not just judgmental, but rather took into account the person's own view of the situation. The person's approaches were not viewed as good or bad in themselves, but as working for the client in some circumstances and for some purposes, and against him or her in others. The assessor's focus on actual events--primary data allowed the client to be an active, genuinely informed participant. The written report reviews this collaborative assessment; it does not surprise, offend, or mystify the client. The assessor need not fear the clients' response to reading the report.

Developing Options

Table 5.1 has illustrated how an assessor can help clients to see that existing patterns may not be necessary patterns, that clients can author their lives differently. However, these discoveries are rarely sufficient to initiate change. A person must find himself or herself already functioning in a different way before that possibility is fully experienced as personally viable. Therefore trying out alternatives during the assessment is intended to serve three related functions: (1) to explore just what is personally viable what fits the person's sense of who he or she has been and where he or she wants to go from there; (2) to help the client recognize landmarks--signs that one is moving toward trouble and to locate pivot points where the client could shift to an optional route to reach the destination; and (3) to practice taking that optional route, so that it feels familiar and reliable and can be taken again on other journeys.

Efforts to develop options continue the assessment of who the person is. The client may discover further aspects of his or her circumstances that should be taken into account. For example, a secretary noted that she could indeed ask her supervisor to clarify instructions, but now she realizes that she could not ask in front of the other secretaries. Moreover, a client may encounter additional motivations that the old comportment served. While practicing drawing Bender designs with lighter strokes and less concern for perfection, another client remarked: "You know it is frightening to feel the heaviness of having to do it just exactly 'their' way; but up here [lightly skimming over the paper instead of darkly tracing] I realized that I'm free to take 'their' demands lightly, and go my own way. But I don't know what my way is." TAT stories later elaborated on the ways the client had resented the burden of others' demands and yet had diligently answered them rather than risk failure on her own. It is in these practicing of alternative approaches that self-deceptions, incompatible goals, and other previously non focal concerns--in short, unconscious motivations become concretely available for collaborative exploration. These pursuits usually occur after the assessment is well under way. Earlier phases of assessment typically emphasize discovering and describing what the client does. Previously unexamined assumptions and habitual, taken-for-granted comportment become apparent well before conflicted, dynamic comportment is evident.

Trying out alternatives early in the assessment serves to explore which of these options are already available for the client. I find it helpful to ask myself the "when/when-not?" question as I notice the person taking some particular approach. To protect myself from assuming that what I am witnessing is the only approach this person takes, I consider the client's present circumstance and how different circumstances might promote different comportment. This reflection leads me to intervene with suggestions that help to clarify where different alternatives should be developed. Although more practicing occurs toward the end of the assessment, it typically arises in earlier form as a "trying out."

I have purposefully used the term "different comportment," rather than "new comportment." For an optional route to be personally viable, it must be a variation of present approaches; it must branch off from where the client is now, and it must accommodate familiar action. Using the client's terms, such as "lightly," "heaviness," and "doing it their way" in the example above, can help the client to recognize what is familiar in a different approach. While inquiring into the "geography" of a client's journey where he or she is going, away from what, among what, and so forth I also ask "for whom?" Sometimes clients know explicitly; other times the answer remains vague. It may be helpful to ask, "Who would be proud to see you do this?" Or who would be surprised, jealous, or angry?

The excerpts in Table 5.2 illustrate the development of personally viable options.

Table 5.2. Developing Options: Excerpts

The client is a 32-year-old woman, referred for assessment of "chronic depression."

Assessor: Some people just automatically turn these cards over, but you waited for me to do it . . .

Client: Oh, I didn't know I was supposed to turn them. You didn't tell me to, did you?

Assessor: No. Either way is fine. But I was reminded of how you waited outside my door instead of knocking. What would you say was the same?

Client: I don't see anything wrong about waiting. I was taught to be polite.

Assessor: I see. And what would be the opposite of polite?

Client: Pushy. Getting what you want at someone else's expense.

Assessor: I wonder if being polite isn't sometimes at your expense? You must have felt a little apprehensive waiting in the hall, wondering if I was going to remember.

Client: No. [Assessor: What then?] Impatient. No offense, but frankly I heard you laughing on the phone, and it was on my time.

(Contd.)

Assessor: I'll bet you were impatient that I was writing instead of turning the cards.

Client: Well, yes. But you're the psychologist.

Assessor: I'd like to try an experiment. Let's start over. [Assessor lays out the Bender cards and new paper.] But this time, turn the cards yourself if you feel like it. [Assessor repeats original instructions.]

Client: [After turning four cards] Are you going to tell me what this experiment is about?

Assessor: Sure. And by the way, your inquiry just now strikes me as quite appropriate, not the least bit impolite. I was wondering if turning the cards felt all right.

Client: Well, yes. You said I could.

Assessor: So it's not just a question of being polite, but also of waiting for permission. [Client looks startled and nods.] And waiting can be frustrating, especially when other people are not being considerate of your deference.

Client: My what?

Assessor: Deference--putting the other person's initiative or plans ahead of yours. I can imagine that sometimes you could become quietly teed-off? [Client makes a dismissing gesture with her hands, but nods.] Being polite while you're wondering if you're being taken advantage of can be awfully wearing. [Testing and discussion continue.]

Client: This [Block Design] was harder than the others. [Assessor: What seemed harder?] You didn't say whether you were counting errors or just timing me or what. I didn't know what to concentrate my effort on. I felt like quitting, but you're not supposed to.

Assessor: And being caught in that bind, you were also a little angry. You did hang in, but you were glaring at me from time to time. [Client nods hesitantly.] You know, in a different situation I might have tried to avoid you so I wouldn't risk having you mad at me.

Client: But I was the one on the spot. You were in charge.

Assessor: Granted, I'm in charge, but let's do another experiment to see how you can avoid being "on the spot." Maybe ask for clarification so you don't have to wonder, or choose what you think is most important. [After re-administering the Block Design subtest twice, up through the fifth design, the assessor pointed out that both she and the client felt more comfortable.

Through the remaining subtests, the client practiced asking for clarification.]

Client: [At the beginning of Rorschach inquiry] You didn't tell me I was supposed to explain everything the first time!

Assessor: You weren't. Going back through the cards this way is standard procedure. What's interesting is that you assumed I was criticizing you. And in turn I felt just now that you were criticizing me for putting you in an awkward place. I'm beginning to see how both you and Marianne [neighbor] are right. I'll bet she does avoid you, leaving you politely waiting again, but that probably happens after she has sensed your unspoken criticism.

Client: Maybe so [silence]. But I don't see what you expect me to do. [Both laugh in recognition of a familiar theme.] Okay, as you've been telling me, I guess the question is what I expect and what I could initiate. But that is not easy to do, you know. [At the end of the session assessor and client summarize the ways the client can recognize when she is setting herself up to become resentful. They role-play successful interchanges with the neighbor. They agree that behaviorally oriented counseling might help her to avoid the trap of becoming resentful in nondirective therapy, and help her to take more responsibility for her own action.]

The client is a 16-year-old high school junior, female, referred for declining grades.

Client: This is horrid [DAP]. I can't draw. This didn't come out right at all.

Assessor: Okay. If you were an artist what would it look like?

Client: Like an artist's drawing! [Assessor smiles, gestures for client to continue.] You know, no erasures, confident lines, perfect rendition of an elegant woman.

Assessor: Uh-huh [both laugh]. So here we are again, with you comparing yourself to perfection! That sure is a rough thing to be doing to yourself so often.

Client: Yeah, and the worst part is that I don't know when I'm doing it.

Assessor: There's hope! You knew you'd done it this time! But I'd like to pursue something else here. If you could draw well, this drawing would have been of an elegant woman? [Client blushes, nods hesitantly.] Let's draw it with words. What about the arms--what effect were you after?

(Contd.)

Client: This arm should be gesturing emphatically but gracefully. This one should fall easily to her side. [Client illustrates, although remaining seated.]

Assessor: Yes! Look at you! You're doing it. Granted, you're not standing, and it was just a quick gesture, but it was certainly more "elegant" than this woman [DAP]. Kind of symbolic, isn't it? Instead of trying out, practicing, being elegant, you and she [DAP] hide your hands behind your back? [Client and assessor chuckle.] Like a lot of young women, you're not sure whether or not to hide the fact that your breasts have developed? [Assessor points to erasures of lines indicating sizes of breasts. Client nods; after further discussion, assessor asks client to draw her elegant woman, even though it won't be perfect.]

The client is a 21-year-old female graduate student who volunteered for a practice assessment during class.

Assessor: So you have often behaved as though things were against you, as was the case in your TAT stories? [Student: I certainly have. This even came up in my peer counseling session last week.] All right. Do you have some concrete instances you wouldn't mind sharing with us?

Student: Well, I barely could believe that I had actually graduated from college, and friends had to convince me that I should apply to a master's program. Now people are telling me I should apply to the doctoral program. I just never thought that I could be that sort of person.

Assessor: Wait a minute. That sounds more like "level of aspiration" than what we were talking about before. [Student: What do you mean?] I'm not sure yet. Tell us some more instances. [Student goes on with further instances until finally she rejects the "against me" theme and renames it "aiming low." Discussion also pursues the student's readiness to agree with others' opinions.] Do you remember this card [TAT #10]? Well, you told a story of two older persons quietly dancing together. Did you know that some describe the man as sneering down at the woman?

Student: Oh my! I didn't see that before. That surely could be.

Assessor: There you go again! [Student laughs and asks a classmate to recount a similar experience they have had together.] Okay, when does this "taking the other's stance" work out well for you? For example, I can see that your classmates feel you understand them and are gentle with them; and they in turn respect you. [Classmates offer other variations along these lines, plus instances of when she had given up her own point of view prematurely.]

Student: Let me summarize the "landmarks" of when I'm moving into "aiming low" or "giving priority to the other's stance." It's when I'm in unfamiliar territory and regard others as experts. I find myself pulling back, both figuratively and literally--like wanting to hide. And from there I find myself glancing into the faces of others, looking for cues.

Assessor: On this card [TAT 3BM], you described a young woman catnapping before finishing cutting out her pattern. Sounds pretty evasive to me! How about this gun here? [The object on the card is ambiguous.]

Student: Each to her own! [We all laugh in celebration.] No, seriously, I can see the gun or maybe it could be a hypodermic in today's times. It surely could be a gun; maybe she's shot somebody or is thinking of killing herself. Yes, I can certainly see your point. But I think that for myself, I'll stick to my story. [More congratulations from the class.] Wow! This stuff is powerful. I mean I've known about those themes, but not in this way. I can do something with it now! Of course, there's a lot more to it, that I'd rather not share in a group. But now I'm beginning to see more clearly how "aspiration" and "aiming low" goes way back into my family's dynamics.

The client is a 9-year-old boy referred for academic problems.

Assessor: Hey Timmy, what are you doing? [During Block Design of WISC-R]

Client: I made a wall [matter-of-factly].

Assessor: Did you make it so this design [pointing to card] is on your side?

Client: Uh-huh [starts to break them apart, to get ready for next design].

Assessor: Hold on! [Assessor gets up, walks to client's corner of the table.] From my side, I can't see whether you did what I asked. My word! You did indeed. [Assessor returns to her seat.] Tim, I'm beginning to see how Ms. Cunningham would say you don't pay attention, even though you say you do. Pretend I'm Ms. Cunningham, and I told you to make this design with these blocks. Okay? And so Tim says, "There, I did what she said." But come over here to Ms. Cunningham's side of the desk. Now look at the wall from her side! See, from her desk, it doesn't look like you did the design at all.

(Contd.)

Client: Oh! [Assessor: What do you think Tim could do so Ms. Cunningham could see that he pays attention?] Turn it around this way after I'm finished?

Assessor: Now that's a good idea. Let's try it. [Assessor administers the next card. Client makes a wall, and then turns it for assessor to see.] Yes, now I can tell that you did it right. Tim, could this be what happened when I was in your room this morning? The art teacher--what is his name? [Client: Mr. Simms.] Mr. Simms got a little impatient with you when he told everyone to clean off their desks. You said you did and he said you didn't. If you were Mr. Simms, looking across the room at your desk, what would you see?

Client: Pieces of construction paper. But I was saving that for recess; it wasn't garbage. I didn't spill any paste or anything, and I put the scissors in my desk.

Assessor: Is there anything you could have done so Mr. Simms could see that you followed his directions?

Client: I guess put the paper in my pocket.

Assessor: Sounds good to me. I think you already know what to do from now on so the grown-ups can see that you're following directions.

Client: Can we do some more [blocks]?

Assessor: Sure. [Later] If I told your mom about the wall and about the construction paper, would she know some other times like that at home? [Client gave examples. A conference was held with Tim, two teachers, and both parents, so all could hear about the examples, what Tim planned to do in the future, and how he would like the adults to help him.]

The clients are a married couple, in their late 20s, who had referred their 6-year-old son for an assessment of "shyness." The following session was held at the family's kitchen table after the psychologist had met with the boy.

Husband: [Card I, Rorschach] Obviously this is a folk festival ethnic dance. Two men with capes swirling, a woman with arms raised in the middle. Yes, definitely. Ukrainian, I'd say. That's it.

Wife: [Pausing, while walking past with coffee pot, to look over husband's shoulder] Oh, now I can see that. The woman is wearing a filmy dress. She's probably on her tiptoes.

Husband: [Card II] This one is more complex. These red parts should be integrated. It's a circus. These are dancing bears; this is an elephant's upturned barrel--the kind they balance on. This red is bunting--the overall impression of center ring.

Wife: [Chair pulled up beside her husband's] Oh my. The bears could be playing patty cake, couldn't they?

Assessor: [Presenting Card III] Miriam, pull your chair over here [to side of table diagonally from husband]. This time, you tell us first, what could this be?

Wife: Oh, well, I . . . I don't know what Dave would say. [Assessor: Go ahead.] Could it be more than one thing? [Assessor: Sure, there are lots of possibilities.] Would it be all right for these to be two native dancers?

Assessor: Why in the world not? Miriam, what's the worst possible thing you can imagine could happen if neither Dave nor I agreed with you?

Wife: I'd feel dumb. I'd be lost. Well, he'd help me, but I'd be afraid I was wasting time. Besides, he's always right, he really is. [Assessor asks if what just happened were familiar--that Dave organized a response, and then Miriam accepted it and filled in. They immediately provided such examples as Dave's buying their new house without Miriam's having seen it (although they had agreed in advance which criteria it should meet), and her then selecting wallpaper, rugs, and furnishings. The same pattern was identified in regard to raising their son, Ricky. They agreed that although Miriam and Dave generally found the pattern comfortable, Ricky's holding back until given directions and permissions was not working well for him.]

Assessor: I suspect that if Ricky saw you [Miriam] being more flexible--initiating plans yourself, and sometimes offering your opinions first, he would begin to do so too.

Wife: You know, I never thought of this before, but sometimes I see him [Ricky] holding back, and my heart just aches. I know what it's like.

Assessor: Holding back has been painful for you too, at times.

Husband: Honey, I sensed that too, even when you say it's okay.

Assessor: [Ricky peers around the kitchen doorway.] Hi, Ricky. You're just in time. Come sit here on your side of the table. Here's what we're going to do. Do you remember these pictures [TAT]? I'll show all of you a picture, and each of you will think to yourself what could be happening in the picture. Then we'll take turns being the first to tell what we thought. [All four tell a story to each card, taking turns being the first. Assessor points

(Contd.)

out that nobody was wrong, that there were many possible stories, and that Dad feels okay about all this.] All right, let's see some other times when Ricky and Mom could "go first." Mom, tell Dad some ideas for this year's vacation--just some random thoughts about what would be nice. [Laughter and apologies are followed by suggestions. Ricky is then asked to pretend the assessor is his teacher, and to make a request for which morning song the class should sing. Other practicing follow. Assessor acknowledges that the family's pattern works very well in many circumstances, but suggests that they all continue the exercise for a week, and then decide whether they would like further guidance from a family counselor who would conduct similar sessions with them.]

The client is a 9-year-old retarded boy, referred by his EMR teacher for reevaluation of his intellectual level.

Assessor: Milton, let's practice that. Tell me how the boy makes a happy ending [TAT card IBM].

Client: His name is Sammy--Sammy rides my bus. This is one of those things you play [violin]. Sammy doesn't know how to play it. [Assessor: What can he do to make a happy ending?] He does what his teacher says to, and once upon a time he makes a song come out. [Assessor: Good. That's a happy ending. What will Sammy do to make a happy ending if Brooks teases him?] Brooks says, "That's gross! That's baby noise." Sammy says, "Go away. My teacher says I play it good."

Assessor: Okay! [Handing Milton his human figure drawing of himself] What can Milton do to make a happy ending?

Client: Milton tells the lady at MacDonald's that he wants a big french fries. She tells him it's not enough money. [Assessor: That's not happy! What will Milton do?] He'll cry.

Assessor: Milton, what would happen if Milton said, "What do I have enough money for?" and the lady said, "A small french fries," and Milton said, "Okay, I want a small french fries," and then he told his mother that he didn't cry and that he did everything by himself?

Client: Milton's mother would go back to her job and Milton would have to live by himself. All alone with Walpole--that's our cat. [Further practicing of "making good endings" confirms Milton's fearfulness that being competent may result in his being abandoned or overwhelmed by increased demands for independent accomplishment.]

Assessor: Let's talk to Mr. Remy [teacher]. I'll bet he would understand if you told him when you were afraid of "too much." [Milton brings Mr. Remy back from the classroom. Assessor retells Milton's stories and explains his fears. They role-play Milton telling Mr. Remy that he wants to finish just one page, so the work won't become "too much"; that is, escalate too quickly. Mr. Remy reassures Milton that nobody will move him to Mr. Bono's class without discussing the move with Milton, that he will visit the class first, and that after transferring he may come back to see Mr. Remy. Similar discussions were later held with Milton and his parents.]

The client is a 55-year-old housewife, self-referred for job guidance.

Assessor: [As client begins to tell a story for TAT card #9GF] Hold it! You're about to tell me that this woman up here looking from behind the tree is thinking that the woman down below running on the beach is going to get somewhere first, that she got a head start!

Client: [Taken aback at first] No, you got there first! I'm not going to give you the satisfaction of telling you how accurate you were! [Both laugh.]

Assessor: That's a nice twist--my getting there first. I'll bet you could imagine all kinds of other stories here. Try a few.

Client: Well, this one [behind tree] could be plotting how to stop the other one. [Assessor: Sure! What else?] Or she could maybe be thinking how to follow her footsteps, so to speak, to get to the same place. [Assessor: Right. I wonder if you could tell me what's happening for this woman who's running?] She probably doesn't even know someone's watching. She's probably just trying to get somewhere on time. You know, I just realized, she looks worried, but determined [laughs]. Pretty tricky! I see what you've just done! But it's true: Whatever I do, whether it's keeping up with volunteer work from home or getting a salaried job, I'll still be worried and determined. So I might as well be getting paid!

Assessor: Okay, so try that out with this picture. Tell me the story here [#17BM].

Client: [Long pause] He's on the way up this rope in some sort of Olympic competition. He's decided it's not so much whether he wins or loses medals, but that under the circumstances he does his best. And how about this: and that he enjoys it!

Assessor: Quite a difference from the story on Card 1! By the way, when you told that first one, were you aware that there were different potential stories?

(Contd.)

Client: Intellectually. But none of them occurred to me.

Assessor: I'd say that you came to me already prepared to try out some different perspectives.

Client: I guess so, in a way. But I didn't realize how much it was me holding myself back. I guess I'd be willing to try that job interview role-play now. But you promise to help me with cues?

The client is a 24-year-old woman bank teller, referred by her counselor for differential diagnosis between neurotic depression and borderline personality disorder.

Assessor: [Client has been protesting that she wants to be more independent but that people won't let her be so.] Look how lightly you've done all your pencil work; it's barely visible! [Assessor holds her penciled notes up by way of comparison.] Here, how about retracing these [Digit Symbol from WAIS-R], making them darker? Press harder, keep going. What's it like to press harder?

Client: It feels good. And nothing's getting messed up.

Assessor: Let's do these again [Presents Bender cards and fresh paper.] Okay. But putting pressure into what you do doesn't have to be laborious. Go faster; you've been here before! Okay, and how shall you sign your name? Ah-ha! Well, I imagine that you could practice putting more pressure into other things you do too. It's like putting yourself more firmly into whatever you do. Let's try that out another way. Let's move over here to these chairs, and pretend I'm Dr. Caligny [counselor] telling you that I want you to see a psychologist, and you tell me just what you think about that. [Role-plays ensue.]

The client is a 23-year-old heroin addict, assessed at a methadone treatment center as part of intake procedures.

Assessor: So this turned out to be worth your while after all?

Client: See, I talked to this shrink at the lockup, and that was nowhere. And my girlfriend, she's had four different therapists, no offense, but they were nothing. Thought they knew it all, and they didn't know nothing.

Assessor: You've met Tom Walker? [counselor; client nods.] Well, after you and I have read and made any changes in my written report of what we learned today, we'll ask Tom to join us. He'll have a copy of the report. We'll tell him what changes we've made, and hell ask us questions to be sure he understands. Then the two of you will continue where we've left off. You can work out different goals as you go along--as we did--and role-play, and hell tell you what impressions you're making. I don't think hell use tests, but otherwise counseling can be very much like what we did today.

Client: That Walker fellow seems okay. . . . See, I thought therapy was getting lectured at. And I get to keep a copy of my own of the suggestions, the same ones hell have?

The last excerpt in Table 5.2 illustrates how the assessor may encourage a client to enter counseling or therapy with positive expectations. The client's success during the assessment is compared with therapy activities to show the client that therapy would be an extension of what he or she is already familiar with (if that would in fact be the case). The absence of any tests in the excerpt is a reminder that assessment does not necessarily involve continuous use of tests. Interviewing, counseling, and therapeutic techniques also are prevalent, but Tables 5.1 and 5.2 focused on testing examples because the other individualized techniques are well known.

The options developed in these excerpts are only those that clients are ready for at the time of the assessment. Often further restructuration will require protracted professional assistance. The assessment report's suggestions may include recommendations for treatment, further evaluation, and environmental changes, in addition to the tried-out options. In addition, many of the assessor's shared observations slowly germinate as the person later goes about his or her life, proving to be helpful at some later point.

The assessor makes use of technical and diagnostic knowledge even when it is not presented as such to the client. These secondary data are the assessor's tools for exploring primary data how the client approaches the assessment tasks and similar daily life situations. Informed observation of these primary events is the most productive information to share.

It is not always necessary to obtain a completed assessee production, such as the "other gender" drawing in the "elegant woman" DAP excerpt in Table 5.2. Just getting started on a task often puts the person in touch with his or her inclinations, resistances, concerns. These responses and their pivot points into options are then available for joint exploration. In an individualized assessment, such exploration, rather than completed "productions," is the point of using test materials.

Finally, in those instances where individualized assessment is appropriate; that is, where testing is not merely for establishing comparative levels of achievement or category of best fit; assessment certainly is broader than administration of tests. Individualized assessment is also a testing of optimal environments, interventions, and ways clients can help themselves.

Concluding the Session

The assessment session draws to a close when individualized responses to referral requests have been formulated and, where appropriate, concrete suggestions have been developed for the client as well as for helping professionals. By this time, what has been learned coheres--it appears as various aspects of a whole. No tortuous reasoning is required to hold findings together, and there are no major gaps in understanding. There remains much that the assessor has not shared, and much that has not been explored, but these aspects were not essential for responding to the referral or to developing tailored suggestions.

On the average, I spend about four hours with the client during which I make use of, for example, a Bender-Gestalt, partial Wechsler, complete Rorschach, and a couple TAT cards. When graduate students are given time constraints, they too can complete the assessment within four hours. Without imposed restraints, however, neophyte assessors typically find themselves talking and counseling rather than assessing, thereby adding hours to the assessment. I prefer to break the assessment into two sessions when possible, allowing the client and myself time and distance to mull what we have experienced together. Ideally, at a third session we review the written report. As the client reads through the entire account, some aspects of it inevitably come across somewhat differently than they had during our previous discussions. Discussion of the report now continues the assessment. The client literally leaves his or her mark on the written account by completing the commentary section and signing it.

Regardless of the number of sessions and whether time and travel contingencies allow for a joint review of the written report, before the client leaves the formal assessment session, I review what will be in the report, first to myself and then with the client. I often hand the person pen and paper and suggest that while I review my notes, he or she may want to jot down any ideas that we have left out or questions that I might try to answer. This suggestion is much more effective than asking "Do you have any questions?" to which clients respond too quickly with "No, I guess not."

During my private review I ask myself if I adequately pursued alternative hypotheses, obtained all the factual information I will need for the background sections, and recorded concrete examples to illustrate my impressions and conclusions. Some assessors prefer to prepare a standard checklist, which they quickly review at this point. Many find that when they conduct assessments regularly, they no longer use the checklist, but that in the meantime it has allowed their interviews to be constructively open-ended.

My review with the client then begins with requests for missing information. Next I ask for the client's summary of what we have learned and of the suggestions we developed. In this way I can see what has been most important from the client's perspective, and we can clarify any misunderstandings. Then I orally fill out the clients' rendition with the remaining themes and suggestions that will be in the report. None of this comes as a surprise, because we have discussed these themes during the session. Elaborations and additional, related suggestions often arise at this point, however. I frequently ask for additional past instances of assessment findings, and sometimes ask for an instance that may be less private or value-laden for the report.

Finally, we review future steps, such as holding a family conference, referring the client for medical evaluation, or arranging for a meeting with a psychotherapist. Although I am careful to leave room for the client to take initiative and to voice reservations, I also try to clear the way by providing lists of resources and phone numbers, and sometimes by placing calls myself. The client signs a release form, specifying who may receive the written report. When the form is not part of the report (which the client has just read), the form also states that the client may have access to the report. I give the client a business card and indicate that if questions occur later or if any problems with the report arise, I can be reached by phone. I also mention that I telephone a sample of my clients months or even years later to see if the assessment has been as helpful as we intended. I ask for permission to call if this assessment turns out to be in the random sample.

The "doorway phenomenon" is one of my criteria for a successful assessment. As the client pauses before leaving, he or she frequently remarks with pleased bemusement, something like, "You know, you didn't tell me anything I didn't already know." This statement is followed by qualifications like, "But I hadn't thought about it this way before. And now I know how to begin to do something about it."

6

Counseling Reports for Adults in Psychological Assessment

Introduction

My introductory assessment course, for which most of these reports were written, begins with training in standardized administration of individual intelligence tests, the Bender-Gestalt, human figure drawings (DAP), and the Thematic Apperception Test. Then each graduate student completes two individualized assessments with undergraduate volunteers before going to a field placement with a partner. The assessors are encouraged to break an assessment into two sessions, so that the client's variations in comportment become more evident. For the field assignments, each partner takes primary responsibility for writing the report for one of the two assessments that they conduct together.

In accordance with the principles of individualized assessment, the graduate students view comportment as primary data and tests as occasions to observe comportment in different situations. Assessors are told to re-present comportment rather than claiming "the tests say." Tests and subtests are chosen for their similarity to referral-relevant situations. When standardized completion of a test would interfere with collaborative exploration of themes, the standardized procedures are forsaken. Nevertheless, the assessors are encouraged to use a range of test materials to allow themselves both to recognize similarities across variations and to be surprised by deviations from their expectations.

Among their early re-presentations the assessors include verbal pictures of the client in action. These images help the reader to picture experiaction that is presented later in the report. Images also help to settle readers' preconceptions, thereby allowing the particular person to emerge with greater individuality. Ideally, the visual image should portray the person in action, thereby intimating how that person shapes his or her environment even while being molded by it. Interventions and the modifications that were developed during the assessment are mentioned again in the Suggestions so that the client and other readers recall how he or she already has varied a habitual style into a personally viable alternative. Continuation and further development of this accomplishment are thus encouraged.

Most test data are reported as observed events (as primary data rather than as derived scores). Moreover, rather than automatically reviewing performance on every test, the graduate student assessors first decide what the major outcome of the sessions was, and then choose illustrative instances to share with readers. References to the assessors are in first person (I and we rather than "the examiner"), and Suggestions are often addressed directly to the client ("John, you may want to . . ."). In this way readers become present to the assessed as a particular person, and to the interpersonal context in which he or she emerged as this particular person. The assesses recalls the actual session(s), now also picturing the events from the assessor's perspective.

All but the last two reports in this chapter were written by first-year M.A. students. The reports were selected to illustrate a range of assessment settings, clients, and styles of reporting. However, one representative setting is missing from this sample, namely the client's home.

I have classified these reports as "counseling" rather than as "clinical" in that most of them were written for the client as either sole reader or as one of the primary readers. Diagnosis of psychopathology was not at issue, and even though most of the assesses were in treatment facilities, the referrals did not deal with choice of treatment. Emphasis was instead on offering understanding and guidance to the client and to the client's employer or helpers. This guidance focused on everyday difficulties and opportunities. However, familiar clinical patterns inevitably emerge through careful re-presentational description even though the graduate student assessors were not yet trained in psychopathology and diagnostic classification.

The reports were written carefully both out of pride in a developing skill and in order to meet grading requirements. The students spent four to ten hours on each report. I reviewed and corrected the reports before they were presented to the client and to the facility staff. Mental health workers sometimes protest that in the midst of multiple assignments, responsibilities, and time constraints, they usually have to write their reports in a single draft. But any draft is of higher quality if one has gone through a training period in which great care was taken to communicate as relevantly, effectively, vividly, and efficiently as possible. That accomplishment improves later work, however hurried.

The most frequent difficulty graduate students encounter in writing individualized reports is not having to write so much, but rather deciding what to leave out. A danger of individualized assessment is the desire to share one's full sense of this person that one has just come to know so well. Another danger for the beginner is the temptation to record all the steps through which one came to an insight. Instead, the report writer must consider how to communicate the client's individuality and fullness strictly in terms of the referral and selected instances of what the reader should know in order to understand the grounds of the Conclusions and Suggestions.

To protect the identity of clients in the reports that follow, clients' names and names of the human-services facilities and of their staff members were invented. Clients' pseudonym signatures, imitating the style of the original signature, accompany reproductions of client commentary on four of the reports. The actual names of the graduate student assessor were retained, but supervisors' names have been deleted.

Each of the following reports is accompanied by a brief introduction and a comments section, to highlight various features of individualized reporting.

These reports are only a sample of the many variations that are possible. The last two reports serve as reminders that reports of individualized assessments need not be comprehensive in order to answer the referral request, and that one must decide case by case whether and to what degree reports should be individualized.

Assessment of an Undergraduate Volunteer

This report was the graduate student's second assessment with undergraduate volunteers. Because this volunteer was not particularly communicative, the assessor did not have the opportunity to try out a full range of individualized assessment practices. Nevertheless, he recognized that Marie's way of being reticent was not merely a defense against becoming involved, but was also her way of participating. In fact, that manner of participating became the focus of their work together. Thus the report illustrates both some of the difficulties that confront the beginning assessor, and some positive ways of responding to them.

In this case, the assessor avoided the trap of accepting "shyness" as a trait. Instead he explored Marie's shy manner by inquiring into its everyday occurrence. He asked about instances when she had been shy and when she had not been shy ("when-nots"). He explored the contexts in which a shy manner worked for Marie, and those in which it resulted in discomfort. Even though Marie was difficult to engage in a collaborative assessment, the assessor remained nonjudgmental. In particular, rather than focusing on her refusals as such, he tried to imagine what it might be like to be in her shoes, and he described how she did participate in the assessment activities. He made use of his feelings during the assessment to acknowledge and reflect on his part in creating a situation in which Marie was uncomfortable. He shared some of these feelings with her as part of the assessment findings. Finally, he avoided the temptation to recount Marie's behavior test by test. Instead, test comportment was given its proper place as an access to Marie's everyday ways of dealing with tasks and with people.

The assessor was a student from the University of Leiden (in the Netherlands), enrolled as a special student in our graduate program in order to learn more about our human-science approach to psychology.

Psychological Assessment of Marie Grabowski

March 8, 19___

Identifying Information

Marie is 18, a freshman at Duquesne University and lives with her parents in Pittsburgh.

Focal Issue

In Marie's psychology course an announcement was made that students could volunteer for practice assessments by graduate students. Marie signed up. But when I called, the long silences on the other end of the line told me that she was uncertain about the project. When we met, I realized that the idea that she should present an issue for exploration had not come across. "I thought there would be some experiments," she said. When I explained again and asked what she would like to concentrate upon, Marie said: "I am shy." Looking back I believe that my ambiguous presentation of the assessment process, followed by my becoming overly directive, contributed to our finding it difficult to work on her issue in a more thorough fashion.

Opportunities for Assessment

We met twice for an hour and a half each time in the Duquesne Psychology Center (March 2 and 6). We worked with the Bender-Gestalt, several subtests of the WAIS, and the Draw-A-Person. The tests presented opportunities for us to observe Marie's more general styles. At times we related what happened with the test material to other aspects of her life.

Introductory Description

I found Marie to be a very attractive girl. That is what first stood out for me. Her figure is slender and elegant, her hair was carefully arranged, and when her brown eyes searched me--which was not often, they were surprisingly twinkling and expressive. I say "surprisingly" because Marie was usually silent, moved slowly, and although she sat upright her head often hung down, her lips firmly closed. Her appearance was still that of a girl, but I could easily imagine her becoming a lady of style.

This first impression of an attractive girl then became overshadowed by her long silences and the uncomfortableness with which she spoke to me. I too felt uncomfortable with these silences. They were not those of a person whose thoughts are elsewhere. She was clearly present, and I believe that at these times she notices nearly everything going on around her and has her own opinions about it all. However, I found it extremely difficult to tell from her conduct what she was thinking. Sometimes I felt that I had to pull words out of her. Especially when we spoke of more personal matters, the silences and pulling gave a certain strain to our dealings with one another. For instance, I asked Marie if she could give me a concrete example of a situation in which she had not been so quiet. Her face lost all movement; she sat upright and stared away from me at the window. As she took a full minute before she spoke, I found myself thinking, "it looks as though you are waiting for a bus." As I looked more closely, though, I could see that she was working on something. Her upper lip moved intriguingly slowly a tiny, tiny bit. Seldom have I noticed such slow, long lasting movements in a face. Under the table her right leg swang back and forth in a contrast that made me curious about what was going on. It seemed to me that she was directing her energies into remaining self-contained.

This picture changed when we worked on the performance-oriented parts of the assessment. While she was doing the Block Designs, Marie was quiet in a charming way. She made me feel more quiet. She looked confident and composed as she completed the designs with few mistakes and at her own pace (125 seconds for #s 9 and 10). To my surprise she said after this subtest: "These blocks drive you crazy." At least to me this had remained invisible. Not being able to tell from her face what was going on and even making wrong guesses made me uneasy. Maybe other people in such situations also feel uneasy with Marie.

The picture shifted again when the focus was not on her nor on her performance, but when she asked me some questions. She had noticed my foreign accent and was interested in where I came from and what I did here. We talked for a while in a different atmosphere. Marie more often looked into my eyes, turned her body away from the table and more toward me. I remember her voice as gaining speed and liveliness.

Marie's Viewpoint

Marie came to the assessment sessions knowing that she can be shy and that she doesn't let people know her easily. However, there are many situations in which Marie does not feel shy. For example, she feels much more at ease in her job as a ticket-taker at a theatre. She is not shy when she is talking with her mother. In general she does not feel greatly distressed about being shy. Rather she sees herself as a serious person with opinions about the things that go on around her. She takes being shy as a fact and as something she has more or less accepted. Early in our meeting she said, "I have nothing more to say about my being shy than that I am shy."

However, as our sessions went on, it became clearer to both of us that Marie's shy manner has occasioned difficulties as well as successes for her. She gave me an example of feeling totally embarrassed in class when the teacher pressured her to tell more when she did not know any more to say. She said she not only felt the teacher's eyes on her but also the eyes of all her classmates, who didn't know her except by this incident. She felt judged.

Marie's Participation in Her Difficulties

It was when I asked Marie about herself that she seemed stuck and awkward, which made me feel the same way. Sometimes I felt left out, as when she seemed to be staring at a blank wall. Other times I felt pushed away and devalued, as when she said of the person drawings, "I can't see that there is something of me in there," and "These drawings are not about me; I have nothing to say." I then pulled harder to get her to say something, becoming more direct in my questions. She was then turned off, and became suspicious and more distanced. She became even less inclined to talk about herself. I wondered if this was like what had happened to her and the teacher in the embarrassing class situation.

Nevertheless we did talk. Eventually Marie told me about other situations in which being shy had been uncomfortable. At first she spoke only of facts and as if we were speaking about someone else. It was also as though she were saying "This is just the way things are; there's no use trying to change them." I realized then that when one is shy, one is faced with a difficult dilemma: it would be nice sometimes to break out of being shy, but being shy it is hard for one to speak about it let alone to try out new forms of behaving. And other peoples' pushing only makes it more difficult to break out of the circle.

Marie and I agreed that she thinks a lot about the things she hears and sees. Toward the end of our sessions, she again remarked that "Tests can't show much; they can be destructive." At that point we began to see a relationship between her holding so many opinions about other people and her feeling so uneasy about the possibility of being judged. Marie didn't tell me exactly what was becoming clear to her, but from her nodding head and her "mmm-mmh" sound I could tell that she had seen something of importance for herself and that she wanted to do something about it. Unlike most of our time together, I felt that in this moment Marie let me see herself considering the desirability and feasibility of change.

Marie's Participation in Her Successes

The above description gives a rather stiff picture of Marie. But that stiffness was present primarily when we focused directly on her, especially when I asked specific questions about her. In other situations, Marie's self contained manner struck me as positive composure and grace. For example, on the Picture Arrangement subtest, her style was one of quietly thinking and then deliberately doing. She took average time--not too slow, not too fast--and made no mistakes. I was reminded again of a lady of elegant style.

On the Digit Span subtest, Marie matter-of-factly repeated the digits, with no signs of self-consciousness, or of being otherwise distracted. She did unusually well (8 digits forward, 7 backward). Here, as in those courses that do not require class participation, her quiet, distanced style was appropriate and effective. She was comfortable and confident.

Although our talking about Marie's life did not proceed smoothly, our relationship did grow. As I learned to share some of my feelings. Marie seemed more open and responsive. When I mentioned feeling left out and sometimes kept out when she held her head and eyes down, she acknowledged that she had heard that from other people. Then from time to time she tried to look more openly into my eyes. I could imagine that she undertakes similar accommodations at work and at home, and that she is appreciated for them. I imagine also that she is appreciated for giving others lots of space. Finally, when Marie is not worried about being judged, others no doubt are responsive to her liveliness and warmth--of which I saw only fleeting moments.

Summary

In the assessment situation with me, Marie was a girl who didn't let me get to know easily who she is or what she thinks. She is quickly embarrassed and suspicious when people want to get to know her in this potentially judgmental way. Working with her was like looking into many grey clouds on a winter day, but every now and then the sun broke through changing everything into a vivid, bright vision.

In our short time together I did not get to know Marie well. But I think that through our sessions she has seen more clearly some of the ways she is shy. She has seen the strengths, but also how her silence can sometimes affect others so that they contribute to a mutual discomfort. I felt uncomfortable during the times when it was impossible for me to tell from Marie's face what her mood was. Often I felt there was something she was about to say but didn't. When she looked directly at me, her face changed, and I felt an invitation to talk.

Marie's Commentary

The introductory description of Marie is notably effective. The contrasting profiles presented there not only foreshadow the report's themes, they also disrupt inclinations (including Marie's) to think of the focal issue as a trans situational trait. Instead, readers are introduced to a sense of dynamics. They also sense that Marie could develop in many directions. In order to present this introductory description, the assessor had to look for such variations during the assessment sessions. Usually it is not until the end of the sessions that the assessor knows how these profiles cohere as different aspects of the same person. Only then can one choose which incidents best reflect what the client and assessor have learned. The most effective illustrations are those that described the person in motion moving through specified situations. Readers are thereby assisted in imagining pivot points into and out of positions in which clients find themselves.

Because Marie was self-referred for the assessment, she was the primary reader of the report. If someone else such as an employer or counselor were the primary reader, additional kinds of information probably would be required. This information might include clarification of Marie's reasons for signing up for the assessment, and a background section on her social and academic life.

In this report, I would like to have seen more sentences on what "I am shy" means to Marie--what she likes about it, when she experiences herself as shy, and when she thinks others experience her as shy. Nevertheless, as Marie's Commentary indicates, recognizing oneself in the simple descriptions of the assessment activities is a powerful experience. The client does not require background sections. In fact, for the client, such sections often distract from and hence diffuse recognition of oneself in the behavioral portrait.

Marie's Commentary also helps us to understand how it was that no interventions were undertaken during the assessment sessions. Even while reading the report, she was coping with still-evolving realizations that others may perceive her differently than she had thought, and that her shy ways influence others' actions toward her. Although she had cognitively understood the suggestions, she is not yet ready to try them, just as she was not ready to participate in developing them with the assessor. Marie may make use of them later. In the meantime, her comments tell the assessor and any other readers that although the assessment was both collaborative and accurate in its particular way, the assessor's report is still ahead of Marie's understandings.

Finally, this report illustrates the importance of allowing readers to see who the assessor was--how he responded to Marie, what he felt and did. Through his various reactions one can imagine how other people too might respond to Marie in similar situations. Moreover, one can readily imagine that Marie's portrait would have varied with either a more directive, task-oriented tester or with a Rogerian, empathy-oriented counselor. An assessment report is always a portrait from a perspective; if that perspective is clear to readers, the report becomes multiperspectival. Readers realize that the client may be understood in different ways, and in fact is different with different people.

Assessment of an Undergraduate

The following report is from another assessment by a master's student. Again, the primary reader is the undergraduate volunteer. Unlike professionals who might read such a report, the subject of this kind of assessment does not find the report too lengthy. Instead, the detail helps the person to recall the assessment and surrounding events. In my courses, the graduate students learn first to describe in detail, and then to present the same material more concisely. Later, the time constraints of most work settings encourage the students to re-present events from the assessment more selectively and hence more efficiently. In the meantime, a report of this length, clearly organized and well written, is helpful to the undergraduate volunteer. The report also provides a good description of what individualized assessment sessions are like, and illustrates the helpfulness of taking mundane problems seriously.

Lea's presenting problem certainly is not unusual, and the report's suggestions are the commonsensical sort that the graduate student could have offered without going through an assessment. However, the assessor knew that common sense was no more sufficient for Lea than for the rest of us when we attempt to change our habits. The graduate student accepted the problem as presented and waited for examples of it to arise during the assessment sessions before suggesting options. Practicing and tailoring some of these options and discussing their similarity to the assessor's life situations rendered the options personally viable. Assessment procedures are not the only route to that end, of course, but they certainly can be efficacious.

Finally, this report illustrates how a working relationship evolved over three assessment sessions (two mandated by course requirements, and one that was due to Lea's and the assessor's scheduling according to the only time slots that were mutually available). In addition, when I asked the graduate student if she would revise the report for use in this chapter, she included an addendum about a fourth meeting. The addendum is representative of what one might write in a clinic, and it attests to the "progress report" character of any individualized assessment write-up.

Date of report: April 24, 19__

Sessions: April 16, 20, 22.

Psychological Assessment

Lea James is a freshman at Duquesne University. She turned eighteen on the last day of this assessment. She plans to major in Political Science and is considering Journalism for her minor. Lea volunteered for this assessment through her Introductory Psychology class.

Presenting Problem

Lea originally volunteered because she was curious about what it would be like to take psychological tests. She was interested to see how she would do on the intelligence test and what new things she could learn about herself. When Lea and I conversed on the phone to arrange our meeting, I suggested that she think about a personal issue or problem that she might wish to explore during the assessment.

Lea proposed as a focal issue that she had too many things to do and not enough time to do them all. She explained that she wanted to do everything at once and usually ended up scheduling too many things in too short a span of time. It has been important for Lea to devote time to her school work, her sports activities, her family, friends, and her boyfriend whom she has been seeing for a year and a half. However, between moving at a fast pace to keep up with all these activities, and feeling cramped by the pressures of time, Lea has been jumpy and tense during much of her day and it has been difficult for her to unwind and relax. She mentioned, for example, that the night before our first meeting she couldn't get to sleep, her thoughts raced, and she mulled over plans a mile a minute. Lea wanted to do "something" during the assessment that related to the stress she was feeling, even though she didn't have a clear idea about what that "something" would or should be.

Assessment Procedures

Lea and I met three times at the Duquesne University Psychology Center, spending a total of five hours for the assessment.

We began the assessment with a brief conversation, then moved on to the following tests:

Bender-Gestalt (Bender)

Wechsler Intelligence Scale for Adults (WAIS)

Draw-A-Person (DAP)

Thematic Apperception Test (TAT) (Cards #1, 2, 3GF, 8GF, 12F, 16, and 17BM)

As we moved through the testing process, Lea and I dialogued our impressions and observations about her style of approaching the assessment situation and how this related to other events in her life. This report presents our findings.

Appearance and Comportment

Lea arrived early for the assessment. She sat waiting for me in the hall of the Psychology Center, leaning back comfortably, with one arm draped over the side of her chair, and her legs crossed and extended straight out in front of her. Her other arm was perched back and resting on the arm of her chair as she twirled strands of her light brown hair in circles around her fingers. She was casually dressed in beige corduroy pants and an off-white, colorfully patterned sweater. She smiled in a bright, friendly manner as we introduced ourselves.

Lea is almost of average height and she has a petite, trim figure. Her big blue eyes looked alert and attentive and her glossy, shoulder-length hair was neatly kept. Her youthful appearance added to her air of healthy, athletic, well-being.

As we began the assessment, Lea sat looking relaxed yet ready to begin. She began each task throughout the assessment readily and self-assuredly, as if confident that she would do well. But when she reached a difficult part in a test, she often paused, knitted her brow, and pursed her lips, as if she were concerned about getting an answer wrong or not performing well on a drawing. When Lea was engaged in the drawing or performance tasks, she sat leaning forward over the test materials, working quietly, quickly, and diligently. She looked thoroughly engrossed in her task. When we talked or when she answered verbal questions, she sat back in her chair looking calm and reflective, yet she delivered her answers quickly and decisively. I had the impression that Lea tried to do her best on each test.

Although Lea was responsive to my questions and easily engaged in conversations about herself, she usually remained quiet until I spoke to her. She seemed to require my overtures before she would talk about herself.

Background Provided by Lea

During our talks, Lea acknowledged that she was confident that she could do well in school and she said that her class work has not been a problem. She mentioned that her parents expect more from her academically than any of the other children because she has, as she put it, "the most brains in the family." She added that even though her parents expect her to do well in school, they don't push or force their expectations upon her. Her boyfriend also expects her to do well, and encourages her to try harder in her studies so that she can go to a better school such as Carnegie-Mellon University, where he will be studying next year.

The Assessment

Squeezing Things In: Just as Lea tries to do too many things in too short a time, she drew the Bender in a similar manner. She worked as quickly as she could and she drew her figures as compactly as she could. When I pointed out that her drawings were close together, she remarked that she usually wrote and drew things that way. When she takes notes or writes letters, she squeezes her writing in closely together. She said, "I feel that I need to conserve space."

When we talked about her having drawn her Bender figures rapidly, she repeated that she usually tried to do things quickly. She also added that when she goes out with friends and she doesn't have much time to be with them, she becomes "worked up" and tries to do as many things with them as possible. Lea ends up moving from one fast-paced activity to another, giving herself little time to slow down.

In contrast to her many fast-paced activities, Lea likes to write essays and poetry. Writing poetry relaxes her because she has to slow down to think carefully. As she slows down she becomes totally absorbed with what she is doing. Writing poetry is one activity that Lea doesn't rush herself with. She gives herself all the time that she needs to work on a poem, so that she can get it just the way that she wants it.

Trying Hard to Do Well All the Time

Lea's feeling pressured and stressed around scheduling so many activities in too short a time is compounded by her simultaneously trying to do the best job she can with the things she does. When Lea drew the Bender drawings she tried to draw them as neatly and as accurately as possible. When I asked her about this she replied, "I figured I can't go wrong if I do them just right!" When Lea got to the fifth Bender card, a dot drawing, she laughed and made a grimace. She described her feelings as: "Oh no, do I have to get these dots exactly right oh forget it, it would take years to get them perfect."

Lea tries to do her best on her school projects. When she cooks she follows the recipe to the tee so that she won't make any mistakes, and she tries to do her chores just right. She becomes frustrated when she can't do a good job on a task. In social situations she puts similar pressure on herself when she is with friends or with her boyfriend because she feels that it is up to her that they share a lot of fun. She becomes upset if she and her friends don't have a good time when they are together. She feels that she has disappointed them and let them down.

I suggested to Lea that she do the Bender over again, only this time dropping her own expectations that she had to do the Bender perfectly and as quickly as possible. Even though she still drew the Bender rapidly the second time around, she looked more relaxed and became playful with the task. She followed the movements of her pencil around with her head as she drew, in a sort of dance, mimicking with these motions the contours of the lines and curves that she put down on the paper. She accompanied her movements with little whistling sounds and laughter as she drew.

When Lea finished the Bender, she looked at me and said, "It was funner that time." She was surprised that she had been almost as accurate on the second Bender as she had been on the first. Seeing this reminded her of her poetry writing. She explained that sometimes when she finally stopped trying so hard on a poem and just let herself go with it, her writing came out as well, if not better, than if she were trying to make it perfect.

Wanting to Please Others

When Lea and I met for the third meeting of the assessment, I asked her if she had any questions or concerns to voice before we moved back into the testing. She made two comments. First, she said that she hoped that I would get all the "stuff" that I needed for my report. Second, she wondered what I thought about how she had done on the test battery. These remarks hit at the heart of an important issue for Lea, and we stayed with this theme for the rest of the session.

Many of the things Lea does, she does in order to keep other people happy. She becomes concerned about what other people think of her. She wants people to like her and to think that she does a good job with things. She mentioned that her boyfriend reminds her, "You can't please everyone."

Lea explained that she often sacrifices what she wants to do in order to go along with what other people want her to do. Lea becomes tense and pressured when too many people place demands on her at the same time. She feels guilty when she says "no" to someone, particularly if that someone is special to her, such as her boyfriend and family members. She also becomes scared that people will be dissatisfied with her if she does something she wants to do just for herself.

Lea realizes the bind she puts herself in when she doesn't say "no" to others' wishes when they are too much for her. She knows this puts her under pressure but she has not felt ready to change.

Lea described a situation that arose over the weekend when she had gone home. Sunday afternoon her mother wanted her to stay home and help her with things around the house, her boyfriend wanted her to go for a walk in the park with him, and at the same time she knew that she had to get some schoolwork done. Lea tried frantically to figure out how she could do all these things in the short time that she had and she ended up becoming very tense and edgy. Somehow she managed to squeeze them all in.

When I gave Lea the blank TAT card (#16), at the end of the session, she described a scene in which a boxer is getting pummeled in the ring. He is losing the fight. He knows that there are better ways to make a living, but he also knows that he is not ready to give up the ring. He'll just keep going back for more beatings.

Her story reminded her of herself in two ways. It reminded her of her present life because she feels defeated when she can't say "no" to people.

However, she does not feel that she can change this pattern yet so that she can "get out of the ring." Her boxer story also invoked some feelings of concern she has about her future. Lea set a goal for herself a long time ago to pursue and to establish a career for herself that she will enjoy. Now she becomes scared sometimes that she'll end up settling for a job that she doesn't enjoy or find creative. The tension that she becomes caught up in on a day-to-day basis, when she foregoes her own wants in order to satisfy others, accentuates her fears that she may compromise herself and not be able to reach her career goal.

When Lea had finished her TAT story, she paused for a moment and said, "Ya know, I feel lousy when I comply with others and sacrifice myself. I don't want to feel lousy and depressed anymore and I have to think of how I can change that." Lea and I then talked about what she would have to do to be able to say "no" to others. She would first have to say "yes" to herself. We talked about how when she feels herself becoming tense and edgy in a pressuring situation, she could stop and reason out what her priorities are. Lea said she would have to make sure that she just wasn't being selfish, that she wasn't hurting anyone else and, most importantly, that her decision would work out for others as well as for herself.

I asked Lea to think back to the tense situation that had arisen the weekend before and to imagine herself saying no to someone's requests in order to take pressure off herself. Lea thought carefully for a moment and said that she would tell her boyfriend, Mike, "I have a lot of things that must be done today. I don't have time to take a walk with you but I do have time to see you while I'm doing chores and packing."

Just Being Herself

When Lea drew herself in the DAP drawings, she enjoyed the picture she drew. She explained that she drew her "carefree and easygoing self in her old bummy jeans." This is the way she likes to be the best, "just being myself, being relaxed, and not caring what other people think of me."

Summary

Lea's presenting problem, that of feeling tense and under pressure with having too many things to do and not enough time to do them in, remained our focus throughout the assessment. The assessment process provided an opportunity to explore and discuss many of the personal elements that combine to create this problem for Lea.

Lea's manner of drawing the Bender is indicative of the way she goes about doing many of her daily activities. She often tries to do the best job she can, giving herelf a minimum amount of time for each of her many tightly scheduled activities. Stress builds up for Lea as she races from one activity to another in this way.

Just as Lea wanted to help me with my assessment project, so she often wants to please other people. She tries to live up to the high expectations that she feels other people have of her. She gets herself in a jam when she tries to do too many things for, and with, too many people. She has had a difficult time saying "no" to others when they request her time, even when she knows she is overtaxing herself by complying with their wishes.

Community Mental Health Center

This is the first of the four assessments in this chapter that were conducted in clinical settings by masters students toward the end of the semester. Because the individualized report is longer than most reports the center's staff were accustomed to, the authors chose to place a summary (General Outcome of the Assessment) immediately after the Presenting Problem section to assure readers that the report responds to the referral. In addition, the Outcome section serves as a preparatory overview for readers, and as a reminder for Linda of what she achieved through the assessment.

The introductory description of Linda is particularly effective. Through its vivid images the reader can picture Linda while reading the remainder of the report. The images were carefully selected to represent (re-present) Linda's contrasting ways of being, and to presage the report's description of how those ways had worked both against and for her. The primary author's responses to Linda's various comportments show Linda and other readers how she helps to shape other people's attitudes toward her. These accomplishments of the introductory description were possible only through concrete instances of Linda in action. Another effective aspect of this report's introductory description is its nonjudgmental frankness. Linda's comments at the end of the report indicate that she recognized herself and felt accepted.

Individualized Assessment of Mrs. Linda Mariani

Date of Report: Nov. 19, 19__

Mrs. Linda Mariani is 44 years old and is currently attending community college. She lives with her husband, Frank, their only child, Leslie (age 22), and her mother in a southern suburb of Pittsburgh.

Presenting Problem

Linda has been in individual psychotherapy at the Community Mental Health Center in Haverford, with Ms. Janice Davis, for the past month and a half. Ms. Davis recently invited her to participate in an assessment so that they both might gain a better understanding of her problems and options. In our first meeting with Linda, she stated that she "wanted to know why (she) wasn't more self-confident" at school, particularly when she is being observed by classmates or teachers. Linda's purpose for going to school is to learn secretarial skills that will help her get a job. As she encountered problems at school, she became discouraged and has questioned whether she will succeed in the outside world of work. She attributes many of her problems at school to the way she becomes anxious: "The hands will shake, the voice will break, and the heart will pound."

General Outcome of the Assessment

During the assessment, Linda became increasingly involved in looking at the situations in which she is uncomfortable and testing out new ways to approach these situations. Her initial approach to the assessment seemed to shift rapidly from expecting to be told about herself to actively exploring with us the problems she has had. Linda seemed to enjoy the venture as she realized it would be cooperative, commenting that she was looking forward to our report and to writing her comments about whatever might strike her as "off the wall." This process of sharing her concerns with others seemed to be, in itself, an important outcome of the assessment. It was a vivid example for her of how, when she spoke honestly and was vulnerable to others, she did not feel weak or anxious, but at ease.

In our work with the assessment materials, we identified several styles of approaching tasks that seemed to hinder Linda in the assessment as well as in everyday situations. As Linda related these ways of working to the times she has felt anxious, she explored with us some alternate approaches. She discovered that she has felt more at ease in what had been anxious situations when she has communicated with others about her feelings and decisions instead of cutting herself off. The most memorable incident of the assessment occurred when Linda role-played a discussion with her husband in which she told him, for the first time, how much she needed and loved him. This was one way that Linda began to experiment with what she called "opening the doors of communication" with her family, her classmates, and her teacher. By doing so, Linda may gain support and guidance as she becomes re-oriented toward what she wants personally and in her marriage [see the last pages for suggestions to the client]. The remainder of this report reviews the process of the assessment.

Opportunities for Assessment

The assessment was conducted over three sessions by Andrea Jones assisted by Kareen Malone, graduate students of the Department of Psychology at Duquesne University. The sessions took place at the Haverford Community Mental Health Center on Nov. 6 (2 hrs.), Nov. 10 (2 1/2 hrs.) and Nov. 14 (1 1/2 hrs.). Test materials used during these sessions were: the BenderGestalt, the

WAIS (Information, Arithmetic, Similarities, Vocabulary, and Block Design subtests), the DAP, and TAT cards #'s 17BM, 16F, 2, and 10.

Introductory Description of Linda Mariani

Linda is a short-statured woman of 44 whose tight, greying curls neatly surrounded an open and expertly powdered face. During the assessment she wore colorful, fashionably loose blouses which made her figure, although slightly heavy, seem attractive. Her dressy earrings complemented the quality of her make-up. She seemed to take great care in her appearance, even as she dressed "casually."

At our first meeting, I invited Linda to take a seat with us at the empty circle of chairs. While commenting that she didn't want to sit in the overstuffed chair, she headed right toward it and then slowly sat down, as if testing it out. When I urged her to take a different chair, she wavered a bit and then seemed relieved to comply. Somehow, in seeing her hesitate as if she wanted to move but couldn't, I had felt called on to help her get what she wanted. It turned out later that Linda rarely allows others to see her hesitation and wants.

Linda perched herself on the wooden swivel chair, her knees held close together and her large purse stationed on her lap. Despite the apparent immobility of Linda's lower body, she seemed poised and ready to leave at any moment.

Scarcely ten minutes into the interview, Linda's voice assumed what seemed later to be an habitual loudness, and her hands moved emphatically with her speech. As she spoke, Linda gazed directly into Kareen's eyes; the strong lines of her face made her delivery seem more forceful. Kareen seemed to become mesmerized. Linda's well-articulated and lengthy descriptions of her current and past problems dominated the first session. Kareen and I both hesitated to interrupt.

During the following sessions and as we moved into using the materials, Linda's posture and speech seemed more relaxed and varied. Her purse was placed on the floor and her lower body no longer seemed static as she shifted in her seat. As the assessment progressed, she moved her gaze more frequently from Kareen to me and back. Reciprocally, the two of us became more active in talking with her and were surprised at how easily we interrupted her when her stories became long.

Linda Mariani's Viewpoint

Over the past several years, Linda began to establish and realize some of her own personal goals, beyond those of caring for her family. She has been a member of Weight Watchers and has lost 70 pounds. Over the past winter, Linda decided that she wanted to get out of the house and find a job as a secretary. She feels that she has received little recognition for the work she has done in the home and would like to pursue a job that would "give [her] a feeling of self-worth." In addition, it is important to her that she feels she can stand independently of her husband's support. In order to achieve this goal, Linda studied for and received her GED this past Spring and began courses at Community College.

Linda's attempt to master shorthand and typing has been a constant struggle for her. She has felt ready to cry when she makes mistakes; her hands have felt frozen at the typewriter during speed tests; she has been afraid of her voice breaking when she speaks up in class or talks with the teacher about her problems.

Despite her past successes, these new difficulties have provoked Linda to question whether she will move away from being "only" a housekeeper toward being an "independent" person who holds a paying job. As Linda told us at the beginning of the second session, she entered the assessment with the fear that she would be told that "there are things that I think I am capable of doing that I am not capable of." Linda has stated emphatically, however, that she "won't go back to being a dowdy, fat, little housewife." She seemed determined to do whatever it took to remove any roadblocks from her path. She seemed to consider both therapy and the assessment as ways she could learn to handle her problems more effectively.

Linda Mariani's Participation in Her Difficulties

One theme that ran through the assessment was how Linda "jumped in" to situations and decisions, without checking out what she was doing until later. Her approach to many new situations has been to plunge ahead without looking like she needed any assistance and without turning to others for support. The problems and the opportunities created by this approach w ere examined within the context of the assessment itself and were related to Linda's life situation (see also "Linda M's Successes and Options"). We discovered ways in which Linda has cut herself off from other people and from her own potential success through this "jumping in" style.

Linda's responses to the questions and tasks of the assessment came with unusual speed. During the WAIS, her eyes became glued on Kareen; her forehead wrinkled and her hands twisted around a pencil as she fired her answers back. Eager to do it right, Linda jumped into the B-G and the Vocabulary subtest, missing key aspects of Kareen 's initial instructions. When questioned, Linda stated that by jumping into the B-G task she prevented herself from thinking about it and thus did not become anxious about her performance. In both instances, however, she had to stop in the middle of the task to request information before proceeding.

Linda has faced similar situations in her typing class and at her new part time job. On two specific occasions, as Linda plunged on with a task at hand, she neglected to listen to the typing teacher's lecture on punctuation marks and to the store owner's explanation of how to make a bank deposit. By concentrating on what was immediately present to her, she avoided worrying about how she might handle these new complications. This approach backfired when she discovered later that these explanations were necessary for doing her job.

On the Vocabulary subtest, Linda's jumping in to answer right away had led Kareen to assume that she understood how the test was set up, and thus Kareen didn't continue to point out the words on the Vocabulary sheet. After four vocabulary words had gone by, Kareen and I were surprised to learn that Linda was confused about the purpose of the Vocabulary sheet.

Linda described other situations in which she put herself out, alone on a limb, by appearing to be in control of a situation while she was really unsure of herself and wanted help. After spending seven weeks struggling to learn shorthand, Linda was told by her teacher that she didn't understand how Linda could be having problems because she seemed so "optimistic." Linda realized that because she had acted as if she didn't have any problems, the teacher probably didn't realize how desperate she was for help. It seemed that the way Linda jumped quickly and enthusiastically into situations that were new and difficult for her made it less likely that she would be offered the consideration and help of those around her.

Linda's experiences of being anxious, "the voice breaking, the heart pounding" and "feeling not able to do it," seemed to occur in situations in which she was afraid of being pitied and seen as emotionally "weak." We talked about this when Linda described how she felt anxious and her hands were clammy as she waited for the second session to begin. She said she was worried that she would "kill her dream" of becoming a self-supporting person. At school, Linda felt anxious when she imagined her teacher would think her "a poor, dumb meathead" if she were honest about her difficulties. Linda felt anxious when she wanted help or support from others but imagined that if she were honest about her problems, she would get put down. By not checking with her teacher, her husband or her friends to see how accepting they might be of her, Linda set herself up for becoming more afraid and anxious.

Linda Mariani's Successes and Options

The same "jumping in" style discussed earlier may also be an asset to Linda in that it is the way she gives herself a critical push towards making a change. For example, being willing to jump into new situations could be considered a strength when it meant that Linda left the well-known world of her housewife duties to do other things of which she has dreamed.

I was impressed also by the determined way in which Linda has pursued her newly formed goals, even after she first experienced failure. On the WAIS, her willingness to stick with something until she had it right was shown in her work with the Block Designs. On several of the most difficult designs, Linda almost completed the design and then realized she wasn't getting it right. Frequently checking with the model, she worked steadily until her figure was correct. Similarly, Linda has realized that her present career "design" may need to be revised. She plans to check out her alternatives more carefully, by attending a career planning seminar.

In addition to Linda's determined way of "jumping in," I also saw a more reflective side of Linda when she listened to our comments and shared with us her thoughts and feelings. She seems also to have established this give and take in her therapy. Linda spoke to us of how she had begun to use this style in her everyday world by beginning to talk with her classmates about what they think, and feel about the class. As she does this, she is finding out that she is not as alone as she thought.

During the assessment Linda practiced saying things she had wanted to say to certain people but had not thought it possible that she ever would. She addressed her typing teacher by whom she has often felt intimidated. Linda hestiated at first to directly address her. She then seemed to gain resolve, however, and looking straight into my eyes (I was the typing teacher) she told me how hard shorthand had been for her and the real reason that she had dropped it. Unlike how Linda had characterized herself, she did not seem weak to me. After the role-play was over, Linda said she realized that she had the option of "opening up" to the teacher about her problems, with the possibility of getting help.

Finally, as we were working with the TAT cards during the last session, Linda came back to speak about the relationship she has with her husband. She described the image of the loving couple on card #10 as something she would like for her own marriage. When I asked her to direct her comments to the man on the card as if he were Frank, she began to speak in earnest. She held the card firmly, but gently; her voice came slowly and often with tears. She said: "I would like to say to him that you don't realize just how much I love you or how much I need you. I never told him I needed him because I never gave that impression. And damn it I do need him. " With tears in her eyes, Linda's voice sounded the strongest and the surest that I had yet heard. She seemed vulnerable but not weak, aware of her past history with her husband, and determined to work for a change.

7

Psychological Reports of Children and Youths

Introduction

Ellipses indicate where material has been deleted for the sake of economy. None of these reports include written commentary by the youngsters. Only rarely have we asked children below age ten to write commentary, because involvement with that activity usually distracts them from the meanings of the assessment. Our reports on older youngsters, however, often do include their comments and signatures. Even without that particular form of collaboration, all of the assessments and reports in this chapter were individualized. Brief camp reports and an Individualized Education Plan (IEP) were included as reminders that even when assessment records are not meant to be full-scale or thoroughly individualized, they can nevertheless address the referral issue in ways that evoke a sense of who the youngster is as an individual. The other reports illustrate more thoroughly how to go beyond considering end products (such as test scores, finished drawings). They show us ways to attend to and to describe the processes through which the end products evolved. The reports point to the mutuality of the comportments of the youngster and of his or her adults. The co-creation of events by youngsters and their adults is represented through individualized assessment report-writing practices: concrete, descriptive re-presentations of comportment, context, intervention, and collaboration. These are followed where appropriate by suggestions tailored to the youngster and to the referral resources.

Kindergarten Referral: Melvin Schreider, the Iron Bunny

The "Iron Bunny" report was written by graduate students in my department's M.A. assessment course. It was written toward the end of the semester as one of the two field assessments assigned to each team. The field setting was an experimental, private preschool, where graduate students from several local programs received training.

Although the authors spent more than six hours with Melvin Schreider, they judiciously selected just a few examples to illustrate their findings. The report is all the more powerful for its brevity. The "iron bunny" metaphor effectively uses the assessors' personal experience of Melvin to integrate two apparently opposite comportments that had been observed previously. Because the report evolves around the two apparently opposite comportments, the metaphor also serves to remind readers of the content of the report. To enhance that function of the metaphor, the authors placed "Iron Bunny" in the report's title. The report sticks to its story line; the connection between testing events and classroom behavior is made explicit, and the Alternatives (suggestions) follow directly from the report.

Psychological Assessment: MELVIN SCHREIDER

Melvin, the Iron Bunny

Age: 5 years, 3 months Dates of assessment: 12-2, 4, 9, 13, 19____

Grade: Kindergarten Date of report: 12-15, 19____

Referral

Ms. Judy Sontag director of the West Side New School, believes Melvin to be seriously distressed, and wondered if our observations might help her staff to minimize the difficulties he now experiences (and that are likely to increase in public school). Specifically, the staff has been concerned about (1) Melvin's "aggression" toward other children, and (2) his "withdrawal," which is accompanied by "a funny look on his face." One of his teachers further explained to us that Melvin hates the children, throws things, and when there is surrounding commotion he goes off by himself.

Opportunities for Assessment

We met with Melvin four times over a two-week period for a total of 6 1/2 hours. We first observed him in his classroom playing with other children, and later played with him ourselves. During our second and third meetings with him he did the Bender-Gestalt, the Draw-A-Person, and parts of the Wechsler Primary and Preschool Scale of Intelligence (WPPSI). In our fourth meeting we participated in a play therapy session with Melvin and Ms. Sandy Harst, a child development intern.

First Impressions

What we noticed first about Melvin was his dirty physical appearance. His hair was uncombed, his hands and face unwashed, his clothes torn, and his body smelled of stale urine. Then Melvin, although only five years old, began to remind us of a little steelworker. His square face, solid chin, and prominent forehead reminded us of the features of a man, not a boy. Similarly, his broad shoulders and a large torso reminded us of a little football player. In our first meeting with him he put on a helmet, took out a football and started throwing it to us or running with it like a halfback.

Melvin also definitely struck us as warm, friendly, and gentle, and he moved with caution when we first began playing football with him. His play with us was discontinuous; he sometimes stood in the corner waiting for us to ask him to join the game. He then quickly joined in, running around with the football and enjoying physical contact. He seemed to like the individual attention from us and smiled appreciatively. When a few other children entered the game and it became noisy, Melvin suddenly ran over to a small space next to the rabbit cage and crawled into it. Melvin's face seemed sad, his mouth was twisted, and his eyes frowned in a faraway gaze; this was the "funny look" that his teacher had told us about.

Melvin as Seen through the Assessment Materials

When we first played with him, we thought that Melvin was not particularly intelligent. He did not talk much and when he did he used baby talk. He was also clumsy, uncoordinated. In trying to catch the football, he did move his arms toward the ball but waited for it to land wherever his hands already were. However, as we began going through the assessment materials with him, we discovered a bright little boy. Here Melvin was attentive to his surroundings. On the Picture Completion subtest of the WPPSI, which requires the identification of the missing part of an everyday situation or object, Melvin got 22 out of 23 questions correct. He carefully scanned the picture, concentrating on it until he found the missing part. Melvin was also quick to learn a manual task. On the Animal House subtest, where the child has to match colored pegs with animal pictures, Melvin finished the task in three minutes, well within the five-minute time limit. He started the task before we actually finished the instructions and he did not make one error. Later, Melvin took out the board and pegs by himself, saying that he wanted to play with them again. He then, from memory, correctly matched the colored pegs with the animals.

There were some things that Melvin could not do initially but it was not because he lacked understanding of the task. For example, when we asked him to draw certain geometrical figures. Melvin took the pencil and tried, but as soon as he made a mistake he stopped drawing and said "can't do that," sometimes slapping the paper or throwing the pencil. When he made one mistake, he quickly gave up. On Figure 6, Melvin started drawing and then threw his pencil down, giving up. When we pointed out to him that he had completed half the figure, and encouraged him to continue, Melvin finished the drawing, pleased and surprised. A similar sequence occurred on the maze subtest of the WPPSI: on the more difficult mazes, Melvin began and after making one mistake jumped away, saying, "I don't want to do it." One of us encouraged him to continue by helping Melvin guide the pencil. Melvin welcomed the help, and continued, even on the most difficult mazes. On the Vocabulary subtest, Melvin refused to talk, despite our encouragement. His face took on that "funny look" again, and he looked as frightened as a scared rabbit, holding his hands to his face, squinting his eyes, and shaking slightly.

Similarities between the Assessment and Classroom Situations: In watching Melvin's behavior in the classroom with other children, we saw many similarities with his behavior on the assessment materials. In both situations, when Melvin did not know what to do to get what he wanted, he behaved in an ineffective manner. Most often these were occasions when other persons could have helped him if he had known how to turn to or otherwise engage them. In the assessment situation he threw down the pencil or hit the paper and in the classroom situation he hit other children or threw some toys. When the situation got out of hand for Melvin, he stopped talking altogether and went away by himself. In the classroom situation this meant going off in a corner, and in the assessment situation this meant avoiding any participation with us on the assessment task at hand, although he remained in his seat. At these points Melvin took on his funny look and said nothing more. In both situations, Melvin apparently wanted to participate actively. He was friendly with us, willing to participate patiently in most of our tasks. Likewise, he sought the company of other children and enthusiastically joined in playing with them. At one point we even saw him walk up to a girl and ask her if she was his friend. At times, Melvin could play effectively with the other children. For example, he cooperatively joined in a game of Twister with us and two little girls in his class. In other words, although Melvin sometimes acts inappropriately with other people, he typically wants contact with others and when given support definitely is an open, friendly boy.

Summary

We have tried to illustrate that Melvin's difficulty is not one of "aggression." Rather, it is that at present when he becomes lost he either hops away into seclusion like a frightened bunny, or he tries to hold his ground by throwing things or hitting children. His steelworker appearance and physical strength probably result in children and adults alike perceiving this inappropriate form of assertiveness as "hostility" or "aggression." Surely both children and adults must be tempted to avoid Melvin not only during these misdirected physical assertions, but also in the face of his apparent unpredictability. And then there's his dirty appearance and the odor of stale urine. Melvin unknowingly contributes to an environment in which others turn away from him.

Alternatives

1. Perhaps Melvin could remain more consistently and constructively engaged with persons and activities if adults

would intervene to help him remain involved. A crucial point in his movement is the moment when he meets the first obstacle, when he makes the first mistake. At that point he often gives up. When Melvin has been helped over the mistake, he usually has continued. This is a matter of saying to him, "Come on, Melvin, you can do it," and showing him how he can correct his mistake. In our interactions, Melvin consistently responded well to individualized encouragement.

2. When put into a situation with a lot of people or commotion, Melvin often has either hit somebody or hopped away. Noisy situations seem to have been aversive and confusing to him. We suggest that, when possible, his group activities be limited to a small number of people. In line with this, when Melvin is involved in a group task, it might help to pair him with a quiet, easygoing child who could help Melvin over his obstacles. Such cumulative experiences may gradually allow him to experience classroom commotion as less threatening.
3. We think it is advisable for Melvin to be referred for a preschool developmental readiness screening. It is possible that some of his perplexity may be due to perceptual difficulties, although admittedly what we observed could equally well be attributable to underdeveloped coordination. The latter could be either constitutional or the outcome of insufficient supervised play at home. Examples of what we noticed are: when playing with dominoes, Melvin held them close to his face in order to count the dots; he also had difficulty catching the football--it seemed as if he did not see where it began its trajectory.
4. Similarly, supportive physical play with Melvin seems in order not only to provide constructive intervention when he becomes lost, but also to provide for the development of motor coordination. An additional example here is that Melvin holds his pencil too far up and hence cannot control it effectively. Although this individualized encouragement and gentle supervised play is of course not always possible for already overloaded teachers or for parents with their complex concerns, the more often it can occur, the better off Melvin will be.

5. After Melvin's parents have studied this report and perhaps devised additional suggestions with the West Side New School staff, this report and the additions could be provided to Melvin's first grade teacher. That teacher will be a critical person in aiding Melvin toward an integration of his assertiveness and sensitivity. At any rate, we feel that this report might help to alert her to whichever aspect of Melvin is not immediately apparent in the public school classroom, whether the steelworker or the bunny.

The straightforward, concise presentation of Melvin helps us to see the seriousness of his situation. Concomitantly, Melvin's responses to the assessors' supportive interventions, as well as their observations of adaptive comportment, alert us to a non pathological side. We see possibilities of relating to Melvin's strengths and of helping him to develop. The graduate students' achievement in this dual presentation is especially remarkable in that they were requested by the West Side faculty to not "scare off" the parents by explicitly mentioning their fear of parental criminal neglect or abuse. West Side teachers were working with the parents, encouraging them to seek guidance for themselves and further care for Melvin. In the event that the school's efforts failed, however, assessors and faculty alike wanted this report to be strong enough to help provide "just cause" for intervention by Child Welfare authorities. The report optimizes chances that upon reading it, the parents would recognize the importance of their responsibility to Melvin and yet not be thrown into rigid defensiveness.

An effective report enables helpers to recognize the person they already know--that is, to see the similarity between their own observations and the report's description. The assessors were successful in this regard partly because of their extended observations in the classroom. Assessment description, however, also transforms readers' earlier perceptions and conceptions of the client into a fuller vision, one that integrates apparent discrepancies, such as the "hostility" and "withdrawal" that had been noted by Melvin's teachers. No underlying causes were posited to account for these behaviors; neither feature was explained in terms of the other. Rather, the way each comportment developed was specified. Readers see the circumstances within which Melvin changes from little man of steel to frightened bunny and back again; readers also recognize that both profiles are the same Melvin. Adults thus see how they participate in Melvin's transformations, and how they might do so more mindfully in the future.

Finally, this report is noteworthy for two other ways of reaching staff and parents. First, both parties were engaged through specific references to them throughout the report. Second, because the assessment took place in Pittsburgh, the metaphor was chosen to speak to Pittsburghers: we are the home of the Steelers football team, named after our men of iron, the steelworkers. The bunny image was a particularly effective contrast because of the staff's and parents' familiarity with the classroom's bunny hutch being Melvin's place of refuge.

Family Assessment

A field placement supervisor in a family service agency asked two M.A. students to assess both a counseling client and her son. The mother, Barbara Harrell, had reported difficulties in coping with her six-year-old son, Bobby. He appeared to be doing well at school in terms of grades and conduct, but he was difficult to control at home. He frequently made excuses to stay home on days his mother would be there. She wondered if other children were teasing Bobby or if teachers expected him to perform beyond his age because he was tall and husky. At home he was often demanding and sometimes threw temper tantrums. Barbara wondered if he had a blood sugar problem and gave him peanut butter or candy when he became irritable. She had not, however, consulted a physician.

The assessment team asked for permission to visit the Harrell home on a Saturday morning. There they encountered Bobby's younger brother and sister and Marlan Harrell, Barbara's husband, who had just returned after living alone for a year. After joining the family's informal breakfast routine and then talking with the parents, the team administered a Bender-Gestalt and Wechsler Intelligence Scale for Children with Bobby, asked him for some drawings, and played tic-tac-toe with him. They returned three days later to talk with Barbara. On that visit they made use of the Bender-Gestalt and the Comprehension and Block Design subtests of the Wechsler Adult Intelligence Scale to explore her ways of coping with challenges.

With parental permission, the team then observed Bobby in his classroom, and discussed the contrast to their home observations with Bobby's teacher and the school counselor.

The team then returned to the Harrell home with a report describing the family interactions, the separate assessment activities with Bobby and with Barbara, the school observations, and their initial suggestions. Barbara and Marlan modified and expanded the suggestions, which encouraged Barbara to be more consistent and explicit in her dealings with Bobby. The assessors then wrote a separate report for Bobby in the form of a fable. The fable was intended to help Bobby understand what the assessors had seen, and how his mother was going to try to be more consistently responsive to his needs for structure and guidance.

The excerpts below present the report's findings, illustrate the assessors' approach to a family, and describe their exploration of two contexts in which a youngster appears to be quite different. The fable turned out to be a remarkably effective means of communicating with all parties. Marlan is not in the fable, just as he is often not in the home. The report indicates that he and Barbara married just out of high school, but his sales job has kept him away from home most of the time. Barbara at first focused her life on Bobby, but then began working as a clerk two days a week, doing outside housework on call, and working on women's social action projects. Marlan, a large-boned, husky man, wore wire-rimmed glasses and spoke softly. His astute but unobtrusive remarks showed that he was genuinely concerned about Bobby. The Harrells were uncertain about their future together.

Barbara was described as 27 years old, tall, slender, attractive, with waistlength brown hair. The following excerpts further describe her.

Generally, through the Bender-Gestalt, Block Design subtest, and the DAP, Barbara assumed what appeared to be a casual posture and attitude, resting her head in one hand and performing the tasks with the other hand. Her drawings were completed quickly, lightly, and without detail.

What at first appeared to us as patience with her children when they were demanding or whiney often later appeared to us as avoiding confrontation with them by giving in (for example, by letting them fill up on cookies and cheese twists before dinner). It also seemed that she didn't let them know what was expected of them in a consistent manner (specification of mealtimes, bedtimes, homework times, and so on). This is partly a result of her work schedule. Barbara admitted that she felt she was both lazy and an avoider. She believed it would be a 24-hour vigil to keep her kids under control she's too tired after a day's work and just wants peace, which she attains by not taking a firm stand with her children concerning their behavior.

During the Block Design subtest, Barbara mentioned that she likes "good precise directions." She said she strongly sensed the absence of lines on the stimulus card, which would have indicated the boundaries of the blocks. Barbara likes boundaries, because they indicate to her straightforward direction. (Would this be an easier way for her to make decisions step by step?) She sometimes becomes lost in general directions (and likewise "gives in" with her children). She told us about an older woman at work who criticizes in general statements. Barbara would rather she would criticize directly. "I don't know where I stand with her." We asked Barbara if she considered herself straightforward with her children. She paused, and answered, "My fault is plain laziness I don't take the time." She also referred to "getting up on two feet when you'd like to sit down."

Is she perhaps confusing being straightforward with being pushy? Concerning her problem with Bobby's behavior at home, Barbara feels, " I don't like to be pushed, therefore, I don't want to be pushy. I don't like to be nagged, therefore, I don't like to nag." Barbara also appreciates straightforwardness and would like to be straightforward in her expectations of Bobby's behavior. But on the other hand, she does not want to nag or push. Herein lies an inconsistency. How is Bobby to know what his boundaries and rules are at home when (1) they are often not made clear or are not even spoken, and (2) Barbara does not consistently stand behind her expectations (allows herself to be pushed, is permissive when tired, and screams when her "fuse burns up")?

Barbara often seemed to evade our questions regarding her role in the referral; at one point she began unloading the dishwasher. Other times we felt strongly pulled by her to discuss only generalities. We felt confused because several times Barbara requested concrete suggestions on how to handle Bobby, yet eluded attempts to delve into areas that we felt might be underlying the problem. Barbara was warm toward us in expressing her concern, opening her home to us, preparing meals and snacks for us. But at the same time, she was cool toward us in that it was often difficult for us to locate where she was in relation to us from moment to moment.

The report describes Bobby as resembling his father in appearance: tall for his age, large-boned, husky, brown-haired. In contrast, though, he was energetic and quick to smile. He bounced into the kitchen, demanded breakfast, and was unafraid to ask questions throughout the assessment. During the testing he often set up his own boundaries, finding ways to do tasks a step at a time. He enjoyed "winning," and took pride in mastery, in terms of both accuracy and completeness of answers. However, without boundaries and discrete steps, and with only a broad time limit, Bobby felt hurried and often seemed agitated. He seemed lost in space when he wasn't given clues or directions as to how to pace himself.

During the assessment sessions, when Bobby floundered with a task for the above reasons, we both felt pulled to help him ("Hey, wait, there's something the matter"). Other times his strength in diversionary tactics made us feel subtly manipulated, and we were angered to find ourselves in this circumstance. He often controlled the test situation, and only firmness and persistence on our part brought us all back to the assessment.

The vulnerable six-year-old who skips school to stay home and to keep his mommy home also was represented in the report. Several times during the WISC Bobby's answers made reference to a television Lassie movie, in which a little boy fell over a cliff and was trapped in a canyon all by himself. Bobby had cried during the movie even though the boy was eventually rescued. When the assessors asked Bobby if he thought he was somehow like the little boy, he squirmed in his chair, and acknowledged, "Yeah."

When Bobby was observed in the classroom, he was involved and cooperative in class activities. He was sometimes slow to leave earlier projects to begin a new assignment, but responded quickly to reminders. He was in the top reading section. His teacher and counselor said they had never seen a tantrum. His size had not been problematic so far as they knew. They had wondered about his occasional failures to return to school after having lunch at home, but had seen no connection with happenings at school. The teacher was described in the report as "handling her classroom in a firm but gentle manner, explaining her expectations of the children carefully and clearly, and consistently enforcing them."

Bobby's Report

This is a story we created for Bobby, as his copy of our report. We attempted to simplify somewhat the situation as we see it, while still retaining essential relationships, movements, and suggestions.

Portraying Bobby as a bright-eyed baby elephant, we sought to emphasize his strength, size, ineffectiveness in coping with situations beyond his control, and his wanting consistent, dependable patterns in his life. Portraying Barbara as the little bird perching on the baby elephant's back, we tried to evoke the lightness (ineffectiveness) of her presence in providing stable, dependable guidelines. In her bird likeness, Barbara is at times "fluttery and flighty"--hovering and hesitating between decisions, moving from one interest to another without establishing or fostering growth of roots, a firm stand. When Bobby trumpets around the house, stamping and stomping, he's asking to be put on track, any track, as long as he is encouraged and prodded to continue in the same directions not pulled several different ways at once or left no alternative but to push in conflicting directions. Bobby's school situation with Mrs. Garlow (lioness) also is described in the report. We hope our implicit suggestion will be understood by Bobby and may clarify some questions or encourage him to raise some questions at the family discussion about rules to teach the bright-eyed baby elephant how to move within the structure he wants.

Bobby used the word "jabby" several times during the Vocabulary subtest. To him, "jabby" means something that can hurt you or be dangerous. Bobby's world is jabby to him in some ways; for the most part, he depends on himself to test out or explore the jungle. But without guidance from the little bird who can see ahead and has lived in the jungle, Bobby gets jabbed.

Jabby Jungle

Once there was a bright-eyed baby elephant, strong for his size, who lived in the jabby jungle. If he saw a branch in the way as he lumbered along, he would say to himself, "I am a strong little baby elephant. I bet I can move that branch!" And he would. He liked finding things that he could do because it made him feel grown up, that he could take care of himself sometimes. He liked to see a job well done, so it often took him a long time, but he was proud when he was done.

The baby elephant had a little bird who perched on his back. He liked this little bird, and she liked the bright-eyed baby elephant. She often rested on his back and thought that she should shoo away the little bugs that might annoy him while he was plodding through the jabby jungle.

When she sensed trouble ahead, she would chirp loudly, with screeching sounds, and become fluttery and flighty; this would make the baby elephant jumpy, and he would begin to trumpet loudly and stomp from side to side, flicking the little bird off his back. Then she would fly away for a little while, and the elephant wouldn't know that she had gone. He could hardly tell whether the bird was there or not, because she was so light and he was often too busy exploring the forest and moving branches out of his way.

Other times the little bird would go away because she had things to do by herself while the baby elephant was busy with other friends. The little baby elephant would go with his friends to learn the ways of the jungle from the likable lioness who shared her wise stories. She knew the ways of the jungle and set limits and rules for the baby animals. She showed them how to live by rules in order to be safe and happy.

The little elephant, so strong, enjoyed her teachings, and although he moved slowly sometimes, as elephants do, he learned quickly. When he lumbered slowly along, the lioness would gently prod him to keep up, and he could follow her firm directions. He and his animal companions knew that by following what the lioness said and did, they would learn how to make the jabby jungle a safe place where they could someday move by themselves.

The baby elephant needed the little bird whenever he left his friends and the lioness. He looked to the little bird to help him remember the rules he had learned from the lioness, because little baby elephants can't always remember.

But the baby elephant would often be confused and not know quite where the flighty little bird could be. Sometimes the little bird was perched on his back so lightly that the baby didn't even know it. One day the baby elephant wanted the little bird to guide him, and got so confused that he threw his head back and trumpeted as loud as he could, and stomped and stamped shaking his jungle home, so that she would know where he was and that he was lost and needed help. Usually when he did this the little bird gave him some peanuts to calm him down or flew away for a little while. But this time, instead of flying away or giving him peanuts, she flew in front of him where he could see her. The little bird looked at the bright-eyed baby elephant and noticed that he was not so big. A baby elephant is strong, but the little bird had realized how important she was to him and how he depended on her to guide him firmly through the jabby jungle. She had lived in the jungle longer and the baby elephant trusted her to see ahead for him. The little bird saw that she should be a guide in front of him on the tip of his trunk, so that he could listen to her and follow her.

Sometimes she would still fly away to her other tasks, and he would be off with his friends. But when he wasn't with his friends and the lioness, the little bird tried to make sure that she gave him directions so that he always knew where he was and wouldn't get lost in the jabby jungle anymore.

This assessment illustrates the usefulness of a flexible approach to referrals. Rather than construing the referral as a request for separate appraisals and reports, the assessors saw an opportunity to go to the heart of the referral issue--Barbara's relation with Bobby. When they discovered Marlan in the home, they included him in the assessment. The counselor who made the referral readily encouraged this approach, although previously she had thought that assessments could only appraise single personalities. This flexibility was possible because the graduate students viewed themselves not as testers but as assessors. They properly saw their task as helping the counselor and the Harrells in their efforts to enhance Bobby's growth through Barbara's development. Testing was helpful as an access to Bobby's and Barbara's approaches to tasks, ways of dealing with others, and their levels of effectiveness.

To find out whether Bobby was in fact getting along well at school, the assessors went there to watch him in that environment and to talk with school personnel. Granted, the pressures of time often require that these inquiries occur less directly, for example via telephone consultations. But the visit to the school was helpful because it showed that the same Bobby who could be problematic at home functioned cooperatively at school. We see how the two environments participate differently in the evolution of Bobby's comportment. I use the word see purposely; we can picture process--how Bobby can change from a bellowing, demanding boy at home to a quietly happy follower at school. It is within this process that we can identify what I have called the "pivot points" at which movement can be smoothly redirected. Therein we also see that Bobby's comportment is not simply a reaction to external stimuli; we see how Bobby and his environment flow along together in unity.

This process of flowing in unity is difficult for authors to express because our language is so linear and partitive. Then as readers, when we are removed from the actual behaviors and environments and are present only to records and reports, we think about what we read in terms of categories and constructs. We then integrate the secondhand data in terms of cause and effect. Here, for example, the assessors might have concluded from school records that "Bobby reacts well to a structured environment." That conclusion, of course, would have been correct but not particularly helpful. Most such correct conclusions are truisms. Individualized description tells how the generality is true of a particular person, and where within that person's movement through particular situations a pivot might be initiated, by either the client or other persons. For example, from the report we see that Bobby and his mother could readily learn to recognize the early stages of stomping and trumpeting as signs that he is becoming lost. Bobby can learn that at these moments he can forthrightly seek direction from his mother, his teacher, or other experienced persons. Now those persons are less likely to be put off by the boisterous nature of those requests, which indicate a change of course. Moreover, the adults now know that the object is not to stop the noisiness, nor even to find something new for Bobby to do. Instead, they try to understand where he was going and what he was trying to do, and to help reconnect him with familiar landmarks, rules, and tools.

The report, excerpted here for reasons of economy, accomplished the above points by virtue of its integrated presentation of family members in relation to one another and of Bobby in relation to different contexts. That report was lengthy--12 double-space pages preceding the fable. The fable then served many functions. It is not just a simplified report for a child, but also is a compact, vivid reminder for adults of the report's themes. Experienced from a fresh perspective, those themes strengthen and enrich readers' understandings. The playful literary device, at least in the present case, helps readers to appreciate both Bobby's and Barbara's circumstances without holding either to blame. In the fable each can see his or her responsibility for future comportment. The condensation provided by the fable encourages focused reflection and planning, while the imaginary quality encourages affective recognition of what it may be like to be that baby elephant and flighty guide.

Bobby understood the report, asked questions ("What's lumbering?"), offered elaborations, and was thoroughly pleased that adults could understand his travels through the jabby jungle. The counselor reported that she could use the fable in family therapy as well as in her work with Barbara.

Child Guidance Center Referral

Rick Ferris had been brought to a local child guidance center toward the end of his first-grade year. Until that time, his parents and teacher had thought that as he matured his indistinct speech and shy ways would ameliorate. Instead, according to Mrs. Ferris, his speech had remained "garbled," he had become "aggressive and disruptive at home," and he had "regressed academically" (reading readiness scores had fallen during the year). The clinical child psychologist who supervised the two graduate student assessors asked them to (1) explore the extent to which Rick's misbehavior might be frustration at not being able to communicate, (2) assess Rick's general abilities, especially in regard to how well he could be expected to achieve in school, and (3) note any indications that Rick's difficulties might be neurologically based.

To provide information pertinent to all these concerns, the assessors wrote a lengthy report. They emphasized that their observations had taken place in only one setting (the Center) for only one session, and that they were not trained to answer the diagnostic questions, but that they hoped their detailed description could serve as a point of comparison for other evaluators (pediatrician, speech therapist, developmental disabilities specialist). The following excerpts illustrate the power of an individualized assessment approach--even with a shy, troubled, inarticulate six-year-old.

First Impressions

When we entered the waiting room of the center, Rick's soft "hello" was blocked by his fingers in his mouth. He turned away shyly as if there were a slight danger approaching, and wandered toward his mother, taking shelter by leaning close to her skirt as she stood over him. As we waited she tucked in his shirt while turning him around. Rick was brought into our room alone, seeming uncertain as he wandered over and sat down. He moved as if the situation were not a place where he could be assertive and take a firm stand. When he sat down his arms were tucked in as if there were nowhere else they could extend with certainty. Rick's nonassertive style also appeared in his words, which could hardly be heard and were difficult to understand. As we began to address him, Rick found something to hold onto, a rock, and he clutched it tightly as we talked.

Rick without Guidance

We asked Rick to copy some geometric designs (Bender-Gestalt), and he politely agreed. He held the pencil very tightly (so much so that it flipped out of his hand upon occasion) and pushed down hard, his whole body moving into each stroke, after which he'd look up at Cathy (the administrator). In looking up so frequently, Rick seemed not so much to be seeking approval or validation of his efforts, as to be keeping tabs on the situation during his bold extending of himself. His activity seemed to involve significant risk for him. Rick's left hand continued to hold tightly onto the rock and his toes tapped on the ground in an up and down motion (seemingly searching for a base). As a consequence of his holding onto the rock, the paper slid around on the table, and his preoccupation with Cathy served to break up his vision of the cards and his work. Also contributing to Rick's not seeing his work fully was his head's intermittent shying down or away, at which times his mouth sometimes opened showing his twisting tongue. Rick continued to work without pause, his gestures bold but shaky.

The drawings Rick produced were twisted and inaccurate. Their order on the page seemed to be random; sometimes they almost ran into each other; a couple of figures were rotated (#A, #1) and a couple were incompletely executed (for example, too few dots on #1). Eventually (at design #6), Rick put the rock down and at our suggestion held the paper. This helped to some extent, but even the last few figures wavered off course. The best way to describe these figures might be to call them "garbled," for they look much like Rick's speech sounds.

Our Intervention: Dormant Possibilities

At this time I was interested to know the extent of Rick's capability of appraising the accuracy of these drawings, assuming responsibility for his errors, formulating how they came about, and carrying out the activities necessary for copying them more correctly. Moreover, I was interested to see if Rick would, if he felt our interested concern and knew precisely what was called for, assume a more direct and active role to meet the task more successfully.

After he was finished I asked Rick if his first design looked like the one on the card, and he answered "no." I said, "Can you move the card to make it look more like yours?" He replied "yes," and with a slight smile turned it vertically without looking up. I continued, "What if I put this card back the way it was and gave you a new piece of paper, could you draw it the way it was?" He nodded his head and sure enough he did it almost perfectly, this time the diamond meeting the circle (both well formed) quite precisely. During this work Rick was holding the paper with his left hand and resting his feet on the floor. His hesitance to move out actively into the world was evident, as he twisted his hands together with the pencil while pondering what he was about to do. (This twisting was very much like twisting his tongue when he turns his head away, opens his mouth, and garbles his speech.) However, as he redrew some of the other rotated and more garbled designs, Rick seemed to become more at home and at ease. In facing the situation now he did not look up at Cathy nor turn his head down or away but concentrated closely on the work. Rick demonstrated during this time that he could recognize all the discrepancies between his original drawings and the cards as well as formulate, to a certain extent, how his errors were made (for example, not watching himself). His performance on the second attempt was far superior to his original attempts and turned out to be more accurate than the average for his age.

In this interaction, Cathy and I did not direct Rick but simply asked him questions about accuracy and whether he could be more accurate. After his more successful attempts we told him he did good work but we did not overwhelm him with praise. Our straightforward and structured participation was essential to Rick's straightening out his garbled efforts. However, as Rick began to experience success, he became more confident on his own (without even looking up). This experience was strengthening and uplifting for Rick and set the tone of the rest of the assessment, although further problems and difficulties were by no means absent.

In situations that were well defined and in which Rick could accomplish what was asked of him, he became engrossed in the activities. Here, extending himself into the world did not seem too risky for him. For instance, in drawing predetermined marks into designated forms--stars, squares, circles (Coding, WISC), he set to work in a sure and effective way, leaning back occasionally to breathe deeply. Similarly, when Rick was asked to find the missing part of a picture (Picture Completion, WISC), he remained intently interested with a single-mindedness that earned him his highest subtest score. When he couldn't find the missing part, he straightforwardly concluded, "I don't know." At one point Rick set out to go to the bathroom and also to show me where it was, and he marched along like he was on top of the world; he knew exactly where it was.

After two hours of hard work, Rick remarked that he liked "the copying" best. It seemed to have been an opportunity for him to take the time to change an uncomfortable way of handling a task in the face of significant others. As Rick left us, he took the lead and marched his family out the door like a little general--quite a contrast with his original shy wandering to his mother's side.

Rick in the Face of Risk

Sometimes when the situation called for a more independently derived understanding and for self-initiated activity, Rick's style changed distinctly. He defined brave as "going somewhere and buying something alone"--indeed a dangerous task for him. In these circumstances, after an attempt, Rick would either move around in the same way he came into our room originally a kind of wandering (for example, turning away from a difficult block task and wandering "aimlessly" to the toys), or he would leap into the risky task as if his mere lunging movement would magically get him through (examples: the original Bender, scattering of blocks, becoming violent with toys).

During the times when Rick literally turned away from the task and wandered to the cupboard, he seemed to have no plan of action. He opened the cupboard as if hoping something would grab his interest. His own agency seemed abandoned as whatever struck him invited his activity. Rick initiated very few conversations in our time with him, again showing his hesitance to engage in complex activity in which he would be "on the line." Even when we addressed him, his voice wandered in a shy, slightly fearful way. Often times we would guess aloud at a word, and Rick would seem caught by it and would repeat it, rather than persist in trying to communicate his own original idea. Sometimes his speech faded away. Apparently, rather than face the risk of self initiated action, Rick, in his wandering style, turns from the possibility of entering danger and latches onto whatever grabs him.

When Rick neither directly faced nor purposefully turned away from risk, he impatiently and impulsively acted without organizing himself. This took the form of a relatively blind attempt to face the task or an attempt to destroy it. Rick drew designs in whatever spaces caught his attention, and his effort was slap-dash, as if he hoped it would somehow magically save him from danger. Often Rick did not integrate the material in front of him, as when he looked only at the card and not at what he was drawing. At other times he tried to do two things at once in an impatient, lunging effort to assert himself. In trying to count a row of blocks, Rick rushed in with both hands, trying to count from both ends at the same time, tangling him up completely. Rick's disorganized (garbled) speech is a combination of his wandering style and of this abortive attempt to engage in a risky activity. His mouth begins to twist as he becomes more anxious and the words become unclear. On other occasions he seized upon a part of the situation and became fascinated with it without seeing the whole, as he did on the Block Design, turning one block around and around without any movement toward integration of the design (he then put the block in his mouth and wandered off to the toys). These rough, twisted, magical, and/or impulsive attempts to assert himself in the face of possible failure are, of course, ineffective.

Possibilities of Change

With a bit of help, but mostly with our straightforward concern, Rick began to develop approaches that were more effective for his purposes and with which he could be more at home. When we could not understand Rick, we asked him to clarify himself and he usually did so without becoming frustrated. Also, when he gave short, incomplete answers he gladly elaborated when asked to. He picked up suggestions very rapidly on many tasks. When he was trying to count with both hands at once, I said "slow down and see what you want to do first," and he paused and began counting with one hand. Another time he attempted in a rough and impatient way to balance a rock on a block tower and I said, "How come it keeps falling?" He smiled and then did it gently and successfully. We discussed with Rick several ways he came to err--such as not watching his hand while drawing. He said he only realized it was wrong after it was done, and we asked him how he could be sure it was right. He then did it again, watching carefully. This carefulness then carried over into the rest of the drawing tasks. After a long time at trying to assemble parts of a puzzle and becoming stuck on a few parts, he said, "I can't do it." I got down on the floor with him and, looking at the other pieces, said, "Have you tried everything?" Rick then brought them into the picture, eventually putting the puzzle together.

Other sections of the report indicated that Rick scored in the Bright Normal range of intelligence on the WISC, and that abstract thinking was not impaired. For example, Similarities was one of his highest WISC subtests, and when asked, he said he could imagine Bender design No. 6 as a kite, bees, or a flock of birds. In addition, the report indicated that at various points in the assessors' work with Rick, his speech became clear and distinct. In consultation with the clinical child psychologist, the authors of the report concluded that in all likelihood Rick's difficulties were not due to any neurological deficit or damage, or to mental retardation, but rather could be understood psychologically in terms of his responses to unfamiliar situations that he was required to assertively structure himself.

Because his fearfulness and his subsequent wandering and lunging had developed within his family, the assessors recommended therapy sessions for the family as well as for Rick. Separate suggestions were presented to parents, teachers, and the future therapist. In essence, the various suggestions encouraged replication of the assessment circumstances and interventions through which Rick had found it possible to be direct, clear, and relatively independent. The assessors recommended that after such changes were in place, and Rick was accustomed to them, a referral for evaluation of developmental disabilities be considered. Just because Rick's behavior could be understood psychologically did not preclude neurological weaknesses that could be complicating his growth. An instrument such as the Illinois Test of Psycholinguistic Ability (ITPA), even if it did not indicate a specific learning disability, might provide clues as to the most effective modes of presenting material to Rick (visual, oral, motoric).

This report answered all the referral issues by making Rick's world visible to us. We saw process--the coming into being of Rick's wandering, being grabbed, lunging, garbling. We became aware that Rick's problematic comportment was at once a bodily, verbal, experiential coping with interpersonally risky situations. In short, we were present to structure--to the mutuality of context, experience, action. The consequences of this structural presence were powerful. Deficits and abilities as such disappeared as focal issues. There was no speech problem leading to "frustration"; rather, garbled speech was one of Rick's ways of getting through dangerous situations. Rick did not "have" a problem; he and his social environment co-created problems. Through the structural perspective we saw how adults could intervene to create opportunities for Rick to maintain an effective course or to find his way back from his wandering.

Rather than focusing entirely on end products (developmental level of Bender, IQ, and the like), the assessors were also attuned to the total situation-of which they too were a part. They observed the process of Rick's comportment unfolding in different ways with different outcomes. They re-presented the concrete when and when-nots of Rick's various comportments. Those descriptions included the assessors' immediate reactions, evolved impressions, and the interventions through which they explored Rick's comportment and his viable options. Especially through the explicitation of the contexts in which interventions were effective (for example "our straightforward and structured participation"), Rick's parents, teachers, and therapist see how they too can step into Rick's life constructively.

Summer Camp Reports

At a summer day camp that enrolled children with physical, intellectual, and interpersonal problems in addition to its regular campers, I consulted with the camp staff in regard to supervising one of the special youngsters. One summer a community mental health and mental retardation center sent 21 youngsters to a four-week camp session, with a request that we provide brief feedback on how each child "looked" while at camp, and on what kind of counselor supervision might be required for the next summer. The idea was to help therapists, family, and teachers to see what difficulties the youngsters continued to experience in a different environment and, more important, to see how adaptively the youngsters grew in that environment. The camp was different for these particular children partly because their immediate staff and fellow campers were not informed that they were special in any way. Most of them remained unidentified as diagnosed children throughout the camp season, even though Mary Harrison and I, along with other senior staff members, made suggestions to counselors about these youngsters as well as about other campers.

Behavioral Excerpts

Jack Tacaks (10 years) Chieftans July 15-August 9, 19_____

Items of Concern

- When uncertain of what was happening in a group activity, and when he felt that he had been unfairly ordered to do something, Jack rebelled. On these occasions he has threatened to throw rocks at another child (he did not follow through, however), has instigated a runaway group, and has loudly muttered "shit," "pee on you," and suchlike.

- Jack's persistent mask-like grin contributed to an uncertain distance between himself and both other campers and staff.

Positive Items

- Jack responded very well to being offered concrete alternatives to assignments (such as helping to set the lunch table rather than gathering up athletic equipment).
- Jack took considerable pride in being genuinely needed. He threw himself into doing a good job with some volunteer "helper" projects (camp maintenance and clean-up).
- At first Jack seemed confused by the staff's consistent positive attention even in the face of his "rebellions." However, he soon formed first-name relations with the Chieftan counselors and with several staff persons outside of his own group. He seemed to revel in staff persons' follow through on promises (providing a missed breakfast, asking the outcome of a project, and so on.)

At camp, Jack requires attention from assigned counselors who can provide a consistent relationship as well as general supervision.

Behavioral Excerpts

Carolyn Meuser (10 years) Chieftans July 15-August 9, 19_____

Items of Concern

- Carolyn did not seem to form friendships with her peers; she instead attached herself to a counselor.
- Initially, she frequently sought attention by tattling, complaining of not feeling well, and hitting some other child. Each time the situation she created was one in which she became the loser.
- Carolyn seemed fearful of trying herself out in the various activities. She instead often made remarks about other children's achievements, either derisively or enviously.

Positive Items

- Carolyn approached people through physical contact, and gradually came to ask directly for favors and attention without being negative and without converting the physical touch into a pulling.
- On several occasions toward the end of camp, Carolyn was able to admit a mistake (such as appropriating another child's craft project) and to entertain ideas of how she could work her way out of such a situation. She seemed unused to being presented with constructive face-saving alternatives but she was tentatively eager to try them out.

At camp Carolyn seems to require the sort of individual attention that provides continual recognition, physical affection, and gentle redirection.

These two selections are reminders of three points: First, assessments do not necessarily require the use of tests. Careful observation across varying situations can provide equally useful data. Second, it is not necessary for assessors to individualize every assessment by collaborating with the subject, outlining an overall portrait, detailing the unfolding of process, or itemizing suggestions. Third, even within brief "feedback" reports, an individualized framework can guide the construction of remarks so that they evoke a sense of the particular person.

The CMH & MR staff was pleased with these feedback reports. The reports were brief enough to be read and utilized quickly. The concrete details lent themselves to comparison of comportment at home and at school. The camp's emphasis on possibilities for growth rather than on diagnosis and limitation. encouraged a similar emphasis at home and at school. Moreover, the specification of positive events within their contexts encouraged therapeutic staff and parents to recreate these positive options for the youngsters. The CMH & MR staff told us that they were amazed that such brief reports did not condense observations into judgmental or diagnostic terms. They were even more impressed by the hints for constructive intervention that were inherent in the contexts accompanying described comportment.

Special Education Referral

Public Law 94-142, the federal legislation assuring handicapped children of quality education in a least restrictive setting, mandates that an Individualized Education Plan (IEP) be drawn up for the handicapped child. The year-long goals and shorter term objectives are to be specified, along with means and criteria for measuring arrival at the goals. In general these plans have been a boon to the involved youngsters. Their educational strengths and weaknesses are assessed, and the former are systematically called into play to assist in developing the weaker areas. Teachers are accountable for reaching goals. The individualizing traditionally is in terms of standard educational tools, however, rather than in terms of who the child is as an individual. For example, an objective might be stated as, "Reach average fourth grade vocabulary by the end of the year, as measured by the Metropolitan Achievement Test. Means: Dolch cards, New Word Club, and third grade Bobbs-Merrill reader for successful experiences while reading at home with parents." As in the above examples, despite the word Individualized in the term "Individualized Education Plan," the IEP rarely addresses the child as a particular person. Nor does it address that child's specific situations at school and at home. Contributing to this problem is the under use of the detailed medical, family history, educational testing, and psychological testing data that all too typically remain undisturbed in the respective specialists' files. A school psychologist, Lois M. Love, and I had often commented both on the non individualized aspect of IEPs and on the other utilization of filed data. Eventually we devised a Child Study Form. The form brings together relevant background information, which school specialists summarize in everyday language, focusing on whatever is directly pertinent to developing the IEP. As needed, a child's team members sometimes summarized another specialist's report, to avoid bureaucratic inefficiencies. The child's IEP team (for example, regular teacher, resource teacher, school psychologist, parents) work from the Child Study Form's summaries to document legal criteria for 94-142 assistance, as well as to develop educational goals and statements about how this particular child may be understood and addressed. Under "Team Meeting Summary," we expanded the IEP into two segments, the Remedial Education Plan (the traditional

IEP) and the Individualized Intervention Plan. The latter alerts teachers and parents to what it might be like to be in the child's situation, and shows how educational principles could apply to this particular child. The headings of the Child Study Form are presented below.

Identifying Information

- Reason for Referral
- Past Interventional Efforts
- Background Information
    - Physical Appearance
    - Health
    - Motor and Athletic Development
    - Social Relationships/Emotional Development
    - Educational Development
        - Achievement tests
        - Classroom performance
    - Family Situation
        - Family members
        - Preferred person to contact regarding this child
        - Developmental history
        - Paternal family
        - Maternal family
        - Siblings
        - Family supportive factors
        - Family complications
    - Summary of Psychological Assessment
    - Team Meeting Summary
    - Introduction
    - Diagnosis
    - Recommendations
- Remedial Education Plan (goals and objectives by subject areas)
- Individualized Intervention Plan (critical incidents and interventions)

The Individualized Intervention Plan arose out of Mrs. Love's observations of Megan Ryan in several settings at school, and through discussion with the parents and with other team members. Together, they agreed about critical times when one could tell that Megan was in trouble, what they thought was going on for her at those times, and what one could do to bypass or restructure those moments. Mrs. Love and I summarized the results as a series of Critical Incidents with accompanying Interventions.

The excerpts from the Child Study Form, which precede the Individualized Plan, provide some background on Megan and demonstrate that IEP documents do not have to be filled with educational and psychological jargon. Classroom and resource teachers later expanded the educational plan to include their respective teaching methods and criteria for success.

Team Meeting Summary

Summarized by: L.M. Love, MS Ed., School Psychologist

Nine-year-old Megan has been making minimal progress in the fourth grade. Her parents and teacher requested an evaluation. The parents are positive toward the assessment and are eager to help in any way.

Megan's level of overall intellectual development is in the average range, but her general educational achievement is 1 ½-2 years below age/grade level.

Megan's language skills are adequate, but her visual and auditory functioning are deficient. This circumstance now is adversely affecting further development of reading, writing, and spelling skills. The deficient reading limits other areas of learning, including social studies and science. Arithmetic is affected in the area of word problems.

Encumbered by the above difficulties, Megan has developed faulty reading habits and inconsistent word attack skills. The result is that much of her effort is directed to sounding out words in a slow, laborious manner that precludes understanding the meaning of what she is reading. When a passage is read to Megan, she comprehends at grade level.

During the present year, Megan has begun to engage in more behaviors that are self-defeating. She does not maintain attention to assignments. disturbs other students by entering alternative activities, and becomes distraught when she fails at play or at competitive class assignments.

Until now Megan's learning difficulties were undetected. Instruction therefore was not differentiated from that for typical learners, and it eventuated in a learning lag. In the face of this lag, Megan is experiencing failure and is developing an antipathy for learning. She has experienced little satisfaction related to school, and hence has not been developing positive learning attitudes.

Megan requires a highly individualized program to ensure successful learning. Work will have to be given at an easier level than her customary assignments. Reading should be required in small units and for short drill periods. Activities should be designed so that reading becomes personally meaningful and purposeful.Megan should be placed in a smaller group, where her attention can be gradually lengthened as she develops satisfactory reading habits. She requires individual reading and writing instruction and practice. Adjustments will have to be made in independent arithmetic work when story problems are assigned. Megan apparently has come to feel inadequate in many situations. She has made comments comparing herself unfavorably with her older brother. She has learned to avoid situations that seem too difficult, and hence has not had opportunities to correct her feeling that she is unable to handle difficult circumstances. She has preferred to remain dependent and be rescued by an adult. Megan requires opportunities for satisfying social experiences. When possible, she should work in small cooperative groups in the regular classroom, so that she can respond personally to other children, rather than on a competitive basis via independent assignments. She needs a secure group where she is not embarrassed to try, and where the teacher demonstrates confidence in Megan's competence. Games and play should be utilized to facilitate learning in a variety of ways and to relieve tension around school work. These efforts will create a happier school experience for Megan. Diagnosis . Megan's difficulties qualify as a learning disability. An educational lag has been identified as significant in relation to her age, grade level, and overall intellectual level. Visual and auditory deficiencies in processing information have been documented. Secondary to the learning disability, Megan now engages in disruptive classroom behaviors, but more often withdraws. She expresses feelings of failure and inadequacy.

Remedial Education Plan

Subject Area: Reading: Year's-end goal: Megan will read with smoothness and accuracy. She will comprehend material written at the third grade level and will apply these skills in all subject areas. Short-term objectives:

- Megan will acquire and use word recognition and structural analysis skills.
- Megan will identify details in stories, select main ideas, sequence events, draw cause-and-effect relationships.

Subject Area: Organizational Skills and Self-Direction

Year's-end goal: Megan will identify for herself when she has lost the concept being taught and will choose tactics to redirect herself to her work.

Short-term objectives:

- Megan will ask directly for assistance from appropriate persons rather than waiting for help or engaging in other behaviors to avoid school tasks.
- Megan will redirect her attention to school tasks with no more than two interventions from the teacher.

Individualized Intervention Plan

Recorded by: L.M.L.

Critical Incident--Independent Work: During independent work time, Megan begins working along with the other students. However, in this instance, she does not understand the written directions. She moves about in her seat, half-heartedly raising her hand, then sits waiting for assistance. If the wait is more than a few minutes, she becomes distracted from the work. She tries to enlist the attention of nearby students by showing them a toy or an article from her desk. In the absence of redirection from the teacher, Megan continues to play with objects, annoying other students until an outburst occurs.

Interventions

1. After students have read the instructions, ask one to explain the directions to the entire group. This will probably help other students in addition to Megan as they process the instructions through a different modality and in student terms. When Megan seems to have understood on her own, she could be asked to provide this group instruction, thereby adding prestige to her class involvement.
2. A "rescue team" of two or three students can be designated to whom Megan (and others) can go when stuck on an assignment. The teams can be established in accordance with individual strengths.
3. Design Megan's assignments so that small units are presented one at a time. Tasks will be more easily achieved when the amount of work is not overwhelming. Worksheets can be folded in half so that only one part of an assignment is visible.
4. If the above measures still leave Megan not understanding a concept, provide alternative tasks that she has previously mastered. Then re-teach the unlearned concept. Megan wants to learn but feels threatened and confused by possible failure. She must begin where she succeeds. If provided with a task at mastery level, she can learn to follow through to the next step. Through this process she can assume increasing responsibility for her school work. She will learn that she does not have to avoid difficult work by withdrawing.

Critical Incident Reading

Megan tries to avoid oral reading, finding it embarrassing to read aloud. When she must read aloud, she reads in a slow, plodding manner, laboring over most words. She glances to the teacher, as if silently seeking her assistance. The longer she is asked to read, the more distressed she becomes. Comprehension has become secondary to getting through the words.

Interventions

1. Limit oral reading initially to individual instruction times, to eliminate embarrassment in front of other students. Establish with Megan the purpose of the reading instruction period. If the goal is comprehension, select a short paragraph at her independent reading level. Allow her to read alone to the teacher, or into a tape recorder, to establish an effective reading rate against which she can compare progress.
2. When instruction is in the basic skills of word recognition and structural analysis, establish with Megan that the purpose is to learn to decode words. Help her to keep charts of her progress.
3. Spend part of each instructional time in interpersonal conversation. Relate recent happenings in class or at home to the reading material or to Megan's general growth.
4. When Megan does read before a group, assign her mastery level material so that she can read with confidence before her peers.

Critical Incident Playground

Megan joins in free play on the playground when invited, but seldom participates in structured games. If chosen for a team, she begins to play, but when accused by teammates of incompetent playing, she ends up crying and leaving the game.

Interventions

1. Youngsters who are less comfortable in group structured play could be given 5 or 10 minutes of formal instruction and practice in rules of the game and skills prior to team selections.
2. If Megan does leave a game in tears, allow her to go to a place that is comfortable for her. Give her time to regain composure and then assist her in sorting out her options.

The above excerpts illustrate that not only psychological assessments, but also educational records and plans can be individualized. Legal requirements and concerns for a child's growth can be addressed simultaneously when specific events are addressed. The Child Study faced facts (for example, 1 ½-2 years learning lag) without positing undemonstrable neurological factors. By using descriptive words, such as "deficient" and "difficulty," rather than hypothetical, technological terms such as deficit or disability and descriptive terms such as "overall intellectual achievement" instead of native ability or intelligence, the assessors enhanced the possibilities of constructive intervention and growth.

The Critical Incidents served several functions. They render the child's world visible; they disrupt adults' slippage into perceptions of the child as "bad," "dumb," or "trouble-making." The next time we witness the critical event, we see the trouble in the process of unfolding, and we are reminded of the IEP--its purpose and its suggestions for intervention.

These excerpts reflected collaboration among the child's adults to gather information, to understand the child, and to devise a responsible, individualized education plan. What was not evident in the excerpts was Megan's participation. In fact, Mrs. Love typically includes not only the parents but also the child in the IEP meetings. The child's presence and involvement makes several contributions. All parties, most of all the youngster, perceive that youngster as presently handicapped but as capable of helping him- or herself to grow. Understanding what his or her adults are up to enables the child to cooperate more fully, and to question and offer suggestions, not just during the team meeting but in class and at home. Often the child corrects adult misperception, for example, "Well I don't care if Mrs. Hauser likes me; I don't like her--she calls me 'honey' and says I'm 'sweet.' Couldn't a different aide work with me?" Finally, when the youngster is present, all parties are more likely to remain mindful of the child's life rather than stepping into bureaucratic processing of the numerous mandated forms.

Residential Treatment Facility

The report appears in its original, unedited form, except for changes in identifying information to protect privacy.

June 15,19_____

Psychological Evaluation

Re: David Massey

DOB: 2-12-_____

DOA: 6-18-_____

Fascinating is the word I think of for David in the way that I am drawn into his world. He allows me to do this but is clear that it will be on his terms. This he expresses not in any assertive manner but more in the aloof position he takes. In fact, David appears mild mannered, even submissive, yet in his quiet way he is assertive; that is, expects to get his way. Of course he expects to control this situation with me as well and is reluctant to give up his position when the dictates of the situation (and me) so indicate. He responds best to my interest in him but with a friendly, firm control. I have the feeling that if I treat him right, he will deign to share his time and thoughts with me.

Contributing to the above impression is David's appearance--an olive skinned young man with dark brown hair, and eyes and manner that are both serious and matter-of-fact. His voice likewise deep in tone with not too much fluctuation, has a matter-of-fact, monotonous quality. It is an indication of his degree of involvement in his activities as will be pointed out later.

David let me know from the opening activity of drawing that he was an unusual child. Even the way he held his pencil was different. He would rotate his drawing in his mind, making a mirror reversal of the design I would present him very unusual. He didn't seem to think so but was surprised to find that I did. Through his drawings he tells me other things about himself: that although he may feel inadequate he can be quite expansive. Yet another contradictory polarity exists between control over his actions and his impulsivity. He lets me know more fully about some of these qualities when he enters into the play situation. Even before he had the play material set up, David had in mind what the plot was going to be: "The devil's gonna try to get the animals." We seem to have something in common since we saw each other at the movie "The Black Stallion" the day before. For a moment it looked as though he would follow up the theme of the play since he was fascinated with the horses. This was not the case, however, because David has a mind of his own and certainly imagination of his own. He soon took over the play not just as director but as leader of the characters in the play, doing so with decisiveness. He becomes more animated as he speaks through the animals' actions and as the scene becomes more assertive as they try to capture the devil. He shows his identification with the devil in the way of being sneaky and clever in tricking others. "He's like a ghost" he repeated a couple of times. And now his voice became more animated as he laughed and talked as the devil. The monotone was gone and the intensity of his actions came through. It was as though he was saying with conviction, "You (adults) can't trick me. I'm stronger."

The following day David continued on this theme but this time through the picture stories and with the powers of a witch instead of a devil. He gives us some understanding of the genesis of such a fantasy system when he begins his first story with "that food's no good won't make us grow. Let's go. Mother won't tell us what to do 'cause she mostly don't tell us what to do." His lack of trust in adults taking care of him leads him to find ways to care for himself.

When he encounters a frightening world, he must invent further powers. This he does in an unusual approach to the pictures when he weaves a story in sequence from one card to the next. At times it was obvious this was difficult for him to do, but regardless of the discrepancies that he would see in the pictures, he would pursue his theme: how to remove the power from the noncaring, frightening parent and give it to the child. This must have some deeply cathected meaning to him since he arbitrarily forces this theme on all of the pictures regardless of my encouragement not to and of my questioning him. For example, when the distortions became increasingly obvious and he was trying to carry through the mistreated chickens from the first card to the last saying "the chickens are trying to get the witch's power." At this point I asked "what are those?" and he answered "apes." My intrusion bothered him very little: "I could say bears. They're bears. They're helping the chickens get the witch's power cause they don't like the witch at all." This was the first indication to me that now he could not even keep the cast of characters straight since the bears were initially on the witch's side. This matters not at all to David. By this time he no longer needs the picture. He has taken off on his own story and he makes no effort to comply with the reality of his surroundings-he doesn't even go through the motions as he did previously. However, it is obvious that he is aware that I did not go along with him and now the mumble comes back to his voice as if he had been hiding this fantasy in his own private world, and by divulging it there is a threat of loss of his own power, which makes him aware of his helplessness. As he said in one point in his story: "the genie tries to attack the bear 'cause a lot of people try to get his powers. It got him furious so he gets ate." For those of you wondering how the story turned out, the witch never finds her power and those who are on her side turn against her. It is implied that since the children do not lose their power, it remains with them after they had taken it from the witch.

If you recall I mentioned David's dividedness in the dimension of control and impulsivity: in the devil and the good horses, and of course, in the baby chicks and the witch. Now we see this same theme continuing even into the Rorschach where on two occasions a discrepancy in a minor detail of the blot allows him to see the symmetry as different. For example: "a seal and a man" and later "a bear and an anteater." This kind of reasoning from detail and imposing arbitrarily his own unique configuration is typical of David, suggesting that he is inclined to arbitrarily make judgments based on a minor fact that he may see as significant and then rigidly hold to his view. That there is a rigidity about this is reflected in the certainty with which he views his percepts, indicating a lack of distance from the cards. To him they are not ink blots, they are what he describes them to be. David seems to be pretty much at ease with his idiosyncratic way. At least, the ease with which he describes shading in the blots is an indication of this, or that his anxiety is well bound in a fixed defensive pattern.

My impression has been that David has gone through an autistic phase in his development in which many of the matters he now speaks about in symbolic form were held more quietly wit in him and they are, at this stage of his development, more blatat and have a fixity about them that promises a continued similar defense pattern. My suggestions for working with David are based on this impression.

The danger in working with David would be in getting caught in his world and not holding sufficiently to one's own. He already knows his "powers." Remember that they exist to protect him from the fear of no adult care. He needs to know that adults' "power" in the sense of their responsibility, caring, and greater knowledge is something he can depend on. Without this he must continue to build his own world and power.

The fact that David is willing to share his inner world is a positive indication of moving toward an outer world. To over-praise him for this move could lead him to further cathect this stage and contribute to his aloofness, rather than allowing him the next step of sharing others' worlds. He could be a very unique individual alone with his uniqueness.

As the above implies there is a danger for this child in being a "good training case." To bring out those factors that would make for good training could be detrimental to David.

We saw the leadership qualities in David, at least in his fantasy world. Can these be used in the living situation with his peers? The dramatic ability shown by David could be used as a therapeutic asset in helping him to role-play and thus learn certain social actions.

David is bright and verbal so that talking therapy may appear indicated. However, the material he has to work through is of such a primitive nature that likely play therapy would be required.

Should things get rough for David in the confrontation that he is needing to face, we have some indication of compulsive defenses that could be called into play and strengthened.

Despite the absence of headings and the unrevised work-a-day dictation, the story of Dr. Lewis's encounter with David unfolds clearly. One source of that clarity is the report's disciplined selection of specific events, which are presented in implicit dialogue with diagnostic and treatment issues. Another major positive feature is that through this report we became acquainted with an understandable youngster. We have a strong sense of who David is--of where he is coming from and of his current concerns. We see the serious limitations of his present options, but we also see that there are ways to meet and engage him.

David's records attest to the helpfulness of this individualized assessment. The background documents furnished by David's residential facility indicate that his established DSM II diagnosis was latent schizophrenia with organic brain syndrome (documented by an EEG consistent with susceptibility to seizures). David had spent most of his life in a series of foster homes. After two years he had formed no strong relations with peers or adults in the program, actively irritated other youngsters, at other times shut out both peers and adults, and often exhibited inappropriate affect and thought disorganization. He was enuretic when not medicated. The house manager's report mentions David's "problems with basic techniques relating to cooking, chores, and personal hygiene, requiring constant repetition of demands and explanation." This report goes on to say:

> *His interactions with his peers in the house are negative, argumentative and unyielding. He spends time in covert activities, which arouses the tension and frustration level of the house. He compounds his problems by attempting to place the responsibility of his negative behavior elsewhere.*

From Dr. Lewis's report we can imagine how all these problems could be true of David. But we also see an understandable youngster. We see something of what his struggles are about, how adults are likely to perpetuate David's power plays, and that adults can bypass that perpetuation. At the staff conference, others presented the "when-nots" of David's problematic comportment. The ensuing treatment plan included provision of some backyard space in which David was to be trusted to work by himself, opportunities for David to carry out responsibilities with adults observing but not hovering, and immediate, quiet but firm interventions to preclude development of squabbles and standoffs. A treatment review two months later attested to dramatic changes. These, of course, were not due solely to the psychological evaluation, but it was an important aspect of the staffs finding access points to work positively with David. The concluding paragraph of the treatment review:

> *Incredible progress has been made with David and by David in most of his documented problem areas. He is no longer a constant management problem for the child care worker staff. He is well on his way to attaining grade level in school. He does not use repulsive behavior to keep the world or adults at a distance. David has begun to accept himself and make the best of what he has. Peer interactions are more appropriate. At this point, Dave has laid to rest the following comment which echoed the staff*

consensus of him two years ago: "David continually challenges one's capacity of control."

Dr. Lewis refers to the style of individualized reports as "prose." As he became more certain of himself and more willing to share his ideas, he could then write in "prose" rather than in the specialized language of testing. Because the primary readers of David's report were professionals and paraprofessionals all working together, he incorporated some of their shared language, such as cathect. Even though the readers share a general theoretical orientation, however, David's comportment with Dr. Lewis remains the clear referent of all the report's conclusions. Dr. Lewis says, after writing hundreds, perhaps thousands, of reports,

> *I don't recall receiving such positive response as I have since adopting this [prose] style. It's not that there is always agreement, but that the readers appreciate the style. They look forward to the next "short story." Enthusiasm about the report invites discussion regarding its content.*

Juvenile Detention and Rehabilitation Center Referral: Colleen Olsen (14 Years)

The author of the following report, Amy Lamson, Ph.D., is also author of a book on the "Relationship between Diagnosis and Treatment". She values both individualized assessment and the mental health field's accumulated knowledge about patterns of psychopathology. That knowledge alerts us to compare the assesses with relevant patterns, thereby learning more about the person than if we relied only on our own data. Knowledge of patterns, both normal and clinical, alerts us to likely points of access for intervention and to difficulties we should take into account in assessment and in treatment planning. However, Dr. Lamson also believes that assessments should address a person in his or her particularity, that the ways in which that person both is and is not representative of a diagnostic category should be presented, and that if the assessment is to be maximally helpful in bringing about positive change, the person should be a collaborative participant--discussing data and implications directly.

Dr. Lamson is a clinical psychologist in a juvenile probation facility in California. The juvenile justice system required a diagnostic understanding of Colleen Olsen's behavior--was it related to brain damage, or to psychosis or to something else, or was it another aspect of her already identified delinquency? Dr. Lamson explores these issues systematically and forthrightly, and provides the required bases for her conclusions. She includes her encounters with Colleen outside of the formal assessment, treating them as of the same order as assessment events. The setting is a juvenile detention and rehabilitation center.

Psychological Evaluation

Name: Colleen J. Olsen
Birthdate: 2-4-______ Age: 14-2 Requested by: John Arrow
Date seen: 5-17-19______ Timothy Palmer
Place seen: Girls' Unit, Juvenile Detention and Rehabilitation Center

Reason for Referral

This evaluation was requested to determine if there is a serious pathology underlying Colleen's behavior. She has an explosive temper, and a package of fecal matter was found in her room.

Behavioral Observations and Data from Interviews

When Colleen first arrived in JDRC, she appeared so poised and composed, she looked much older than her 14 years and I wondered whether she was a new Volunteer in Probation. Although on occasions she has since exhibited gleeful spirits in the manner of a younger child, there is still something about Colleen that seems older than her years. Whether it is the fact that she has been on her own and self-supporting for a long time or that she presents a picture of herself as supremely self-satisfied, she does not exhibit the floundering, searching quality of most girls her age.

Colleen has been consistently eager to talk with the psychologist (myself). However, she has not used the time to discuss any problems she may have. Rather, she has delightedly related her past experiences in an apparent effort to re-live the fun she had. When confronted with difficulties she is having on the unit, she has repeatedly passed them off as inconsequential. When it was pointed out that if she kept up the way she was going she would probably have extra time at JDRC, she laughed and stated she had already had two weeks added. On the other hand, when it was suggested that perhaps she likes it in JDRC and wants to stay a long time, she adamantly insisted that was not true. Recently she related several promises of rewards from her mother and her PO if she does better in the program. When asked if she plans to try to do better, she answered, as if that were a ridiculous question, that she would be crazy not to, now that she had been promised those things.

When Colleen first heard that she had been referred for testing, she seemed opposed to the idea. However, the very next day she started asking when she would be tested. It appeared that she had decided that this would be another arena for her to get attention and that she would revel in it. On previous occasions she had stated that she is "weird crazy not like other people," and she warned that the tests would show how weird she is.

After the evaluation, Colleen was told that the tests did indeed show that her thinking is different from others, but the problem is not so much that she is disturbed, as that her values are different, and she does not want to go along with the rules of society. She heartily concurred. When possible reasons why she became this way were suggested to Colleen, she strongly indicated that it was not because she was not taught right from wrong. She believes it was because she did not get enough attention from her mother to make it worth her while to go along with her mother's teachings. She feels her mother always favored her younger sister but had little time for either of them because she was always involved in getting married or getting divorced. When it was pointed out that she would have to change her thinking, at least to some degree, or else she would be in serious trouble the rest of her life, Colleen said she knows that and she is determined not to be locked up again.

Colleen expressed a lot of warm feelings for several girls she has met in Juvenile Hall. When one of these girls was suicidal, Colleen offered to speak with her to cheer her up. During several meetings with this girl, Colleen made many appropriate gestures and remarks to reassure her that she is cared for and to point out how foolish it is for her to think of killing herself. However, it was obvious from Colleen's reactions on another day when she did not see the girl, that her interest in others is rather short-lived and that she is basically self-centered.

After the incident in which fecal matter was discovered in her room, Colleen stated that she could not wait the hour until the rooms would be opened and she could go to the bathroom. She felt it was better to go on the paper rather than press her "E" light and risk having a lowered grade. It was difficult for me to believe that her judgment was that poor and I suspected that her defecating on the paper reflected a deeper motivation. I pointed out to her that she would not have that dilemma again because she was now in a room with a toilet. During a discussion in her room, my suspicions about deeper motivation were confirmed when I noticed a smell in the room and saw some fecal matter in the toilet. She denied that it was hers and insisted that it had been in the toilet before she was placed in that room. When these incidents were discussed again after the testing and it was suggested to her that they symbolically represent her desire to "shit on society," she laughed in agreement. It is obvious, however, from other behavior and remarks that these incidents also reflect an anal preoccupation. She is so messy and dirty in her room and on her person that other girls refer to her as "scuzzy." In addition, one day at lunch while I was eating cheese, she commented that cheese causes constipation.

Tests Administered

Her high Performance IQ was due to a high score on Picture Completion, a test of visual alertness. Her other Performance subtests were all in an average range. Her Similarities and Vocabulary subtest scores were in an average range but her score on Comprehension, which tests practical judgment and understanding of rules and behavior, was significantly higher. Evidently, Colleen is skillful in scanning her environment for important clues and is shrewd in practical matters. Her responses on Comprehension also indicate that she knows the difference between right and wrong, though she does not necessarily do what is right. In response to the question about what you should do if you find a wallet in a store, she said: "Turn it in to Security or take it to Security. That's what you're supposed to do."

Colleen's Bender-Gestalt drawings were very neat and well organized. They gave no evidence of organicity or impulsive tendencies. Colleen's projective test responses reflect deviant thinking, attitudes, and feelings. Instead of seeing the usual Rorschach percepts of animals, people, and objects, she saw all kinds of bugs (for example, squished bug swarm of dragonflies") which frequently are associated with frustrated needs for nurturance, as well as with acting out and psychopathic tendencies. Her TAT stories are similarily filled with maladaptive themes. One boy is "mad at his violin 'cause he couldn't play anything right." A girl "really hated school and wants to stay home." After suffering some losses, another girl "decided there wasn't anything left to live for so she killed herself." One little girl "didn't like to do anything she didn't want to. She was a brat."

Violent tendencies were also evident in one of her Rorschach percepts and in two of her TAT stories. "He really wanted to kill this guy." "She was about to scream. He threw a sack over her head and started strangling her." Colleen's most striking TAT story, however, was one which vividly demonstrated the shallowness of her feelings. She described a couple whose newborn grandchild died. "The old lady started crying, the man hugged her and said it would be O.K. They went home to bed and in the morning they forgot about everything."

Colleen's rather grotesque human drawings appear to be intentional caricatures of people rather than serious drawings. They seem to reflect a sneering, rebellious attitude toward people. Her choice of the animal she would most like to be ("A tiger, 'cause tigers are big and real majestic and pretty much rule where they go") is a further demonstration that Colleen wants to be a law unto herself.

Although Colleen gives evidence of faulty reality testing in her decidedly deviant thinking, she does not appear to be psychotic. Her responses on the Rorschach during testing of the limits, and her house drawing, indicate that she is fully capable of perceiving and behaving in conventional ways. Furthermore, she gives absolutely no evidence in any of the tests of the marked confusion and disorganization evident in psychosis. In other words, it appears that Colleen's deviant behavior is fully under her control.

Summary and Conclusions

Colleen is a 14-year-old girl of Bright Normal intellectual potential who has exhibited markedly deviant behavior. Her remarks and her test responses indicate that her deviant behavior is due to her antisocial values, rather than to any significant emotional disturbance. There is evidence in her social history that she has been hurt in the past due to insufficient nurturance and that these unfulfilled dependency needs are at the root of her antisocial thinking. However, it is apparent that she has succeeded in pushing these feelings aside and that she is very well defended against feeling pain. As a result, Colleen is a poor candidate for traditional psychotherapy to change her behavior. Nevertheless, the situation is not entirely hopeless. Colleen is a clever girl who cannot help but see the wisdom of modifying her behavior, at least to some degree, in order to avoid punishment. In addition, when sufficient rewards are held out to her she can be motivated to behave better. She has recently begun to see her mother as a more giving figure. If her mother continues to show interest in Colleen and to offer rewards for Colleen's good behavior, it is very possible that Colleen will begin to behave in more socially acceptable ways. To this end it is recommended that Colleen and her mother participate in counseling aimed at improving their relationship.

This succinct, to the point, balanced report presents a nonjudgmental, vivid sense of Colleen. She makes sense to us. We see her positive potential, but we also see the seriousness of her sociopathy ("antisocial" orientation). The brevity, clarity, and vividness of the report are due in part to Dr. Lamson 's presentation of test data as firsthand events, that is, as selected instances of Colleen's comportment. There is no test-by-test overkill, obfuscating jargon, or refuge in theoretical constructs. We know the everyday life events as well as the test findings that led to the conclusions.

Dr. Lamson was not afraid to integrate activities that are too often maintained as separate roles for different professions: history-taker, assessor, therapist, family consultant. Nor was she afraid to move beyond her office to be with Colleen in her room or to eat lunch with the Center residents. In all these settings, Dr. Lamson inquires directly about Colleen's understandings, and integrates these into the assessment report. She knows that to help Colleen to help herself, her understandings must be directly addressed and taken seriously. But in this process Dr. Lamson remains clear about her own, broader comprehensions, through which she challenges Colleen.

A follow-up letter from Dr. Lamson reports, "Through counseling with her mother, Colleen made some dramatic changes in her outlook on life. These were reflected in a subsequent testing where she gave many high-level Rorschach percepts. She was placed in the Center one more time after her return home, but has been staying out of trouble for several months since then."

Probation Referral: Douglas Whitman

The concluding report in this chapter illustrates a different format: occasionally the report is written in the form of numbered suggestions with accompanying rationales. The graduate student who assessed Douglas Whitman had discovered by the end of the assessment sessions that his test data added little to what Doug's helpers already understood. Rather than go through the motions of making independent discoveries via testing, the assessor chose to cite test comportment only when it filled out the rationale for or extended current staff efforts to be of help to Doug. This format would be helpful to the judge, who would have to think in terms of options. In this instance, inclusion of more test findings would have added little, except the risk of obfuscating the conclusions.

Dates of assessment: December 9, 12,
13, 19______
Date of report: December 17, 19______

Psychological Assessment of Douglas Whitman

Doug is currently on probation for having broken into a Fullertown drugstore with several friends. As part of the conditions of his probation, Doug has been forbidden by the court to be in the company of his co-defendants and must be off the streets after 9:30 P.M. Recently Doug was found in the company of his co-defendants after his curfew (at 10:30 P.M.). He was referred to the Fuller town

Mental Health and Retardation Clinic for assessment, with judgment by the court on his probation violation to take place in January.

Mrs. Borckovitch, Staff Coordinator at the MH/RC, has asked me to work on an assessment with Doug in the hope of finding ways of breaking through the pattern of recidivism which seems to be emerging.

Assessment Opportunities

Wechsler Intelligence Scale for Children (WISC-R), Bender-Gestalt, Thematic Apperception Test (partial), mutual discussion of my impressions.

My Impressions of Doug

In spite of his size (5'10"), age (16 later this month), and considerable composure and poise in the face of the uncertainty and stigma for him of a psychological assessment, my overriding impression of Doug after our first session was one of a likeable little boy. This impression materialized for me most vividly while Doug and I worked on various parts of the WISC-R. In particular, I noted his willingness to guess at answers, his obvious smiles and pleasure at getting answers right, and his vocal displeasure with himself when he couldn't answer a question, or when he knew his answer was wrong. Doug was immediately willing to attempt tasks with which he had difficulty, at the same time enlisting my aid in a childlike, unembarrassed way. On the Arithmetic section, which involved reading problems aloud, Doug looked up to me for help on words he didn't know. This unusual childlike enthusiasm, friendliness, affability, and ease has been noticed by several other people who have worked with Doug. His probation officer, professionals at the MH/RC, and his Volunteer in Probation all seem to agree that Doug can be a likeable and enjoyable person.

However, when we spoke of the "trouble" Doug was in and when I asked more personal questions about his family, I had the impression that Doug had formed a wall of pat answers between us. Much of the enthusiasm, ease, and open expression was flattened out. Although Doug initially painted a picture in short repeated sentences of a loving and comfortable home life, in another session he came close to tears in relating his perception that his family, particularly his mother, wanted to get rid of him, and wanted him to be sentenced to a term in jail. Despite his pat answers about his crimes and sophisticated sociological rationales for his not being sentenced, Doug admitted being terrified of the prospect of a jail term.

Through the three sessions that we spent together I developed a perception of Doug as being at odds with his world much of the time. His lying (which I have described as pat answers) is a form of self-protection, which occurs when he feels that something about his conduct, if revealed, will lead to punishment or reprisal by an angry adult. Pat remarks are his way of attempting to get people to like or accept him in spite of his behavior. Although Doug and I did not talk directly about this aspect of his pat answers, I believe that they arise in part out of alienation: a sense of being unknown and unlike other people. The only adult Doug expressed some feelings of similarity to was his Volunteer in Probation, Mr. Sallis. I had the impression that pat answers also may function for Doug as a way of claiming the concern and affection he misses. For example, he blithely told me about unnamed friends who help him to stay out of trouble and who visit him at his house, only to leave at the time of his curfew. I wonder if Doug's friends do show the concern and affection for him implied in this account. Surely, Doug must wish someone would. I think he believed that if he told me that he had such friends my opinion of him would be improved.

Suggestions and Their Rationales

Suggestion 1: Doug should continue to see his Volunteer in Probation, Mr. Sallis, as often as possible. The topics of their meetings should be at least partially set in advance and the time formalized in terms of a definite hour and day of the week. Taking into account the limitations of Mr. Sallis' time and the importance of Doug spending time with sympathetic adults who can help him understand what is happening in his life and ways of planning for the future, I would suggest that an additional Volunteer in Probation, preferably a man, spend time with Doug every week.

Rationale: Doug never knows when he will see Mr. Sallis. For Doug this seems to mean that he has nothing certain and enjoyable in his life to which he can look forward. In order to increase the consistency and possibility of satisfying experiences in his life, I believe that it would help if Doug and Mr. Sallis attempted to set a schedule for their times together.

Doug and I talked about his need and desire to "stay out of trouble." But, as with other goals in his life, Doug has no clear sense of the procedures leading to its accomplishment. For example, Doug would like to find work as a bricklayer, or some other skill offering union wages, but has no sense of the difficulty or of what's involved in union work. Mr. Sallis could point such things out to Doug and help him move through the step-by-step processes involved.

Spending time with Mr. Sallis, whom he likes and admires, would also present Doug with an alternative style of life to his own. Perhaps Mr. Sallis could help point out to Doug the real consequences of his actions and increase Doug's sense of being in control of his own life instead of having things just happen to him. (Doug anticipates that he will get a prison sentence not for what he has done, but because he got caught and the judge, he believes, doesn't like him. He tends to blame his present situation on other people and circumstances.)

Doug tends to give up when he encounters some obstacle to achievement. On the intelligence test this often occurred when his method of breaking down problems into units small enough for him to deal with was thwarted. At these times, though, with any encouragement and pointing out of his steps and missteps, Doug was often able to proceed. I believe that he responds to complicated, confusing situations outside of our assessment in the same way.

Suggestion 2: It would help Doug if he could have a job (or jobs) which he could do every day after school and on weekends when he is not in the detention center. We spoke both of volunteer work and of jobs for which he would be paid a salary. Good work experience might increase his confidence and self-worth. Volunteer work in which he is helping other people would be particularly helpful. Since Doug perceives the detention center as a place from which he emerges frustrated and angry, I would suggest that work might be offered as a form of "alternative service" with an explicit understanding that unexcused absences from work would have to be made up for by time in the detention center. At first, Doug might test this out by missing work, but if the consequences were immediate and clear I believe he would come to develop the sufficient, immediate personal reason he needs for doing something well. With time on the job the benefits for Doug of this kind of work might emerge.

However, if a full-time job or apprenticeship in which Doug could learn a skill can be found, I believe that he should take it. In the meantime, since Doug will be sixteen this month, perhaps Mr. Sallis or someone at the clinic could guide him toward obtaining a social security card.

Rationale: Doug's interest in working conscientiously and successfully at a job seems to be associated for him with the meaningfulness of the task in terms of personal gain. For example, we spoke of his drawing geometrical designs (Bender-Gestalt) as meaningless to him, resulting in his not copying the designs with precision. Similarly, Doug spoke of not caring about how carefully he cleaned up around the house unless someone was coming over. The ideal work situation would be one in which Doug worked around other people, and where he could see that his contribution made a difference. His boyish enthusiasm, likeability, and willingness to ask questions would get him off to a good start. But his supervisor, Mr. Sallis, and perhaps others would have to help him keep sight of where his work was getting him.

Doug's score in the low Average range on the intelligence test was much higher than it had been on previous administrations. This may reflect Doug's increased comfort and sense of belonging at the school he is now attending, Wrights High School. The vice-principal there, Mr. Donatelli, reported that Doug has not presented any serious problems this year. He genuinely seems to enjoy his classes at Wrights and referred laughingly to how his teachers in social studies and science would be upset with his not remembering the capital of Greece, or what a barometer was. In this circumstance, his grades well might improve from his record of Ds and Fs. Since only 50 percent of the persons with an IQ of 100 or lower graduate from academic high schools, however, C's in competitive standard courses would be superb for him. If Doug does remain in high school it is important for him to be in one of the vocation oriented tracks. However, the abstract meaning of a high school diploma is too distant. The immediate monetary rewards of work might well give Doug the incentive he needs to perform up to his capabilities.

Doug brought up the possibility of jobs before I had a chance to suggest it. He explained the motivation for his robbery of the Fuller town drugstore to be getting money in the only way available to him. Doug also mentioned wanting to help out his mother at home.

I agree with Doug that having a job(s) would be important for him in many ways. I told him that having something to do was an important way of staying out of trouble. Throughout the time we spent together Doug often referred to the environment in which his crimes were planned as "just sitting around with some friends." Similarly, on the Vocabulary section of the WISC-R Doug defined join in terms of "having something to do." Doug's tendency to go with whatever else is happening can lead him into constructive or destructive behavior, according to what is going on around him. His difficulty making plans and his desire to be a part of something would seem to suggest his crimes were adventures for him in which he went along with the group. In a work situation Doug might become involved with a group with more constructive values.

At times, while working on a problem on the WISC-R, Doug would give up. With encouragement he would return to the task and finish it. This, plus his allusions to his family wanting him to be "sent away" suggested to me that Doug has very few experiences in which he can feel some sense of accomplishment, worth, and success.

Suggestion 3 and Rationale: Would a prison sentence have the desired effect? I doubt this since Doug blames his circumstances on bad luck. Whatever lessons he would learn probably would have more to do with becoming more devious or with the advisability of staying away from authorities. Confinement also might disrupt his relationship with Mr. Sallis which seems to hold the greatest possibility of rehabilitation at the moment. Part of Doug's attachment to Mr. Sallis has to do with the latter's not challenging Doug's pat answers or likewise talking down to him. Doug responds negatively to punishment, but does gradually learn through encouragement and positive example.

Several features of this report might be adapted by other assessors. The author distinguished explicitly his direct observations and his inferences and projections ("I developed a perception," "I had the impression," "might well give Doug"). He specified the issues that were and were not explicitly and collaboratively discussed with Doug ("when we spoke of the 'trouble' Doug was in," "although Doug and I did not talk directly about this aspect of his pat answers"). Finally, the author integrated data provided by Doug's other helpers (the vice principal's review of academic records and his impressions of Doug's behavior, the multiple affirmations of Doug's affability). This integration provided the MH/MRC staff and the judge with a cohesive picture that was preferable to separate, lengthy reports of the various professionals' records. Of course, to arrive at integrated suggestions, the assessor had to go beyond his tests to talk with those other professionals. The resulting report was one that Doug's helpers identified with, which in turn encouraged future cooperation in Doug's treatment.

This report's format foregoes the drama of test-based data unfolding toward conclusions and subsequent suggestions. What is gained is a sense of the obviousness of the suggestions. In many ways the suggestions are standard for cases like Doug's, but here the reader sees how they are relevant for Doug in particular. The suggestions would not be mistaken as soft-hearted appeals for liberality. Doug was not presented as a poor misguided child, nor as a sick child who should be excused. On the other hand, he was not presented as essentially evil or deviant. The reader sees that the affable boy, the kid with pat answers, the youngster who blames others for his own troubles, and the youngster who wants to belong and to achieve are all Doug. The Suggestion/ Rationale format shows readers that there are ways of helping him to avoid a recidivist career. Current helpers are reminded of the particular ways in which they can best assist Doug.

BIBLIOGRAPHY

Alemi F., Stephens R., Parran T., Llorens S., Bhatt P., Ghadiri A., and Eisenstein E., (1994), "Automated Monitoring of Outcomes: Application to Treatment of Drug Abuse". *Medical Decision Making*, 14.

American Psychiatric Association, (1994), *Diagnostic and Statistical Manual of Mental Disorders* (4th ed.), Washington, DC: Author.

Atkinson M.M. (1996), "Psychiatric Clinical Nurse Specialists as Intensive Case Managers for the Seriously Mentally Ill". *Seminars for Nurse Managers*, 4.

Balas E.A., Austin S.M., Mitchell J.A., Ewigman B.G., Bopp K.D., and Brown G. D., (1996), "The clinical value of computerized information services: A review of 98 randomized clinical trials". *Archives of Family Medicine*, 5.

Balas E.A., Jaffrey F., Kuperman G.J., Boren S. A., Brown G.D., Pinciroli F., and Mitchell J.A., (1997), "Electronic communication with patients: Evaluation of Distance Medicine Technology". *Journal of the American Medical Association*, 278.

Campbell T.L., (1987), "Is Screening for Mental Health Problems Worthwhile in Family Practice? An Opposing View". *Journal of Family Practice*, 25, 184-187.

Carlin A.S., Hoffman H.G., and Weghorst S., (1997), "Virtual Reality and Tactile Augmentation in the Treatment of Spider Phobia: A case report". *Behaviour Research and Therapy*, 35, 153-58.

Carr A.C., and Ghosh A., (1983), "Response of Phobic Patients to Direct Computer Assessment". *British journal of Psychiatry*, 142, 60-65.

Dyer J.G., Hammill K., Regan-Kubinski M.J., Yurick A., and Kobert S., (1997), "The Psychiatric-primary Care Nurse Practitioner: a Futuristic Model for Advanced Practice Psychiatric-mental Health Nursing". *Archives of Psychaitric Nursing,* 11, 2-12.

Erdman H., Klein M.H., and Greist J.H., (1983), "The Reliability Of A Computer Interview for Drug Use/Abuse Information". *Behavior Research Methods & Instrumentation,* 15, 66-68.

Erickson S.M., (1997), "Managing Case Management across the Continuum: An Organized Response to Managed Care". *Seminars for Nurse Managers,* 5, 124-128.

Fiore M.C., Novotny T.E., Pierce J.P., Giovino G.A., Hatziandreu E.J., Newcomb P.A., Surawicz T.S., and Davis R.M., (1990), "Methods Used to Quit Smoking in the United States". *Journal of the American Medical Association,* 263, 2760-2765.

Greist J.H., Gustafson D.H., Stauss F.F., Rowse G.L., Laughren T.P., and Chiles J.A., (1973), "A Computer Interview for Suicide-risk Prevention". *American Journal of Psychiatry,* 130, 1327-1332.

Greist J.H., Jefferson J.W., Wenzel K., Kobak K.A., Bailey T., Katzelnick D.J., Hagerson S.J., and Dottl S.L., (1997), "Telephone Assessment Program: Efficient Patient Monitoring and Clinician Feedback". *MD Computing, 14,* 382-387.

Hamilton M., (1960), "A Rating Scale for Depression". *Journal of Neurology, Neurosurgery and Psychiatry,* 23, 56-62.

Heather N., Kissoon-Singh J., and Fenton G.W., (1990), "Assisted Natural Recovery from Alcohol Problems: Effects of a Self-help Manual with and Without Supplementary Telephone Contact". *British Journal of Addiction,* 85, 1177-1185.

Katzelnick D.J., Kobak K.A., Greist J.H., Jefferson J.W., and Henk H.J., (1997a). "Effect of Primary Care Treatment of Depression on Service use by Patients with High Medical Expenditures". *Psychiatric Services,* 48, 59-64.

Katzelnick D.J., Kobak K.A., Greist J.H., Jefferson J.W., and Henk H.J., (1997b), "Predictors of Adequate Dose and Duration of Antidepressant Medication for Depression in a HMO". *Psychopharmacology Bulletin,* 33, 534.

Katzelnick D.J., Kobak K.A., Greist J.H., Jefferson J.W., Mantle J.M., and Serlin R.C., (1995), "Sertraline for Social Phobia: A Double-blind, Placebo-controlled Crossover Study". *American Journal of Psychiatry,* 152, 1368-1371.

Marlatt G.A., (1985), "Situational Determinants of Relapse and Skill-training Interventions". In G. A. Marlatt & J. R. Gordon (Eds.), *Relapse Prevention: Maintenance Strategies in the Treatment of Addictive Behaviors* (pp. 71-127). New York: Guilford Press.

Newman M.G., Consoli A.J., and Taylor C.B. (in press). "A Palmtop Computer Program for the Treatment of Generalized Anxiety Disorder". *Behavior Modification.*

Newman M.G., Kenardy J., Herman S., and Taylor C.B., (1997), "Comparison of Palmtop-computer-assisted Brief Cognitive-behavioral Treatment to Cognitive-behavioral Treatment for Panic Disorder". *Journal of Consulting and Clinical Psychology,* 65, 178-183.

NIH Consensus Development Panel on Depression in Late Life. (1992), "Diagnosis and Treatment of Depression in late Life". *Journal of the American Medical Association,* 268, 1018-24.

Orleans C.T., George L.K., Houpt J.L., and Brodie H.K.H., (1985), "How Primary Care Physicians Treat Psychiatric Disorders: A National Survey of Family Practitioners". *American Journal of Psychiatry,* 142, 52-57.

Osgood-Hynes D.J., Greist J.H., Marks I.M., Baer L., Heneman S.W., Wenzel K.W., Manzo P.A., Parkin J.R., Spierings C.J., Dottl S.L., and Vitse H.M., (1998), "Self-administered Psychotherapy for Derpession Using a Telephone-accessed Computer System Plus Booklets: An Open U.S.-U.K. Study". *Journal of Clinical Psychiatry,* 59, 358-365.

Pfeffer R.I., Kurosaki T.T., Harrah C.H., Chance J.M., Bates D., Detels R., Filos S., and Butzke C., (1981), "A Survey of Diagnostic Tools for Senile Dementia". *American Journal of Epidemiology,* 114, 515-527.

Piette J.D., and Mah C.A., (1997), "The Feasibility of Automated Voice Messaging as an Adjunct to Diabetes Outpatinent Care". *Diabetes Care,* 20, 15-21.

Reynolds W.M., and Kobak K.A., (1995b), "Development and Validation of the Hamilton Depression Inventory: A Self-report

Version of the Hamilton Depression Rating Scale". *Psychological Assessment,* 7, 472-483.

Reynolds W.R., Kobak K.A., & Greist J.H., (1992, August), "Diagnostic Utility of the Hamilton Depression Rating Scale". Paper presented at the meeting of the American Psychological Association, 100th Annual Convention, Washington, DC.

Risser J., Biros M., Hodroff M., Kobak K.A., and Mandell M. (1997, October), "Prevalence of Unsuspected Psychiatric Disease in Emergency Department Patients". Paper presented at the meeting of the American College of Emergency Physicians, Scientific Assembly, San Francisco, CA.

Selmi P.M., Klein M.H., Greist M.H., Sorrell S.P., and Erdman H.P., (1990), "Computer-administered Cognitive-behavioral Therapy for Depression". *American Journal of Psychiatry,* 147, 51-56.

Simon G.E., Lin E.H.B., Katon W., Saunders K., Von M. Korff, Walker E., Bush T., and Robinson P., (1995), "Outcomes of Inadequate Antidepressant Treatment". *Journal of General Internal Medicine* 10, 663-670.

Ware J.E., (1993), "SF-36 Health Survey". *Manual and Interpretation Guide.* Boston, MA: Health Institute, New England Medical Center.

Ware J.E., Kosinski M., and Keller S.D., (1995), *SF-12: How to score the SF-12 Physical and Mental Health Summary Scales.* Boston: Health Institute, New England Medical Center.

Yesavage J.A., Brink T.L., Rose T.L., Lum O., Huang V., Adey M., and Leirer V.O. (1983). "Development and Validation of a Geriatric Depression Screening Scale: A preliminary Report". *Journal of Psychiatric Research,* 17, 37-49.

Zhu S.-H., Stretch V., Balabanis M., Rosbrook B., Sadler G., and Pierce J.P., (1996), "Telephone Counseling for Smoking Cessation: Effects of Single-session and Multiple-session Interventions". *Journal of Consulting and Clinical Psychology,* 64, 202-211.

Zimmerman M., Coryell W., Wilson S., et al., (1986), "Evaluation of Symptoms of Major Depressive Disorder: Self-report vs. Clinician Ratings". *Journal of Nervous and Mental Disorders,* 174, 150-153.

INDEX

W